Informed Consent
to Human
Experimentation

Informed Consent to Human Experimentation:

The Subject's Dilemma

George J. Annas, J.D., M.P.H.
Leonard H. Glantz, J.D.
Barbara F. Katz, J.D.

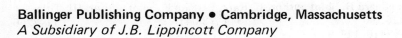
Ballinger Publishing Company • Cambridge, Massachusetts
A Subsidiary of J.B. Lippincott Company

This book is printed on recycled paper.

International Standard Book Number: 0-88410-147-9

Library of Congress Catalog Card Number: 77-2266

Printed in the United States of America

Library of Congress Cataloging in Publication Data

Annas, George J.
  Informed consent to human experimentation.

  Includes bibliographical references.
  1. Informed consent (Medical law)—United States. 2. Human experimentation in medicine—Law and legislation—United States. 3. Informed consent (Medical law) 4. Human experimentation in medicine—Law and legislation. I. Glantz, Leonard H., joint author. II. Katz, Barbara F., joint author. III. Title.
KF3827.I5A95   344'.73'041   77-2266
ISBN 0-88410-147-9

Dedicated to Our Parents.

Margaret and George Annas
Edith and Irving Glantz
Faye and Albert Katz

Contents

Foreword   xi

Acknowledgements   xv

Introduction   xvii

Chapter One
Origins of the Law of Informed Consent to
Human Experimentation   1

Pre-Nuremberg Appellate Cases   2
The Nuremberg Code   6
Post-Nuremberg Cases   9
    Therapeutic Experiments   10
    Nontherapeutic Experiments   18
Summary and Conclusions   21
References   22

Chapter Two
The Current Status of the Law of Informed Consent
to Human Experimentation   27

Informed Consent in Therapy   27
    Battery or Negligence?   27
    Informed Consent as a Negligence Action   29
    Functions of the Informed Consent Doctrine   33

State Laws on Informed Consent   38
Federal Regulations on Informed Consent   42
Therapy vs. Experimentation: Some Conclusions   44
The Law's View of "Risk"   45
Legal Limits of an Individual's Ability to Consent
  to Experimentation   50
Summary and Conclusions   53
References   55

Chapter Three
Research with Children: Legal Incapacity and
Proxy Consent   63

Who Is a Minor?   64
Consent to Therapeutic Treatment   68
The Child's Consent to Medical Care   70
The Child's Consent to Take Risks   73
Nontherapeutic Experimentation on Minors   75
The Kidney and Bone Marrow Transplantation Cases   80
Proxy Consent   87
Summary   93
Conclusions and Recommendations   94
References   96

Chapter Four
Research with Prisoners: The Problem of Voluntariness   103

Biomedical Research   103
Motivation   106
Duress and Coercion, and Undue Influence   110
  Duress   110
  Undue Influence   112
Duress and Undue Influence in the Prison Setting   113
Waiver of Rights   117
Behavior Modification in Prisons   119
  Prisoner Autonomy in Consenting to Medical Treatment   119
  Behavior Modification Cases   122
Legislative and Regulatory Responses   128
Summary and Conclusion   132
References   134

Chapter Five
Research with the Institutionalized Mentally Infirm:
The Dual Problems of Incapacity and Voluntariness   139

Capacity to Consent 144
Barriers to Capacity 147
 Effects of "Institutionalization" 147
 Ability to "Comprehend" 151
Proxy Consent 153
Therapeutic Experimentation 155
 Biomedical Procedures 155
 Behavior Modification 159
Nontherapeutic Experimentation 172
Conclusions and Recommendations 182
References 183

Chapter Six
Fetal Research: The Limited Role of Informed
Consent in Protecting the Unborn 195

Types of Fetal Research 196
 Growth and Development in Utero 196
 Diagnosis of Fetal Disease or Abnormality 196
 Fetal Therapy and Pharmacology 197
 Research on Previable Fetuses Outside the Uterus 197
Ethical Issues 198
The Fetus and the Law 200
 Roe v. Wade 201
 Consent 204
 The Dead Fetus 204
 Therapeutic Research 205
 Nontherapeutic Research 205
 Laws and Regulations 206
British Guidelines 210
Conclusion 211
References 211

Chapter Seven
Psychosurgery: The Regulation of Surgical Innovation 215

Traditional Mechanisms of Legal Regulation 216
 Historical Overview 216
 Private Actions 217
 Public Actions 222
Current Legal Responses to Psychosurgery 224
 Judicial Action 224
 Legislative Action 228
 Administrative Action 233

Conclusions on Review Committees for Psychosurgery   243
References   245

Chapter Eight
Compensation for Harm: An Additional
Protection for Human Subjects   257

Examples of Indemnification Problems   258
Liability Without Fault   261
    Automobile Accident Insurance   263
    Medical Malpractice Insurance   264
    Worker's Compensation   265
    Price-Anderson Act   266
An Indemnification Proposal   268
Summary and Conclusions   274
References   274

Appendixes

I   The Nuremberg Code   279
II   Declaration of Helsinki   283
III AMA Ethical Guidelines for Clinical Investigation   285
IV   H.E.W. Regulations on the Protection of Human Subjects 290
V   Human Experimentation in the Armed Forces   305
VI   H.E.W. Draft Working Document on Experimentation
     with Children   313
VII H.E.W. Proposed Rules on Experimentation
     with Prisoners   317
VIII H.E.W. Proposed Rules on Experimentation with the
     Institutionalized Mentally Disabled   321

Index   325

About the Authors   335

Foreword

Medicine, as art and science, always has had a component of experimentation, linked with the many uncertainties that have accompanied the healer's efforts to understand and intervene in states of *dis-ease*. But in the long span of medical history, formalized clinical research, and the roles of professional investigator and of human subject, are recent developments. With the acceptance of man as the "animal of necessity" at certain phases in the testing of new medical and behavioral procedures, techniques, and agents, we have acquired as well a responsibility to deal with a complex network of social, ethical, and legal issues that surround experimentation with human subjects.

This responsibility devolves, most immediately, upon the major groups of participants that have become involved in the conduct and control of human experimentation. These include investigators and subjects, governmental and private sponsors of research, institutional review boards, regulatory agencies, and the legal system. Just as the process of research with human subjects itself is fraught with problems of uncertainty, these participants must grapple with many uncertainties as to how that research *ought* to proceed.

With the promulgation of the Nuremberg Code, the obtaining of a potential subject's informed, voluntary consent to participate in research began to be accepted as a central ethical norm for guiding the conduct of human experimentation. The principles of informed consent, in essence and ideal, serve to protect and promote individual autonomy. But in seeking to translate these principles into practice, those involved in the arena of human experimentation have found that interpreting and applying ethical ideals in the myriad types of research with human subjects is, at best, a difficult and uncertain task.

In this richly-detailed volume, George Annas, Leonard Glantz, and Barbara Katz trace and analyze the legal system's efforts to articulate the law of informed consent to human experimentation for various types of research and with various types of subjects. The authors demonstrate that, along with the dilemmas facing those involved in research as subjects, investigators, lawyers, and judges confront numerous and complex problems in their determination of how to implement the ethical and legal requirement of "competent, voluntary, informed, and understanding" consent. Setting forth an informed consent doctrine for the competent adult, whether a (medically) normal subject or a patient-subject, has been a slow and arduous legal task. The magnitude of the task grows apace as the law deals with the meaning and exercise of consent for other categories of subjects, such as fetuses, children, and the mentally infirm.

The authors provide an in-depth analysis of the law in these and other areas, ending each chapter with a concise summary of the issues and the authors' suggestions for dealing with them. For example, they discuss whether the bonds inherent in the therapeutic relationship between a normal patient and his physician destroy the ability to obtain legally-valid consent to experimentation. Does the consent of the mother to experimentation on a fetus provide sufficient protection for the interests of the fetus? Are minors unable to give consent to experimentation on themselves due to their incompetency? Does the mere fact of incarceration prevent a prisoner from being able to give voluntary consent to participate as a research subject? Are all institutionalized mental patients precluded from giving competent and voluntary consent because of their diminished mental capacity and their presence in an institution?

What the law has said or not said, and why, about consent for various types of medical and behavioral research is knowledge that should be available to and utilized by all those concerned with human experimentation. In providing us with this knowledge, in a single, comprehensive, and highly readable source, the authors of *Informed Consent to Human Experimentation* have performed a major service for the many participants in research with human subjects. Not only is this the first time that this has been done, but it has been accomplished in a manner and style which should appeal to layperson and lawyer alike. Reading this book, one comes away with the realization that those formulating the law of human experimentation, just as those who are investigators and subjects, have learned the truth of Hippocrates Aphorism:

> Life is short
> And the art long
> The occasion instant
> Experiment perilous
> Decision difficult.

Judith P. Swazey, Ph.D.
February, 1977

Acknowledgements

Acknowledgements

This book would not have been possible without the dedicated work of a number of individuals. We wish to especially thank our secretarial and editorial staff, Elizabeth Ollen, Patricia Callahan and Carolyn Harrelson, all of whom contributed heroically to the final product. Law students Richard Wayne, Robert Trakimas, Alice Kupler, Mitch Simon, Sandy Schussel, Barbara Keshen, Barbara Alsop, Jean Kelly provided us with invaluable research assistance.

Professor John Robertson of the University of Wisconsin Law School and Professor Frances Miller of the Boston University School of Law reviewed parts of earlier drafts of the manuscript and provided us with helpful comments.

Finally, we wish to thank Michael Yesley, Staff Director of the National Commission for the Protection of Human Subjects of Biomedical and Behavioral Research, and his staff for their support and cooperation in preparing the report upon which much of this book is based.

Introduction

Of all the controversial issues surrounding human experimentation, the most central and least understood is informed consent. While almost everyone agrees that society would ultimately suffer from a total ban on human experimentation, most are uncomfortable with present mechanisms designed to protect human subjects. Some are vexed because they believe they go too far, others because they believe they are insufficient and ineffective. It has come to be almost universally accepted that no person should be experimented on without his informed consent. But what this means in practice and how the doctrine is to be applied to children, prisoners, mental patients, and other populations particularly vulnerable to abuse, is not well articulated.

Two forces have combined to make informed consent a focal point in the debate over human experimentation. These are the medical malpractice insurance "crisis," and increased federal involvement with regulating research to protect human subjects. In response to the former, for example, more than forty states passed statutes in 1975 and 1976 making it more difficult for physicians to be successfully sued by their patients. Almost half of these statutes contained provisions concerning the doctrine of informed consent, because it is (erroneously) viewed by many physicians as a principal cause of malpractice lawsuits. Federal involvement in human experimentation through grants for research led to the creation in 1975 of a National Commission for the Protection of Human Subjects of Biomedical and Behavioral Research. The Commission was assigned, among other things, the drafting of proposed regulations concerning research on children, prisoners, mental patients, fetuses, and candidates for psychosurgery. As part of their research effort, the authors, through the Center for Law and Health Sciences at Boston University, prepared papers for the Commission under N.I.H. contract No. N01-HU-6-2120 from January to July, 1976. Chapters 1-5 of this book are based on work done under this contract.

The purpose of our Report to the Commission was to summarize the law of informed consent to human experimentation, especially as it related to specific populations, and to make recommendations to the Commission concerning the proper role and content of federal regulations. Many focuses were possible. The person who procures informed consent, for example, may be as important as the forms and procedures used in obtaining it. The time at which informed consent is obtained may also be the most critical issue in certain circumstances. Relevant issues may vary from one research setting to another. For example, consent requirements for survey research may be drastically different from consent requirements for invasive, experimental surgery. We decided to concentrate on the medical research model, and to explore the development of the informed consent doctrine in this context.

The reasons for this focus are, we believe, compelling. First, almost all the judicial pronouncements that exist concerning informed consent involve medical procedures. Secondly, the great majority of all the research currently funded by the United States Department of Health, Education and Welfare on human subjects involves medical research. Third, the law of informed consent was applied to the medical experimental setting long before it found acceptance in the therapeutic setting. To this day, the most complete and comprehensive statement on informed consent remains the Nuremberg Code—a document based on "natural law" principles and enunciated following a trial of Nazi physicians for their genocidal and barbarous medical experimentation on German prisoners of war.

As with any focus, however, this one has limitations. Almost no space is devoted to social science research, survey research, or retrospective research based on an examination of personal data. As important as these issues are, we feel that this book is not the place to try to address them. These types of research present a number of issues completely divorced from those we believe essential to discuss. For example, the very concept of "risk" differs in the biomedical and social science areas, and many of the questions are not as much related to informed consent as they are to privacy.

Our research has led us to conclude that prior to experimenting on a human subject, the experimenter must obtain that subject's voluntary, competent, informed and understanding consent. How the law arrived at this conclusion, the functions of informed consent and its limitations and major problems are discussed in chapters one and two. The problems of the "normal" volunteer are discussed, centering on the issues of information and understanding. The third chapter, on children, concentrates on a population for which the primary issue is competency. The next chapter deals with prisoners, where the emphasis shifts to voluntariness. The fifth chapter explores the problems with consent by mental patients, and incompetency and voluntariness hold center-stage together. Each of these chapters is concluded with a short summary of our major conclusions concerning obtaining informed consent from these populations, and some suggestions for future regulators.

In the final three chapters the emphasis is on somewhat more specific issues. The chapter on fetal research examines what is perhaps the most emotionally-charged area in the human experimentation debate. The chapter on psychosurgery examines the most controversial type of human experimentation currently being performed, and the chapter on compensation for harm explores the major issues raised by a potential additional protection for the subjects of human experimentation. While we make no pretense that we have discovered any ultimate truths in this volume, we believe that we have identified and discussed the most critical issues concerning informed consent to human experimentation.

We, of course, understand that in many instances informed consent, while necessary, is not sufficient protection. Other mechanisms, such as review committees, research subject advocates, monitoring committees, etc. merit continued exploration. The goal is to find that combination of protection mechanisms which will adequately safeguard the rights of subjects without unduly burdening scientific advance.

We have very much enjoyed struggling with and debating the issues discussed in the following chapters. It was unpredictable and somewhat remarkable that we managed to find basic agreement on all of them—but we have. Even though each of us was primarily responsible for certain parts of this book, we worked together on all of them and take joint responsibility for all conclusions drawn. If this book has the effect of increasing the understanding of, and promoting the more reasonable use, of the doctrine of informed consent in the experimental setting, we will be able to consider the effort not only enjoyable, but worthwhile as well.

February, 1977   George J. Annas
Boston, Mass.   Leonard H. Glantz
                                     Barbara F. Katz

Informed Consent
to Human
Experimentation

Chapter 1

Origins of the Law of Informed Consent to Human Experimentation

The law's attitude toward human experimentation has undergone a relatively radical shift during the last two centuries. In this introductory chapter, we review most of the appellate court decisions in the human experimentation field as well as some pioneering work that did not reach the courts. These cases deal almost exclusively with patients undergoing experimentation, either in ignorance or with the hope that they will benefit from it. Most are hospitalized. While there are few legal precedents, the normal volunteer's status is also explored since most courts deal with special populations, like prisoners, by defining the ways in which they are different from "normal" individuals.

The most comprehensive and definitive statement of the law of informed consent in the experimental setting is contained in the Nuremberg Code, and reference is made to it in each chapter of this book. None of the case law prior to this Code is of much help in determining the standards that should be applied to modern experimentation. Indeed, a discussion of the facts of these early cases is much more instructive than an analysis of the law the courts applied to them. There is only one court case involving experimentation in the nontherapeutic setting, *Bonner v. Moran*,[1] that reached an appellate court prior to the enunciation of the Nuremberg Code.

A brief outline of the facts of these cases will reveal that all involved what we would now classify as malpractice, rather than legitimate human experimentation, and accordingly should not be used to guide present policymaking. In these cases the courts are simply using the term "experimentation" as shorthand for deviation from accepted or standard medical practice. While such a deviation may be a necessary element of medical experimentation, as used in this book the term experimentation is defined functionally as the deviation from standard medical procedure for the primary purpose of obtaining new knowledge.[2] Moreover, while the term therapeutic experimentation is used to designate procedures that may be of direct benefit to the subject, the intent of the researcher will not always be viewed as controlling. Rather where the risks to the subject are very great and the benefits uncertain, we believe the procedure must be considered legally nontherapeutic regardless of the motivation of the researcher and subject.

PRE-NUREMBERG APPELLATE CASES

The first case involving human experimentation to reach an appellate court was decided in 1767 in England.[3] In that case an individual had broken his leg, and when it healed, a bulge formed at the union. "There was a little protuberance, but not more than usual." The surgeon attending the patient, however, decided to rebreak the leg and "extend" it using "a heavy steel thing that had teeth" to "stretch and lengthen the leg." Four months later the patient was still very ill and had not recovered. A jury awarded him damages against the surgeon and his associate, an apothecary. On appeal, the court, in affirming the verdict, made two points—neither of which is good law today:

1. Since it appeared from the evidence that this was the first time this device had ever been used, "it was a rash action, and he who has acted rashly acts ignorantly," and is accordingly responsible for the consequences of his actions.

2. The surgeon should have informed the patient about what he planned to do before he rebroke the patient's leg so that the patient "may take courage and put himself in such a situation as to enable him to undergo the operation."[4]

The mere fact that something is done for the first time no longer subjects one to absolute liability for its consequences, nor is the primary purpose of informed consent to enable the subject to "take courage." The issues of rashness and consent have, however, remained with us to the present date. Moreover, this British court at least recognized the necessity of a subject's consent more than 150 years before any American court discussed it.

Approximately one hundred years later in 1871, a case involving treatment of a dislocated arm was tried in New York.[5] The jury awarded the plaintiff $2,000, an extremely large verdict at that time. After relocating the bones, the physician had failed to inform the patient that his arm should either remain in a sling or be held on a pillow at a right angle for a period of time. The giving of such advice was found to be standard medical practice.

The physician defended by arguing that he should be permitted to try new modes of treatment. The rule the court announced is probably too strict regarding common ailments, and too lenient regarding novel diseases:

> *If the case is a new one, the patient must trust to the skill and experience of the surgeon* he calls; so must he . . . [if] there is no established mode of treatment. But when the case is one as to which *a system of treatment has been followed for a long time, there should be no departure* from it unless the surgeon who does it is prepared to take the risk of establishing, by his success, the propriety and safety of his experiment.
>
> The rule protects the community against *reckless experiments*, while it admits the adoption of new remedies and modes of treatment only when their benefits have been demonstrated, or when, from the necessity of the case, the surgeon or physician must be left to the exercise of his own skill and experience.[6] (emphasis supplied)

This rule was followed by the Colorado Supreme Court in 1895 when it affirmed a jury verdict of $5,000 against a physician.[7] The doctor had been employed to treat the man's swollen penis, a condition caused by an adherence of the foreskin to the head of the penis. The plaintiff alleged that instead of splitting the skin, as was standard medical practice, the physician applied a "flaxseed meal poultice" which aggravated the condition, caused gangrene, and led to amputation of the penis. Citing with approval the language quoted from the New York case, the court said:

> [I]f a physician sees fit to experiement with some other mode, he should do so at his peril. In other words, he must be able, in the case of deleterious results, to satisfy the jury that he had *reason for the faith* that was in him, and *justify his experiment by some reasonable theory*.[8] (emphasis supplied)

Less than a dozen additional cases dealt with these issues prior to World War II, and almost all dealt with them in a substantially similar manner, *i.e.*, treating any departure from standard medical practice as "experimentation," and treating experimentation as something improper. As the Washington Supreme Court expressed it in 1902 in the case of a broken leg that healed unsatisfactorily:

> [The physician] must not experiment in his treatment of the injury. On the contrary, if he desires to avoid liability for his mistakes, he must treat it in some method recognized and approved by his profession as the most likely to produce favorable results.[9]

The court did, however, go on to say that if a difference of opinion regarding the proper treatment existed in the profession, the physician would not be liable for an "honest mistake in judgment" in picking one over the other.[10]

Other cases that courts characterized as experimentation cases would now be categorized as gross negligence. In one a physician sought to cure asthma by injecting a drug into the nasal cavity. He missed and destroyed the patient's optic nerve instead.[11] In another an osteopath unsuccessfully treated a girl with a severe infection in her leg with a black box that emitted "radio waves." The California Supreme Court, reviewing the case, concluded that the physician assumes "the risk of the quality and accuracy of his genius or inventions," noting that if a treatment is both novel and unsuccessful, it is *de facto* unreasonable.[12] Likewise a physician who used an injection for hemorrhoids, the result of which was an ulceration of the rectum, drew harsh words on experimentation from a Missouri court in 1926: "A failure to employ the methods followed or approved by his school of practice evidences *either ignorance or experimentation* on his part. *The law tolerates neither.*"[13] (emphasis supplied)

The Wisconsin Supreme Court had used similar language two decades earlier in a case involving complications resulting from an operation performed in unsanitary conditions:

> We have little doubt that, if the first case of vaccination had proved disastrous and injured the patient, the physician should have been held liable. Nor do we believe that a physician of standing and loyalty to his patients will subject them to *mere experiment the safety or virtue of which has not been established by experience of the profession, save possibly when the patient is in extremis*, and fatal results substantially certain unless the experiment may succeed.[14] (emphasis supplied)

While more cases of this nature could be discussed,[15] only one adds anything to those already mentioned. That case was decided in Michigan during the Depression. A sixty-year-old man was suffering from a swollen knee.[16] The physician diagnosed bone cancer, and prescribed injections. The condition got progressively worse until the knee broke open and raised a "cauliflower mass," causing sharp pain. The man consulted another physician who performed various diagnostic tests, including a Wasserman, which showed that the man was suffering from syphilis. He was treated for this disease, and shortly thereafter returned to work. A jury awarded him $25,000, which the judge reduced to $7,000.

The appeals court commented on the failure of the first physician to perform standard diagnostic testing:

> We recognize the fact that, if the general practice of medicine and surgery is to progress, there must be a certain amount of experimentation carried on; but such experiments must be done with the *knowledge and consent* of the patient or those responsible for him, and *must not vary too radically from the accepted method of* procedure.[17] (emphasis supplied)

This is the first case in which experiments were viewed as legitimate as long as they were not "too radical" and were done with the patient's consent. It is worth reemphasizing, however, that like the other cases reviewed, this one involved what we would now call simply negligence or gross negligence in the physician's failure to employ an indicated, standard diagnostic test. Thus the court's language on experimentation can probably best be described as interesting dicta.

Nevertheless, while all of the cases outlined emphasize the importance of following "standard medical procedures," this is the first United States case that discusses the consent of the patient as a prerequisite to performing an experiment. More importantly, it bears repeating that in all of the prior cases the courts, either directly or indirectly, treated experimentation as something that was presumed to be "reckless" or careless, and placed the burden on the experimenter to demonstrate to the jury's satisfaction that what they were doing was, in fact, reasonable.

A 1941 New York case brings us even closer to present day judicial thinking. In that case a physician was found guilty of fraud and deceit by the state's licensing authority for using an experimental cancer treatment, and his license to practice medicine suspended. The physician appealed. The court found that the physician had used a topical medication for face cancer. The medication had been developed by another patient of his and was used only after he had tried it on himself to be sure there were no side-effects. He had informed the patient that the treatment was experimental and that it might do some good and could not do any harm. In fact, a complete cure was effected and the physician, who made more than 100 calls on the patient, never submitted a bill. In reversing the determination of the Board the court said:

This doctor effected a cure when so-called orthodox methods of treatment had failed and now he has been punished for it. It is not fraud or deceit for one already skilled in the medical art, *with the consent of his patient*, to attempt new methods when all other known methods of treatment had proved futile and least of all when the patient's very life has been despaired of. *Initiative and originality should not be thus effectively stifled, especially when undertaken with the patient's full knowledge and consent, and as a last resort.* (emphasis supplied)[18]

THE NUREMBERG CODE

The Nuremberg Code, reprinted in its entirety in Appendix I, represents the most comprehensive statement on the law of informed consent to human experimentation. As is well known, the Code was articulated in a court opinion concerning the trial of twenty-three German physicians for "war crimes and crimes against humanity" during World War II. The court rejected the defendants' contention that their experiments with both prisoners of war and civilians were consistent with the ethics of the medical profession as evidenced by previously published experiments on venereal diseases, plague, and malaria, among others. Instead the court found that only "certain types of medical experiments on human beings, when *kept within reasonably well-defined bounds*, conform to the ethics of the medical profession generally."[19] These "bounds" were described by the court in what is now known as the Nuremberg Code.

The basis of the Code is a type of natural law reasoning. In the court's words: "All agree . . . that certain basic principles must be observed in order to satisfy moral, ethical, and legal concepts." Principle one demonstrates the primacy the court placed on the concept of individual consent:

1. The voluntary consent of the human subject is absolutely essential.

   This means that the person involved should have *legal capacity to give consent*; should be so situated as to be able to exercise *free power of choice*, without the intervention of any element of force, fraud, deceit, duress, over-reaching, or other ulterior form of constraint or coercion; and should have *sufficient knowledge* and *comprehension* of the elements of the subject matter involved as to enable him to make an understanding and enlightened decision. This latter element requires that before the acceptance of an affirmative decision by the experimental subject there should be made known to him the nature, duration and purpose of the experiment; the method and means by which it is to be conducted; all inconveniences and hazards reasonably to be expected; and the effects upon his health or person which may *possibly* come from his participation in the experiment.

The duty and responsibility for ascertaining the quality of the consent rests upon each individual who initiates, directs, or engages in the experiment. It is a personal duty and responsibility which may not be delegated to another with impunity.[20] (emphasis supplied)

The Nuremberg Code thus requires that the consent of the experimental subject have at least four characteristics. It must be competent, voluntary, informed, and understanding (or comprehending). As will be discussed later, the element of comprehension differentiates the quality of consent necessary in the experimental setting from the typical therapeutic setting. Another point worth noting is that no exceptions are made to full disclosure in the Code.

The court went on to find that the Nazi experiments were contrary to "the principles of the law of nations as they result from the usages established among civilized peoples, from the laws of humanity, and from the dictates of public conscience." The question that remains is the legal standing of the Nuremberg Code in the United States.

An approach to this difficult issue must begin with a careful review of the composition and jurisdiction of the court rendering the decision. On August 8, 1945, the United States, Great Britain, Russia, and France executed the London Agreement which established an International Military Tribunal for the trial of war criminals. On December 20, 1945, the Allied Control Council of Germany, comprised of the same signatory nations, issued Control Law No. 10, which authorized the arrest and prosecution of suspected war criminals. Subsequently the military governor of the American Zone issued Ordinance No. 7, which established the Military Tribunals to try the war criminals.[21]

Each such Tribunal was to consist of three member judges and an alternate selected by the Military Governor. All judges were required to be American lawyers. Because of this, the international character of the trials has been denied by some writers.[22] Nevertheless, the United States Supreme Court declined to hear any appeals from the Tribunal stating that it did not have the power to review the proceedings of an "international court."[23] The judges were mainly past or present United States judges, and were recruited by the War Department. The prosecutors were predominantly American, and the procedural rules followed were American.[24]

It is tempting to argue that this court was making United States common law because of its composition, the procedures it followed, and its own stated conclusion that it was simply codifying the common law of nations that all men were bound by. Strictly speaking, however, this argument is difficult since the Tribunal was set up under military, not civilian authority, and tried only individuals who were acting under orders of a state in a military or quasi-military context against the citizens of foreign countries. In addition, one must recognize that the military tribunals at Nuremberg were not established by treaty, and in none of the agreements did the United States submit itself to the jurisdiction of similar tribunals in the future.[25]

While disputed as international law by some, its adoption by the United Nations General Assembly on December 11, 1946, and its use as a basis for other international documents, such as the Declaration of Helsinki (Appendix II) lead to the almost inescapable conclusion that the decision is properly viewed as part of international customary or common law.[26] The next issue, then, is the status of such customary international law in the United States.

This question is not completely agreed upon by international law scholars. However, there is judicial authority for the proposition that "International law is part of our law, and must be ascertained and administered by courts of justice of appropriate jurisdiction, as often as questions of right depending upon it are duly presented for their determination."[27] While some authorities have argued that state courts may apply international customary law in the same manner that they apply the common law, such a view would mean that "fifty states could have fifty different views on some issue of international law while the federal courts might have still another."[28] Recent scholarship, however, supports the more reasonable position that the application of international law is properly regarded as a federal function, dealing with foreign affairs. Accordingly, international law should be determined or made by federal courts as though it were federal law, and their view of it should bind the state courts. In this view, issues of international law could always be appealed to the Supreme Court as involving a federal question, and the Court could determine and establish a uniform law for the entire United States.[29]

Whichever view of the role and applicability of international law one accepts, the result is that state courts could adopt and apply the principles of the Nuremberg Code as a basis for a *criminal* prosecution against a researcher who violated the provisions of the Code. In the second, or more "reasonable" view, federal courts could also apply it in this manner, and violation of the Code would be a federal offense. More likely, however, the Code can be used in courts of the United States in *civil* litigation alleging negligent experimentation. In such a suit the Code could be introduced into evidence to establish a *duty* or standard of care applicable to all medical experimenters. The

Code could be introduced either as customary international criminal law, violation of which could be considered as evidence of a dereliction of duty, or as a standard accepted by the research community, violation of which could also be considered as evidence of a dereliction of duty.

To date, however, the Nuremberg Code has only been used as authority by one United States court in the experimental context. In that case, which involved a psychosurgical procedure, the court did not find it necessary to go through any of the above analysis before concluding that the Nuremberg Code was a proper standard against which to judge the sufficiency of the consent obtained for the proposed experimental brain surgery.[30]

Other codes, such as the Declaration of Helsinki and the AMA Ethical Guidelines for Clinical Investigation (see Appendix II and III), can also be viewed as "law" in this sense. If they have been adopted by the medical profession as standards of conduct or care, they can be introduced into evidence in a malpractice case.[31] The purpose of the document or code would be to establish the experimenter's duty to the subject on the basis of the wording of the code. The jury would then be permitted to determine if the provisions of the code were violated by the experimenter. If they were, and if the violation caused the subject damage, the jury could bring in a verdict for the subject.[32]

POST-NUREMBERG CASES

After World War II the shift in the courts' emphasis from a concentration on "standard medical procedure" to a primary concern with the quality of the subjects' consent to the experiment continued. The probable reason was the change in the courts' perception of medical experimentation. Previously viewed as quackery, it is now generally regarded as responsible and legitimate scientific investigation.

Appellate court decisions involving true human experimentation were rare after World War II with one exception: a series of cases involving tissue transplants from minor donors. Since they are dealt with in detail in the chapter on children, they will not be examined here. In all of these cases the primary concern of the courts is with either the quality of the consent of the minor donor, or with the power of someone else to consent to the procedure for the donor. Those appellate decisions that do exist will be summarized under two headings: therapeutic experiments and nontherapeutic experiments.

Therapeutic Experiments

Perhaps the case which best illustrates the judiciary's new perception of medical experimentation is *Baldor v. Rogers*, a case involving the treatment of cancer.[33] The plaintiff, a farmer, was suffering from cancer of the lip. He told the physician that he did not want surgery, and accordingly was treated with drug injections for nine months. After that time the cancer had spread so much that the physician discharged the patient and sent him home. The patient sued the physician, alleging both wrongful experimentation and abandonment. The court's comments on the role of the medical profession in attempting to develop a cure for cancer are especially relevant to our discussion:

> [W]e believe the pivotal question is whether a physician who uses a method other than X-ray, radium and surgery in treating cancer, by that act alone, indulges in malpractice. The appellant concedes that these three methods "have the blessing of the American Medical Association" but he contends that there is no sure cure for the ailment and "no unanimity of opinion as to which of said procedures should be employed on [sic] a particular case."
>
> This Court will take judicial notice of the supreme effort being made by the members of the medical profession and by the citizenry as well to conquer the great human killer, cancer. The fight is unrelenting . . . The reason, of course, for the intensive campaign is that the disease is out of hand because *the remedy is so far unfound* . . .
>
> We do not propose to indicate what from the record in this case would appear to be the proper treatment in a given case . . . But we do have a conviction that the heroic effort being made by members of the medical profession and other scientists only emphasizes that *an enemy is so far being fought in the dark and that one man should not be condemned from the fact alone that he chooses a weapon that another may consider a reed* . . .[34] (emphasis supplied)

The court then went on to conclude that "If there is no certain cure and if the physician did not indulge in quackery by representing he had one, . . ." then no malpractice can be found solely for experimenting with possible cures. The court thus firmly breaks with almost all previous cases, and finds not only that experimentation is a legitimate undertaking, but also that it is to be encouraged, at least in areas where no effective treatments exist. On rehearing the court did, however, place the responsibility on the investigator to disclose options to the subject-patient when it became clear that the experimental treatment was ineffective:

> All of the medical testimony emphasizes the fact that time is of the essence in treating cancer. It is the doctor, and not the patient, who holds

himself out to be, and must be, best equipped to detect the warning signs. And *when treatment is ineffective, it is the doctor who must know it first and recommend other action.*[35] (emphasis supplied)

The next case also involves a novel approach to disease. It is a 1966 New York opinion, which involved a physician who was the only one in the country who performed surgery for scoliosis (curvature of the spine) in a particular manner.[36] The surgeon had developed the technique himself five years before using it on the plaintiff. He had used it thirty-five times. Five times it had produced "unexpected and untoward results," including one case that resulted in complete paralysis and the withdrawal by the hospital of permission to perform this procedure in its facility. The plaintiff's fourteen-year-old son underwent the procedure for scoliosis, which involved the insertion of a steel bar or "spinal jack" screwed into the vertebral column. He died from an "exsanguinating hemorrhage" as a result.

The issue was not the appropriateness of experimentation, but the necessity to disclose the known risks of the procedure. The court found that, because the procedure was "novel and unorthodox," the physician was obligated to make a disclosure to the parents concerning the "risks incident to or possible in its use."[37] The court went even further to hold that the hospital was also liable for failure "to ascertain that the physician had made such a disclosure before permitting the operation to take place."[38] This latter finding drew a dissent from one of the judges who argued that it was not an independent obligation of the hospital "to go behind such consent to ascertain whether . . . an informed consent had been given."[39] A judgment for the parents against both the physician and hospital was affirmed.

While this New York court had found a procedure to be experimental even though the physician had used it thirty-five times over a five year period, two Texas courts found the first (and only) implantation of an artificial heart into a human being to be exclusively "therapeutic" in perhaps the most remarkable case of human experimentation on record.[40] This case will be outlined in more detail than the others discussed thus far because it illustrates the point that consent is now seen by many courts as much more important than the intrinsically experimental nature of the medical procedure—at least in cases where the court finds that the primary purpose is therapeutic and the patient's chances of survival without the experimental procedure are minimal.

In April 1969 Dr. Denton Cooley implanted an artificial heart, developed by Dr. Domingo Liotto, in the chest of Haskel Karp. Mr.

Karp survived for approximately sixty-four hours on the device, but died about a day after it was replaced by a human donor heart.

After a period of praising Dr. Cooley's efforts to keep her husband alive, Mrs. Karp changed her mind and sued Drs. Cooley and Liotta for malpractice, alleging, among other things, failure to obtain informed consent. A verdict was directed by the trial court in favor of the doctors in October 1972, and affirmed on appeal in April 1974 by the Fifth Circuit of the United States Court of Appeals.[41]

Mrs. Karp's major contention was that Dr. Cooley had failed to obtain adequate informed consent for this exceptional and experimental procedure. At the trial it was established that Dr. Cooley had discussed the procedure with Mr. Karp on at least two occasions, and that Mr. Karp had signed two consent forms on two other occasions. The first form was the hospital's general consent form which he signed upon admission. It read as follows:

> I hereby authorize the physician or physicians in charge of Haskel Karp to administer any treatment; or to administer such anesthetics and perform such operation as may be deemed necessary or advisable in the diagnosis and treatment of this patient.[42]

This is often termed a "blanket" consent form and is usually held by the courts to be insufficient consent for surgical procedures because of its lack of specificity. If Dr. Cooley had relied exclusively upon this consent form he would probably have lost this case instead of winning. About three weeks after hospitalization, however, and prior to the operation, Mr. Karp signed, and Mrs. Karp witnessed, the following consent form:

> I, Haskell Karp, request and authorize Dr. Denton Cooley and such other surgeons as he may designate, to perform upon me, in St. Luke's Episcopal Hospital of Houston, Texas, cardiac surgery for advanced cardiac decompensation and myocardial insufficiency as a result of numerous coronary occlusions. The risk of the surgery has been explained to me. In the event cardiac function cannot be restored by excision of destroyed heart muscle and plastic reconstruction of the ventricle and death seems to be imminent, I authorize Dr. Cooley and his staff to remove my diseased heart and insert a mechanical cardiac substitute. I understand that this mechanical device will not be permanent and ultimately will require replacement by a heart transplant. I realize that this device has been tested in the laboratory but has not been used to sustain a human being and that no assurance of success can be made. I expect the surgeons to exercise every effort to preserve my life through any of these means. No assurance has been made by anyone as to the results that may be obtained.

I understand that the operating surgeon will be occupied solely with the surgery and that the administration of the anesthetic(s) is an independent function. I hereby request and authorize Dr. Arthur S. Keats, or others he may designate, to administer such anesthetics as he or they may deem advisable.

I hereby consent to the photographing of the operation to be performed, including appropriate portions of my body, for medical, scientific, and educational purposes.[43]

While far superior to the first, there is no suggestion that this form is flawless. It contains a number of medical terms not rendered in lay language (*e.g.*, cardiac decompensation), describes the possibilities of success and failure only in the most general terms, and gives a far broader anesthetic authorization than is necessary. The form also fails to spell out clearly the experimental nature of the artificial heart and the probability of its both being implanted and functioning successfully. There was evidence that Dr. Cooley told Mrs. Karp orally that her husband had a 70–30 chance of surviving the ventriculoplasty (plastic reconstruction of the ventricle) operation.

Mrs. Karp's first allegation, that she did not understand how experimental this procedure was, was rejected as irrelevant. The court noted that under the law only Mr. Karp had the power to consent to this surgery. Her second argument, that her husband did not read the document, was also rejected by the court since Texas law (the law which this federal court had to apply to the case) required that the jury be instructed that Mr. Karp was charged with reading the consent document by the fact of his signature, even though he in fact did not. Her final major argument—and the one which both courts spent most of their time examining—was that Dr. Cooley did not give Mr. Karp sufficient information concerning the nature of the artificial heart to enable Mr. Karp to give a valid informed consent.

While this case involved a first-of-its-kind human experiment done with debatable pretesting on animals and without formal peer review of protocol, these issues were not dealt with by the court. Indeed, the appeals court summarily dismissed the experimentation argument by noting that "the record contains no evidence that Mr. Karp's treatment was other than therapeutic and we agree that in this context an action for experimentation must be measured by traditional malpractice evidentiary standards."[44]

We would argue that while the case points up the great utility of a consent form that at least attempts some specificity, the proposition that this was not primarily an experiment (albeit a "therapeutic" one) is untenable. The court's conclusion can only mean that the judge was not presented with sufficient evidence at the trial level on this issue, or viewed the magnitude of the risks involved as irrelevant.

If the procedure was considered experimental, the court could have properly applied federal Health, Education and Welfare guidelines concerning consent forms, which required at that time—among other things—a complete disclosure of the possible risks and benefits of the experimental procedure.[45]

In this regard it is worthy of note that in 1974 the National Heart and Lung Institute announced supplemental criteria for the human testing of therapeutic devices under its research contracts which include the following:

> The device is to be used only in a situation in which it offers at least as likely benefit as any known accepted technique or any experimental technique which is available for clinical trial in the same setting by the same group.
>
> There must be experimental evidence from laboratory animal studies of beneficial effect.
>
> Definitive criteria for patient selection must be included in the investigation protocol.
>
> The approval of local institutional research committee and other appropriate committees and conformity to the Institutional Guide to DHEW Policy on Protection of Human Subjects is required.
>
> Prior to the clinical use, the complete research protocol must be approved by NHLI.[46]

Anyone currently doing research on human beings whose funding derives from HEW or whose hospital requires institutional review prior to investigation on humans, could be found guilty of malpractice for failure to follow these and other NHLI guidelines. Dr. Cooley's case could have been resolved differently had the court viewed the issue as experimentation rather than therapy. The NHLI Regulations also illustrate how specific a federal agency can get in regulating human experimentation.

The major distinguishing characteristic of the *Karp* case as compared with other first-of-their kind implant and transplant cases was that it got to court. In almost every other example of completely novel surgical intervention of this type, the patient was given less information concerning the procedure than Haskell Karp, and in some instances not even told of the specifics of the procedure, let alone of its highly experimental nature. A few of these cases merit discussion, even though they never reached the courts, because they illustrate many of the problems, both perceived and real, of informed consent to potentially therapeutic experimentation by the terminally ill patient—the one most likely to be the subject of such drastic forms of experimentation.

The first patient to survive the implantation of an artificial heart valve, Mary Richardson, for example, was not even told about the implant prior to the procedure. Instead she was led to believe that the operation was merely a repeat of a more routine one that had previously been performed on her. The surgeon, Dr. Dwight Harkin, not only did not tell her about the procedure (even after the operation), but inaccurately denied that she could hear the clicking sound made by her artificial valve. She did not actually see the type of artificial valve that was used in the procedure until she left the hospital and was confronted by a group of newspaper photographers and a nurse who held the valve in her hands.[47]

While Ruth Tucker, the first recipient of a human kidney, was informed about the nature of the procedure before the operation, the surgeon, Dr. Richard Lawler, refused to tell her that the operation had been a failure. Instead, he made this information known at a medical meeting, and it was transmitted to Ms. Tucker by a reporter, who came to her house to get her reaction to the doctor's report on her case. She is quoted as having said, "What a way to get your death sentence—from a newspaper reporter."[48]

The first recipient of monkey kidneys, Jefferson Davis, a black patient in a New Orleans charity hospital, indicated that he didn't think he had any choice but to accept. In his words, to his surgeon, Dr. Keith Reemtsma, "You told me it gonna be animal kidneys. Well, I ain't got no choice." His wife indicated even less knowledge, "They said, the doctors, that they'd do a transplant, but they never said it'd be a monkey, a chimp, you know. I didn't know that until they did it. When it came out in the papers . . . that's the first I knew about it."[49]

The recipient of the first heart transplant, Boyd Rush, had a similar experience. His sister signed the following consent form:

I hereby give full permission for left leg amputation and heart surgery on Boyd Rush. I understand that any clots present will be removed from the heart to stop them from going to still more arteries of his body. I further understand that his heart is in extremely poor condition. If for any unanticipated reason the heart should fail completely during either operation and it should be impossible to start it, I agree to the insertion of a *suitable heart transplant* if such should be available at the time. I further understand that hundreds of heart transplants have been performed in laboratories throughout the world but that any heart transplant would represent the *initial transplant in man*. (emphasis supplied)[50]

At the time of the operation no human donor was available so Dr. James D. Hardy performed the heart transplant using a large chimpanzee as a donor. The words "suitable heart" were thought to be broad enough to justify this. The operation was unsuccessful, and the furor in the medical community that it evoked helped insure that the first human heart transplant would not take place in the United States.[51]

The first recipient of a human heart was told about the proposed procedure, but not about the risks it entailed and the probability of success. Instead Dr. Christiaan Barnard purposely led Louis Washkansky to believe that the procedure had an eighty percent success probability, instead of telling him that the eighty percent referred only to his chances of coming out of the operation alive, not to getting better as a result of it.[52] In Dr. Barnard's words:

> He had not asked for odds or any details . . . He was ready to accept it because he was at the end of the line, waiting for a transfer. What else was there to say? Either you got it, or you folded up . . . Since then many people have said it was very brave of Mr. Washkansky to accept a heart transplant. They really mean it would be brave for them to accept a heart transplant—not Washkansky. *For a dying man, it is not a difficult decision because he is at the end.* If a lion chases you to the bank of a river filled with crocodiles, you will leap into the water convinced you have a chance to swim to the other side. But you would never accept such odds if there were no lion.[53] (emphasis supplied)

Barnard did not add, although he could have, that it is much easier to "accept such odds" when they are presented as being heavily in your favor, instead of the way they really are. His view of the dying patient, however, is not uncommon among transplant surgeons, and was echoed later by Dr. Denton Cooley in describing his relationship with Haskell Karp, the case which initiated this discussion: "He was a drowning man. *A drowning man can't be too particular what he's going to use as a possible life preserver.* It was a desperate thing and he knew it."[54] (emphasis supplied)

Heart transplants and the use of artificial hearts or assist devices remain controversial. In response to the attitudes of many thoracic surgeons, and the difficulties of obtaining an informed consent from a dying patient to such experimental procedures, the Committee on Ethics of the American Heart Association in early 1976 published some guidelines regarding the clinical use of the left ventricular assist device (LVAD), a device which is a partially implanted artificial heart for temporary use following some forms of heart surgery. Noting the likelihood of a "strong mutual dependency" existing between the surgeon and the patient, the committee suggested that both the patient and his family may have lost their ability to give a meaningful consent. The cases just reviewed would certainly support this view. Consequently, the committee recommended the participation of a third party in the consent procedure. In the committee's words:

> The participation of a third party, which may be more than one person, to mediate the consent process without being caught up in the force of its dependencies ought to make the consent decision more genuine. It should also be a source of reassurance and comfort to both family and paramedical personnel, as well as to the patient and his doctor.[55]

The committee further went on to recommend that in cases where even with this assistance the patient and family are so faced with anxiety and distress as to make the in-depth communication necessary for informed consent impossible, that such patients be excluded from the initial LVAD trials. The committee also explicitly rejected the view that the terminal condition of the patient itself justified the use of this experimental device: "It is insufficient to claim in a narrow context of high-risk treatment that the patient would be dead had he not been revived. The joint context of both innovative therapy and of research ought to comprise an ethical sensitivity to outcome that goes beyond the mere completion of the trial."[56]

While these recommendations have not been universally adopted, the question of having some knowledgeable third party aid in the consent procedure is one which is well on its way to acceptance in other contexts. The most notable of these is psychosurgery, to which we have devoted an entire chapter. It is, however, fitting to end this section with a discussion of the only other major case of therapeutic experimentation to reach the courts, as it involved a proposed psychosurgical operation.

While this case seems to fit the pattern of concentrating more on consent than on the type of procedure proposed, the court actually reverts to 18th and 19th century case law in viewing the proposed operation as *de facto* quackery. The case involved an institutionalized person convicted of murder and rape of a nurse.[57] He had been in a mental institution for over fifteen years and the proposal was to perform an experimental amygdalotomy on him to see if it would decrease his aggression. While the court spent most of its opinion dealing with the issue of a valid consent, it seems clear from a careful reading of the case that the court believed no consent in this case was possible since the operation was *per se* too experimental and the dangerous consequences *too* uncertain.

Even though a full and detailed consent form had been signed,[58] the court seemed to be saying that signing such a form proved one of two things: Either the person did not understand the form's content, or if he did understand the content, his signature indicated that he was either incompetent or was coerced into signing. Put another way, the court found that the performance of this particular experiment was to be considered against public policy, much the way self-mutilation and suicide are against public policy and will not be sanctioned by the courts. Therefore the experiment was forbidden altogether—an approach not previously taken by any court.[59]

Nontherapeutic Experiments

Excluding the kidney transplant cases involving minors, there are no post-Nuremberg appellate court decisions involving nontherapeutic experimentation in the United States. United States courts would, however, probably resolve the issues the same way one Canadian appeals court and one New York administrative agency did. These two cases will, therefore, be used as a basis for defining the law of consent relating to the nontherapeutic setting. Both were decided in 1965.

The Canadian case, *Halushka v. University of Saskatchewan*,[60] is the only post-Nuremberg case we have located involving a normal volunteer. A student, looking for a job, was advised by the employment office that he could earn $50 by being a subject of a test at University Hospital at the University of Saskatchewan. He went to the hospital and was informed that the test involved a new drug, but that it was "perfectly safe" and "had been conducted many times before." He was informed also that it involved an incision in his arm and the insertion of a catheter into his vein. He signed a consent form which read:

. . . I have volunteered for tests upon my person for the purpose of study of *Heart & Blood Circulation Response under General Anesthesia.*

The tests to be undertaken in connection with this study have been explained to me and I understand fully what is proposed to be done. I agree of my own free will to submit to these tests, and in consideration of the remuneration hereafter set forth, I do release the chief investigators.

Dr. G.M. Wyant and J.E. Merriman, their associates, technicians, and each thereof, other personnel involved in these studies, the University Hospital Board, and the University of Saskatchewan are absolved from all responsibility and claims whatsoever, for any untoward effects or accidents due to or arising out of said tests, either directly or indirectly.

I understand that I shall receive a remuneration of $50.00 for *one* test . . .[61]

After asking, he was informed that "accidents" in the form referred to accidents that might occur in his home, not in the hospital.
When he reported for the test a catheter was inserted into his arm
and threaded through his heart and out into the pulmonary artery
where it was positioned. Surgical anesthesia was then introduced.
After about forty-five minutes his heart unexpectedly stopped. His
chest was cut open, and his heart beat restored by manual massage
after about ninety seconds. He was unconscious for four days, and
remained in the hospital for an additional ten days before discharge.
The day before discharge he was given $50.00 by the experimenters.
He asked if that was all he would get for what he'd been through,
and the experimenters said he could get more if his mother and elder
sister would execute a release.

The subject sued the experimenters and was awarded $22,500 by a
jury. The experimenters appealed on the ground that the subject had
consented. The trial judge had charged the jury that the duty of disclosure in these circumstances was the same as in a doctor-patient
relationship. The appeals court found that the duty was "at least as
great as, if not greater than" that duty, and went on to say:

> There can be *no exceptions* to the ordinary requirements of disclosure in
> the case of research as there may well be in ordinary medical practice. The
> researcher does not have to balance the probable effect of lack of treat-
> ment against the risk involved in the treatment itself. The example of risks
> being properly hidden from a patient when it is important that he should
> not worry can have no application in the field of research. *The subject of
> medical experimentation is entitled to a full and frank disclosure of all the
> facts, probabilities and opinions which a reasonable man might be ex-
> pected to consider before giving his consent.* (emphasis supplied)[62]

The court noted further that the subject had not been told the new
drug was an anesthetic, that there were specific risks, or that this particular anesthetic had *never* been tested before, and that accordingly
his consent had not been properly obtained. The jury verdict was
therefore affirmed.

The other case of nontherapeutic experimentation involves disciplinary proceedings against physician-researchers before the state
licensing board in New York. It has come to be known as the Jewish
Chronic Disease Hospital Case. The facts are well known, and many
of the legal documents involved are reproduced in the first chapter of
Jay Katz's casebook, *Experimentation with Human Beings.*[63] It is
sufficient for our purposes to note that at least twenty-two debili-
tated, chronically ill hospital patients were injected under the skin
with live cancer cells to determine how long it would take them to

reject such cells. The major purpose was to study the immune reaction. The principle investigator, Dr. Chester Southam, expressed his opinion on consent prior to the experiment:

> It is, of course, inconsequential whether these are cancer cells or not, since they are foreign to the recipient and hence are rejected. The only drawback to the use of cancer cells is the phobia and ignorance that surrounds the word *cancer*. It would be possible to study the same process by experimental skin grafts, but this is less satisfactory for quantitation, is much more difficult technically, and is unacceptably annoying to your patients . . . You asked me if I obtained (written) permission from our patients before doing these studies. We do not do so at Memorial or James Ewing Hospital since we now regard it as a routine study, much less dramatic and hazardous than other routine procedures such as bone marrow aspiration and lumbar puncture.
>
> We do get signed permits from our volunteers at the Ohio State Penitentiary but this is because of the law-oriented personalities of these men, rather than for any medical reason.[64] (emphasis in original)

As a result of publicity arising from this study, the Attorney General of New York brought an action before the state licensing authority, then the Board of Regents,[65] to revoke the medical licenses of the principal investigators. The Board ultimately decided that their licenses should be suspended for one year, and this sentence was suspended and the physicians placed on probation. An opinion written by the Board of Regents Discipline Committee contained the following language concerning the necessity for full disclosure, including in this case the fact that the cells being used were cancer cells, in the nontherapeutic setting:

> What form such an actual consent must take is a matter of applying common sense to the particular facts of the case. No consent is valid unless it is made by a person with legal and mental capacity to make it and is *based on a disclosure of all material facts. Any fact which might influence the giving or withholding of consent is material.* A patient has the right to know he is being asked to volunteer and to refuse to participate in an experiment for any reason, intelligent or otherwise, well-informed or prejudiced. *A physician has no right to withhold from a prospective volunteer any fact which he knows may influence the decision.* It is the volunteer's decision to make, and the physician may not take it away from him by the manner in which he asks the question or explains or fails to explain the circumstances.[66] (emphasis supplied)

The Board's Discipline Committee then went on to chide the

physicians for assuming to know what was in the patient's best interests:

> There is evidenced in the record in this proceeding an attitude on the part of some physicians that they can go ahead and do anything which they conclude is good for the patient, or which is of benefit experimentally or educationally and is not harmful to the patient, and the patient's consent is an empty formality. With this we cannot agree.[67]

The Committee further made it clear that this case did not concern "the usual doctor-patient relationship," but an experimenter-subject relationship, and therefore there was "no basis for the exercise of the usual professional judgment [regarding disclosures that are potentially harmful to the patient] applicable to patient care." To underline their major point the Board continued:

> No person can be said to have volunteered for an experiment unless he has first *understood* what he was volunteering for. *Any matter which might influence him in giving or withholding his consent is material.* Deliberate nondisclosure of the material fact is no different from deliberate misrepresentation of such a fact . . . The alleged oral consents that they obtained after deliberately withholding this information [that the cells were cancer cells] were not informed consents and were, for this reason, fraudulently obtained.[68] (emphasis supplied)

Both of these cases underscore the point that a normal volunteer can *never* be considered a patient. Therefore the exceptions to full disclosure of all material facts, such as the "therapeutic privilege," that might apply in a doctor-patient relationship can never apply in an experimenter-subject relationship. The importance of distinguishing between the physician-patient relationship and the investigator-subject relationship is well illustrated by an examination of the evolving doctrine of informed consent in the doctor-patient relationship from an action sounding in battery to an action in negligence. This and other issues are explored in the following chapter.

SUMMARY AND CONCLUSIONS

1. The most complete and authoritative statement of the law of informed consent to human experimentation is the Nuremberg Code. This Code is part of international common law and may be applied, in both civil and criminal cases, by state, federal and municipal courts in the United States.

2.   Almost all of the cases decided by courts concerning experimentation before the enunciation of the Nuremberg Code dealt with experimentation as the equivalent of either rash or ignorant activity, and usually held physicians strictly liable for the consequences of their experiments on patients. All of these cases involved what we would now classify as malpractice or quackery.

3.   After World War II the attitude toward human experimentation shifted and courts began to view it as an important and legitimate enterprise, and put emphasis on the necessity of obtaining the patient's informed consent rather than the novelty of the procedure.

4.   Examples of "medical firsts" in artificial implants and organ transplantation indicate that the doctrine of informed consent may not be a useful one in terms of protecting the patient's right of self-determination because of the patient's distress and dependency on the surgeon. In such cases it may be appropriate to have a third party or group of persons who act as mediators or patient advocates to insure that the patient understands the procedure and its probable consequences before the patient-subject's consent is obtained.

5.   There is no "therapeutic privilege" available to the physician in cases of nontherapeutic experimentation, and all information material to the subject's decision concerning participation must be presented to the subject.

REFERENCES

1. Bonner v. Moran, a 1941 District of Columbia case discussed in detail in the chapter on Children, *infra*.

2. Annas, The Rights of Hospital Patients, 100 (1975).

3. Slater v. Baker and Stapleton, C.B. Eng. Rptr. 860 (Michelmas Term, 8 Geo III, 1767).

4. *Id.*

5. Carpenter v. Blake, 60 Barb. 488 (N.Y. Sup. Ct. 1871).

6. *Id.*

7. Jackson v. Burnham, 20 Colo. 532, 39 P. 577 (1895) *reversing* Burnham v. Jackson, 1 Colo. A. 237, 28 P. 250 (1891).

8. *Id.*

9. Sawdey v. Spokane Falls and N. Ry. Co., 30 Wash. 349, 70 P. 972, 975 (1902).

10. *Id.*

11. Langford v. Kosterlitz, 107 Ca. 175, 290 P. 80, 86 (Cal. App. 1930).

12. Kershaw v. Tilbury, 214 Cal. 679, 8 P. 2d 109, 115 (1932).

13. Owens v. McCleary, 313 Mo. 213, 281 S.W. 682, 685 (1926).

14. Allen v. Voje, 114 Wis. 1, 89 N.W. 924, 931 (1902).

15. *E.g.*, Brinkley v. Hassig, 83 F.2d 351 (10th Cir. 1936) (use of a "compound operation" to cure impotency, high blood pressure, prostate and kidney

condition); Graham v. Dr. Pratt Institute, 163 Ill. App. 91 (1911) (use of carbolic acid to remove small pox pittings from face); Brown v. Hughes, 94 Colo. 295, 30 P.2d 259 (1934) (removal of sixteen teeth and tonsils in same operation); Smith v. Beard, 56 Wyo. 375, 110 P.2d 260 (1941) (unsuccessful skin graft procedure).

16. Fortner v. Koch, 272 Mich. 273, 261 N.W. 762 (1935).

17. *Id.* at 261 N.W. 765.

18. Stammer v. Bd. of Regents, 262 App. Div. 372, 29 N.Y.S.2d 38 (1941) *aff'd.* 287 N.Y. 359, 39 N.E.2d 913 (1942).

19. United States of America v. Karl Brandt, No. 1, Trials of War Criminals, vol. 11, at 181. For a description of the specified criminal acts charged regarding human experimentation *see A. Mitscherlich F. Mielke* translated by Heinz Norden, Doctors of Infany (1949), and Mant, The Medical Services in the Concentration Camp of Ravensbruck, 17 Medico-Legal J. 99 (1950).

20. *Id.* at 181–186.

21. Woetzel, The Nuremberg Trials in International Law, 218–226 (1960).

22. *Id.* at 177–189, and 222 n. 6. For the rationale concerning the criminal jurisdiction of the United States over World War II war criminals see Cowles, Universality of Jurisdiction Over War Crimes, 33 Cal. L. Rev. 177 (1945). While the jurisdictional rationale set forth by Cowles applies to crimes with an international dimension (*e.g.* piracy), and thus could apply to human experimentation done on foreign nationals, it probably has no direct application to research done in the United States by United States citizens on United States citizens.

23. Flick v. Johnson, 174 F.2d 983, *cert. den.*, 338 U.S. 879 (1949).

24. Woetzel, The Nuremberg Trials in International Law, 222 (1960).

25. *Id.*

26. *Id.* at 243, n. 26, and *see generally* Henkin, Foreign Affairs and the Constitution, 221–224 (1972).

27. The Paquete Habana, 175 U.S. 677, 700 (1900).

28. Henkin, Foreign Affairs and the Constitution, 223 (1972).

29. *Id.* and *see* Banco Macional de Cuba v. Sabbatino, 376 U.S. 398, 432–33 (1964); Dickinson, The Law of Nationas as Part of the National Law of the United States, 101 U. Pa. L. Rev. 26 (1952), and Note, The Federal Common Law and Article III, 74 Yale L. J. 325, 335–36 (1964).

30. Kaimowitz v. Mich. Dept. Mental Health, discussed in detail in the chapter on the Mentally Infirm. *infra.*

31. Annas, The Rights of Hospital Patients, 31 (1975).

32. *E.g.*, Steeves v. United States, 294 F. Supp. 446 (D.S.C. 1968); Darling v. Charleston Comm. Mem. Hosp., 33 Ill. 2d 326, 211 N.E.2d 253 (1965), *cert. den.*, 383 U.S. 946 (1966). The elements necessary to win a malpractice suit are discussed in more detail in section on informed consent in the therapeutic setting, *infra*; and *see supra*, note 22.

33. Baldor v. Rogers, 81 So. 2d 658 (Fla. 1955); and *cf.* Stammers v. Bd. of Regents, *supra*, note 18 and accompanying text. Similar issues are currently being debated in the controversy over Laetrile as a cancer cure. *See, e.g.*, Case Study on Laetrile, *The Hastings Center Report*, Dec. 1976, 18–20.

34. *Id.* at 660.

35. *Id.* at 662, and *see* the following language in a case involving use of mas-

sive dosages of radiation to treat nonoperable colon cancer: "In order for a physician to avoid liability by engaging in drastic or experimental treatment, which exceeds the bounds of established medical standards, his patient must always be fully informed of the experimental nature of the treatment and of the forseeable consequences of that treatment." Ahern v. Veterans Admin., 537 F.2d 1098, 1102 (10 Cir. 1976).

36. Fiorentino v. Wenger, 26 App. Div. 2d 693, 272 N.Y.S.2d 557 (1966).

37. *Id.* at 272 N.Y.S.2d 559.

38. *Id.*

39. *Id.*

40. Karp v. Cooley, 349 F. Supp. 827 (S.D. Tex. 1972); Karp v. Cooley, 493 F.2d 408 (5th Cir. 1974).

41. *Id.*

42. Karp v. Cooley, 349 F. Supp. 827, 829 (S.D. Tex. 1972).

43. *Id.* at 831.

44. Karp v. Cooley, 493 F.2d 408, 423 (5th Cir. 1974).

45. *See*, notes 31-32 *supra* and accompanying text.

46. NIH Guide, 3:11 (Aug. 7, 1974).

47. Thorwald, The Patients (1971) at 57-63. Ms. Richardson was the second person to receive an artificial implant at the hands of Dr. Dwight Harkin, and the only one of his first five recipients to survive.

48. *Id.* at 92-101. As reported in the *Chicago Tribune* of May 23, 1951.

49. Thorwald, The Patients (1971) at 200-205.

50. *Id.* at 246.

51. *Id.* at 248-250.

52. Barnard, One Life (1969) at 348.

53. *Id.* at 310-311.

54. Thorwald, The Patients (1971) at 402.

55. Committee on Ethics of the American Heart Association, Ethical Considerations of the Left Ventricular Assist Device, 235 JAMA 823 (Feb. 23, 1976). *Cf.* Annas & Healey, The Patient Rights Advocate—Redefining the Doctor-Patient Relationship in the Hospital Context, 27 Vanderbilt L. Rev. 243 (1974).

56. *Id.* at 824.

57. Kaimowitz v. Mich. Dept. Mental Health, discussed in detail in the chapter on the Mentally Infirm, *infra*.

58. The text of this form is set forth at 149, *infra*.

59. But see the kidney transplant cases discussed in the chapter on Children. At least two courts have refused to sanction kidney donations where the potential donors were mentally incompetent.

60. Halushka v. University of Saskatchewan, 52 W.W.R. 608 (Sask. 1965).

61. *Id.*

62. *Id.*

63. Katz, Experimentation with Human Beings (1972).

64. *Id.* at 11 (letter from Chester M. Southam to Emmanuel Mandel, July 5, 1963).

65. This function was given to a new body under the 1975 "malpractice" act.

66. *Id.* at 60; and *see* In the Matter of Southam and Mandel, Report of the Regents Committee on Discipline (Nos. 158, 159, undated opinion), at 5-6.

67. *Id.* at 6.

68. *Id.* at 7-8.

Chapter 2

The Current Status of the Law of Informed Consent to Human Experimentation

In the first chapter we explored the historical development of the law of informed consent to human experimentation as seen through the eyes of the appellate courts. This chapter continues that discussion by examining informed consent in an analogous situation—the doctor-patient relationship. The hope is that such an examination will expose the major issues in the current debate concerning informed consent, and will serve to highlight the differences between the therapeutic and experimental setting. These differences explain why the requirements for informed consent should be more stringent in the experimental setting. After this is done, we will examine the different approaches state legislatures have taken to the issue of informed consent. Finally we will explore the difficult questions of defining "risks" raised by both the courts and current HEW regulations designed to protect human subjects, and then examine the limits of the informed consent doctrine.

INFORMED CONSENT IN THERAPY

Battery or Negligence?

In the doctor-patient relationship, failure to obtain proper consent has traditionally been treated as a battery (unconsented-to touching) action.[1] The most frequently tried cases involve those in which the physician has operated on the wrong part of the body (and therefore one for which consent has not been obtained), or cases in which the physician has failed to adequately advise the patient of the potential consequences of a certain course of treatment.[2] In one Texas case, for example, the court relied on the battery theory to hold a physician liable for failure to advise a patient of the potential total loss of hearing which occurs in one percent of all stapedectomy operations.[3] In both of these types of cases, the patient can recover damages from a physician if he can demonstrate that he did not consent to the procedure performed. Where material information has been withheld, the consent obtained is simply found to be ineffective. The basis of these suits is the oft-cited principle that "every human being of adult years and sound mind has a right to determine what shall be done with his own body . . ."[4] Consent, it is said, "entails an opportunity to evaluate knowledgeably the options available and the risks attendant upon each."[5]

The modern trend in the courts is to view failure to provide adequate disclosure of alternatives and risks as a breach of the physician's *duty* to the patient, and thus to require the patient to sue in *negligence* instead of battery. As a negligence action the patient must prove not simply that the treatment was unconsented to, but that he was injured by the treatment, and had the physician fulfilled his duty of disclosure, the patient would not have consented to the treatment, and therefore would not have been harmed. The Supreme Court of Wisconsin has listed a number of reasons for preferring the negligence theory over the battery approach:

1. Rather than intending an unlawful touching, as in traditional battery cases, physicians are "invariably acting in good faith and for the benefit of the patient . . . the act complained of is surely not of an antisocial nature usually associated with the tort of assault and battery."

2. The failure to inform adequately is "probably not, in the usual case, an intentional act and hence not within the traditional concept of intentional torts."

3. The act complained of "is not within the traditional idea of 'contact' or 'touching' . . . the physician [usually] performs the surgery or other treatment" impeccably. The complaint is the reactions which were unanticipated.

4. The physician's malpractice insurance may not cover intentional torts, such as battery, which may amount to a criminal act.

5. No punitive damages (also called exemplary or "punishment" damages) should be awarded for failure to warn cases.[6]

The court is probably correct with reasons 1 and 3, but the others would seem either wrong (#2 and #5) or irrelevant (#4). Whether one finds this analysis persuasive or not, however, the fact is that the patient in the therapeutic setting faces an *extremely* difficult task in prevailing against a physician for nondisclosure of risks in all but the grossest of malpractice cases, such as some of those from the 19th and early 20th century outlined in Chapter One.[7] The reason for this is best understood by analyzing the elements of proof in this type of negligence or malpractice suit.

Informed Consent as a Negligence Action

Instead of simply proving lack of consent and a "touching," in a negligence action the patient must establish: (1) that the physician had a *duty* toward him; (2) that the duty was *breached*; (3) that *damages* occurred to the patient; and (4) that the damages were *caused* by the breach of duty. If any of these elements cannot be demonstrated, the physician will prevail. Moreover, even if all of the elements are proven, the physician in an informed consent case has a number of affirmative *defenses*, the most important one in this context being the *therapeutic privilege*, which may also allow him to prevail. Each of these elements merits discussion.

A patient can sue only if one of the undisclosed risks actually occurs and causes him physical or mental damage. Thus, even though a physician made no disclosures and the patient can demonstrate that had he been aware of the risks he would not have consented, no action would be possible against the physician under a negligence theory unless the patient suffered an injury. In a battery action, on the other hand, the patient could sue successfully.

Secondly, a majority of the courts still permit the medical profession to define the scope of the physician's duty. Thus the physician is required to make only those disclosures that other members of his profession would make in similar circumstances and the plaintiff is required to produce an expert witness on this issue. Therefore, if standard medical practice was not to disclose the risks of a particular operation, no physician would have any legal obligation to make such disclosures.

A number of recent cases, however, have abandoned this rule in favor of one which would base the physician's duty on the patient's need to know, rather than on standard medical practice. In the words of one court:

> The patient's right to make up his mind should not be delegated to a local medical group—many of whom have no idea as to his informational needs. The doctor-patient relationship is a one-on-one affair. What is reasonable disclosure in one instance may not be reasonable in another.[8]

Put another way, by a different court, "Respect for the patient's right of self-determination on particular therapy demands a standard set by law rather than one which physicians may or may not impose upon themselves."[9] Based on the patient's need to know, the so-called "legal" standard, the physician is required to disclose, in lay language:

1. A description of the proposed treatment;
2. Alternatives to the proposed treatment;
3. Inherent risks of death or serious bodily injury in the proposed treatment;
4. Problems of recuperation that are anticipated; *and*
5. Any additional information other physicians would disclose in similar circumstances.[10]

No disclosure at all is necessary for common procedures where the risks are small and generally appreciated, *e.g.*, blood drawing.[11] The basis of this duty is usually said to be the *fiduciary qualities of the doctor-patient relationship.*[12] The patient is described as having an abject dependence on the physician for medical information, and must necessarily trust his physician to be truthful and completely candid with him.[13] Because of this trust and dependence, which are inherent in the doctor-patient relationship, the physician has an affirmative duty to make the disclosures outlined above to his patient prior to commencing treatment. A breach of duty, of course, occurs when the disclosure required by whichever rule is adopted in the particular jurisdiction is not given.

Perhaps the most difficult questions in an informed consent case, however, involve causation and the defense of the therapeutic privilege. As previously noted, the patient must prove to the satisfaction of the jury that had the disclosure been made he would not have consented to the proposed treatment, and therefore would not have been injured. Two approaches to this question are possible. The battery rationale considers the doctrine of informed consent to be based primarily on an individual's right of self-determination, and holds that an individual can refuse medical treatment for himself for *any* reason, no matter how silly or unsound it may seem to the physician or the community. Under this theory the proper question to the jury should be, would *this* injured patient have consented to the treatment if the risks had been properly disclosed? Such things as the individual's fear of losing a particular body part or organ, his business schedule, and his personal quirks would be especially relevant to this question, as would the individual's own sworn testimony on this subject.

Courts adopting the "patient's need" or "legal" standard to define the scope of the physician's duty to disclose have, however, consistently refused to adopt this "self-determination" approach on causation. Instead the courts have worried out loud about the jury's ability to judge the veracity of an injured patient who testifies (based on "20-20 hindsight") as to what he would have done if . . . , and have labeled such questions as "hypothetical."[14] They have also been concerned that physicians would be burdened by determining what, if any, individual quirks the patient might have that would cause him to reject an otherwise commonly accepted medical treatment.[15] Therefore, rather than adopt the strictly subjective standard that protects patient autonomy, the courts have adopted a somewhat more objective standard to protect the physician. The jury is asked to find not what the individual patient would have decided with proper information, but what a "reasonable person" in the patient's position would have decided. Thus if a "reasonable person" with a duodenal ulcer would have agreed to surgery knowing of a five percent risk that an ulcer would soon develop in his stomach, no disclosure of this five percent risk need be made![16] Moreover, the person who valued his stomach for some particular reason would not be able to successfully sue a physician for failure to disclose this information to him—even though he could prove he would have refused the treatment had he known about it!

Finally, as if all this were not enough to guarantee that the nonquack would prevail in almost every informed consent case on the issue of causation alone, the courts have also given physicians some *affirmative defenses*. The most commonly stated ones are that no disclosures need be made:

1. In an emergency;
2. If the patient does not want to be informed;
3. If the procedure is simple and the danger remote and commonly appreciated as remote;
4. If in the physician's judgment it is not in the patient's best interests to know.[17]

Whatever the applicability of these defenses to the therapeutic setting, only the third should be permitted any place in the experimental setting. The first defense, of course, should never be applicable to the nontherapeutic experimental setting, since proper experimentation cannot be carried out on an emergency basis with volunteers. Nor would the second be applicable, as a subject should not be permitted, as a matter of public policy, to volunteer for an experiment that he does not know anything about. We would take this so far as to argue that both for the protection of the subject and to insure basic minimal procedures are followed in all cases of human experimentation, the subject should not even be permitted to waive his right to this information. The third should apply, if at all, only to things like drawing an extra c.c. or two of blood from an otherwise necessary venipuncture. The fourth is by far the most troublesome and, like waiver, should never be allowed into the experimental setting, even where therapy is a primary purpose, because of the great potential for abuse.

The doctrine of *therapeutic privilege* has been variously stated. Broadly it "obtains when risk-disclosure poses such a threat of detriment to the patient as to become unfeasible or contraindicated from a medical point of view."[18] Specific examples include extreme illness or emotional upset that could lead to inability to form a rational decision, complicate or hinder treatment, or cause psychological damage to the patient.[19] Stated more narrowly the privilege attaches "when a doctor can prove by a preponderance of the evidence he relied upon facts which would demonstrate to a reasonable man the disclosure would have so seriously upset the patient that the patient would not have been able to dispassionately weigh the risks of refusing to undergo the recommended treatment."[20] Suffice it to say that the purpose of the doctrine is to make sure patients get treatment that physicians believe they need, and it therefore has no application to nontherapeutic experimentation where no treatment is involved.

Because of the great potential for abuse, *e.g.*, the withholding of information for convenience or to assure the patient will not reject the treatment, and because the probability of success with an experimental treatment is either not known or very low, this exception should also not be permitted in the case of therapeutic experimentation. Indeed, as has been noted by a number of commentators, in this situation the physician-experimenter may have much more ability to obtain consent for an experiment than he would have from a normal volunteer, who neither has an established dependency relation with him, nor expects that the proposed experiment might be personally beneficial to him. As Professor Alexander Capron has observed:

> The "normal volunteer" solicited for an experiment is in a good position to consider the physical, psychological, and monetary risks and benefits to him when he consents to participate. How much harder that is for the patient to whom an experimental technique is offered during a course of treatment! The man proposing the experiment is one to whom the patient

may be deeply indebted for past care (emotionally as well as financially) and on whom he is probably dependent for his future well-being. The procedure may be offered, despite unknown risks, because more conventional methods have proved ineffective. Even when a successful but slow recovery is being made, patients offered new therapy often have eyes only for its novelty and not for the risks.[21]

In order to protect self-determination and promote rational decisionmaking, more, not less, information should probably be required to be disclosed in the experimental therapy situation than in the purely experimental setting with a normal volunteer. If the negligence model is adopted in the experimental setting, causation should be subjectively based and the therapeutic privilege found, as it was in the Jewish Chronic Disease case and the *Halushka* case, to be inapplicable.

Functions of the Informed Consent Doctrine

Of the approximately two hundred appellate decisions to date dealing with the issue of informed consent, fewer than twenty-five percent (forty-five cases) mention the basis on which the court found or failed to find informed consent necessary. Of those that do give a basis, twenty-five rely on the patient's right of self-determination, thirteen citing *Schloendorff*.[22] The other cases tend to rely on the fiduciary qualities of the doctor-patient relationship—seventeen cases basing their conclusions on it, four in conjunction with a self-determination rationale. Just as rationales vary from jurisdiction to jurisdiction, so do specific rules concerning the law of informed consent.

Nevertheless, there are certain broad conclusions that can be drawn concerning the functions of the informed consent doctrine from these cases. For example, with Professor Jay Katz of Yale, Professor Capron has argued that informed consent performs six distinct functions in cases involving medical intervention:

1. To promote individual autonomy;
2. To protect the patient-subject's status as a human being;
3. To avoid fraud and duress;
4. To encourage self-scrutiny by the physician-investigator;
5. To encourage rational decision making; and
6. To involve the public.[23]

While this is a well thought out list, it is probably correct to say that number (6) is illusory, or at best a potential byproduct, rather than a function. Moreover, numbers (1), (2) and (3) are simply different ways of stating the same basic proposition, i.e. the promotion of individual autonomy. Further, number (5) is simply another way of stating number (4) i.e. the promotion of rational decision making. It would thus seem correct to conclude that the primary functions of the doctrine of informed consent are two: to promote individual autonomy, and to encourage rational decision making.

Since the functions of the doctrine are its justifications for existence and use, it is worth spending a moment exploring them. Initially, it should be pointed out that the primary reason for "disclosure statements" is the *promotion of equity and fairness* among parties who otherwise have inherently unequal bargaining positions. This is a more general proposition, and can be said to include both the promotion of individual autonomy and of rational decision making. Thus in many other analogous areas of law courts and legislatures have redefined previously—protected relationship by requiring some minimal disclosures prior to any binding agreement. Examples include the Securities Exchange Act which required certain disclosures to stockholders and purchasers,[24] the Uniform Commercial Code, regulating transactions between buyers and sellers,[25] and laws requiring certain disclosures to debtors by creditors, especially concerning interest rates and repayment terms.[26] Perhaps the most controversial and best-known example, however, is the *Miranda* rule, requiring police to give certain "warnings" before questioning a suspect.[27]

While these disclosure requirements are all analogous, and remind us that the requirement of informed consent in the medical arena is certainly not unique, they cannot serve a precise analogy for two reasons. The first is that unlike the general suspicion a purchaser has of a seller (summarized in the statement, "buyer beware"), that a debtor has of a creditor, a suspect of the police, a prisoner of a warden, etc., the patient usually has a tremendous amount of trust and confidence in his physician.[28] This promotes what some courts have referred to as the "abject dependency" on the physician. Moreover, since medical care may be an absolute necessity of life in some circumstances, the real options open to the patient may be extremely limited. This means that more than legislative formulas are necessary to insure that the patient is adequately informed of such things as risks and alternatives. An affirmative, albeit sometimes difficult, burden must be placed on the physician to insure that these disclosures are made. No formula is possible (as it is, for example, in the case of annual interest rates) since risks and alternatives will vary from procedure to procedure, and perhaps from patient to patient.

The second major difference between medical decision making and the other examples we reviewed is that the consequences of medical treatment (and experimentation) are often irreversible. This is especially true of significant physical disabilities. Under these circumstances decisions once acted upon cannot effectively be changed, and the importance of making the "right" decision initially becomes that much more important. Keeping these two distinctions in mind, we now examine the two major functions (or subfunctions, if the promotion of equity and fairness is viewed as the primary function) of the informed consent doctrine in the doctor-patient and investigator-subject relationship.

To promote individual autonomy. The purpose of autonomy is to protect the individual's integrity as a person or "human being" by denying anyone the right to invade his body without his consent. This simple proposition can be restated in a number of ways and approached from a variety of directions—the ultimate conclusion, however, remains the same. For example, one can term this the "right to be left alone,"[29] or the "right to privacy" in terms of bodily decision making.[30] Another approach is the view that research on human subjects must always be viewed as a "joint enterprise" between the researcher and subject to prevent the subject from becoming a means or thing to be used, instead of an end or human being.[31] Viewed from this perspective, informed consent is necessary to prevent the gross advantage-taking of subjects to the point where their "humanness" is in such question that the types of procedures that are performed on them is expanded beyond that which society would view as tolerable on members of the human race.[32]

Still another approach notes that the purpose of human experimentation is ultimately to benefit all through medical progress, but that the burdens or risks of such experimentation will of necessity fall on only a few. In this view the subject is giving a "gift" to society—a gift that cannot rightfully be forceably taken, and one that is devalued (and the giver debased) insofar as the gift is based on a false assumption concerning the risks involved.[33] As with all of the other approaches, the conclusion is that to adequately protect an individual's autonomy and personhood, it is essential to provide him with enough information to permit him to make up his own mind concerning participation in the proposed experiment.

The view that such promotion of individual autonomy comes at the price of sometimes delaying scientific advances is, we think, adequately dealt with by the oft-quoted argument of Hans Jonas:

Let us not forget that progress is an optional goal, not an unconditional commitment, and that its tempo in particular, compulsive as it may become, has nothing sacred about it. Let us also remember that a slower progress in the conquest of disease would not threaten society, grievous as it is to those who have to deplore that their particular disease be not yet conquered, but that society would indeed be threatened by the erosion of those moral values whose loss, probably caused by too ruthless a pursuit of scientific progress, would make its most dazzling triumphs not worth having.[34]

To encourage rational decision making. While this goal is clearly viewed as a secondary one by the courts, it is, in fact, an extremely important function of the informed consent doctrine at least to the extent that if this goal was not achieved in any instance, the entire concept would be called into serious question. Katz and Capron, for example, note that the requirement that the researcher catalogue and explain the risks inherent in any research proposal to the subject requires him to review the literature and animal experiments before embarking on human experimentation.[35] They quote Professor Paul •
Freund as noting that:

> To analyze an experiment in terms of risks and benefits to particular groups by way of presentation for consent is a salutary procedure for self-scrutiny by the investigator—like the preparation of a registration statement by a corporation issuing securities.[36]

The hope is that this self-scrutiny will prevent a number of research projects from being performed, or at least postpone their initiation until adequate animal testing has been done. Related to this, of course, is the role of the subject. One would anticipate, for example, that after a candid review of extreme risks, the subjects would refuse to participate with such regularity as to make experiments that are inherently too dangerous to be ethically performed on humans *de facto* impossible. It is suggested that this ability to refuse to participate is what is really at stake here, rather than the ability of the subject to fully comprehend all of the aspects of the research proposal and make an independent judgment as to its merit. As Katz and Capron point out, "[W]ho other than the patient-subjects, can determine whether the benefits of a procedure, conventional or experimental, outweigh the burdens that will be imposed on them?"[37]
It should thus be clear that the function of informed consent in this instance is to help insure that those who bear the risks of experimentation will have the final decision as to whether or not it is performed. The argument is that this type of market or voluntary decision based on proper information, will help minimize the costs to the system for scientific advance.[38] The idea is not that "Two heads

are better than one" (a refrain or popular proverb that as Sancho Panza illustrated, can often be refuted by another, such as "Too many cooks spoil the broth"), but that rational decisions are more likely to be made if they are left in the hands of those who bear the risk of those decisions rather than those who might have ulterior motives, such as career advancement, in making the decision.[39]

The traditional argument against the subject-patient having a major role in the decision making process is twofold: (1) the patient will never be able to comprehend the information related; and (2) the information will unduly frighten the patient, and he will therefore not participate in research projects that actually entail only a minimal risk. The conclusion drawn by those who make this argument is that ultimately we must rely not on the transaction between the subject and the investigator, but on the individual ethical responsibility of the investigator himself to insure that the rights of subjects are properly protected.[40] The reality of the informed subject is explained by Beecher:

> The experienced clinician knows that if he has a good rapport with his patients they will often knowingly submit, for the sake of 'science', to inconvenience and even to discomfort, if it doesn't take very long; but excepting the extremely rare individual, the reality is, patients will not knowingly seriously risk their health or their lives for a scientific experiment. It is ridiculous to assume otherwise. They will not do it.[41]

The answer to the argument is that reliance on the beneficence of the investigator is completely insufficient and sometimes misplaced (as the examples of first-of-its kind surgical implants reviewed in Chapter One illustrate).[42] It is the physician's proper duty to inform and educate the subject sufficiently to enable him to make up his own mind. If the physician-investigator argues this is not possible, he may in fact be saying one of two things: he cannot properly explain the risks and alternatives because he does not understand them himself, or he believes if he does properly explain them, the subject will not consent. In either case the answer is that rational decision making will be promoted by both the development of an adequate disclosure statement, and the requirement that the subject be given final authority concerning the application of the experimental method to him.

To accomplish these functions in the experimental setting it is, of course, essential not only that full information be given to the subject but also that the subject be able to comprehend this information well enough to base a reasonable decision on it. Since we have argued that subjects should not be permitted to waive disclosure of such information, it may be appropriate to develop criteria for comprehension of the information disclosed. For example, Bradford Gray has demonstrated in his studies of women involved in trials using an experimental method of labor induction, that even though they had signed a consent form which indicated the experimental nature and risks of the study, forty percent did not realize that they were in an experimental study when their participation began and forty-one percent did not realize that any risks were involved.[43] If this is typical, and there is little reason to suppose it is not, new mechanisms must be developed to supplement oral and printed form disclosures to insure that the subjects comprehend the information disclosed.

One such mechanism might be a series of true-false questions on the informed consent form itself. Failure to answer them all correctly (e.g. Does this study entail any risk of death?) would require additional explanations to the subject until he either comprehended the information or was rejected for the study because of inability to comprehend the information. Other mechanisms, mentioned elsewhere in this book, include the use of a consent review committee, or a patient-subject advocate whose task it would be to insure that the subject gave an informed and comprehending consent.[44]

State Laws on Informed Consent

In states with statutes on the subject, the statutory language defining and/or limiting the doctrine of informed consent will be controlling. Prior to 1975 few states had any laws dealing specifically with this subject. In 1975 and 1976, however, at least eighteen states[45] enacted statutes that either defined or restricted the application of the doctrine of informed consent in reaction to the malpractice insurance crisis.[46] A brief review of some of the provisions of these statutes is useful because it identifies issues that state legislatures currently view as important in this area.

None of the statutes specifically mentions or deals with experimental procedures, although the Florida statute applies only to treatment that is in accordance with "an accepted standard of medical practice . . ."[47] Most of the statutes attempt, in one way or another, to make it more difficult for a patient to be successful in a suit against a physician for failure to obtain informed consent.

Statutes in nine states provide that a patient's signature on a consent form shall be conclusive evidence that the information was provided to the patient and that the consent was valid.[48] Florida's statute, for example, provides that the signed consent shall be "conclusively presumed to be valid consent."[49] This presumption "may be rebutted if there was a *fraudulent misrepresentation of a material fact* in obtaining the signature."[50] (emphasis supplied) Idaho's statute likewise provides that "such written consent, in the absence of convincing proof that it was *secured maliciously or by fraud*, is presumed to be valid . . . and the advice and disclosures of the attending physician or dentist, as well as the *level of informed awareness* of the given of such consent, shall be presumed sufficient."[51] (emphasis supplied)

In Iowa:

A consent in writing to any medical or surgical procedure or course of procedures *in patient care* which meets the requirements of this section *shall create a presumption* that informed consent was given.[52] (emphasis supplied)

And in Ohio:

Written consent to a surgical or medical procedure or course of procedures shall, to the extent that it fulfills . . . [certain requirements] *be presumed to be valid and effective*, in the absence of proof by a preponderance of the evidence that the person who sought such consent was *not acting in good faith*, or that the execution of the consent was induced by *fraudulent misrepresentation of material* facts, or that the person executing the consent was *not able to communicate effectively in* spoken or written *English* or any other language in which the consent is written.[53] (emphasis supplied)

Both in Iowa and Ohio statutes also certain lists of the types of risks the legislatures require that physicians disclose. The language of each is set forth because it gives an indication of the types of risks a legislature (as opposed to a court) has found to be of significance to patients in the therapeutic setting. The argument, of course, is that such risks must *a fortiori* be disclosed in the experimental setting. The lists are identical, both statutes requiring disclosure of the following risks: "death, brain damage, quadriplegia, paraplegia, the loss of function of any organ or limb, or disfiguring scars . . . with the probability of each such risk if reasonably determinable."[54] The approach of eight [55] other statutes follows that of New York, in which the physician is required to disclose only those "risks and benefits involved as a reasonable medical practitioner under similar circumstances would have disclosed . . ."[56] Five other states (in addition to Ohio and Iowa), Colorado, Utah, Nevada, Alaska, and Idaho adopt their own definitions of informed consent, while Pennsylvania and Washington base disclosure on the "risks and alternatives to treatment or diagnosis that a reasonable patient would consider material to the decision whether or not to undergo treatment or diagnosis."[57]

Two other provisions are of interest. Colorado attempts to clarify the type of disclosure required in probability terms in cases involving a risk of death or serious injury. The physician is required to quantify such risk by approximating "the percentage within two percent of the risk associated with the procedure, which percentage is either contained in a recognized medical publication or is measured by the experience of the physician out of a substantial number of the same or similar procedures."[58] The unstated, but probably intentional implication is that risks having less than a two percent probability need not be disclosed. Ohio goes one step further, and is the only state legislature which sets forth a model consent form in its statute, providing that if this form is properly used, consent shall be presumed to be valid. Because of its uniqueness, the entire text of the form is set forth here:

CONSENT FOR MEDICAL PROCEDURE AND ACKNOWLEDGMENT OF RECEIPT OF RISK INFORMATION

State law requires us to obtain your consent to your contemplated surgery or other medical procedure. What you are being asked to sign is simply a confirmation that we have discussed your contemplated operation or medical procedure and that we have given you sufficient information upon which to make a decision whether to have the operation or medical procedure and any choice as to the type of operation or medical procedure of your own free will. We have already discussed with you the common problems or undesired results that sometimes occur. We wish to inform you, not to alarm you. If you wish, however, we can go into more elaborate details or more unlikely problems. If you do not, that is also your privilege. Please read the form carefully and check the appropriate boxes. Ask about anything that you do not understand. We will be pleased to explain it. I hereby authorize and direct _____ , with associate or assistants of his choice to perform the following surgical, diagnostic, or medical procedure on _____ , my _____ , as we have agreed upon.   relationship

---

I further authorize the doctors to perform any other procedure that in their judgment is advisable for my well being. Details of this operation have been explained to me. Alternative methods of treatment, if any, have also been explained to me as have the advantages and disadvantages of each. I am advised that though good results are expected, the possibility and nature of complications cannot be accurately anticipated and that therefore there can be no guarantee as expressed or implied either as to the result of surgery or as to cure.

Degree and kind of risks known to be associated with this procedure, including anesthesia; each marked box indicates some risks that are associated with this procedure:

<table>
<tr><td></td><td>Comments</td></tr>
</table>

Death   _____
Brain Damage   _____
Quadriplegia (paralysis of all arms and legs)   _____
Paraplegia (paralysis of both legs)   _____
Loss of organ   _____
Loss of an arm or leg   _____
Loss of function of organ   _____
Loss of function of an arm or leg   _____
Disfiguring scars   _____

The doctor has explained to me the most likely complications or undesired results that might occur in this operation or medical procedure and I understand them. The doctor has offered to detail the less likely complications of [sic] undesired results which, even if rare, could occur.

_____ I do _____ I do not wish to have a full description of all the possible complications given to me.

I hereby authorize and direct the above named physician with associates or assistants to provide such additional services as they might deem reasonable and necessary including, but not limited to, the administration of any anesthetic agent, or the services of the X-ray department or laboratories, and I hereby consent thereto.

I hereby state that I have read and understand this consent and that all blanks were filled in prior to my signature.

Date: _____ _____ Time _____ a.m. p.m.

Signature of Patient _____
Signature of Relative (where required) _____
Witness _____

I certify that I have personally completed all blanks in this form and explained them to the patient or his representative before requesting the patient or his representative to sign it.

_____ (signature of named physician)[59]

The purpose of this form seems to strike a balance between requiring physicians to prepare unique forms for each procedure and using a standard form for all procedures. Here, for example, a standard form is used, but each case is treated uniquely based on the manner in which the blanks are filled in. The danger exists, however, that providing this time-saving device to the physician may detract from the goal of promoting individual autonomy and encouraging rational

decision-making. The more routine and standard the procedure becomes, the less likely it will be that these goals will be attained. Informed consent is a *process* of giving and receiving information. The
consent form, on the other hand, is merely physical evidence that the
process has taken place. Its traditional role has been to help protect
the physician in case the patient later denies that informed consent
was in fact obtained.

It would be a tragedy if the promotion of a uniform consent form
led to making the process itself just one step that both physician and
patient come to regard as unnecessary red tape, and consequently do
not engage in the dialogue envisioned by the doctrine. While this is
not a necessary outcome, it is a potential one and is one of the reasons that we do not anywhere in this book set forth a "model" consent form. Each procedure has its own unique risks, and each patient
is in some manner unique. Only by going through the difficult task
of tailoring information to fit the procedure and the patient is it
likely that either individual autonomy or rational decision-making
will be promoted. If neither of these functions is furthered, the
process becomes meaningless.

While few conclusions can be drawn from this group of statutes,
one can see a trend toward treating the written consent form as a
complete defense in an informed consent case (barring fraud or misrepresentation). What most legislatures that have acted on this question to date are concerned with is *disclosure* on the part of the
physician, rather than *understanding* on the part of the patient. In
this approach they are consistent with the appellate courts. Where
some are less consistent is in their permitting the physician to limit
disclosures based on "standard medical practice" rather than on the
patient's need to know. In this regard many of the statutes must be
seen as anti-self-determination measures. Again, however, it should
be emphasized that *none* of the statutes specifically deals with the
experimental setting, and arguably none is applicable to it.

Federal Regulations on Informed Consent

Current federal regulations define informed consent in the research setting as follows:

[T]he knowing consent of an individual or his legally authorized representative, so situated as to be able to exercise free power of choice without
undue inducement or any element of force, fraud, deceit, duress, or other
form of constraint or coercion. The basic elements of information necessary to such consent include:
(1) A fair explanation of the procedure to be followed, and their pur-

poses, including identification of any procedures which are experimental;

(2) A description of any attendant discomforts and risks reasonably to be expected;

(3) A description of any benefits reasonably to be expected;

(4) A disclosure of any appropriate alternative procedures that might be advantageous for the subject;

(5) An offer to answer any inquiries concerning the procedures; and

(6) An instruction that the person is free to withdraw his consent and to discontinue participation in the project or activity at any time without prejudice to the subject.[60]

The regulations further prohibit the use of "any exculpatory language through which the subject is made to waive, or to appear to waive, any of his legal rights, including any release of the institution or its agents from liability for negligence."[61] The regulations require that all consents obtained be "fully documented" in one of the following three ways. (1) By a signed written consent form containing all of the elements outlined above; (2) by a signed written consent form indicating that all of the elements above have been orally transmitted; or (3) by any other method approved by the institution's Institutional Review Board, but only if the Board finds: (1) That the risk to any subject is minimal, (b) that use of either of the primary procedures for obtaining informed consent would surely invalidate objectives of considerable immediate importance; and (c) that any reasonable alternative means for attaining these objectives would be less advantageous to the subjects.[62] The IRB is also required to specify its reasons for such modification in the minutes of its meeting, and to review the modification "regularly."[63]

From this description it can be seen that HEW views the consent form itself as a major means of protecting human subjects, and the requirement of documentation of the consent is not viewed primarily as protection for the researcher (as it is usually), but as protection for the subject himself. This probably explains the great emphasis put on the content of such forms by most IRB's, and the almost exclusive concern with this issue at IRB meetings.[64] While we would argue that use of such guidelines, rather than use of a model form as that in Ohio, makes good sense in that it requires that some thought be given to each issue and how it relates to the proposed research, it is not at all clear that so much emphasis on the content of the form itself is appropriate. This is not to say that content is unimportant, but only to reemphasize that the end is the *process of decision-making*, not the documentation of it. If forms become routinely signed, as was evidenced by the study of Bradford Gray at a large teaching hospital,[65] documentation will prove nothing, and the signing of the form will not indicate that a process has taken place—it will, instead, substitute for the process itself. These issues, of course, become even more critical when "special populations," like children, prisoners, or mental patients, (discussed in separate chapters) are the proposed subjects of human experimentation.

Therapy vs. Experimentation: Some Conclusions

The law of informed consent in the therapeutic setting is more evolving and uncertain than in the area of experimentation—even though there is "more" of it. The discussion of it, in this much detail, is meant primarily to attempt to demonstrate what aspects of the doctrine of informed consent in therapy might be applicable to the experimental setting, and which aspects are not. *The general conclusion is that more detailed disclosures and no therapeutic privileges should be the rule in the experimental setting.* Moreover, it may be appropriate to permit noninjured experimental subjects to sue for battery and punitive damages as a deterrent to investigators who routinely fail to obtain informed consent from their subjects.

No case law, statute, or regulation has been found that is as comprehensive as the Nuremberg Code. That Code requires the competent, voluntary, informed, and *understanding* consent of the subject. While "understanding" is implicit in some of the cases discussed in this section, use of the objective causation standard in the more recent cases makes it clear that the critical element is *disclosure* (*i.e.,* information), not understanding. As one court put it in the leading modern case on informed consent:

> Adequate disclosure and informed consent are, of course, two sides of the same coin—the former a *sine qua non* of the latter. But *the vital inquiry on duty to disclose relates to the physician's performance of an obligation* while one of the difficulties with analysis in terms of "informed consent" is its tendency to imply that what is decisive is the degree of the patient's comprehension. As we later emphasize, *the physician discharges the duty when he makes a reasonable effort to convey sufficient information although the patient, without fault of the physician, may not fully grasp it.*[66] (emphasis supplied)

The legal implication is clear: In theory the patient need not understand to effectively consent. Some recent state statutes likewise provide that a patient's signature on a consent form is an *irrebuttable* (except in cases of fraud or misrepresentation) presumption that he understood the contents of the forms. This is not, and should not be, the rule in experimentation. Indeed, we would argue this approach is defective even in the therapeutic situation.

The physician need not be put at the mercy of an "odd" patient with peculiar needs or beliefs. Simple questions can be asked to expose these, and risks can be detailed and explained—first in writing and then in person. If doubts exist as to a patient's comprehension, a short multiple choice questionnaire can be filled out. The patient's responses will indicate his level of comprehension. The question of which risks should be disclosed is explored in the next section.

THE LAW'S VIEW OF "RISK"

The meaning of "risk" in the law is generally confined to death and bodily injury, and only in rare instances to psychological or emotional trauma. Courts tend to look at risks in qualitative terms, and tend not to deal with quantitative terms like probabilities. When they do, their analyses are not always consistent. While some of this inconsistency can be explained by the unique facts at work in each case, this explanation is not always adequate. For example, Table 2-1 lists nineteen qualitative risks that courts have found important enough to require that they be disclosed to patients prior to treatment. Table 2-2, on the other hand, lists nineteen risks that courts have determined did *not* have to be disclosed. This listing covers almost all of the cases which found that specific risks had to be disclosed, and most of them that found they did not. The only conclusion that can be drawn is that there is no general agreement among courts on the quality of the risks that must be disclosed. In fact, there is no significant difference between these two lists.

Nor have courts been much more helpful in discussing probabilities. Some courts have simply said "all risks potentially affecting the patient's decision" must be disclosed,[105] without attempting to deal with probabilities. One court, on the other hand, has gone so far as to require a drug manufacturer to disclose directly to the recipient of a polio vaccine that the vaccine carried a *one in a million* chance of producing polio in the recipient.[106] That court, however, said it was specifically *rejecting* the "purely statistical" approach. Their test is, "[w]hen, in a particular case, the risk qualitatively (*e.g.*, of death or major disability) as well as quantitatively, on balance with the end sought to be achieved, is such as to call for a true choice judgment, medical or personal, the warning must be given."[107] In this case the court found that the individual plaintiff had less than a one in a million chance of contracting polio without the vaccine, so that the

Table 2-1.   Examples of Risks That Must Be Disclosed

Sterility from prostate operation[67]
Amputation from finger operation[68]
Paralysis from arteriogram (3% risk of serious adverse results)[69]
Inability to open mouth completely after jaw operation[70]
Paralyzed vocal cords after thyroidectomy[71]
Brain lesion in test involving drilling holes in child's skull[72]
Injuries from gold injections for arthritis[73]
Defective child as a result of rubella during pregnancy[74]
Death from hysterectomy[75]
Amputation from hypothermia treatment[76]
Nerve damage from spinal anesthesia[66]
Paralysis from laminectomy (1% risk)[78]
Deafness from drugs[79]
Bone fracture from insulin treatment[80]
Skin damage from radiation treatment[81]
Change in leg length from hip operation[82]
Deafness from ear operation[83]
Bone fracture from electroshock treatment[84]
Paralysis from radiation treatment[85]

Table 2-2.   Examples of Risks That Courts Have Found Need Not Be Disclosed

Paralysis from contrast media use in X-rays[86]
Injury to vocal cords from anesthesia[87]
Vesicovaginal fistula from hysterectomy[88]
Ureter injury leading to loss of kidney from hysterectomy[89]
Dead facial tissue after face lift[90]
Facial bone injury after plastic surgery[91]
Head injury to child from use of forceps at birth[92]
Pregnancy after sterilization operation[93]
Loss of voice from thyroidectomy[94]
Puncture of esophagus during stomach procedure[95]
Cardiac arrest during childbirth[96]
Sinus fistula from tooth extract[97]
Hepatitis from blood transfusion[98]
Septicemia and death from ectopic pregnancy[99]
Paralysis from anesthesia[100]
Paralysis from laminectomy[101]
Fractures from electroshock treatment[102]
Death from cardiac catheterization[103]
Jaundice from gold injections[104]

decision concerning immunization was real, and should have been his to make. The drug was administered at a clinic by a nurse. Had a physician been involved, the court would have required the drug manufacturer to warn only the physician, and would have left it to the physician's discretion whether or not to warn the patient.[108]

Courts in kidney transplant cases have mentioned probabilities, but only to justify their conclusion to permit the donation. One court found that with a kidney transplant "there is substantially 100 percent probability of both twins living out a noraml life span—emotionally and physically," and accordingly sanctioned the donation which involved twin seven-year-olds.[109]

Another court concluded that the risks of kidney donation were "minimal to both the donor and the donee,"[110] citing the following language from a medical article:

> The immediate operative risk . . . in a healthy subject has been calculated as approximately 0.05 per cent . . . the long-term risk has been estimated at 0.07 per cent . . . this is an increase in risk equal to that incurred by driving a car 16 miles every working day . . .[111]

The fact that the donee in this case was an institutionalized patient who did not drive anywhere was not mentioned. The court, however, seemed to be saying that if certain risks are accepted by society as "minimal," other risks of the same magnitude should also be accepted in different contexts.

An almost identical analysis was used in a study on Atomic Reactor Safety commissioned by the Atomic Energy Commission.[112] That study, which concentrated on risks of death, concluded that society in general finds risks of death in the 1 in 1,000 range unacceptable, attempts to control and limit accidents that occur with a probability of more than 1 in 10,000 a year, is not quite as concerned with risks in the 1 in 100,000 per year range, and disregards risks in the 1 in 1,000,000 per year range.[113] The accidents examined occurred with the probabilities set forth in Table 2-3.

One need not agree with the study's conclusion that the safety of nuclear reactors should be judged against these other risks which society "accepts" to use this analysis in the experimentation setting. The study, for example, deals mainly with risks which are taken *involuntarily* (one-fifth of all people killed in auto accidents are pedestrians and one-fourth of all people killed in plane accidents were killed by planes crashing into them), and the risks are averaged over a year.

Experimentation risks are voluntary, and usually last for periods much shorter than a year. Accordingly, if we as a society take mortality risks of 1 in 100,000 seriously enough to spend large sums to decrease the risk, we should *a fortiori* require risks of this magnitude to be disclosed prior to asking individuals to volunteer as subjects for an experiment. Indeed, one can make a good argument that *any* risk of death, even 1 in a billion, should be disclosed since a significant segment of the population may avoid even this risk if given the choice. As one judge has put it, "it should be borne in mind that it is the patient who is taking the risk, not the surgeon . . ."[115]

Table 2-3. Individual Fatality Risks per Year

Type of Accident	Individual Chances per Year
Motor Vehicle	1 in 4,000
Falls	1 in 10,000
Fires	1 in 25,000
Drownings	1 in 30,000
Firearms	1 in 100,000
Air Travel	1 in 100,000
Electrocution	1 in 160,000
Lightning	1 in 1,200,000
Tornadoes	1 in 2,500,000
Hurricanes	1 in 2,500,000
Nuclear Reactor Accidents	1 in 300,000,000[114]

A case involving informed consent in a nonmedical, nonexperimental setting provides even stronger language concerning the risks that must be disclosed.[116] The plaintiff, a physician, alleged that the airline failed to warn its passengers before takeoff of expected turbulent weather on route. He was thrown into a window during the flight, breaking his glasses and experiencing angina pectoris. The evidence showed that the pilot had information that predicted heavy thunderstorms, surface wind gusts of 50 to 70 miles, cloud tops to 45,000 feet, and isolated tornadoes and hail storms which could cause "moderate to severe turbulence."[117] On these facts the court concluded that the airline had a duty to warn its passengers:

> Such conditions aloft, although possibly not extreme enough to prevent take-off, are sufficiently serious to be a matter of significant concern to prospective travellers. Although an airline must bear the ultimate responsibility for deciding whether conditions permit a safe flight, it need not and, we think, must not arrogate to itself a decision which rightly belongs to each passenger, namely whether to fly under conditions which, although not hazardous, might prove to be emotionally or physically traumatizing.[118]

By substituting subject for passenger and researcher for airline we have a test that requires disclosure of any aspect of the experiment that "might prove to be emotionally or physically traumatizing." The reason for this rule is so the passengers (subjects) "can choose for themselves whether they are physically and emotionally capable of undertaking the trip and wish to do so."[119] A strong argument can be made to support the proposition that researchers owe their subjects at least this measure of disclosure. As noted previously, the only legislative pronouncement on this issue comes from Colorado, whose statute requires disclosure, in the therapeutic setting, of all risks of death or serious liability that occur with a greater than two percent probability.[120]

It must ultimately, however, be concluded that neither the courts nor the legislatures have defined with precision either the quality or probability of the risks that must be disclosed in the experimental setting. Since this is a matter of great concern to both researchers and subjects, and since current definitions are so vague as to be almost meaningless, federal regulations should address these issues as concretely as possible. Current regulations define "subject at risk" as follows:

'Subject at risk' means any individual who may be exposed to the possibility of injury, including physical, psychological, or social injury, as a consequence of participation as a subject in any research, development, or related activity which departs from the application of those established and accepted methods necessary to meet his needs, or which increases the ordinary risks of daily life, including the recognized risks inherent in a chosen occupation or field of service.[121]

A not uncommon response to this vague and overly-inclusive definition is stated by a social scientist, David Mechanic:

Speaking as an investigator myself, I can say that I regard the statement on social risk [in the federal regulations] . . . as an unrealistic standard for social research which, if taken seriously, would interfere with research clearly in the public interest. The statement on social risk does not heighten my ethical sensitivities; the lack of reality, and even hypocrisy, of the statement just frustrates me. Yet the statement is sufficiently imprecise and ambiguous to cause no real problem in obtaining approval of research. *It breeds cynicism*, which is hardly the purpose of stating ethical rules. (emphasis supplied)[122]

Mechanic goes on to argue persuasively that if rules are to have the effect we desire, "their legitimacy must be accepted and they must appear reasonable in light of the circumstances. What we need is a framework of regulation that is simple, that is responsive to the conflict between patient rights and societal needs, and that stimulates ethical concern . . ."[123] This statement is difficult to disagree with, and we have seen, in the area of risk definition at least, that little agreement has been reached by the courts, state legislatures, or federal agencies on the issue of how "risk" is to be defined and quantified. While not as often discussed, it is worth at least noting that a definition of "benefit" is also lacking, and that these may be every bit as ill-defined and conjectural as risks.[124] All this makes weighing risks against benefits an almost impossible task.

LEGAL LIMITS OF AN INDIVIDUAL'S ABILITY TO CONSENT TO EXPERIMENTATION

Two old legal doctrines deserve discussion in the context of consent to experimentation. The first is *de minimis non curat lex*, the law does not recognize trifles. It has been argued that this doctrine means that "an extra drop of blood to build up a control group for a research study, or the use of tissue that has been properly severed would not be condemned by the court."[125] While such a result is certainly possible, and probable, it is not necessary. The doctrine's major role is to provide the court with a *discretionary* power to ignore certain very minor wrongs. In one case, for example, a one penny error in a computation of a judgment was raised as a reason to overturn it. The court held that errors of such magnitude were insufficient to warrant such action.[126] However, there are more examples of the doctrine *not* being applied than being applied. In one case a court held that the sum of six cents was not to be considered a trifle,"[127] and in another that "The smallness of the damage to a commoner for injury done to the common by taking away thence the manure which was dropped on it by the cattle is no ground for a nonsuit."[128] And in a more modern case a court held that a one in a million risk of contracting polio from the vaccine is not "so trifling in comparison with the advantage to be gained as to be *de minimis*."[129]

The *de minimis* doctrine will also not defeat an action for nominal damages where one alleges the invasion of one's person or property, or where a statute has been violated.[130] Accordingly, any federal regulations on the subject of experiments that may be permitted without documented consent should be extremely explicit. The experimenter will in most cases have to rely on federal policy as expressed in such regulations, rather than the *de minimis* doctrine, in cases where the subject alleges experimentation without consent.

While at this extreme courts would probably and properly ignore the requirements of informed consent, at the other extreme of dangerousness courts may find that the experiment is improper no matter how complete and informed the consent of the subject.

In this regard a second legal doctrine is relevant, *volenti non fit injuria*, to one who is willing no wrong is done. This general rule allows persons to consent to a wide range of activities, such as sporting contests and dangerous occupations, in which they risk serious and permanent injury. There are, however, exceptions to this rule. One may not consent to his own murder, to a duel, to a brawl in a barroom, to a maiming, or to other such activities which are regarded as a "breach of the peace" or a violation of "public policy."

The public policy against maiming (mayhem being defined as an unlawful maiming) was early recognized in Britain. There it was said that the crown had an interest in the fighting ability of its subjects and could, accordingly, punish those who diminished it by mutilation of their bodies. The rule survives due to the state's interest in maintaining the health of its citizens and in preventing them from becoming wards of the state. Maiming is therefore analogous to murder in that consent on the part of the victim is no defense. In a modern case, for example, a physician was convicted as an accessory before the fact of mayhem for anesthetizing the fingers of an individual who desired to amputate them to obtain insurance proceeds.[131] The amputation was performed by the individual when the doctor refused to perform the actual procedure himself.

While no court has specifically applied this rationale to a legitimate experimentation case, at least one case indicates that the possibility exists. In that case a seventy-five-year-old individual who claimed to be a physician, but who was not licensed in the state, treated a fifty-year-old woman with cancer of the nose using three salves.[132] She died ten months later, shortly after the defendant was indicted. By the time of her death her nose was almost completely eroded. An analysis of the salves prescribed showed that they contained zinc chloride, "a strong corrosive chemical that would eat tissue, flesh or even metal."[133] Physicians testified that use of this chemical was "not approved or recognized in the medical profession." The court found that consent "is no excuse for recklessness."[134] The case was, however, remanded for a new trial on assault and battery so that the jury could be properly instructed on the questions of intent and criminal negligence.

The case illustrates that no one can consent to an experiment that is done in "such reckless, wanton or flagrant nature as to show utter disregard of the safety of others under circumstances likely to cause injury." Accordingly, one who performs such an experiment is subject to criminal charges of mayhem, assault and battery, and manslaughter if the subject dies as a result, and consent will not be a defense.[135]

Not only is an individual's right to consent to danger circumscribed by existing criminal law, it is also relatively certain that the state could, if it so chose, make all forms of dangerous human experimentation illegal. Such a statute would be based on the general proposition that "the interests of the public require such interference, and that the means are reasonably necessary for the accomplishment of the purpose, and not unduly oppressive upon individuals."[136] Statutes making boxing subject to specific regulations, for example, do not violate the United States Constitution. In one case such a statute was challenged by a fifty-one-year-old prize fighter who had fought in more than 300 bouts.[137] The court found that the athletic commission could rightfully conclude that to allow him "to engage in such a contest would be to run the risk of serious injury to him."[138] The court went on to say that this risk was "not a consideration purely personal to him" but that the state also had a legitimate interest in his health.[139] In the court's words:

> Two main purposes have prompted such legislation: First, the desire to prevent as far as possible certain brutal and degrading features which have in the past sometimes attended such contests, and, second to promote and protect such contests when conducted within the legitimate limits of a sport.[140]

By analogy, it can be concluded that any individual state, or the federal government, could regulate dangerous human experimentation to prevent reckless experiments and to promote and protect experimentation done according to specified rules.

If the state found, however, that certain types of experimentation were so dangerous that they could not be properly controlled, a statute to outlaw such experimentation altogether would probably also be valid. In a recent case, currently on appeal to the United States Supreme Court, the Supreme Court of Tennessee outlawed the handling of snakes in religious ceremonies conducted by The Holiness Church of God in Jesus Name.[141] The court noted that while the First Amendment regarding freedom of religion was broad, it did not include the right to violate a statute or the right to commit or maintain a nuisance. In concluding that the handling of poisonous snakes by church members constituted an unlawful nuisance the court said:

> *Tennessee has the right to guard against the unnecessary creation of widows and orphans.* Our state and nation have *an interest in having a strong, healthy, robust, taxpaying citizenry* capable of bearing arms and adding to the resources and reserves of manpower. We, therefore, have a substantial and compelling state interest in the face of a clear and present danger so grave as to endanger paramount public interests . . . Yes, *the*

state has a right to protect a person from himself and to demand that he protect his own life.[142] (emphasis supplied)

In accord with this view are the statutes of a majority of states that require riders of motorcycles to wear helmets under pain of criminal penalties. These statutes have almost universally been upheld on grounds similar to those used in the boxing and snake handling cases.[143]

The conclusion is that in the absence of any law to the contrary, an individual can consent to any reasonable experiment where the risks are not so great that it would amount to consenting to murder or mayhem. The state may, however, greatly circumscribe the conditions under which an individual can consent to be a subject of human experimentation, and can probably forbid dangerous experiments altogether if it so chooses.[144]

SUMMARY AND CONCLUSIONS

1. To be legally valid, an individual's consent to human experimentation must be competent, voluntary, informed, and understanding. Only the first three elements are required in the nonexperimental therapeutic setting, but all are essential in experimentation.

2. The primary functions of the informed consent doctrine are to promote individual autonomy and encourage rational decision-making. The purpose of the required disclosures is to help promote equity and fairness in the doctor-patient and investigator-subject relationship to promote these two ends. If full information is not both disclosed and comprehended before the patient or subject is asked to make a decision, the functions of the doctrine cannot be attained, and it becomes a useless rule.

3. The law of informed consent to nonexperimental therapy varies in certain respects from state to state and has undergone significant changes during the past five years—including statutory revisions in eighteen states during the past two years alone. The most significant trend is found in court decisions shifting the cause of action from battery to negligence in informed consent cases. These courts base the physician's duty to disclose on his fiduciary relationship with the patient, and consequently determine what must be disclosed by the patient's view of what is material for him to know in deciding upon the recommended treatment. Nevertheless, the courts adopting this standard have universally determined that the jury must consider not what the particular patient would have done if the proper infor-

mation had been disclosed, but what the average "reasonable person" would have done. This undercuts the patient's self-determination. Moreover, physicians in the doctor-patient setting are given a "therapeutic privilege" which permits them to withhold risk information from their patients under certain circumstances. While many physicians complain bitterly about the informed consent doctrine, it is, in fact, almost impossible for a patient to win a suit founded on failure to obtain informed consent in the absence of independent negligence in the treatment by the physician.

4. Neither the "reasonable person" causation test nor the therapeutic privilege should apply in the experimental setting whether therapeutic or nontherapeutic. Where the procedure is nontherapeutic, failure to disclose material risks would amount to fraud and should be condemned. In the experimental therapeutic setting the physician may have more influence over his patient, and the consent is not likely to be either voluntary or informed if material information is withheld.

5. Informed consent is a process. The signing of a consent form can be evidence that this process took place. However, if too much emphasis is placed on the form itself there is a danger that the informed consent will be viewed simply as a bureaucratic barrier to treatment or experimentation, rather than as a process through which a joint decision is reached. Such a result would render the signature on a consent form meaningless.

6. The meaning of "risk" in the law is generally confined to death and bodily injury, and only in rare instances to psychological or emotional trauma. However, neither courts nor the legislatures have defined with precision either the quality or the probability of the risks that must be disclosed in the experimental setting. This is an appropriate subject for specific federal regulation, and current federal regulations on the subject are so vague as to be counterproductive.

7. While a subject's informed consent is necessary, it is not a sufficient condition of lawful experimentation. The experiment itself must not be so radical as to amount to a breach of the peace, mayhem, or manslaughter—since consent is not a defense to any of these crimes.

8. There does not seem to be a constitutional right either to conduct research or to be a research subject. Accordingly, the state may adopt laws limiting an individual's ability to conduct or participate in research, and may, under certain circumstances, proscribe dangerous human experimentation altogether.

REFERENCES

1. The complaint in a battery case will allege that the physician's failure to disclose rendered invalid any generalized consent obtained from the patient and accordingly terminated the physician's privilege to touch his body. No expert testimony is required since the doctor's privilege to touch ends when the patient's consent is invalidly obtained. *See, generally,* Waltz and Inbau, Medical Jurisprudence, 152–156 (1971).

2. *Id.*

3. Scott v. Wilson, 396 S.W.2d 532 (Tex. Civ. App. 1965).

4. Schloendorff v. Society of N.Y. Hosp. 211 N.Y. 125, 105 N.E. 92, 93 (1914).

5. Canterbury v. Spence, 464 F.2d 772, 780 (D.C. Cir. 1972).

6. Trogun v. Fruchtman, 58 Wis.2d 596, 207 N.W.2d 297, 313 (1973).

7. *See,* Annas, Avoiding Malpractice Suits Through the Use of Informed Consent, Current Problems in Pediatrics, (March, 1976).

8. Wilkenson v. Vesey, 110 R.I. 606, 295 A.2d 676 (1972).

9. Canterbury v. Spence, 464 F.2d 772 (D.C. Cir. 1972).

10. Cobbs v. Grant, 8 Cal.3d 229, 502 P.2d 1 (1972).

11. *Id.* at 502 P.2d 1.

12. Wilkenson v. Vesey, 295 A.2d 676 (R.I. 1972); Canterbury v. Spence, 464 F.2d 772 (D.C. Cir. 1972); Cobbs v. Grant, 8 Cal.3d 229, 502 P.2d 1 (1972).

13. Cobbs v. Grant, 8 Cal.3d 229, 502 P.2d 1 (1972).

14. *E.g., Id,* and Canterbury v. Spence, 464 F.2d 772 (D.C. Cir. 1972).

15. Id.

16. *See,* Cobbs v. Grant, 8 Cal.3d 229, 502 P.2d 1 (1972).

17. *Id.,* and Canterbury v. Spence, 464 F.2d 772, 789 (D.C. Cir. 1972).

18. Canterbury v. Spence, 464 F.2d 772, 789 (D.C. Cir. 1972).

19. *Id.*

20. Cobbs v. Grant, 8 Cal.3d 229, 502 P.2d 1 (1972).

21. Capron, Genetic Therapy: A Lawyer's Response in Hamilton, ed., The New Genetics and the Future of Man, 151 (1972).

22. Schloendorff v. Society of N.Y. Hosp., 211 N.Y. 125, 105 N.E. 92, 93 (1914).

23. Katz, & Capron, Catastrophic Disease: Who Decides What? (1975) at 82-90.

24. Perhpas no relationship has been regulated more persuasively than that between the purchaser and the seller of securities. For example, the registration requirements centering around §5 of the Securities Act of 1933, 15 U.S.C. §77e (1970), provide a detailed set of rights and duties applicable to the participants in a distribution of securities. *See, e.g.,* Escott v. BarChris Constr. Corp., 283 F. Supp. 643 (S.D.N.Y. 1968) and one of the most striking judicial definitions of a relationship has come in the context of the expanding civil liability under §10(b) of the Securities Exchange Act of 1934, 15 U.S.C. §78j (1970), and under SEC

Rule 10b-5, 17 C.F.R. §240.10b-5 (1973). The courts have given detailed substantive content to the terse provisions of the Rule, thereby redefining the purchaser-seller relationship according to the changing judicial theories of securities regulation. *See* Superintendent of Ins. v. Bankers Life & Cas. Co., 404 U.S. 6 (1971) (10b-5 invoked as a remedy for corporate mismanagement); Shapiro v. Merrill Lynch, Pierce, Fenner & Smith, Inc., 353 F. Supp. 264 (S.D.N.Y. 1972) (duty of disclosure placed on insider who trades on exchange).

25. Article 2 of the Uniform Commercial Code constitutes a general redefinition and codification of the purchaser-seller relationship. Of particular note is §2-302, which allows a court to refuse enforcement of a clause or contract that it finds unconscionable. This section apparently is a legislative mandate for continuing judicial readjustment of commercial consumer relationships. *See* State v. ITM, Inc., 52 Misc.2d 39, 275 N.Y.S.2d 303 (Sup. Ct. 1966) (fraudulent referral sales program); cf. Henningsen v. Bloomfield Motors, Inc. 32 N.J. 358, 161 A.2d 69 (1960) (disclaimer of warranty on automobile).

26. Although enacted by only a handful of states, the Uniform Consumer Credit Code would define and harmonize the debtor-creditor relationship in the context of small loans, installment loans, and other consumer credit transactions. *See generally* Malcolm, The Uniform Consumer Credit Code, 25 Bus. Law 937 (1970). Congress also acted to define the rights and duties between debtor and creditor when it passed the Consumer Credit Protection Act, 15 U.S.C. §§1601–77 (1970), and the Fair Credit Reporting Act, 15 U.S.C. §§1681–81t (1970). Even in the absence of a specific statute, the courts have been active in shaping the debtor-creditor relationship. *See* Fuentes v. Shevin, 407 U.S. 67 (1972) (use of provisional remedies without notice and hearing violates due process); Unico v. Owen, 50 N.J. 101, 232 A.2d 405 (1967) (holder in due course status denied to financier closely related to original seller).

27. Miranda v. Arizona, 384 U.S. 436 (1966); other relationships that have been redefined include warden-prisoner, *see* Rudovsky, The Rights of Prisoners (1973); mental patient-administrator, *see* Wyatt v. Stickney, 344 F.Supp. 373 (M.D. Ala. 1972); Ennis & Siegel, The Rights of Mental Patients (1973); student-teacher, especially with regard to the expression of political opinions, *see* Tinker v. Des Moines Independent Community School Dist., 393 U.S. 503 (1969); Burnside v. Byars, 363 F.2d 744 (5th Cir. 1966); and officer-soldier, *see* Rivkin, The Rights of Servicemen (1972); Rivkin, GI Rights and Army Justice (1970).

28. Charles Fried describes the trust relationship in the following terms: "Although trust has to do with reliance on a disposition of another person, it is reliance on a disposition of a special sort: the disposition to act morally, to deal fairly with others, to live up to one's understandings, and so on. Thus to trust another is first of all to expect him to accept the principle of morality in his dealings with you, to respect your status as a person, your personality." Privacy, Hughes, ed. Law, Reason and Justice (1969) at 52. But *see* Bernard Shaw's opinion in his Preface on Doctors to his Doctor's Dilemma (1913): "I do not know of a single thoughtful person who does not feel that the tragedy of illness at present is that it delivers you helplessly into the hands of a profession which you deeply mistrust . . ."

29. *E.g.*, Warren & Brandeis, The Right to Privacy, 4 Harv. L. Rev. 193 (1890).

30. *E.g.*, Roe v. Wade, 410 U.S. 113 (1973).

31. *See, e.g.*, Ramsey, The Patient as Person (1970) at 5.

32. *See, e.g.*, Mead, Research with Human Beings: A Model Derived from An Anthropological Field Practice, 98 Daedalus 361 (1969).

33. *See, e.g.*, Tittmuss, The Gift Relationship (1971).

34. Jonas, Philosophical Reflections on Experimenting with Human Subjects, 98 Daedalus 29 (Spring, 1969).

35. Katz & Capron, supra, note 23 at 87.

36. *Id.* at 88; Freund, Legal Frameworks for Human Experimentation, 98 Daedalus 315, 323 (1969), and *see supra.*, note 24, and accompanying text.

37. Katz & Capron, *supra.*, note 23 at 89.

38. *Cf. Id.* and Calabresi, G. The Cost of Accidents (1969).

39. *E.g.*, the following quotation from Dr. Francis Moore, "There can be little question that personal ambition, usually for career advancement or public acclaim, underlies much intense motivation in research work and in the trial of new ideas, drugs, operations, or treatment. Such personal ambition is usually well hidden under the sophisticated affect of the dedicated clinical scientist and, far from being remiss, is the sign of a healthy society . . . But ambition, no matter how praiseworthy, can certainly lead individuals astray." As quoted by Mechanic, in The Growth of Bureaucratic Medicine (1976) at 261.

40. *See, e.g.*, Ingelfinger, Informed (But Uneducated) Consent, 287 New Eng. J. Med. 465 (1972).

41. Quote by Mechanic, *supra.*, note 39 at 262.

42. *See supra.*, pages 11–16.

43. Gray, Human Subjects in Medical Experimentation (1975) 67 and 114.

44. *See, e.g.*, the chapter on Psychosurgery, *infra.* for a discussion of the possible role of a review committee for experimental surgery.

45. Alaska, c. 102, Sess. 1976; Colorado, 13 CRS 20–304; Delaware, c. 373, Sess. 1976; Florida, F.S.A. s. 768.132; Idaho, s. 41–400 et seq.; Iowa, c. 147.137; Kentucky, KRS 311.377(1) as amended, 1976; Nebraska, L.B. 434, s. 16, 1976; Nevada, c. 41A.110; New York, Pub. Health 2805-d et seq.; North Carolina, c. 977, sec. 8–94, 1975; Ohio, H.B. 682, 1975; Pennsylvania, c. 40.1301 et seq.; Rhode Island, H.B. 7796, 1976; Tennessee, c. 23–3401 et seq.; Utah H.B. 35, December 5, 1976; Vermont, 12 V.S.A. s. 1910; Washington, c. 56, s. 10–11, 1975–76. In addition, Hawaii enacted a statute that directed its board of medical examiners to set standards for informed consent. H.B. 2700, p. 1172. One of the states that had a statute before 1975, for example, was Georgia. Its statute provides, among other things, that "A consent to medical and surgical treatment which discloses in general terms the treatment or course of treatment in connection with which it is given and which is duly evidenced in writing and signed by the patient . . . shall be conclusively presumed to be a valid consent in the absence of fraudulent misrepresentation of material facts in obtaining same." Georgia Health Code, §88–2906 (Acts, 1971). The statute has been used as a basis for a directed verdict in favor of a physician who failed to disclose a .05 risk of hypertrophic scarring in a facelift operation. Young v.

Yarn, 222 S.E.2d 113 (Ga. App. Ct. 1975). We gratefully acknowledge the assistance of Richard L. Krause of the American Medical Association's Legislative Dept. in providing us with copies of some of the more recently enacted statutes. He is, of course, in no way responsible for our analysis of them. All of the statutes are on file at the Center for Law and Health Sciences, Boston University.

46. For a discussion of the malpractice insurance crisis *see*, Annas, Katz & Trakimas, Medical Malpractice Litigation under National Health Insurance; Essential or Expendable?, 1975 Duke Law Journal 1335.

47. Fla. Stats. Ann., §768.132(3)(a).

48. Colorado, Florida, Iowa, Idaho, Nevada, North Carolina, Ohio, Utah, and Washington.

49. Fla. Stats. Ann. §768.132(4)(a)

50. *Id.*, Nevada's statute has no such exception, and its consent provisions are stated in the vaguest terms of any of those examined. 41A.110.

51. Idaho Code 439–4305.

52. Iowa Code Ann. ch. 147 § (added by H.B. 803, §16, 1975).

53. Ohio Revised Code Ann. §2317.54.

54. *See*, notes 32 and 33 *supra*.

55. Delaware, Florida, Nebraska, New York, North Carolina, Kentucky, Vermont and Tennessee.

56. N.Y. Public Health Laws, s. 2805–d.

57. Penn. st. s. 1301.103.

58. Col. st. s. 13–20–302(2).

59. Ohio St. §2317.54(D).

60. Protection of Human Subjects, 45 C.F.R. 46.103(c).

61. *Id.* §46.109.

62. *Id.* §46.110

63. *Id.*

64. *See, e.g.*, Survey Research Center, Research Involving Human Subjects (Institute for Social Research, U. Michigan) Oct. 2, 1976. Results of a survey done for the National Commission for the Protection of Human Subjects of Biomedical and Behavioral Research.

65. Gray, *supra*, note 43.

66. Canterbury v. Spence, 464 F.2d 772, 780 n.15 (D.C. Cir. 1972).

67. Bang v. Charles T. Miller Hosp., 251 Minn. 427, 88 N.W.2d 186 (1958).

68. Barnette v. Potenza, 79 Misc.2d 51, 359 N.Y.S.2d 432 (1974).

69. Bowers v. Talmage, 159 So.2d 888 (Fla. App. 1963).

70. Campbell v. Oliva, 424 F.2d 1244 (6th Cir. 1970).

71. Congrove v. Holmes, 37 Ohio Misc. 95, 308 N.E.2d 765 (1973).

72. Darrah v. Kite, 32 App. Div.2d 208, 301 N.Y.S.2d 286 (1969).

73. DiRosse v. Wien, 24 App. Div.2d 510, 261 N.Y.S.2d 623 (1965).

74. Dumer v. St. Michael's Hosp. 69 Wis.2d 766, 233 N.W.2d 372 (1975); Jacobs v. Theimer, 519 S.W.2d 846 (Tex. 1975); Stewart v. Long Island Hosp., 58 Misc.2d 432, 296 N.Y.S.2d 41 (1965).

75. Dunbar v. Wright, 423 F.2d 940 (3d Cir. 1970).

76. Fogel v. Genesee Hosp., 41 App. Div.2d 468, 344 N.Y.S.2d 552 (1973).

77. Funke V. Fieldman, 212 Kan. 524, 512 P.2d 539 (1973).

78. Gray v. Grunnage, 423 Pa. 144, 223 A.2d 663 (1966); Canterbury v. Spence, 464 F.2d 772 (D.C. Cir. 1972).

79. Koury v. Fallo, 272 N.C. 366, 158 S.E.2d 548 (1968).

80. Mitchell v. Robinson, 334 S.W.2d 11 (Mo. 1960).

81. Nathanson v. Kline, 186 Kan. 393, 350 P.2d 1093 (1960), *rehearing denied*, 187 Kan. 186, 354 P.2d 670 (1960).

82. Russell v. Harwick, 166 S.2d 904 (Fla. 1964).

83. Wilson v. Scott, 412 S.W.2d 299 (Tex. 1967).

84. Woods v. Brumlop, 71 N.M. 221, 377 P.2d 520 (1962).

85. ZeBarth v. Swedish Hosp. Medical Center, 81 Wash.2d 12, 499 P.2d 1 (1972).

86. Ball v. Mallinkrodt Chemical Works, 53 Tenn App. 218, 381 S.W.2d 563 (1964); Ciccarone v. United States, 350 F. Supp. 554 (E.D. Pa. 1972); Nishi v. Hartwell, 52 Haw. 188, 473 P.2d 116 (1970).

87. Bell v. Umstattd, 401 S.W.2d 306 (Tex. 1966); Riedinger v. Colburn, 361 F. Supp. 1073 (D. Idaho 1973).

88. Bowers v. Garfield, 382 F. Supp. 503 (E.D. Pa. 1974); Longmire v. Hoey, 512 S.W.2d 307 (Tenn. App. 1974); Riedisser v. Nelson, 111 Ariz. 542, 534 P.2d 1052 (1975); Tatro v. Lueken, 212 Kan. 606, 512 P.2d 529 (1973).

89. Bryant v. St. Paul Fire & Marine Ins. Co., 272 So.2d 448 (La. 1973).

90. Bush v. St. Paul Fire & Marine Ins. Co., 264 So.2d 717 (La. 1972).

91. Butler v. Berkely, 25 N.C. App. 325, 213 S.E.2d 571 (1975).

92. Charley v. Cameron, 215 Kan. 750, 528 P.2d 1205 (1974).

93. Coleman v. Garrison, 327 A.2d 757 (Del. Super. 1974).

94. DiFilippo v. Preston, 53 Del. 539, 173 A.2d 333 (1961); Roberts v. Wood, 206 F. Supp. 579 (S.D. Ala. 1962); Watson V. Clutts, 262 N.C. 153, 136 S.E.2d 617 (1964); *Cf.* Patrick v. Sedwick, 391 P.2d 453 (Alaska 1964) (paralysis from thyroidectomy).

95. Diltow v. Kaplan, 181 So.2d 226 (Fla. 1966); Mason v. Ellsworth, 3 Wash. App. 298, 474 P.2d 909 (1970); Starnes v. Taylor, 272 N.C. 386, 158 S.E.2d 339 (1968).

96. Dunlop v. Marine, 242 Cal. App.2d 162, 51 Cal. Rptr. 158 (1966).

97. Ericksen v. Wilson, 266 Minn. 401, 123 N.W.2d 687 (1963); Watkins v. Parpala, 2 Wash. App. 484, 469 P.2d 974 (1970).

98. Fischer v. Wilmington Gen. Hosp. 51 Del. 554, 149 A.2d 749 (1959); Sawyer v. Methodist Hosp. of Memphis, 383 F. Supp. 563 (W.D. Tenn. 1974) (.013% risk).

99. George v. Travelers Ins. Co., 215 F. Supp. 340 (E.D. La. 1963).

100. Gravis v. Physicians & Surgeon's Hosp. of Alice, 415 S.W.2d 674 (Tex. 1967); Hall v. United States, 136 F. Supp. 187 (W.D. La. 1955); Martin v. Stratton, 515 P.2d 1366 (Okla. 1973).

101. Karriman v. Orthopedic Clinic, 516 P.2d 534 (Okla. 1973).

102. Lester v. Aetna Casualty & Surety Co., 240 F.2d 676 (5th Cir. 1957).

103. Williams v. Menehan, 191 Kan. 6, 379 P.2d 292 (1963); *Cf.* Walsted v. U. of Minnesota Hosp., 442 F.2d 634 (8th Cir. 1971) (loss of child's leg during cardiac catheterization).

104. Woods v. Pommerening, 44 Wash.2d 867, 271 P.2d 705 (1954).

105. Canterbury v. Spence, 464 F.2d 772, 787 (D.C. Cir. 1972).

106. Davis v. Wyeth Laboratories, 399 F.2d 121 (9th Cir. 1968).

107. *Id.*

108. *Cf.*, Wright v. Carter Products, 244 F.2d 53 (2d Cir. 1957) in which the court also rejected a purely statistical approach to warnings in requiring a cosmetic manufacturer to warn a small hypersensitive group about a potential side effect.

109. Hart v. Brown, 29 Conn. Supp. 368, 289 A.2d 386 (1972). Discussed in more detail in the chapter on Children.

110. Strunk v. Strunk, 445 S.W.2d 145, 148 (Ky. 1969).

111. *Id.*, citing Hamburger and Crosneir, Moral and Ethical Problems in Transplantation in Rappaport and Dausset, eds., Human Transplantation (1968).

112. Reactor Safety Study: An Assessment of Accident Risk in U.S. Commercial Nuclear Power Plants, (WASH-1400) Oct., 1975.

113. *Id.* at 11-12.

114. *Id.* at 112.

115. Haggerty v. McCarthy, 344 Mass. 136, 143 (Spiegel, J. dissenting). A 1976 survey of 547 principal investigators in H.E.W. funded research concluded that the percentage of trivial injuries, disabling injuries and fatal injuries for therapeutic research was 8.3, 2.1, and 0.1% respectively. For nontherapeutic experiments the rates were 0.7, 0.1, and 0%—rates which the surgeons described as seemingly not "greater than those of every day life." Cardon, Dommel & Trumble, Injuries to Research Subjects, 295 New Eng. J. Med. 650 (1976). While one can agree with the authors that their figures may provide an adequate "first approximation" of the risks involved in human experimentation done under H.E.W. auspices, one is reasonably skeptical of the responses to the basic question asked: How many subjects have *you* injured? Further, as Mechanic has noted, it is likely that the most dangerous and risky human experimentation is being conducted by private physicians in their own offices with no monitoring or peer review whatsoever. Mechanic, The Growth of Bureaucratic Medicine (1976) at 264.

116. Fleming v. Delta Airlines, 359 F. Supp. 339 (S.D.N.Y. 1973).

117. *Id.* at 341.

118. *Id.*

119. *Id.*

120. *See, supra* note 58, and accompanying text.

121. Protection of Human Subjects §46.3(b).

122. Mechanic, *supra*, note 39 at 266.

123. *Id.* at 267.

124. *See*, for example, the discussion of this issue in the chapter on Psychosurgery at pages 238-242.

125. Kidd, Limits of the Rights of a Person to Consent to Experimentation on Himself, 117 Science 212 (Feb. 27, 1953).

126. Nawoski v. Pallotto, 63 Ill. App.2d 50, 211 N.E.2d 600 (1965).

127. Grosevenor v. Chesley, 48 Me. 369 (1859).

128. Pindar v. Wadsworth, 102 Eng. Rptr. 328 (1802).

129. Davis v. Wyeth Laboratories, 399 F.2d 121 (9th Cir. 1968).

130. *E.g.*, McCullough v. Hartpence, 141 N.J.E. 499, 58 A.2d 233 (1948); and *see*, 22 Am. Jr.2d Damages, §5.

131. State v. Bass, 255 N.C. 42, 120 S.E.2d 580, 583 (1961). And *see*, discussion in Annas and Glantz, Psychosurgery: The Law's Response, 54 B.U.L.Rev. 249, 255–256 (1974).

132. Banovitch v. Commonwealth, 196 Va. 210, 83 S.E.2d 369 (1954).

133. *Id.* at 371.

134. *Id.* at 375.

135. In another case an individual convicted of aggravated battery sought a reversal on the grounds that the injured person had consented. He and the victim had been drinking heavily and argued. He told the victim that if he had a gun he would shoot him. The victim went to his car, got a gun, and gave it to the defendant saying, "If you want to shoot me, go ahead." Defendant picked up the gun and shot the victim in the head, seriously wounding him. The court held that the consent was no defense stating, "whether or not the victims of crime have so little regard for their own safety as to request injury, the public has a stronger interest in preventing acts such as these." State v. Fransua, 85 N.M. 173, 510 P.2d 106 (Ct. App. 1973).

136. Lawton v. Steele, 152 U.S. 133, 137 (1894); and *see*, Goldblatt v. Hempstead, 369 U.S. 590, 594 (1962).

137. Fitzsimmons v. New York State Athletic Commission, 146 N.Y. Supp. 117 (1914), *aff'd without opinion*, 147 N.Y. Supp. 1111 (1914).

138. *Id.* at 122.

139. *Id.*

140. *Id.* at 120.

141. Tennessee v. Pack, 527 S.W.2d 99 (Tenn. 1975).

142. *Id.* at 113.

143. *E.G.*, People v. Newhouse, 55 Misc.2d 1064, 287 N.Y.S.2d 713 (1968); State v. Mele, 247 A.2d 176 (N.J. 1968); State v. Odegaard, 165 N.W.2d 667 (N.D. 1969); Bisenius v. Karns, 42 Wisc.2d 42, 165 N.W.2d 377 (1969); *Contra*, American Motorcycle Assoc. v. Davids, 11 Mich. App. 351, 158 N.W.2d 72 (1968).

144. The "state" in this context refers either to the individual states or the federal government.

Chapter 3

Research with Children: Legal Incapacity and Proxy Consent

Before an investigator can use any person as a subject in biomedical or behavioral research, he must obtain that person's informed consent. This consent must be voluntary, competent, and understanding.[1] There are two questions that arise in regard to experimentation on children. First, is a child legally capable of giving an informed and understanding consent? Second, do parents have the legal capacity to consent to the performance of research on their children? This chapter will attempt to answer both of these questions.

More than a decade ago, the renowned legal scholar, Paul Freund, wrote, ". . . the law cannot now be expected to yield precise answers to the ethical problems of human experimentation."[2] Unfortunately, in regard to the law respecting research on children, this statement is equally true today.

Research on children has provided society with substantial benefits. Studies of normal mineral and water composition of healthy infants have led to effective parenteral fluid therapy and regimens with which to combat serious complications of diarrheal diseases.[3] Research on healthy children is the only method by which one can establish normal patterns of growth and metabolism.[4] In addition, the Kefauver-Harris amendments to the Food, Drug and Cosmetics Act[5] require that drugs to be distributed in interstate commerce for use in children be tested in children to determine their safety and efficacy. Due to the fact that children are not simply "little people," drug testing on adults does not provide adequate information regarding dosage, contraindications, toxicity, efficacy, or side effects for children.[6]

The beneficial nature of research on children does not, however, establish its legality. Before going on to examine the law regulating therapeutic medical procedures that are performed on minors, we should first examine the issue of how the law has come to define minority.

WHO IS A MINOR?

Under both American and English common law an individual was a minor until he reached the age of twenty-one.[7] Recently, almost all the states have lowered the age of majority to eighteen.[8] It is not entirely clear how it was originally determined that the attainment of twenty-one years of age should be the dividing line between minority and adulthood.

In Roman law at the time of Justinian there were three age groups that determined legal capacities and incapacities. First, *infantia*, when the child was incapable of speech, but by 407 A.D. this was fixed at below seven years of age. Second, *tutela impuberes* ceased at puberty, as a tutor was no longer required when a child could have children. At later law this was fixed at fourteen for males and twelve for females. Third, *cura minoris* was the reaching of adulthood, and was later set at twenty-five years of age.[9]

Among the barbarian tribes fifteen was both the age of majority and the age of combat. In thirteenth-century France if either the challenger or the challenged in judicial combat (the forerunner of dueling) was under fifteen years of age, there could be no combat.[10] Between the ninth and eleventh centuries, fifteen seemed to be the age of majority in Northern Europe.[11] The basis on which the age of majority was adopted was quite different in Europe and in Rome. In Rome the question was: Had the male "pupil" both understanding and judgment as to acts in law, particularly in relation to property rights? It was presumed these capacities arose at puberty, later set at fourteen. In Europe, the choice of age fifteen seems to be connected to the capacity to bear arms.[12] Apparently, the raising of the age of majority from fifteen to twenty-one was due to the increase in weight of arms. It was not until the late eleventh century that a military revolution involving a mounted knight occurred, and knighthood became a social distinction. In the twelfth century, knights began riding horses into battle and by the thirteenth century, armor became very heavy. The combination of the heavy armor and the use of horses in combat required a stronger and better trained knight, thus requiring extra years of training and physical development.[13]

During this time, however, socage tenants (those who owned and worked land) recognized fifteen as the age of majority, which was later reduced to fourteen. In socage tenure, one came to majority when he was capable of "attaining to husbandry and 'of conducting his rustic employs.' "[14]

Until 1753 when the Marriage Act was passed, a minor could marry at the age of fourteen without the consent of his parents. After the passage of the Marriage Act, this age was raised to twenty-one for males. A statute of Phillip and Mary raised the age when a female could marry without consent from fourteen to sixteen. It seems that this is responsible for fixing the woman's age of consent to sexual intercourse at sixteen.[15]

A commentator who wrote over a hundred years ago acknowledged the fact that setting any one age for the termination of infancy was inequitable, but states that twenty-one years of age is as good as any other.[16] He points out that human life is divided into four periods, each of which is a multiple of seven.

> Natural infancy ends at seven years, puberty begins at fourteen, legal infancy ends at twenty-one years, and the natural life of man is three-score years and ten.[17]

It is generally believed that the legal status of minority offers children certain protections. As Blackstone put it:

> Infants have various privileges, and various disabilities; but their very disabilities are privileges; in order to secure them from hurting themselves by their own improvident acts.[18]

From an historical perspective, this is not readily apparent. Under ancient Roman law a father had the power of life and death over his children until they reached adulthood. He could kill, mutilate, sell or offer his child in sacrifice.[19] Such was also the case in ancient Greece.[20]

In feudal law if a tenant died leaving a minor heir, the lord was allowed the profitable rights of wardship and marriage. The lord had full use of the child's land and had no obligation to render an account to the minor. Upon obtaining majority, the ward had to sue the lord for possession and pay a half year's profit to the lord to receive his own land. Although the minor is protected from squandering his inheritance, it is a rather expensive means of protection.[21]

It has also been argued that a minor's reduced capacity to contract was not for the minor's protection. Under the common law a father was entitled to all the earnings of his child. One way of assuring the father's receipt of these earnings was to prevent the minor from spending them. This was accomplished by rendering the minor incapable of entering into a binding contract. It also protected the father's goods in that the minor could not sell any of his father's property and convert the proceeds to his own use.[22]

According to Blackstone,[23] at common law minors were given the power to enter into a number of serious endeavors. A male at the age of twelve could take the oath of allegiance; at fourteen, he reached the age of discretion and, as discussed above, could consent to or disagree to marriage, could choose his guardian, and, if discretion was actually proved, could make a testament of his personal estate; and at seventeen he could be an executor. A female could be given in marriage or betrothed at seven; at nine she was entitled to dower; at twelve she could consent to or disagree to marriage, and, if found to have sufficient discretion, could bequeath her personal estate; and at seventeen she could be an executrix.

A three-judge Federal District Court in deciding that some minor women are capable of consenting to abortions stated:

> [W]hatever may be the value of conclusive presumptions making the 18th birthday a turning point for such matters as voting, the purchase of liquor, and entering into contracts other than certain contracts for necessaries, . . . we can attach no such factual magic to that birthday.[24]

This short review of how we have come to adopt an age of majority not only demonstrates that one cannot attach any "factual magic" to that age, but that our choice of an age of majority is based on feudal law and custom with no relevance to the needs of a modern society.

As a result of this fact some courts have taken a more operative approach to resolving age of consent problems in certain specific circumstances. Thus, in another case dealing with a minor woman's capacity to consent to an abortion, the Washington Supreme Court held that:

> The age of fertility provides a practical minimum age requirement for consent to abortion, reducing the need for a legal one.[25]

One commentator writing about the criminal responsibility of children also pointed to the arbitrary ages set for determining their criminal responsibility. The general rule is that a child younger than seven is conclusively presumed to be incapable of committing a crime.[26] Between the ages of seven and fourteen a child is presumed to be incapable of committing a crime, but this presumption is rebuttable by the state.[27] The author then discussed the psychological research that has been conducted concerning the development of moral judgment and a sense of justice in children.[28] She concludes that at approximately the age of twelve

> a juvenile should have reached a sufficient degree of maturation when he is able to assume the consequences of his acts. He has then reached a subjective responsibility and acquired consideration of equity, internalized orientation of right and wrong as well as distributive justice. The child younger than twelve years of age should not be presumed to possess a moral development sufficient to be considered as legally responsible.[29]

Whether or not one agrees with this conclusion, this paper has taken a giant step in its approach to rationally setting an age of criminal responsibility. Instead of basing the choice of an age of responsibility on the weight of armor, she attempted to use modern psychological research for some guidance. Basically, the paper states that one cannot commit a crime until one understands the meaning of moral responsibility, and one does not reach this stage until about the age of twelve.

One attempt has been made at rationally setting an age limit on participation in a particular experimental procedure. Proposed Massachusetts regulations state:

> Psychosurgery shall not be performed on the following categories of patients; a) all patients under the age of thirty [30] years old where there is still the possibility of developmental maturation. . . .[30]

The physiological fact that developmental maturation continues until the age of thirty was used as the criterion for setting this age limit.

Unfortunately, no such analysis exists in regard to consent of a minor to medical treatment. It would be most helpful to know at what age a child obtains a true sense of his body and mind, knows what it means to take risks, knows what it means to be harmed or suffer discomfort, knows how to balance risks and benefits, and so forth. If we had this knowledge it might be possible to rationally determine an age at which most people could give an informed consent to medical treatment and experimentation. In the absence of such an anlysis the courts have constructed their own rules, as we shall now examine.

CONSENT TO THERAPEUTIC TREATMENT

As a general rule, "a surgeon who performs an operation without his patient's consent commits an assault and battery for which he is liable in damages."[31] The law of battery is designed to protect the individual's interest in freedom from intentional unpermitted contacts. In proving battery, hostile intent need not be shown. One is only required to prove the absence of consent to the contact.[32] The problem of providing medical treatment to children is that they are deemed to be legally incapable of giving such consent.[33] Thus, prior to conducting a therapeutic procedure on a child, the consent of the parent is generally obtained. There is case law that would indicate that the giving of such consent is a parental right that is not tied to any protective function. In the only case that analyzes the basis for the parental consent requirement it is said:

> This rule [that a minor cannot consent to medical treatment] is not based upon the capacity of the minor to consent, so far as he is personally concerned, within the field of the law of torts or law of crimes, but is based upon the right of parents whose liability for support and maintenance of their child may be greatly increased by an unfavorable result from the operational procedures upon the part of the surgeon. . . . [S]ince the parents of such a child are responsible for his nurture and training and are liable for his maintenance and support, others will not be permitted to interfere with such relationship or with matters touching the child's personal welfare.[34]

The court in effect is stating that since the parent of a child might be financially damaged as the result of a procedure performed on his child, he must consent before such a result may occur.

In another case[35] an eleven-year-old child died after an operation to remove her tonsils and adenoids. Although there was no parental consent to the operation, the operation was consented to by the child's adult sister. The court held that only the parent could give such a consent and therefore the doctor committed an assault and battery. What is especially interesting here is that the adult sister was in her third year of training as a nurse, and could probably better understand the necessity for, and risks inherent in, the operation, thereby being better able to protect the child's interest. The court was clearly not concerned with protecting the child's interests but in protecting the parents' prerogatives.

It must be noted that the parental prerogative to consent to medical care for the child is not without its limitations. Where it appears that the parents' decision not to consent to medical treatment will cause the child serious injury, the court will intervene to protect the child's interest. Thus, in *In re Clark*,[36] the parents would not consent to blood transfusions that were necessary in order to treat their three-year-old child who was suffering from second and third degree burns over forty percent of his body. The court found that:

> [The child] has rights of his own—the right to live and grow up without disfigurement.
>
> The child is a citizen of the State. While he "belongs" to his parents, he belongs also to the state. Their rights in him entail many duties. Likewise the fact that the child belongs to the State imposes upon the State many duties. Chief among them is to protect his right to live and to grow up with a sound mind in a sound body, and to brook no interference with that right by any person or organization.[37]

The recent lower court cases, *Maine Medical Center v. Houle*[38] and *In the Matter of Karen Quinlan*,[39] hold that parents may not order the termination of treatment that is required to keep their children alive, even when the parents believe that such action would be in the best interests of their child. The protective role courts take is amply demonstrated by the *Houle* case where the doctors, agreeing with the parents, stated that withholding treatment would be in the child's best interests.[40] However, as is discussed in detail in the section on proxy consent, the appeals court in the *Quinlan* case has reduced the protective role of the court.

Moreover, where the courts are not presented with a life-threatening situation, the refusal of a parent to give consent will not be overruled by the courts. For example, in *In re Seiferth*,[41] a parent would not consent to an operation on a fourteen-year-old boy that was needed to repair a harelip and cleft palate. Although physicians and social workers claimed that it was important for this child to undergo such procedures, the court refused to overrule the parental judgment.

However, there is some indication from more recent cases that courts are beginning to take a more protective role even where the situation does not threaten the child's life. In *In re Sampson*,[42] a fifteen-year-old boy suffered from Von Recklinghausen's disease which caused a "massive deformity" of the right side of his face. Although he was excused from school as a result of his deformity and had no friends, this condition did not threaten his physical well-being. Neither his sight nor his hearing was affected. Physicians testified that they could not cure the problem, although it could be alleviated, and that the surgery that would take from six to eight hours to perform was "risky." One physician stated that the risk of the procedure would decrease as the child became older because the relative blood loss would be smaller. He suggested that the court wait until the child reached twenty-one years of age so he could make his own decision, and that nothing would be lost by waiting. The court, finding that psychological harm would result from not performing the procedure now, overruled the mother's refusal to give her consent. This decision is some indication of how far a court will go in protecting the interests of the child by limiting the prerogative of the parent.

THE CHILD'S CONSENT TO MEDICAL CARE

While somewhat limiting the parents' ability to make decisions regarding their child's health care, courts and legislatures are at the same time expanding the child's capacity to give consent to such care. A number of doctrines have developed that enable a child to receive health care services without parental consent. First, if an emergency exists, a physician need not wait to receive consent prior to the commencement of treatment. This rule applies to minors as well as adults.[43] However, determining whether or not an emergency exists requires, in at least some cases, a subjective judgment, and if the physician is wrong in his determination, he may be liable for damages.[44]

Second, an emancipated minor may, in some jurisdictions, consent to medical treatment.[45] Children become emancipated by marriage, judicial decree, consent of the parent, or failure of the parents to meet their legal responsibilities.[46] In addition, a minor who is self-supporting and lives separate and apart from his parents is often deemed to be emancipated.

It is noteworthy that although some courts and legislatures allow emancipated minors to consent to health care, emancipation does not generally give a minor the rights of an adult. Generally, a minor is emancipated against his parents and not the whole world. That is to say, he is no longer under their control and guidance, and they are no longer obligated to support and nurture the child. When a California court ruled that "an emancipated child is in all respects his own man . . . with the same independence as though he had attained the age of majority,"[47] a commentator wrote that this case made a "radical departure" from the general rule.[48] The general rule is readily stated in the ancient Massachusetts case of *The Inhabitants of Taunton v. The Inhabitants of Plymouth*,[49] wherein it was held that the emancipation of a son "did not give him capacity to make binding contracts, beyond other infants; or any political or municipal rights, which do not belong by law to minors."[50]

Some statutes merely state that an emancipated minor may consent to medical care.[51] Some statutes are more explicit, stating, for example, that a minor who is fifteen years of age or older, and who is living apart from his parents regardless of duration, and who is managing his own financial affairs, regardless of the source of income, may consent to medical and surgical treatment.[52]

In the absence of a statute some courts have adopted the emancipated minor rule. Thus an eighteen-year-old (the age of majority in this case being twenty-one) who was married, employed, self-supporting and a father, was held to be legally capable of consenting to a vasectomy.[53] The court looked to the age, intelligence, maturity, training, experience, economic independence, and general conduct as an adult in determining the emancipated status of this minor.

Courts and legislatures in adopting the emancipated minor rule have responded creatively to a specific problem. If a minor is living separate and apart from his parents, requiring parental consent would be a serious barrier to the minor's receiving medical treatment. Additionally, since the parent of an emancipated child is no longer responsible for the maintenance and support of that child, a bad result will not increase that parent's obligation.

Finally, the last exception to the general rule is that "mature minors" can consent to receiving medical treatment. In one seventy-year-old case,[54] a seventeen-year-old boy who was accompanied to the hospital by an adult aunt and adult sister, died during a surgical procedure to remove a tumor from his ear. Although his father had not consented to the procedure, the court held that no battery was committed since he was accompanied by adult relatives, and since the boy, who was almost grown into manhood, gave his consent.

In *Lacey v. Laird*,[55] an eighteen-year-old underwent plastic surgery on her nose without parental consent. One judge in a concurring opinion found that since she was a minor she could not legally consent to the procedure, and therefore a technical battery occurred. However, since the battery was of a merely technical nature only nominal damages, one dollar or less, could be awarded.[56] Another judge, also concurring in the outcome of the case, said that an eighteen-year-old could consent to simple surgical procedures.[57]

In *Bishop v. Shurly*,[58] a court found that a nineteen-year-old could consent to the administration of a local anesthetic although his mother requested the use of a general anesthetic. And in *Younts v. St. Francis Hospital,*[59] a seventeen-year-old intelligent minor was allowed to consent to a skin transplant to treat a seriously damaged finger. The court found that she was of sufficient age and maturity to know and understand the nature of the procedure.[60]

Several states have legislatively adopted the mature minor doctrine to a greater or lesser degree.

In Oregon, any person fifteen years of age or older may consent to medical or surgical care.[61] In Alabama, the age of consent to medical care is fourteen.[62] Mississippi has what may be the most liberal statute which states that:

> Any unemancipated minor of sufficient intelligence to understand and appreciate the consequences of the proposed surgical or medical treatment or procedures [may consent to such procedures].[63]

Basically, the mature minor rule states that anyone who is mature and intelligent enough to give informed consent to a procedure can undergo that procedure without parental consent. Or to put it another way, if you can understand the risks you can consent to them.

The Supreme Court of the United States has, to some extent, validated the mature minor rule, at least insofar as abortion is concerned. The Missouri legislature responded to the Supreme Court's 1973 *Roe v. Wade*[64] decision that required the liberalization of state abortion laws, by passing a statute that prohibited minors from obtaining abortions unless one of the minor's parents consented to the procedure.[65] This requirement was challenged in the case entitled *Planned Parenthood of Central Missouri v. Danforth.*[66] The Court held that the parental consent requirement was unconstitutional, stating,

> Constitutional rights do not mature and come into being magically only when one attains the state defined age of majority. Minors, as well as adults, are protected by the Constitution and possess constitutional rights.[67]

However, the Court did not find that "every minor, regardless of age or maturity may give effective consent for termination of pregnancy."[68] This statement does indicate that if a minor is sufficiently mature then that minor is capable of consenting to an abortion. The determination of maturity must be made on a case by case basis.

The Court decided a similar case[69] on the same day concerning a Massachusetts statute prohibiting abortions on minors unless both parents consented to it. Unlike the Missouri statute, if one or both parents refused to consent, consent could be obtained by order of a judge of superior court for "good cause shown."[70]

The Massachusetts Attorney General argued that this statute did not give parents a veto power over a minor's decision to have an abortion. If the parents refuse to consent the minor has recourse to the courts, and, according to the Attorney General, if the court finds that a minor is "capable of giving an informed consent" it must permit the abortion.[71] This retains the mature minor rule and merely requires a court to determine the minor's maturity. The state also argued that a minor could petition the court regardless of whether the parents had been consulted or had withheld consent.

The Court strongly implied that if this interpretation of the statute, which indicates a preference for parental consultation and consent but gives the parents no veto power, and deems mature minors as being legally capable of giving consent, is correct, then the statute would be constitutional. However the Court decided that it would not decide the case until the Massachusetts Supreme Judicial Court had a chance to interpret the statute.

For our purposes it is enough to say that in both of these cases the Supreme Court found that mature minors were capable of giving a valid informed consent to undergo a serious medical procedure.

THE CHILD'S CONSENT TO TAKE RISKS

Under our legal system the capacity of a child to consent to risky undertakings is not novel. Indeed, the doctrine of "assumption of risk" has been applied to minors a number of times. Assumption of risk is a defense in a negligence action. It means that the plaintiff, in advance, has expressly given his consent to relieve the defendant of an obligation of conduct toward him, and to accept the chance of injury from a known risk arising out of the defendant's actions. This doctrine is summarized in the Latin phrase, *volenti non fit injuria*—to one who is willing no wrong is done.

To successfully invoke the assumption of risk defense the defendant must show that the plaintiff knew and understood the risk he was incurring, and that his choice to incur the risk was entirely free and voluntary.[72] The defendant must not only know the facts that created the danger, but must comprehend and appreciate the danger itself.[73] If one cannot comprehend the risk because of his age, he will not be taken to have consented. Aside from the most exceptional cases, courts do not hold that children cannot assume the risks of certain activities. For example, a California court held that as a matter of law a three-and-a-half-year-old child could not assume risks.[74] But for the most part whether or not a child can assume the risk inherent in a certain situation is a question of fact.

In one Massachusetts case, a ten-year-old child was struck on the head with a golf ball while he was in the process of collecting golf balls that had been hit from practice tees.[75] The court found that the boy had caddied six or eight times before and had been collecting golf balls for about half an hour prior to being struck. With the knowledge derived from this experience, the court found that this child voluntarily exposed himself to a known and appreciated risk, and therefore could not recover damages.

In *Porter v. Toledo Terminal Railway Co.*,[76] a thirteen-year-old was injured when he rode his bicycle over rotted railroad tracks, and in *Centrello v. Basky*,[77] a ten-year-old boy fell and caught his hand in a cement mixer while playing near a construction site. In both of these cases the defendants successfully utilized the assumption of risk defense. In another case, a fifteen-year-old high school freshman had his neck broken in a football game.[78] He sued the school system which entered a defense based, among other things, on assumption of risk. The court held:

> One who enters into a sport, game or contest may be taken to consent to physical contact consistent with the understood rules of the game.[79]

Thus, whether or not a child is capable of understanding the risks inherent in undertaking a dangerous endeavor, and whether or not those risks were voluntarily incurred are questions of fact, and the courts do not find that children are never capable of assuming such risks.[80]

In an unrelated line of cases, courts have also found that minors may waive certain constitutional rights. In the Supreme Court case of *Haley v. Ohio*,[81] which involved a fifteen-year-old, and *Gallegos v. Colorado*,[82] which involved a fourteen-year-old, the question presented to the Court was the validity of confessions made by these minors. The Court did not hold that fourteen- and fifteen-year-old children could not give their consent, but held that such confessions would be valid where the minor had the counsel of a lawyer, parent, or adult friend. In a 1971 Pennsylvania case the court found that "a fifteen-year-old boy with an I.Q. of 76 and a mental age of eight to eleven-and-a-half was held to have the required understanding of his constitutional rights to render his confession obtained after four hours of interrogation admissible."[83]

In summary, certain points can be made regarding how courts view parental and children's rights to make decisions concerning risk-taking.

1. The general rule concerning majority and the age of consent is not based on a scientific or logical rationale. It is the result of generally irrelevant feudal law doctrine.
2. Parents can consent to therapeutic medical care for their young children.
3. The trend is that older children who can understand the consequences of a therapeutic medical procedure can consent to that procedure.
4. In the area of consent to therapeutic medical treatment courts require either the consent of the minor or of the parent, but not of both.
5. In areas outside the field of medical treatment, courts find that children may consent to take risks or waive rights, but base their decisions on the factual circumstances of the specific case.

NONTHERAPEUTIC EXPERIMENTATION ON MINORS

It has been stated that a resolution of the legal problems surrounding nontherapeutic experimentation on minors is made extremely difficult due to the fact that statutory law is nonexistent and case law is largely irrelevant.[84] Unfortunately, this observation is correct. Two questions are presented that must be dealt with. First, since it is generally understood that the law allows a parent to consent to the invasion of his child's body only if such invasion is for the child's benefit or welfare,[85] can the parent consent to the conducting of nonbeneficial experimentation on the child? Second, at what point must the child give his consent (or assent) to a nontherapeutic procedure as a precondition to its performance?

In trying to answer these questions, Professor Paul Freund has explained how the law approaches novel questions.[86] Law is a basically conservative field—no Nobel Prize is awarded for the most revolutionary judicial decision of the year. The law fears setting a bad precedent. To expand on this point Freund cites F.M. Cornford's book, *Micro-Cosmographia Academica* where it is stated in a somewhat tongue-in-cheek fashion:

The principle of the dangerous precedent is that you should not now do an admittedly right action for fear that you or your equally timid successors should not have the courage to do right in some future time, which *ex hypothesi* is substantially different but superficially resembles the present one. Every public action which is not customary is either wrong or, if it is right, is a dangerous precedent. It follows that nothing should ever be done for the first time.[87]

Law also tends to generalize on the basis of balancing risks and is deeply protective of human integrity and life. Finally, law is creative and responsive—if the reason for a rule of law ceases to exist, the rule of law should also cease to exist.[88]

With this as a background, we can examine how the problems set forth above have been dealt with.

Codes of conduct that are often referred to for guidance in this area of human experimentation do not directly confront this issue. The Nuremberg Code's first principle is that:

> The voluntary consent of the human subject is absolutely essential.
>
> This means that the person involved should have legal capacity to give consent . . . and should have sufficient knowledge and comprehension of the elements of the subject matter involved as to enable him to make an understanding and enlightened decision.[81]

As the previous examination of the law has demonstrated, minors are generally deemed legally incapable of giving their consent to medical treatment. For emancipated and mature minors, courts and legislatures have decided that they may consent to medical treatment that is rendered for their benefit. It is not all clear that such minors could consent to nontherapeutic procedures. But assuming that minors are legally competent to give such a consent, they must have "knowledge and comprehension of the elements of the subject matter involved" in order to give such consent. This sounds very much like the mature minor rule discussed earlier. Some argument could be made that under the Nuremberg Code, older minors can and must consent to nontherapeutic research in order for such research to be conducted on them.

It also appears that the Nuremberg Code outlaws proxy consent. It is the consent of the "human subject" that is required, not the consent of a guardian or representative.

The Helsinki Declaration, on the other hand, states that a subject must give his free consent, but "if he is legally incompetent the consent of the legal guardian should be procured."[90] It is not clear, however, whether or not the guardian's consent is in addition to the incompetent's consent, or if it acts as a substitute for the subject's consent.

The *only* case that exists which deals with this issue is *Bonner v. Moran.*[91] Because it is quoted so often we will explore it in some detail. At the time of the incident involved, John M. Bonner was a fifteen-year-old junior high student. His cousin, Clara Howard, had been so severely burned that she was a "hopeless cripple." Her aunt (who was also Bonner's aunt) took her to a charity clinic in Washington, D.C. that specialized in plastic surgery. It was decided that a skin graft was required, and a donor with the same blood type as Clara's was sought. After a number of unsuccessful attempts at finding a qualified donor, the aunt persuaded Bonner to go to the hospital for a blood test where it was discovered that he had the same blood type as his cousin. At this time the physician, Dr. Robert Moran, performed the first operation on the boy's side. His mother, with whom he lived, was ill and knew nothing about the procedure. After the operation he returned home and told his mother he was going back to the hospital to get "fixed up." However, once in the hospital more operations were done in order to cut and form a "tube of flesh" from his armpit to his waist. After the tube was surgically formed, it was attached to his cousin forming a literal flesh and blood bond between them. The results were unsatisfactory because of improper blood circulation in the tube, and it was severed after Bonner had lost so much blood he required transfusions. From beginning to end he was hospitalized for two months.

Bonner sued the physician who performed the surgery for assault and battery. The trial court adopted section 59 of the *Restatement of the Law of Torts* which then stated that if a child were capable of appreciating the nature, extent, and consequences of the invasion, he could consent to the medical procedure. Judgment was accordingly rendered by the trial court in favor of the physician which means that it had to find that the child understood the nature of the procedure and consented to it.

The appeals court began its analysis by noting that the general rule was that a minor could not consent to undergoing a medical procedure, but that there were exceptions to this rule when a minor was emancipated or close to maturity.

> But in all such cases [in which the exceptions apply] the basic consideration is whether the proposed operation is for the benefit of the child and is done with the purpose of saving his life or limb. The circumstances of the instant case are wholly without the compass of any of these exceptions. Here the operation was entirely for the benefit of another and involved sacrifice on the part of the infant of fully two months of schooling, in addition to serious pain and possible results affecting his future life.

> This immature colored boy was subjected several times to treatment involving anesthesia, blood letting, and the removal of skin from his body, with at least some permanent marks of disfigurement.[92]

The appeals court held that the trial court should have instructed the jury that the consent of the parent was also necessary. The court went on to find that during her son's confinement in the hospital his mother may have learned of what was transpiring, and by doing nothing about it may have ratified her son's consent. If his mother learned about the procedure and publicly expressed pride in her son's courage, such action would have been "tantamount to consent by implication; and that, in the circumstances, would be sufficient."[93]

The court's opinion is both confused and confusing on this point. Clearly the mother could not give her implied consent after the battery occurred. Consent must occur before the fact. The court must be basing its opinion on the mother's ratification of the child's consent, which was given before the second procedure was performed to form the tube of flesh. As a result the appeals court had to agree with the finding of the trial court that Bonner did consent to the procedure.

There is some dispute over the meaning of this case, Curran and Beecher[94] argue that the case holds that nonbeneficial procedures "can be legally permitted as long as the parents (or other guardians) consent to the procedure."[95]

Professor Alexander Capron argues that the interpretation "casts more weight onto the opinion that it can bear."[96] Capron suggests that the outcome of the case is based on the court's finding that Bonner was too immature to understand the complications involved, with the issue of lack of benefit "thrown in as a mere addition."[97] He goes on to say that the case is really one of ratification of the minor's consent by the parent, but that it nowhere suggests a parent has independent authority to give consent for a nonbeneficial intervention in which a child refuses or is too young to give his consent.[98]

Regardless of scholarly speculation about the meaning of this case, two statements can be made with authority. First, the trial court found as a matter of fact that Bonner understood and consented to the procedure discussed. Second, the appeals court found that as a matter of law, Bonner's mother could ratify his consent. The only conclusion that one can reach with any element of certainty is that if a child *and* his parent consent to a procedure that does not provide the minor with any benefits, and, indeed, may cause him harm, the procedure may be performed.

One must remember, however, that this case was decided before the Nuremberg Trials were held, and it is conceivable that the outcome would have been different if this case had arisen after the promulgation of the Nuremberg Code. The Nuremberg Code makes no provision for proxy consent, and if the court viewed this as a proxy consent case and found the Nuremberg Code to be controlling, it could have decided that this procedure could not be done under any circumstances.

There is no case that even suggests that children can consent to nonbeneficial research without parental consent. However, the British Medical Research Council, in its statement on children, does suggest that such is the case in England.[99] The statement starts with the premise that in the strict view of English law parents of minors may not, on behalf of the minor, consent to any procedures which carry some risk of harm and do not benefit the minor. It goes on to say that it may "safely be assumed" that no court would regard a child of younger than twelve years of age as having the capacity to consent to "any procedure that may involve him in an injury."[100] Above this age the reality of a purported consent by the minor would be a question of fact, and one would have to show the person involved fully understood the procedures. However

[e]ven when true consent has been given by a minor. . . . Considerations of ethics and prudence still require that, if possible, the assent of parents or guardians or relatives, as the case may be, should be obtained.[101]

In the English view one cannot perform nontherapeutic procedures that involve risk on any minor under the age of twelve, or on any minor over the age of twelve, unless he can give "true consent." In cases in which such consent is obtained, parental consent is not required by law, although it might be prudent and ethically desirable.

In a limited way the Michigan legislature had adopted a variation of this rule, Section 27.3178(19b) of the Michigan Code states:

A person of fourteen years of age or older may give one of his two kidneys to a father, mother, son, daughter, brother, or sister for a transplantation needed by him, when authorized by order of the probate court. . . .

If the court determines that the prospective donor is sufficiently sound of mind to understand the needs and probable consequences of the gift to both the donor and donee and agrees to the gift, the court may enter an order authorizing the making of the gift.

Thus, the only determination the probate court must make is whether or not the minor can give "true consent" to the procedure. If he can, then the minor will be allowed to consent and the transplant can go forward. There is no mention of the need for parental consent, and the statute would seem to ban organ donation by younger children. This procedure has one advantage over the English rule. In England it would appear that the determination of the existence of a valid consent would occur after the experiment had been performed, whereas in Michigan the before the fact determination better protects all the parties involved.

One transplant surgeon has adopted elements of both the English rule and the Michigan statute. He does not use children under the age of twelve as kidney donors because they are too young to understand the possibility of physical and psychological harm to themselves in the future and are unable to evaluate the present and future state of their health. However he believes children in their teens are acceptable to use as kidney donors.[102]

THE KIDNEY AND BONE MARROW TRANSPLANTATION CASES

The Michigan statute is the result of the existence of a body of case law that deals with the problems of organ transplantation in a confusing and ambiguous manner. Although, as discussed below, these cases are not strictly analogous to the nontherapeutic research situation, they do offer some insights into how courts tend to resolve the issue of proxy consent to nonbeneficial procedures.

Kidney transplantation has been conducted with adults since 1954, with the first case involving minors arising in 1957.[103] This case[104] involved nineteen-year-old twins. Although the healthy twin, Leonard, and his parents consented to the procedure, the physicians refused to operate because of the uncertainty concerning the validity of the parents' and the minor's consent to undergo a surgical procedure not for his benefit. To resolve this problem, an action for declaratory judgment was brought before a single justice of the Massachusetts Supreme Judicial Court. During the hearing, psychiatric testimony was offered to the effect that if the sick twin, Leon, died, it would have a "grave emotional impact" on the healthy twin. A finding was made that the operation was required to save the life of Leon and that Leonard had been fully informed and understood the consequences of the procedure and consented. Unfortunately, the court did not stop here and specifically adopt the mature minor rule in this situation. Instead, it went on to find that the emotional disturbance resulting from his brother's death could affect the health and emotional well-being of Leonard for the rest of his life. Therefore the operation was necessary for the continued good health and future well-being of Leonard and that in performing the operation the defendants are conferring a benefit upon Leonard as well as upon Leon.[105]

By finding "benefit" to Leonard, the court was able to circumvent the hard issue, since if the healthy donor received a "benefit" the validity of parental consent would no longer be a problem.

This "benefit" theory was used two more times the same year in cases that involved kidney transplants between fourteen-year-old identical twins.[106] In both of these cases the court found that the fourteen-year-olds understood the probable consequences and risks of the procedures, and gave their consent free of pressure or coercion. But the court still went on to use the psychological benefit theory, thereby avoiding the true issue. In all these early Massachusetts cases the courts found that the minors consented, the parents consented, and there was psychological benefit to the donor. If any one of these elements was missing the outcomes might have been different.

Several cases concerning kidney transplants between siblings have arisen since 1957. Perhaps the most discussed is *Strunk v. Strunk.*[107] In this case the donor, Jerry Strunk, was not a minor but a twenty-seven-year-old incompetent with an I.Q. of 35 and a mental age of six, who was committed to a state institution. The donee, Tommy Strunk, was twenty-eight years old, married, employed and a part-time university student who was suffering from chronic glomerulus nephritis. No other member of the family qualified as a donor due to blood type incompatibility. Because of the apparent lack of benefit to Jerry a court action was instituted, and a guardian *ad litem* (a guardian appointed for the purposes of litigation) was appointed. The guardian questioned the authority of the state to approve the transplant. Psychiatric testimony was offered that alleged Tommy's death would have an "extremely traumatic effect"[108] on Jerry, and that "Tom's life is vital to the continuity of Jerry's improvement"[109] at the state hospital. The court also found that renal transplantation was becoming relatively common and that over 2500 transplants had been done up to the date of the trial. It found that the chances of the transplant being successful increase when the donor and donee are genetically related and that the risk of transplantation to the donee is small, 0.05 to 0.07 percent. The court then adopted the doctrine of "substituted judgment" in which a court acts in a manner it believes the incompetent would act if he had his faculties. The seriously divided court (4–3) allowed the transplant to go forward, becoming the first case in which such an operation was done without the consent of the donor.

In a strong dissent Judge Steinfeld stated "My sympathies and emotions are torn between a compassion to aid an ailing young man and a duty to fully protect unfortunate members of society."[110] The dissenters, recalling the experiments in Nazi Germany found that guardians must act to "protect and maintain the ward."[111] They found that opinions concerning psychological trauma are "most nebulous," that it is well known that transplants are frequently rejected, and that the life of the incompetent is not in danger but that the surgical procedure creates some peril.[112] According to the dissenters, the ability to fully understand and consent is a prerequisite to the donation of a body part and a transplant should not be done on an incompetent until it can be "conclusively demonstrated that it will be of significant benefit to the individual."[113]

Several years later the case of *Hart v. Brown*[114] was decided in Connecticut. This case dealt with a kidney transplant between identical twins who were seven years, ten months old. The court found that although Kathleen, the sick twin, was undergoing regular hemodialysis, she could not do so indefinitely and a kidney transplant was required to sustain her life. It also found that, since immunosuppressive drugs would not be required because the twins were identical, such a transplant would be much less risky for Kathleen than a transplant from a different donor, and that there was substantially a 100 percent chance that both twins would live out a normal life upon following the procedure. The family's clergyman felt the decision was morally and ethically sound and a psychiatrist found that a successful operation would be of "immense benefit to the donor in that the donor would be better off in a family that was happy than in a family that was distressed. . . ."[115] The donor was informed of the procedure and "insofar as she may be capable of understanding"[116] desired to donate her kidney. The guardian *ad litem* also consented. The court specifically noted the limited value of the psychiatric testimony but instead found that

> [i]t would appear that the natural parents would be able to substitute their consent for that of their minor children after a close, independent and objective investigation of their motivation and reasoning. This has been accomplished in this matter by the participation of a clergyman, the defendant physicians, and attorney guardian *ad litem* for the donee, and indeed, this court itself.[117]

It was also found that this procedure was not "clinical experimentation but rather medical treatment."[118] The court held that

> natural parents of a minor should have the right to give their consent to

an isograft kidney transplantation procedure when their motivation and reasoning are favorably reviewed by a community representation which includes a court of equity.[119]

The right to consent on behalf of a minor was given to the parent as long as the parents' motivation was proper.

In a Georgia case, the court substituted its judgment for a moderately mentally retarded fifteen-year-old girl who was to serve as a donor for her dying mother, and permitted the transplant.[120]

There are two recent cases in which organ donation by a minor was not permitted. In the first, *In re Richardson*,[121] the prospective donor was a seventeen-year-old mental retardate with a mental age of three or four, and the prospective donee was his thirty-two-year-old sister, Beverly. An examination of the court's use of the facts in this case is instructive. It found that although a kidney transplant would be beneficial, it was not immediately necessary to preserve Beverly's life. In the first place, there was evidence that she could be sustained indefinitely by kidney dialysis. Second, although Roy would be the best donor available, as there was only a 3–5 percent chance of rejection with his kidney, there were other donors that could donate with a 20–30 percent chance of rejection. And if these were rejected, other transplant procedures could be done. Thus, a transplant from Roy might be the best alternative for Beverly, but there were other, if less desirable, options open to her. The court discussed the *Strunk* case but found that Louisiana law differs from Kentucky law in that the law of Louisiana "is designed to promote and protect the ultimate best interests of the minor."[122] Under Louisiana's statutes, a minor is not allowed to make any *inter vivos* transfers of property and a parent is absolutely prohibited from transferring a minor's property. The court reasoned that if the law affords such protection against intrusion into a "comparatively mere" property right, it was inconceivable that the minor's right to be free from bodily intrusion would be any less protected.[123] The argument that Roy would benefit from the procedure because Beverly could care for him after his parents died was rejected as "highly speculative . . . and highly unlikely."[124] The fact that the transplant was the most desirable course of action for Beverly was not enough to convince the court of equity to permit the transplant, since less detrimental alternatives were available. But from the legal analysis performed by the court, even if a transplant from Roy was the only way to keep Beverly alive, it would not have had the authority to permit such a transplant.

In the second case, the Wisconsin Court resolved the problem in a similar manner. In this case, *In re Pescinski*,[125] a petition was filed with the court asking it to permit a kidney transplant from Richard, a thirty-nine-year-old catatonic schizophrenic who had been institutionalized for sixteen years and who had a mental age of twelve, to his thirty-eight-year-old sister who was the mother of six minor children. The physician involved said he would not use her parents, who were aged seventy and sixty-seven, since "as a matter of principle"[126] he would not do the operation on a person over sixty. The physician also refused to use a kidney from any of her minor children as a matter of his "own moral conviction."[127] Another brother forty-three-years-old who owned a dairy farm and had ten children refused to be a donor because there would be no one to take care of his farm. Additionally, he said he had a stomach problem that required a special diet, and a rupture on his left side. The court's opinion implied that there were a number of competent, healthy potential donors, who were excluded for "moral reasons" or for personal reservations, and who were not asked or did not volunteer to donate their kidneys because of the existence of Richard.

The court held that since Richard did not consent to the procedure, it could not be done.[128] Additionally, a guardian must act "loyally in the best interests of his ward"[129] and there was absolutely no evidence here that any interests of the ward would be served. The concept of substituted judgment was forthrightly rejected.[130] In summarizing its opinion the court stated:

> An incompetent particularly should have his own interests protected. Certainly no advantage should be taken of him. In the absence of real consent on his part, and in a situation where no benefit to him has been established, we fail to find any authority for the county court, or this court, to approve the operation.[131]

Following this line of kidney transplant cases, a separate but similar line of cases resulted from the advent of bone marrow transplantation procedures.[132] The bone marrow cases provide less of a physical intrusion into the donor's body as no body cavity is opened, and unlike kidneys, the bone marrow regenerates itself. The donor is subjected to as many as 200 aspirations of the pelvic bone with a needle specially designed to remove bone marrow.[133] The Attorney General of the state of Washington has determined that written consent of the guardian is sufficient to authorize a bone marrow donation by a minor.[134]

The practice in Massachusetts, however, is still to acquire a court decree prior to the transplant. The court that created the "psychological benefit" mischief is currently dealing with the problem in a more straightforward manner. Thus in *Rappeport v. Stott*,[135] a bone marrow transplant case, the judge held that a seventeen-year-old was "capable of consenting to the proposed procedure," and did not bother to find that he received psychological benefit.

The most illuminating bone marrow transplant case is probably *Nathan v. Farinelli*,[136] because of its forthright approach. Toni Farinelli was a healthy six-year-old and her ten-year-old brother, William, was suffering from aplastic anemia, which, left untreated, is fatal in eighty-five percent of the cases. The parents consented to a bone marrow transplant but the physicians refused to operate in the absence of a court authorization. The court found that the risk to Toni was minimal, but also found that she would receive no benefit. The petitioners took the standard approach and called a psychiatrist as a witness. Surprisingly, she testified that she would be speculating if she ventured any opinion about the psychological effect of either allowing or preventing the intended donor from furnishing the bone marrow.[137] The court appreciated her honesty and found that

> [t]o require a finding of benefit to the donor, and particularly to accept a psychological benefit as sufficient, often seems to invite testimony conjured to satisfy the requirement by words but not by substance.[138]

The court also rejected the "substituted judgment" theory as being irrelevant in these situations.[139]

> It is the court's opinion that a better approach to the issue involved in this case is to consider that the primary right and responsibility for deciding the delicate question of whether bone marrow should be taken from Toni and transplanted in William is that of the parents with reference to both children.[140]

The requirement that the parents' decision be reviewed arises out of the possible conflict between the parents' responsibility for the care and custody of one child, and their similar responsibility for the other. In what can serve as a summary of all these cases, the court wrote, "It would be more truthful to recognize that the parents themselves are making decisions for their children,"[141] and are not substituting their judgment for that of the child. Finding that the parents' decision was "fair and reasonable" the court permitted the procedure to be done.[142]

The reason for setting out these cases so extensively is that, with the exception of *Bonner*, they are the only cases that deal with consent to nonbeneficial procedures. But we can learn a number of lessons from these cases, as diverse as they may be, that are applicable to research conducted on children.

Although never explicitly stated, courts will permit parents to consent to therapeutic research on children, even where the risks are high, if the benefits are great. In the bone marrow transplant cases, the transplanted bone marrow might cause adverse reactions in the recipient's body. This condition, called graft-versus-host disease, can lead to an agonizing death.[143] However, since the experimental procedure might save the life of a doomed child, no question is raised as to the ability of the parent to consent on his behalf.[144]

As to these cases' importance in regard to nontherapeutic experimentation, we must look at the differences between the transplant cases and nontherapeutic research. First, the procedures that were performed on the donors in the transplant cases were not experimental. Neither the removal of a kidney nor bone marrow aspiration is considered an innovative procedure.

Second, in the average nontherapeutic research setting, parents will not have to struggle with the conflict of interest problem. One commentator has pointed out that one reason why experimentation must be more closely regulated than therapy, is because during therapy the doctor sees the patient as an end and not a means, and in nontherapeutic experimentation the subject is seen as the means and not the end.[145] In the transplant cases the parent must also view the donor child as a means, and the cure of the ill child as the end. As a result, the parent's role as the protector of the donor child might be negatively influenced. Courts should be especially aware of this in cases in which the donor is mentally ill or retarded and it may be suspected that parents and physicians may not value the life of the donor as highly as the life of the donee. This is made all the more apparent by the fact that in all the transplant cases involving mentally ill or retarded adults or children, all the mentally ill or retarded individuals were donors, never recipients. Indeed, during the hearings in the *Strunk* case, the Director of the Renal Division, University of Kentucky Medical Center, testified that if something should later happen to the retarded donor's remaining kidney, based on selection criteria at the Medical Center, the donor would not be eligible for either hemodialysis or transplantation.[146] Because of the possibility of exploitation, it is not surprising that the two cases in which the courts denied permission to conduct the transplant involved a mentally retarded and a mentally ill individual.

In the absence of such a conflict, parents should be better able to protect the interests of their child when an investigator asks their permission to use their child as a subject in nontherapeutic research. It might be presumed that parents could put all their energies into protecting their healthy child, because they need not be concerned about the welfare of a sick child.

Both parents and children might be better able to make protective decisions concerning the child's welfare in nontherapeutic research than in the transplant situation because no duress should exist. When a transplant is needed by a sick child, and the healthy child is the only available donor, one essentially communicates the point to both the parent and the child that unless consent is received from all concerned, the child or sibling will die. Truly voluntary consents are hard to imagine in such a situation.[147] But where neither the parent nor child receives any benefit, duress should be entirely absent.

From this analysis it would appear that children involved in non-therapeutic research need *less* outside protection than transplant donors.

But if one looks behind the logic involved in these cases one can see why these cases are resolved the way they have been. The transplant cases revolve around the power of the family to protect its own members. When a child is sick the family as a unit is permitted to use its resources and make sacrifices to help the sick member. All the courts agree on one point, however—the general rule is that parents must act in the best interests of their children and not subject them to harmful situations. The courts that permit transplants have gone through incredible feats of mental gymnastics, such as finding benefit where none exists, to overcome the general rule. The *Farinelli* case, tired of these maneuvers, directly confronted the issue and held that the family could protect its members, and made its decision on that basis.

In addition, as discussed above by Freund, in the transplant cases the courts are balancing risks and being deeply protective of life. Where the risks are relatively minimal and a life hangs in the balance, the courts will decide in favor of life.

PROXY CONSENT

All the transplant cases have had to struggle with the problem of proxy consent to nonbeneficial procedures. As has been demonstrated by these cases, the issue of who can consent to nonbeneficial procedures that are to be conducted on another person is far from resolved. Part of the problem springs from the fact that the very term "proxy consent" is a contradiction in terms. If the major purposes of the doctrine of informed consent are to protect *self* autonomy and *self* determination, it is difficult to conceptualize how these very personal rights can be exercised by a third party. The courts have confused the matter even more by not clearly setting forth the grounds upon which they have validated the exercise of proxy consents.

There are three tests courts have used in determining whether or not proxy consent on behalf of an incompetent organ donor is valid—the "substituted judgment" test, the "best interests of the donor" test, and the "fair and reasonable" test.[148]

The substituted judgment concept has a lengthy history that predates *Strunk*, the first transplant case to adopt the doctrine. It appears to have originated in the 1816 English case of *Ex parte Whitbread*,[149] in which it was held that a portion of the money in the estate of a "lunatic" could be given to his next-of-kin to rescue them from poverty. In deciding that such a use of the incompetent's resources was permissible although he did not directly benefit from the use of the funds, the court looked "at what it is likely the lunatic himself would do, if he were in a capacity to act. . . ."[150] The court merely placed itself in the position of the incompetent and determined how it thought he would act if he were competent. There was apparently no evidence as to how this specific individual truly desired to have his funds used in this circumstance, but the court decided he would have acted in the same fashion as would a reasonable person.

More recent American opinions have required courts to actually try to determine how the particular incompetent would act in a given situation. In so doing, courts have imputed to incompetents motives of charity, altruism, self-interest, and the desire to reduce estate taxes in upholding gifts from their estates.[151] Courts have also taken into account evidence that the incompetent had previously made gifts to a particular person or persons, or had stated an intention to make such gifts prior to becoming incompetent.[152] In addition, it has been inferred by courts that the incompetent would have made such transfers to his immediate family, and sometimes has extended this inference to more distant relatives.[153]

Thus, the historical basis for the substituted judgment test is a line of cases dealing with the transfers of property from an incompetent to a family member who was in need of funds. The question that presents itself is whether or not this principle should be transferred to the organ donation and nontherapeutic research situation. Certainly the court in the *Strunk* case had no problem making this conceptual leap. However, an invasion of a person's body is a more serious undertaking than the invasion of a person's property under our system of jurisprudence. Additionally, determining what a "reasonable person" would do when confronted with the decision to donate an organ is not an easy task. In the *Pescinski* case, it was noted that a number of possible donors did not volunteer to donate a kidney to a relative. However, in the cases of competent donors, we do see relatives readily donating their organs to members of their immediate families who suffer from kidney disease. In one study of kidney donors, it was discovered that fourteen out of the twenty questioned stated that their decision to donate was made in a "split second" or "instantaneously" after learning of the need for the donation.[154] It appeared that their decision-making process was "irrational" and could not be said to meet the requirements of informed consent.[155] If this is an accurate indication of how "reasonable people" make their decision to donate their kidneys to relatives, a court substituting its judgment on behalf of an incompetent could use this information as guidance in determining how a "reasonable person" would act in a similar situation. Thus, if a court found that "reasonable people" act irrationally when faced with the decision to donate an organ, and often agree to donate an organ without taking the risks into account, it could use this finding to permit the donation by the incompetent. Although the Wisconsin[156] and Louisiana[157] courts have rejected the use of the substituted judgment test in regard to kidney donations, one commentator has suggested that such an approach deprives the incompetent of the benefits that might be derived from donation.[158]

Regardless of the validity of the substituted judgment doctrine as applied to the organ transplant situation, it would seem to have no bearing in the nontherapeutic research situation. Both the historical basis for the doctrine and its recent applications indicate that the doctrine is only to be used to benefit a close relative in need of either funds or a body organ. Nontherapeutic research is usually conducted to benefit society in general at some future date, and therefore the doctrine would not seem to be applicable. In addition, it is far from clear that "reasonable people" generally consent to undergo, for the benefit of society as a whole, nontherapeutic experimental procedures that carry a risk of harm.

The second test under consideration, the "best interests" test is closely allied with the substituted judgment doctrine. Under this test, one has to demonstrate that the donor will directly benefit from the donation of an organ. This is the test that was utilized in the first three kidney donation cases involving minors.[159] In these cases, it was found that the donors would receive a "psychological benefit" as a result of donating a kidney to their sick twin. By establishing the presence of a benefit, the court was able to avoid the difficult issue of the validity of proxy consent to nonbeneficial procedures. Once a benefit to the donor was established, there was no question that the parents could give their consent. In the *Strunk* case, the court found that the survival of the sick sibling was necessary for the "treatment and eventual rehabilitation" of the incompetent and institutionalized donor.[160] In the *Richardson* case, it was argued that the transplant was in the best interests of the donor because, if the sick sibling survived, she could care for the incompetent after the deaths of their parents.[161] The court rejected the argument as being both "highly speculative" and "highly unlikely."[162] The best interests doctrine would also appear to have no applicability to the nontherapeutic research situation. It is difficult, if not impossible, to think of how subjecting a child to nontherapeutic research that carries a risk of harm could be in that child's best interests. This doctrine, would, of course, apply to therapeutic research.

Finally, the "fair and reasonable" test has been adopted by one court in Massachusetts in the case of *Nathan v. Farinelli*.[163] As discussed earlier, the court found that the parents of a minor donor have the primary responsibility in deciding whether or not their child can serve as a donor in a bone marrow transplantation procedure. The only determination the court made was to decide whether or not the parents' decision was fair and reasonable in the particular circumstances.[164]

This test would be applicable in the nontherapeutic research setting. It is conceivable that the parents' decision to subject their child to a nontherapeutic research procedure that did not involve any risk or involved a very minimal amount of risk could be deemed to be fair and reasonable. The problem with this test is that it is very subjective, since what may appear to be fair and reasonable to one person might be considered unfair or unreasonable by another.

The most recent, and perhaps the most drastic, proxy consent case involves the right of a parent to terminate medical procedures that are required to sustain the life of his comatose adult child. In this case, *In the Matter of Karen Quinlan*,[165] Joseph Quinlin, Karen's father, petitioned the lower court to appoint him guardian of the person and property of his comatose daughter, with the specific authority to order cessation of life-sustaining procedures. The lower court denied this petition[166] but was reversed by the New Jersey Supreme Court. The Supreme Court found that Karen's right to privacy would enable her to order cessation of extraordinary life-sustaining procedures if she were competent to do so.[167] It went on to find that she was grossly incompetent to assert this right, but that such a right could be asserted on her behalf by a guardian.[168] The court reasoned that not to permit such action by the guardian would be to deprive Karen of her right to privacy. The court found:

> The only practical way to prevent destruction of the right [to privacy] is to permit the guardian and family of Karen to render their best judgment, subject to the qualifications hereinafter stated, as to whether she would exercise it in these circumstances. If their conclusion is in the affirmative this decision should be accepted by a society the overwhelming majority of whose members would, we think, in similar circumstances, exercise such a choice in the same way for themselves or for those closest to them.[169]

This would seem to be an acceptance of the substituted judgment doctrine. The court also seems to accept the fact that it must evaluate the "interests" of the patient as seen by her guardian.[170] This would appear to be some recognition of the best interests test. Finally, the court seems compelled to examine the "motivation and purpose" of the guardian, which might indicate that it is concerned with whether or not he would act in his ward's best interest, and in a fair and reasonable manner. Thus, the court touched on all the tests, although it seemed to adopt the substituted judgment test. As an additional precaution, the court requires the incompetent's physician and an "ethics committee" to be in agreement with the guardian's decision.[171] Regardless of these additional safeguards, the *Quinlan* case would seem to expand the power of a parent or guardian to substitute his judgment for his child or ward. However, the facts of this case are very different from either the organ transplant situation or the nontherapeutic research situation, and therefore the holding cannot be applied to those instances.

We should not expect that courts will permit nontherapeutic research on children without their consent, where there is a chance that harm will occur. At this point one must recall the pronouncement in *In re Clark that:*

> [T]he fact the child belongs to the state imposes upon the state many duties. Chief among them is to protect his right to live and to grow up with a sound mind in a sound body, and to brook no interference with that right by any person or organization.[172]

Although someday we might all benefit from the results, no specific life will be immediately prolonged by such participation. One commentator has pointed out that allowing nonbeneficial procedures to be performed on minors without their consent, but requiring the consent of adults prior to such procedures being performed on such adults, enables us to force children to participate in activities that may harm them, but not force adults to participate in similar programs.[173] One might compare this to lowering the age of conscription to include only those from birth to eighteen. It can be concluded that neither parents nor courts can consent to nontherapeutic research on minors who have not also given informed and voluntary consent. The consent of the minor to nontherapeutic research that puts him at risk of harm is essential.

Hopefully, the question of the limits of parental proxy consent to nontherapeutic research on children will be resolved by a case now pending in California, *Nielsen v. Board of Regents*.[174] In this case, the plaintiffs are seeking to bar the use of normal, healthy infants, ranging in age from two months, to four years, as controls in an asthma research project. Blood samples were to be drawn and drugs injected to determine the children's tolerance to such substances and stresses.[175] The study was to last five years and the parents were to be paid $300 per year for their children's participation.[176] There is no question that the children cannot give their consent due to their young age, and the complaint alleges that California law prohibits parents from consenting to such research. California Penal Code § 273(a) states:

> (1) Any person who, under circumstances or conditions likely to produce great bodily harm or death, willfully causes or permits any child to suffer, or inflicts thereon unjustifiable physical pain or mental suffering, or having the care or custody of any child, willfully causes or permits such child to be placed in such situation that its person or health is endangered, is punishable by imprisonment in the county jail not exceeding one year, or in the state prison for not less than one year nor more than 10 years.

> (2) Any person who, under circumstances or conditions other than those likely to produce great bodily harm or death, willfully causes or permits any child to suffer, or inflicts thereon unjustifiable physical pain or mental suffering or having the care or custody of any child, willfully causes or permits the person or health of such child to be injured, or willfully causes or permits such child to be placed in such situation that its person or health may be endangered, is guilty of a misdemeanor.

One writer argues that the complaint does not go far enough.[177] The experimental group consists of children who are "at-risk" of becoming asthmatics, as indicated by their family medical histories. The complaint does not allege that parents cannot consent to the participation of these children. These children are not now ill, and the drugs given to them are not designed to cure them of a present illness. If they do become ill this research may be of help to them at that future time, but it is argued, at the moment it must be deemed nontherapeutic: And therefore parents may not give consent to their child's participation.

The difference between therapeutic and nontherapeutic research is not obvious. In testing the polio vaccine which was supposed to prevent a clinically rare disease, but could, and sometimes did, cause the disease, one might ask, "Were these children subject to therapeutic or nontherapeutic procedures?" None were being treated for an existing condition, and the large majority would never contract the disease. Or were the controls who did not receive the vaccine the ones who were put at risk?[178]

Some research may have elements of both therapeutic and non-therapeutic procedures. In one study of phenylketonuria (PKU) and diet, a two-year-old child who could not stand, walk or talk, and who spent her time crying, groaning and banging her head as a result of PKU, was given an experimental diet. Within a few months she improved greatly. This was clearly therapeutic. To establish that the improvement was due to the special diet rather than to natural development, the investigators added five grams of L-phenylalanine to the diet without telling the child's mother, so that her observations would not be biased. The child rapidly deteriorated. Could the determination that the diet made the difference in the developmental progress be considered therapeutic? The diet is both expensive and restrictive and it would be an injustice to keep the person on the diet forever if it wasn't required.[179]

SUMMARY

1. The general rule is that one must obtain the informed and voluntary consent of the subject prior to his participation in biomedical or behavioral research.

2. There are no decided cases or statutes that specifically deal with the problem of the validity of the consent of the parent or child to participation in nontherapeutic research.

3. The one case that comes closest to confronting this problem, *Bonner v. Moran,* held that if the trial court found that both a fifteen-year-old and his mother consented to his undergoing a procedure that posed serious risks to his health, while offering him no benefits, that such consent would free the physician from liability.

4. Although in the kidney and bone marrow transplantation cases courts permit parents to consent to nonbeneficial procedures

on behalf of the minor donors, the cases are factually distinguishable from the nontherapeutic research situation. In the transplantation cases, one family member acts to save the life of another family member. Even in these cases, courts generally require some sort of consent from the donor, and require prior court review of the parents' decision to permit the transplant.

5.   Courts have not questioned the right and ability of parents to consent to the performance of therapeutic research on their sick child.

6.   Courts are expanding their role as the protectors of the best interests of the child.

7.   Courts will closely scrutinize the facts of a particular situation to ensure that one who is not capable of protecting his own interests is not being exploited.

8.   Parents have the legal duty to protect the health, well-being and best interests of their children.

9.   Courts have found that with adequate safeguards children are capable of waiving important rights, and can consent to incurring serious risks.

CONCLUSIONS AND RECOMMENDATIONS

Therapeutic Research • Where research is designed to cure a specific disease or condition from which the child is suffering, and no other drug or procedure is available to treat such condition or disease, or the existing procedure is more dangerous or produces greater discomfort than the proposed procedure, such therapeutic research should be allowed to be conducted with the informed consent of both parents, or one parent if both are not available.

In such a case the parents are consenting to therapy. Or to put it another way, they are consenting to a procedure that is carried out with the purpose of furthering the best interests of the child. As such, the law will enable parents to consent to such procedures. Although the consent of one parent would probably be sufficient, because of the experimental nature of the procedure it would be prudent to allow both parents to decide that the standard procedure is not to be used, since the new procedure might not be efficacious.

Nontherapeutic Research • For nontherapeutic research that carries a risk of harm, such procedures should only be done when the risks are extremely small and the benefits to society are very great. When it has been determined that the risk-benefit ratio of a certain procedure falls into this category, courts, performing their own balancing test, would probably uphold the parental right to consent to their child's participation in such a study. What constitutes a high-risk procedure is not readily determined. Is a high-risk procedure that which has a one-in-a-million chance of causing death, or one that has a fifty percent chance of causing a headache? Though no definitive answers are available, the Ethical Review Board, the Institutional Review Board and the Consent or Protection Committees should all be given the authority to make an independent determination of this issue regarding any proposed research.

When a minor is capable of understanding these procedures his consent should also be required. Or, in other words, he should have the absolute right to refuse to participate in such nontherapeutic procedures. The problem is setting an age at which a minor has such understanding of risk-taking, benefits and harm, and is able to weigh these factors, so that he can give a truly informed consent. One can establish a subjective rule and say that a minor of sufficient intelligence and maturity to understand the consequences of the proposed experimental procedure may consent to such procedures. Investigators would probably be unhappy with this because they would have to make such a determination, and if they are wrong, liability might result. However, investigators must also make this determination in adults. If an adult is incapable of understanding the risks inherent in undergoing an experimental procedure, an investigator cannot get his informed consent.

Alternatively, one could have all minor subjects of this type of research screened by a protection committee which would make the determination. Or we could ask the courts to make such a finding, as is the case in Michigan in regard to kidney transplants.

The advantage of setting a specific age at which a child can participate or refuse to participate is its objective nature. But it must not be set too low. Draft proposed federal regulations state that research cannot be done on a child above the age of six without his consent.[180] A child of this age will probably agree to do almost anything an authority figure requests. Although it gives the child the right to say no, it is probably a right that will not be forcefully exercised. The age should be set higher, hopefully on a scientific basis with the help of experts in child development. The Michigan statute uses the age of fourteen, Professor Curran suggests fourteen,[181] and the British Medical Research Council suggests twelve.[182]

The consent of both parents should be required if both are alive. Since their child might be injured, they should be able to veto his decision since such an injury would have a negative impact on them and would not benefit their child in any way. In addition, since it can be presumed that they will protect the interests of their child when no conflict exists, their counsel should be sought, and their protective role utilized. Children who have no parents and institutionalized children should not be allowed to participate in such studies. The institutionalized child has the duel burden of his minority and the effects of institutionalization.

Children below the age of consent that have been selected, or who are too young to understand the nature and consequences of a procedure, may be subjects in nontherapeutic research when there is no chance of harm occurring, or, as discussed above, the risks are minimal. When harm cannot occur, the need for consent declines considerably, and one need not worry about the exploitation of the child. Of course, the consent of the parents should still be required.

Federal regulation of research can only add to the protections already required by state law. Thus, if California outlaws all nontherapeutic research on minors, federal regulations cannot permit such activities in that state.

We believe these recommendations are fair. They protect the children-subjects as well as the parents of these children, but do not unduly burden the research community. Such regulation of research will permit it to continue without exploiting the children who deserve our utmost protection.

REFERENCES

1. United States of America v. Karl Brandt, in Katz, Experimentation with Human Beings, 305–306 (1972). *See* Appendix I.

2. Freund, Ethical Problems in Human Experimentation, 273 New Eng. J. Med. 687 (1965).

3. Lowe, Alexander and Mishkin, Non-Therapeutic Research in Children: An Ethical Dilemma, 84 J. Ped. 468 (1974).

4. *Id.* at 469.

5. 21 U.S.C. 5301 *et seq.*

6. Capron, Legal Considerations Affecting Clinical Pharmacological Studies in Children, 21 Clin. Res. 141, 142 (1972).

7. 1 Blackstone, Commentaries at *463; Bardwell v. Purrington, 107 Mass. 419, 425 (1871).

8. Time, November 25, 1974 at 92.

9. James, The Age of Majority, 4 Am. J. of Leg. Hist. 22, 24 (1960).

10. *Id.*

11. *Id.* at 25.

12. *Id.*

13. *Id.* at 26–28.

14. *Id.* at 30.

15. *Id.* at 31–32.

16. Tyler, Law of Infancy and Coverture, 34 (1868).

17. *Id.*

18. Blackstone, *supra* note 7, at *464.

19. Thomas, Child Abuse and Neglect, Part I: Historical Overview, Legal Matrix, and Sociological Perspectives, 50 N. Car. L. Rev. 293, 295 (1972).

20. *Id.* at 294.

21. Edge, Voidability of Minors' Contracts; A Feudal Doctrine in a Modern Economy, 1 Ga. L. Rev. 205, 220 (1966-67).

22. *Id.* at 221-222.

23. Blackstone, *supra* note 7, at *463.

24. Baird v. Bellotti, 393 F. Supp. 847, 855 (1975), *vacated*, 44 U.S.L.W. 5221 (June 29, 1976).

25. State v. Koome, 1 F.L.R. 2236, 2237 (Feb. 18, 1975).

26. Cote-Harper, Age, Delinquent Responsibility and Moral Judgment, 11 Les Cahiers de Droit 480, 496 (1970).

27. *Id.*

28. *Id.* at 500-505.

29. *Id.* at 506.

30. Proposed Mass. Dept. of Mental Health Reg. § 220.18, 5 Mass. J. of Ment. Health 53 (1975).

31. Schloendorff v. Society of N.Y. Hosp. 211, N.Y. 125, 105 N.E. 92, 93 (1914).

32. Prosser, Law of Torts, 34-36 (4 ed. 1971).

33. *Id.* at 102.

34. Lacey v. Laird, 166 Ohio St. 12, 139 N.E.2d 25, 30 (1956).

35. Moss v. Rishworth, 222 S.W. 225 (Texas, 1920).

36. 185 N.E.2d 128 (Ohio, 1962).

37. *Id.* at 132.

38. Maine Sup. Ct. Civ. No. 74-145 (Feb. 14, 1974).

39. New Jersey Sup. Ct. Chancery Div. No. C-201-75 (Nov. 10, 1975).

40. *Supra* note 38, at 3.

41. 309 N.Y. 80, 127 N.E.2d 820 (1955).

42. 317 N.Y.S.2d 641 (1970), *aff'd*, 29 N.Y.2d 900 (1972).

43. Prosser, *supra* note 32, at 103; Mass. Gen. Laws. Ann. ch. 112 § 12F; Ann. Code of Md. Art. 43 § 135.

44. Roger v. Sells, 61 P.2d 1018 (Okl. 1936).

45. Pilpel, Minors' Right to Medical Care, 36 Alb. L. Rev. 462, 464 (1972).

46. *Id.* at 465; *See*, Katz, Schroeder and Sidman, Emancipating Our Children—Coming of Legal Age in America, 7 Fam. L.Q. 211 (1973).

47. Jolicoeur v. Mihaly, 5 Cal. 3d 565, 96 Cal. Rptr. 697, 488 P.2d 1 at 10 (1971), cited in Katz, *et al.*, *supra* note 46, at 231.

48. Katz, *et al.*, *supra* note 46, at 231.

49. 15 Mass. 203 (1818).

50. *Id.*

51. *See, e.g.*, Nev. Rev. Stat. § 12.030(1).

52. *See, e.g.*, Ca. Civ. Code § 34.6.

53. Smith v. Seibly, 431 P.2d 719 (Wash. 1967).

54. Bakker v. Welsh, 144 Mich. 632, 108 N.W. 94 (1906).
55. *Supra* note 34.
56. *Id.* at 30–31.
57. *Id.* at 34.
58. 237 Mich. 76, 211 N.W. 75 (1926).
59. 205 Kan. 292, 469 P.2d 330 (1970).
60. *Id.* at 338.
61. Ore. Rev. Stat. ch. 381 §1-3.
62. Code of Ala. ch. 22 §104(15).
63. Miss. Code Ann. §41-41-3(h).
64. 410 U.S. 113 (1973).
65. H.C.S. House Bill No. 1211 §3(4).
66. 44 U.S.L.W. 5198 (June 29, 1976).
67. *Id.* at 5204.
68. *Id.*
69. Bellotti v. Baird, 44 U.S.L.W. 5221 (June 19, 1976).
70. Mass. Gen. Laws Ch. 112 §12P.
71. *Id.* at 5224.
72. Prosser, *supra* note 32, at 447.
73. *Id.*
74. Greene v. Watts, 21 Cal. App. 2d 103, 26 Cal. Rptr. 334 (1962).
75. Pouliot v. Black, 341 Mass. 531 (1960).
76. 152 Ohio St. 463, 90 N.E.2d 142 (1950).
77. 164 Ohio St. 41, 128 N.E.2d 80 (1955).
78. Vendrell v. School District No. 26c, 23 Ore. 1, 376 P.2d 406 (1962).
79. *Id.*
80. Aldes v. St. Paul Ball Club, 88 N.W.2d 94, 251 Minn. 440 (1958).
81. 332 U.S. 596 (1948).
82. 370 U.S. 49 (1962).
83. Note, The Admissibility of Juvenile Confessions: Is an Intelligent and Knowing Waiver of Constitutional Rights Possible Without Adult Guidance?, 34 U. of Pitt. L. Rev. 321, 324 (1972), citing Commonwealth v. Darden, 441 Pa. 41, 271 A.2d 257 (1971).
84. Lowe, *et al.*, *supra* note 3, at 468.
85. Freund, *supra* note 2, at 671.
86. Freund, *supra* note 2.
87. *Id.* at 687–688.
88. *Id.* at 688.
89. United States of America v. Karl Brandt, *supra* note 1.
90. *See*, Mitchell, Experimentation on Minors: What Ever Happened to Prince v. Massachusetts?, 13 Duquesne L. Rev. 919, 925 (1975).
91. 126 F.2d 121 (D.C. Cir. 1941).
92. *Id.* at 123.
93. *Id.*
94. Curran and Beecher, Experimentation in Children, 210 J.A.M.A. 77, (1969).
95. *Id.* at 79.

96. Capron, *supra* note 6, at 889.

97. *Id.*

98. *Id.*

99. Curran and Beecher, *supra* note 94, at 80.

100. *Id.* at 81.

101. *Id.*

102. Moore, Transplant: The Give and Take of Tissue Transplantation 107 (Simon & Schuster, 1972).

103. *See*, Curran, A Problem of Consent: Kidney Transplantation in Minors, 34 N.Y.U.L. Rev. 891 (1959).

104. Masden v. Harrison, No. 68651 Eq., Mass. Sup. Jud. Ct. (June 12, 1957).

105. Curran, *supra* note 94, at 893, citing Masden v. Harrison, at 4.

106. Huskey v. Harrison, 68666 Eq., Mass. Sup. Jud. Ct. (Aug. 30, 1957); Fostor v. Harrison, 68674 Eq., Mass. Sup. Jud. Ct. (Nov. 20, 1957).

107. 445 S.W.2d 145 (Ky. 1969).

108. *Id.* at 146.

109. *Id.*

110. *Id.* at 149.

111. *Id.*

112. *Id.* at 150.

113. *Id.* at 151.

114. 29 Conn. Sup. 368, 289 A.2d 386 (1972).

115. *Id.* at 289 A.2d at 389.

116. *Id.*

117. *Id.* at 390.

118. *Id.*

119. *Id.* at 391.

120. Howard v. Fulton-DeKalb Hosp. Authority, 42 U.S.L.W. 2322 (Ga. Sup. Ct., Fulton, Nov. 29, 1973).

121. 284 S.2d 185 (La. App. 1973).

122. *Id.* at 187.

123. *Id.*

124. *Id.*

125. 67 Wis. 2d 4, 226 N.W.2d 180 (1975).

126. *Id.* at 181.

127. *Id.* at 182. When the physician was asked to explain his moral stance he replied:

> Sir, there are many difficult moral judgments in the field of transplantation to make and each transplant surgeon has to build his own philosophy. That just happens to be mine. I don't care to defend it. It just happens to be my personal philosophy, sir.

Robertson, Incompetent Organ Donors and the Substituted Judgment Doctrine, 44 (unpublished manuscript, 1975).

128. 226 N.W.2d at 181.

129. *Id.*

130. *Id.*

131. *Id.* at 182.

132. *See,* Baron, Botsford and Cole, Live Organ and Tissue Transplants from Minor Donors in Massachusetts, 55 B.U.L. Rev. 159 (1975).

133. *Id.* at 164 n.20.

134. *Id.* at 162 n.16.

135. Civ. No. J74-57 (Mass. Aug. 28, 1974).

136. Civ. No. 74-87 (Mass. July 3, 1974).

137. *Id.* at 7.

138. *Id.*

139. *Id.* at 8-9.

140. *Id.* at 10.

141. *Id.*

142. It is noteworthy that this court ordered both parties to try to procure insurance that would compensate the donor for any harm that might come to her. *Id.* at 12. The court must have realized that although the requirement of informed consent serves to protect the child, there are other mechanisms which would offer additional protection.

143. *See,* Baron, *et al., supra* note 132, at 159-160 n.4, citing Bach and Bach, Immunogenetic Disparity and Graft-Versus-Host Reactions, 11 Seminars in Hematology 291 (1974).

144. Although at least one Massachusetts Probate Court judge appoints a guardian *ad litem* for the donee child as well as for the donor child, the role of the donee's guardian is not clear. *See,* Baron, *et al., supra* note 132, at 163 n.19.

145. *See,* Freund, *supra* note 2, at 689.

146. Savage, Organ Transplantation with an Incompetent Donor: Kentucky Resolves the Dilemma of *Strunk v. Strunk,* 58 Ken. L.J. 129, 146 (1970).

147. *See,* Sharpe, The Minor Transplant Donor, 7 Ottowa L. Rev. 85, 98 (1975).

148. *See,* Baron, *et al., supra* note 132, at 169-181. A fourth test would be to determine if the donor is sufficiently mature to personally consent. Since this does not involve proxy consent it is not discussed here.

149. 2 Mer. 99 (1816).

150. *Id.* at 102.

151. Robertson, Organ Donations by Incompetents and the Substituted Judgment Doctrine, 76 Col. L. Rev. 48, 58 (1976).

152. *Id.* at 59-60.

153. *Id.* at 60-61.

154. Fellner and Marshall, Kidney Donors—The Myth of Informed Consent, 126 Am. J. Psychiatry 1245 (1970).

155. *Id.*

156. *Supra* note 125.

157. *Supra* note 121.

158. Roberston, *supra* note 151, at 70.

159. *See,* Curran, *supra* note 94.

160. *Supra* note 107, at 147.

161. *Supra* note 121, at 187.

162. *Id.*

163. *Supra* note 136.

164. *Id.* at 10–11.

165. Sup. Ct. of New Jersey, A-116 (1976).

166. *Supra* note 39.

167. *Supra* note 165, at 33–38.

168. *Id.* at 38.

169. *Id.* at 38–39.

170. *Id.* at 37.

171. *Id.* at 58–59.

172. 185 N.E.2d at 132.

173. Baron, *et al.*, *supra* note 132, at 176.

174. Civ. No. 665-049 (Super. Ct. San Francisco. Cal., filed Aug. 23, 1973).

175. *See*, Mitchell, *supra* note 90 at 929.

176. *See*, Lowe, *et al.*, *supra* note 3, at 470.

177. Mitchell, *supra* note 90, at 930–931 n.49.

178. *See*, Lasagna, Special Subjects in Human Experimentation, 98 Daedalus 449, 458 (1969).

179. Bickel, Garrard and Hickmans, Influence of Phenylalanine Intake on Phenylketonuria, 2 The Lancet 812–813 (1953), reprinted in Katz, Experimentation with Human Beings, 958–959 (1972).

180. 38 Fed. Reg. 31746 §46.27(e), Nov. 16, 1973.

181. Curran and Beecher, *supra* note 94, at 82.

182. *Id.* at 80.

Chapter 4

Research with Prisoners: The Problem of Voluntariness

Unlike a minor or a severely mentally ill person, prisoners are not incompetent to give informed consent. It is not usually alleged that prisoners are less able to understand the risks, discomforts, and benefits that may be the result of experimentation than free-living individuals. The problem in obtaining informed consent from prisoners is that the very fact of their incarceration may prevent them from giving their consent voluntarily.

The issue of experimentation on prisoners is not a new one. It is reported that Persian kings allowed their physicians to use prisoners as experimental subjects. In the sixteenth century the Duke of Tuscany permitted Fallopius to use prisoners for his experiments. Queen Caroline, the wife of King George IV, let her physician use six condemned criminals for experimental smallpox vaccinations before submitting her own children to the procedure.[2]

For many reasons prisons are almost ideal places to conduct research. Life is routine and subject to few variations. The population is relatively stable, which makes long-range studies feasible. The imposition of experimental procedures that might inconvenience free-living subjects is not a burden on prisoners. It is also less expensive to use prison subjects than it would be to use free-living subjects.[3]

BIOMEDICAL RESEARCH

Regardless of these considerations, there has been a great deal of controversy concerning whether or not prisoners are capable of giving an informed consent to such research. Because of the very nature of incarceration it can be argued that prisoners do not have a real choice concerning their participation in these activities. This concern is articulated in the Nuremberg Code where it is stated:

> 1. The voluntary consent of the human subject is absolutely essential. This means that the person involved should have legal capacity to given consent; *should be so situated as to be able to exercise free power of choice, without the intervention of any element of force, fraud, deceit, duress, over-reaching, or other ulterior form of constraint or coercion*; and should have sufficient knowledge and comprehension of the elements of the subject matter involved as to enable him to make an understanding and enlightened decision.[4] (emphasis supplied)

The issue in regard to prisoners is whether they are so situated as to prevent them from exercising free choice.

Some argue that not only are prisoners without free choice, but that they are used as research subjects because they are not able to choose otherwise.[5] Indeed, one defense tactic at the Nuremberg Trial was to try to demonstrate that prisoners were exploited by researchers in the United States. Dr. Andrew Ivy was called by the prosecution as an expert witness in high altitude experiments and medical ethics. During the cross-examination Dr. Ivy was questioned concerning malaria experiments that were done in the United States penitentiaries. The prisoners who participated were paid $50 at the commencement of the experiment, and $50 when it was terminated. Some of Dr. Ivy's testimony, presented during cross-examination by the defense lawyers, follows:

> *Q.* Witness, you said yesterday that the prisoner who ordinarily had to sign a waiver according to which, if I understand you correctly, that they gave up any claim if it proved a fatality, did I understand you correctly?
>
> *A.* Yes. They signed an agreement, if I recall it correctly they would make plans for themselves in case of accident.
>
> *Q.* Not only if they were injured, but if the patient should be a fatality?
>
> *A.* I believe the expression, "heirs and assigns" was included, yes.
>
> *Q.* Then the people gave up all claims for their heirs too. Now, witness, in your experiments did you have such waivers signed by the subjects?
>
> *A.* No. Our subjects, conscientious objectors, were given insurance against possible damage or injury.
>
> *Q.* Insurance. Why did your subjects get insurance, and why did the prisoners have to give up all claims? Why this distinction?
>
> *A.* I do not know.

Q. Witness, on the basis of your great experience, don't you have any idea why there was this distinction? You are an expert in all these fields.

A. Well, I presume it was out of sympathy for the C.O.'s. The soldiers in the Army were insured by the government, and, I thought—I should believe that might have been thought to be a good idea to insure the C.O.'s for the same reasons that they were taking experiments that had a small amount of hazard in them.

Q. Was there sympathy not felt in the case of prisoners who had volunteered for experiments on behalf of the general public?

A. I had nothing to do with that or determining the conditions. Thus I cannot answer "yes" or "no."[6]

[Dr. Ivy was asked if it was ethical to carry out experiments on prisoners who were asked to waive all their rights.]

A. Yes, I believe it can be reconciled with the basic medical ethics.[7]

[Dr. Ivy went on to state that he thought prisoners participated in experiments for idealistic reasons. He said that prisoners had stated that they participated in the malaria tests because they were patriotic, wanted to help our soldiers, or had a friend or relative who might contract malaria.]

Q. If all the persons apply for idealistic reasons, why are they offered pecuniary recompense?

A. I suppose it is to serve as a small reward for the unpleasantness of the experience.

Q. Don't you believe that money was the motive for many of them—a hundred dollars?

A. That is rather small. From the point of view of prisoners in the penitentiary in the United States. A hundred dollars isn't much money.

Q. For a prisoner that would be quite a lot of money it would seem to me, for someone at liberty it is not so much.

A. Our prisoners in the penitentiary in the United States, when they work in factories in the prisons receive pecuniary compensation for that work.[8]

Q. If one declares one's self to be a volunteer, must one not weigh the advantages against the disadvantages?

A. I believe so.

Q. The disadvantages being the risk of serious disease, the advantage is fifty or a hundred dollars.

A. I should say the advantage is being able to serve for the good of humanity.

Q. For what reason was the money not paid immediately—but in two payments? . . .

A. I presume that that is just the common way of doing business in the United States when an agreement is involved. I presume the lawyers had something to do with that.

Q. Was the reason not this: that the prisoner would lose his enthusiasm for the experiment and would cease to cooperate? Could that have been the reason for being a little circumspect in the payment?

A. I doubt it.[9]

[In addition to defending the malaria experiments, Dr. Ivy defended the work of Colonel R.P. Strong who injected attenuated plague organisms into 900 condemned prisoners in Manila in the early 1900s. After demonstrating disbelief in the fact that there were 900 condemned convicts in a city the size of Manila the defense asked Dr. Ivy about the safety of the procedure. Dr. Ivy responded that Dr. Strong did work on guinea pigs first and knew the procedure was safe.]

Q. Regarding Strong's experiments . . . you said the experimental subjects had a temperature of one degree Farenheit [above normal], and that the harmlessness of the experiment was absolutely no surprise to the author because he could foretell the successful results. Did I understand you correctly?

A. On the basis of animal experiments.

Q. For what reasons were criminals who had been condemned to death used for these experiments, in view of those facts?

A. I do not know.[10]

Thus the defense tried to demonstrate that in the United States prisoners are coerced into being experimental subjects by the offer of rewards including payment of money, that they are not as well protected as are other subjects, and that they are subjected to dangerous experiments for which other groups would not volunteer.

MOTIVATION

In determining the voluntary or involuntary nature of a prisoner's consent, his motivation becomes an important factor. If he is motivated to participate in an experiment for improper reasons, or by forces that are coercive or that unduly influence him, his consent may be involuntary and therefore invalid.

The issue of what motivates prisoners to participate in research has been discussed in the medical literature. Two individuals who have worked with prisoners since 1949 have stated that they believe participation in research relieves some of the monotony and oppressiveness of the prison routine, and that for some, money may act as a motive, although prisoners can earn almost as much in other prison activities as they can as experimental subjects. Some prisoners are less reluctant to be visited by their children in the hospital environment, and some are motivated by altruism. There is also the hope held by some prisoners of more favorable treatment in the future by prison authorities.[11]

Dr. Frank Ayd lists eleven motivating reasons, the first being financial reward. He agrees with Freund's statement that the "amount paid should not be so large as to constitute undue influence—that is, so large as to obscure an appreciation of the risk and weaken the will to self-preservation. We ought not be put in the business of buying lives."[12] The other motives Ayd lists are hope for reduction of sentence, direct or indirect seeking of medical or psychiatric help, escape from a lonely and tedious existence, curiosity, and a few other factors.[13]

Although much of this work is speculative in nature, some objective studies have been done. Arnold, *et al.*, found that whether or not a prisoner volunteers as a research subjects depends to a great extent on the type of penal institution in which the prisoner is incarcerated, and the prisoner's value scale.[14] Dr. Arnold did his research in a county prison in which two types of studies were being conducted—one dealing with the treatment of malaria and the other with the effects of drugs on certain body functions. In this prison there was very little constructive activity provided for the prisoners and therefore little competition for their time and interest.

The prisoners who volunteered for such studies were moved to a special part of the prison where they were treated more like members of a free society. Clean linens were provided, there were beds instead of bunks, the quality of the food was better, and food was available twenty-four hours a day. When asked, most of the prisoners described the general living conditions in the prison as "impossible situations."[15] More than fifty percent indicated that their decision to volunteer was based in part on their desire for better living conditions. Most of the volunteers were "loners" who were not members of any of the cliques that were found in the prison. The third factor was the general level of fear within the prison, which exists in many state and county prisons. Many prisoners stated that it was safer in the research project than in the prison itself. One prisoner stated that you could go to sleep without being afraid that someone would "bust you in the head," or "set fire" to your bunk while you were asleep.[16]

In giving an informed consent, one must evaluate the risks involved in the research project. Arnold found that risk taking is an integral part of the life of many of the prisoners. Many of these men are dedicated professional criminals whose "professional lives are often devoted to activities that expose them to personal risk." The very fact that risk is involved may give an activity status[17] in certain inmate groups. The fact of incarceration affected the prisoners' willingness to take risks. In one group of thirteen volunteers, twelve indicated that the risk of adverse physical effects had little influence on their decision to volunteer as long as they were in jail. In some cases they were attracted by the risk. However, only eight would volunteer for a similar experiment if they were free-living.

In another group of fourteen inmates, three expressed no concern about long-range effects because they rarely planned ahead for anything. One prisoner stated he would volunteer for anything regardless of risk. "As a professional thief, he regarded life as just one long chance [and] viewed his long-range survival with much doubt."[18]

Prisoners also felt that they needed money to ease their way back into society when they were released. Without money they knew they would have to return to crime, at least immediately following their release. One way to obtain some money while in prison was to become an experimental subject. However, most of the money earned was spent while in prison.[19]

Finally, a number of prisoners stated that by becoming research subjects they could make a positive contribution to society, about half of those interviewed felt that it would improve their chances of getting a job once released, and a very few felt it would increase their chances of getting paroled.[20]

Martin, *et al.*, conducted several studies to determine why individuals volunteer as research subjects.[21] One study involved two groups of prisoners, volunteers and nonvolunteers, for the Malaria Project at Jackson County Jail, in Missouri. Inmates with sentences of less than one year were asked to participate. The project and risks involved were carefully detailed and each inmate was told he would be paid but that there would be no reduction in sentence. Inmates who volunteered received additional information, whereas nonvolunteers did not. Thirty-six inmates who volunteered and twenty-four who did not comprised the sample. It was found that those who volunteered understood the nature of the disease and its threat to human life no better than nonvolunteers although the volunteers were given much more information. Sixty percent of the volunteers described the project in terms of high-risk although it had been explained that it was a low-risk experiment. About half of the volunteers gave altruism and half gave money as the reason for volunteering. Almost all the nonvolunteers stated respect for the volunteers. The authors express the belief that this respect may be the most important consideration in deciding to volunteer.

The second study involved four groups of people—low income individuals, policemen and firemen, professionals (scientists, lawyers, and educators) and prisoners—who were asked whether or not they would volunteer for four hypothetical experiments. The experiments involved investigating malaria, new-drug toxicity, the common cold, and the effects of air pollution. These experiments presented different degrees of risk, different time demands, varying requirements for interrupting family life and employment, and different degrees of social importance. Little information was given to the "subjects," but all questions were answered.

The following table shows the results.[22]

Volunteer Group	Malaria		Test Drugs		Cold		Air Pollution	
	Yes	No	Yes	No	Yes	No	Yes	No
Prisoners	40	20	44	16	49	11	50	10
Low Income	7	19	9	17	10	16	17	9
Fire & Police	3	37	5	35	11	29	28	12
Professional	0	28	1	27	2	26	26	2

Clearly prisoners and low-income individuals were more likely to volunteer for risky experiments. However, all groups were more willing to volunteer for the less risky experiments than for those that had higher risks. Thus, the element of risk certainly entered into the decision-making process for all the people involved.

This study also found that there was a greater willingness to volunteer when the volunteer was not obligated to others. Half of the persons living alone would have volunteered for the malaria experiment whereas only a fifth of those who had family responsibilities would have volunteered for this experiment.[23]

From these studies one sees that prisoners are motivated by a variety of factors to volunteer for research. The need for money certainly enters into it. This is demonstrated not only by these studies but by the statements of prisoners. One prisoner has stated that the only way he could raise bail money was to participate in experiments in a county jail.[24] He also testified he needed money for books and writing materials.[25] Another prisoner commented, "Yeah, I was on research, but I couldn't keep my chow down. Like I lost about thirty-five pounds my first year in the joint, so I started getting scared. I hated to give it up because it was a good pay test."[26] One prisoner who made $30 a month participating in a study of the topical application of dimethylsulfoxide (DMSO) said that he knew a couple of inmates who were burned so badly by it that they were hospitalized. But, he said, "Thirty is a full canteen draw [all one can buy in the prison store] and I wish the thing would go on for years— I'd be lost without it."[27]

There are more subtle reasons stated such as altruism, the need for respect, lack of concern regarding risks or a desire to encounter such risks, relief from boredom, and curiosity. The true impact of these subtle motivations is for social scientists, not lawyers, to decide. Assuming, however, that these motivations do exist, do they work to invalidate the ability of a prisoner to give his informed consent? Or, to put it another way, do these motivations unduly influence the prisoner, coerce him to participate, or cause such duress, as these terms are defined by law, as to deprive him of his consensual capacity?

DURESS AND COERCION, AND UNDUE INFLUENCE

Duress

In order to review the law that relates to duress (or coercion) and undue influence, one must look to areas of the law that have little to do with experimentation—the law of contracts, wills, and criminal procedure. It is very difficult to simply state the law of duress or undue influence. One authority on contract law has stated that the cases on this subject are far from uniform and are inconsistent due to the very different fact patterns involved.[28]

Duress is generally evidenced by the following:

1. Personal violence or threats thereof;
2. Imprisonment or threats of imprisonment;
3. Threats of physical injury or of wrongful imprisonment or prosecution of a husband, wife or child, or some other close relative;
4. Threats of wrongfully destroying, injuring, seizing or withholding land or other things; or
5. Any other wrongful acts that compel a person to manifest apparent assent to a transactions without his volition, or cause such fear as to preclude him from exercising free will and judgment in entering into a transaction.[29]

To establish coercion the facts must indicate that he was actually induced by the duress to give his consent and would not have done so otherwise. This must be to such an extent that "the action is not based on a voluntary personal judgment previously made."[30] The pressure that is brought to bear on the person must be wrongful. It can be wrongful even if it is lawful and nontortious. Contracts that are made under duress or coercion are voidable, but they are not void and can be ratified by later acts.

Thus, to establish duress or coercion one must demonstrate a threat, or threatening situation, of such intensity that the person threatened loses the ability to choose or to act freely. A review of one case may further explain how courts view this problem. In *Fox v. Piercey*,[31] the plaintiff, a fireman, became drunk and disorderly at a party and was arrested for drunkenness. The chief of the department asked for his resignation, but Fox refused. Fox claimed the chief said, "If you do not resign, I will blast you and smear you in every newspaper in Salt Lake City. I will make it so miserable you can't get a job in the city." According to Fox he resigned as a result of this threat. He went to the civil service commission and then to court in an attempt to rescind his resignation. Fox claimed it was void because it was made under duress.

The trial court found that the chief did not make the alleged threat. It did find, however, that the chief said that unless he resigned he would be discharged, and that the discharge would attract publicity that would adversely affect future employment opportunities. It decided that Fox resigned when "frightened and alarmed and under the influence of duress"[32] and the resignation was therefore void.

The appeals court reversed the decision of the trial court. It said, "Duress is unlawful constraint whereby one is forced to do some act against one's will."[33] The threats must be such as to overcome the will of an ordinarily reasonable man. It stated that the modern rule is "that any wrongful act or threat which actually puts the victim in such fear as to compel him to act against his will constitutes duress."[34] Since the chief could discharge Fox for his offense, his statement was not wrongful. In addition, he did not state or imply he would publicize the discharge, but merely advised Fox what the consequences of discharge would be.

Even though this situation "created great fear for the economic welfare of himself and his family,"[35] duress was not established. Thus duress is not inherent in a particular situation. One cannot merely look objectively at the threatening situation but most look to "the state of mind induced [by threats] in the victim."[36] in that particular situation in order to establish duress.

Ascertaining the state of mind of an individual is a difficult task. One must look to the external factors that make up the particular situation and determine if the situation is so threatening as to prevent a person from acting freely. Surely if one acts at the point of a gun we can safely assume that he is acting under duress. Threats to ruin one's business have been found to cause duress.[37] However, prison conditions pose much subtler problems in determining the existence of duress. After a short discussion of undue influence we will analyze a specific prison situation in an attempt to determine whether coercive conditions exist.

Undue Influence

Undue influence is similar to duress but is different in one important factor. For undue influence to exist, there must be evidence of a confidential or fiduciary relationship of some sort. If a party in whom another reposes confidence misuses that confidence to gain his own advantage while the other has been made to feel that the party in question will not act against his welfare, the transaction is the result of undue influence. The victim must act in a way contrary to his own wishes.[38]

Under the law of wills, "anyone in a position to influence the testator" is in a confidential relationship with him.[39] In certain circumstances confidential relationships have occurred between patient and nurse, father and son, and neighbors who did housework for an infirm individual. There is nothing wrong with influencing a person. One may comfort an elderly or dying person in the hope that he will leave you a large bequest, or reward you in some way.[40] The influence must be "undue," that is, it must lead to the destruction of a person's ability to weigh various influences.[41]

In most cases dealing with undue influence, the testator's state of mind is usually weakened by illness or some other incapacity, the suspected beneficiary actively participated in the execution of the will, and the will is "unnatural," that is to say that the natural objects of the testator's bounty have been ignored.

Thus, where an eighty-three-year-old woman suffering from Parkinson's disease, hypertension, nephritis, and arteriosclerosis made a gift of $6,000 worth of stock to a doctor who treated her daily for a period of years, the gift was overturned as being the result of undue influence.[42] The court found that a confidential relationship of the "highest sort" existed and that the transaction was therefore subject to "close scrutiny."[43] If it was shown that she had received independent advice in making the gift, the outcome may have been different.[44]

In recognition of this problem Rhode Island has adopted a statute denying convicts the right to make wills while in prison, without judicial permission. The apparent reason for this is to prevent undue influence upon a prisoner to name a prison authority as a beneficiary or to aid the convict in making a will.[45]

DURESS AND UNDUE INFLUENCE
IN THE PRISON SETTING

To demonstrate that coercion exists in prisons in regard to experimentation, the poor state of prison conditions is often mentioned. If the conditions are sufficiently poor, and the enticements to participate are sufficiently great, there is little question that coercion can exist.

Because a finding of duress or undue influence must be based on the facts of a specific situation, it is necessary to present the circumstances of the following case in a lengthy and detailed manner. Since this case has not yet been decided there is no opinion by the court.

This case[46] involves nontherapeutic experimentation that took place at the Maryland House of Corrections. The research consisted of exposing prisoners to a number of diseases, including typhoid, dysentery, shigella, malaria, Rocky Mountain spotted fever, cholera and influenza, and then treating them with drugs to determine the drugs' efficacy.

According to the complaint, the prison housed 1640 inmates, 700 beyond its capacity. There was unremitting noise, violence, and homosexual attacks. Two men occupied a cell measuring 5 × 8 × 7 feet equipped with two bunks and an open toilet. Prisoners were not provided with sufficient necessities to maintain health and personal hygiene. It was necessary to purchase food from the commissary to supplement the prison diet. Clothing, toothpaste, soap, razor blades, deodorant, paper, envelopes, stamps, cigarettes, etc., had to be bought at the prison commissary at a cost equal to or greater than the cost of these items at a private supermarket. It was estimated that necessary supplies cost a minimum of $11.00 every two weeks. Money could be obtained from outside sources, the prison welfare fund, prison wages, or by participating in experiments. 500 of the 1640 prisoners did not have jobs. Except for brief recreation periods, these prisoners were not allowed to leave their cells. The average pay for prison jobs was $.65 per day. The prisoners' welfare fund was available only to indigent prisoners who had less than $2.00 in their commissary account and had no prison job. The fund did not provide enough money to maintain even minimum personal hygiene.

The Infectious Disease Area (IDA) where the studies were conducted contained thirty-three beds divided into three wards. It was spacious, well-lighted, air-conditioned, quiet, equipped with a color television, radios, and a kitchen for snacks and sandwiches. Frequent private showers were permitted. The IDA paid $10.00 per prisoner per day. The prisoner received $2.00 plus $1.00 for each stool or blood sample taken. The remaining $8.00 went to a special fund for use by the hospital. At the time of the suit the fund contained approximately $28,000. Among other things, the complaint stated that because of the disparity in conditions between the IDA and the general prison facilities, the defendants were coerced into participating in the research studies.

The allegations of duress can be examined on an issue by issue basis. Averring that money motivates and influences prisoners to participate is not a radical stand to take. When C. Joseph Stetler, President of the Pharmaceutical Manufacturers Association, testified on this issue before a Congressional subcommittee, he readily acknowledged that financial reward is "the most important factor behind prisoner participation" in experimentation.[47] It is beyond question that money influences free-living individuals as well as prison inmates. It can be safely assumed that most of the work force would not report to work but for the promise of a paycheck. But in the case under discussion the promise of financial reward probably resulted in coercion or undue influence. The pay for participation in the prison research was more than three times as great as that paid for other employment found within the prison. But more important than this, participation in experimentation was the *only* way prisoners could earn enough money to maintain a minimum standard of living. If the charges were accurate one had to participate in the experiments to acquire a minimally required diet, and to be able to obtain those items needed to maintain personal hygiene. As a result, one's physical well-being was threatened by refusing to participate in the experiments and trying to live on the prison wages. For those who did not have a job and had to rely on the prison welfare fund, the coercive factors are even more egregious.

The disparity in living conditions provided further coercive force. If an investigator said to a prisoner, "Unless you participate in our experiment, you will be sent to live in crowded, unsanitary and dangerous living conditions," a "wrongful" threat of the type discussed above would be established. For all intents and purposes, this is what was alleged in the case under discussion. Indeed, the disparity in living conditions was so great that one who lived in the IDA was virtually "released" from the prison, the most coercive promise that can be made.

One professor of ethics and law has analyzed this problem as follows:[48]

[T]here are certain basic freedoms and rights which we possess that *entitle* us (morally) to certain things (or states of affairs). We would all, no doubt, draw up different lists of these rights and freedoms: but included in them would be safety of person, freedom of conscience and religion, a right to a certain level of education, and, for some of us, a right to some level of health care. When the "reward" is such as only to give us the necessary conditions of these rights and freedoms—when all that the reward does is to bring us up to a level of living to which we are entitled, and of which we have been deprived by man—then the "reward," I think, constitutes duress. A reward which accrues to one who has achieved this level, or who can easily achieve it (other than by taking the reward-option), and which hence serves only to grant us "luxury" items, does not constitute duress, and hence does not render choice unfree, no matter how great this reward may be.

The final evidence of duress or undue influence in this case is the "unnatural" result, a standard similar to "unnatural" wills discussed above. For $2.00 per day, the prisoners were willing to risk contracting a number of serious diseases which could have serious and debilitating effects. But this fact, without more, would not establish duress.

If the prisoners in this case lived in a prison that provided them with the minimal requisites for a decent standard of living so that the prisoner would not *have* to participate in experiments to acquire this standard of living, the offer of $2.00 per day and better living conditions would not be coercive. It might be fairer to say that the prison environment, not the offer by the IDA, is what was coercive. The IDA merely provided the prisoners with what they should have been given in the first place. But the prisoners should not have had to risk their lives or health to get those things which they deserve.

The Maryland House of Corrections is not particularly unique in its conditions. In Statesville Prison in Illinois, where a project to test antimalarial drugs was carried out, the element of fear of attack was so pervasive that in 1974 nearly forty men were placed in solitary confinement at their request for their own safety.[49]

In Texas State Penitentiary at Huntsville where studies of respiratory diseases and cholera vaccines were conducted, inmates were paid $5.00 per day for participation in research, and nothing for prison work.[50]

Promise of release or reduction of the sentence as a reward for participation in a study must always be considered inherently coercive. As discussed above, threat of imprisonment produces duress under the law. By offering to release a prisoner or to reduce his sentence for his participation in an experiment, one is also saying that failure to participate will keep him imprisoned. It is safe to assume that more than anything else, a prisoner desires his freedom. He should not be goaded into bartering his body to obtain this strongly desired goal.

This point of view has not always been adopted, however. When

Goldberger, in 1915, conducted pellagra experiments on convict volunteers, formal agreements were drawn up prior to the experiment with the prisoners' lawyers for their subsequent pardon and release.[51]

In 1948, Governor Dwight Green of Illinois formed a committee to examine the practice of paroling prisoners for participation in the malaria studies that were the focus of the cross-examination of Dr. Ivy discussed above.[52] The Green Committee readily acknowledged that the possibility of reduction in sentence may influence a prisoner's decision to volunteer. The report stated that the parole system exists to reward "good conduct and industry" and "exceptional bravery or fidelity in a good cause."[53] As participation in an experiment is a form of good conduct, parole for such participation was permissible. The committee report did recognize that, "A reduction of sentence in prison, if excessive or drastic, can amount to undue influence."[54]

An indication that any reduction in sentence unduly influences prisoners to participate in experimentation is a widely accepted concept today can be seen from surveys conducted by Jessica Mitford, Urban Information Interpreters and the Health Policy Program of the School of Medicine, University of California, San Francisco, in 1973, 1974 and 1975. All the states that responded stated that no special parole considerations are given to inmates who participate in medical experimentation.[55] However, policy and practice are not always the same. Connecticut was one of the states that replied that parole considerations are not influenced by such prisoner participation in experiments.[56] In 1975 a suit was filed in the United States District Court in Connecticut alleging that such was the practice.[57] Although this case involves behavior modification, it is included in this section because it is an excellent example of coercive forces and undue influence.

The three plaintiffs were incarcerated in the Connecticut Correctional Institute in Somers, Connecticut and, allegedly, were coerced to join the experimental behavior modification program for pedophiles. Two of the plaintiffs had been denied parole and had been informed that this was due to their lack of participation in the program. The third plaintiff, who also had not participated, was about to become eligible for parole and was told by prisoners and members of the staff that his failure to join the program would result in the denial of parole.

The behavior modification techniques included the use of faradic aversive conditioning and covert sensitization. In the faradic electric conditioning portion of the program, electrodes were placed on the upper thighs of the prisoner. He was then shown slides of adults and slides of children. When a slide of a child was shown, the prisoner received a painful electric shock unless he asked for a change of slides within three seconds. In a second situation, the prisoner could not avoid the shock regardless of what he did. In the third situation, the prisoner received a shock whenever he told the researchers that he fantasized a sexual situation after being shown a slide of a child. This behavior modification program consisted of twenty twenty-minute sessions.

The covert sensitization portion of the program consisted of interviewing the prisoner regarding his previous involvement with children, his pedophilic fantasies, and his phobic, anxiety-provoking and disgust-invoking fantasies. These were then combined in a taped narrative and played to a hypnotized prisoner. In the narrative, the prisoner's sexual fantasies were paired with suggestions of aversive events, such as becoming violently ill, being attacked by rats, dogs or hornets, being unable to breathe, and being castrated with a hot iron. The covert sensitization sessions lasted sixty to seventy minutes and were conducted twenty times.

The plaintiffs had the program explained to them by the investigator and were told they could refuse to participate. They were also told the parole board favored participation. At various times during the incarceration, several correctional officers stated to the plaintiffs that participation in the program was essential for a favorable parole decision.

Clearly this situation constitutes duress and undue influence. It can be safely said that correctional officers and the parole board are in a "confidential relationship" with the prisoners as that term was explained above, *i.e.*, they are in a position to influence the prisoners. This suit never came to trial as it was settled shortly after it was filed. The behavior modification program was closed. The prisoners were given new parole hearings in front of a board which was not familiar with the program, and no mention of the program permitted. All three plaintiffs were granted parole.[58]

WAIVER OF RIGHTS

Before leaving this topic there is a final analogy that should be drawn. After arrest but prior to conviction, there is much opportunity for coercion to be brought to bear on the suspect to either confess to the crime, or to plea bargain and plead guilty in hope of obtaining a shorter prison term. As the suspect is in custody or about to be imprisoned, the analogy to the prison situation is obvious.

The first case to be discussed is *Miranda v. Arizona,*[59] the famous coerced confession case. The court recognized certain facts concerning in-custody interrogation. First, that modern interrogation techniques were "psychologically rather than physically oriented."[60] Second, that "the very fact of custodial interrogation exacts a heavy toll on individual liberty and trades on the weakness of individuals,"[61] and third, that "the process of in-custody interrogation of persons suspected or accused of a crime contains inherently compelling pressures which work to undermine the individual's will to resist and compel him to speak where he would not otherwise do so freely."[62] After acknowledging all the pressures and stresses that were brought to bear on an arrested person, the court did not prohibit the use of custodial confessions. It allowed the use of these confessions if certain warnings were given.[63] The warnings that are now required prior to incustody interrogation serve the same purpose that informed consent serves in the experimental situation. The police are about to put their prisoner "at risk" by asking him certain questions and must therefore inform him of these risks as well as his right not to participate in the interrogation. Perhaps the most important warning is that the prisoner has the right to counsel. This right assures the prisoner that someone acting in his interest will be present if he so desires. This rule is applicable to the prison experimentation situation—that even if certain coercive factors are present, safeguards can be constructed to reduce the effect of the coercion which would enable the prisoner to give informed consent.

The second case, *Brady v. United States*,[64] involved the voluntary nature of guilty pleas. Brady was charged with kidnapping and not liberating his victim unharmed. Under the statute then in effect a person could be sentenced to death only upon the recommendation of the jury. The judge was unwilling to try the case without a jury and Brady claimed he pleaded guilty so that a jury would not be able to make such a recommendation. In addition, his codefendant had pleaded guilty and was prepared to testify against him. Brady was asked twice by the trial judge if his plea was entered voluntarily and without coercion of any kind. He answered "yes" both times and was sentenced to thirty years imprisonment.

The court stated that "waiver of constitutional rights not only must be voluntary but must be knowing, intelligent acts done with sufficient awareness of the relevant circumstances and likely consequences."[65] Brady claimed that the Fifth Amendment was violated if he was encouraged or influenced to plead guilty by an opportunity or promise of leniency, and that it is "coerced and invalid if influenced by the fear of a possibly higher penalty."[66] The Court stated that "we decline to hold, however, that a guilty plea is compelled and invalid under the Fifth Amendment whenever motivated by the defendant's desire to accept the certainty or probability of a lesser penalty rather than face a wider range of possibilities extending from acquittal to conviction and a higher penalty authorized by law for the crime charged."[67] It found that the situation in this case was no different than (1) a defendant who pleaded guilty because his lawyer advised that the judge would probably be more lenient than the jury, (2) a defendant who was advised by counsel that the judge is more lenient on those who plead guilty than those who go to trial, (3) the defendant who was permitted to plead guilty to a lesser included offense, (4) a defendant who pleaded guilty with the understanding all other charges would be dropped.[68] The Court also pointed out that the defendant had competent counsel at all times.[69]

These two cases are included here to demonstrate that an individual may be placed in situations which appear to be inherently coercive, but may waive very important rights if adequate safeguards are provided. However, it must be pointed out that the plea bargaining cases are not strictly applicable to the issue of experimentation on prisoners. The Court realized that if plea bargaining were outlawed due to its coercive nature, the criminal justice system would collapse. If, however, experimentation on prisoners were prohibited because of its coercive nature, the consequences would be relatively minor—inconvenience and added expense for drug companies testing new drugs.

BEHAVIOR MODIFICATION IN PRISONS

Prisoner Autonomy in Consenting to Medical Treatment

As was discussed in Chapter One, prior to undergoing any invasive medical procedure, an individual must give his consent or the touching will constitute a battery.[70] It is not clear, however, that this general rule applies to prisoners.[71] A number of cases would seem to hold otherwise.

In *Haynes v. Harris*,[72] a prisoner maintained that he should be allowed to determine whether or not he should obtain medical treatment. He claimed that in the absence of consent, the treatment constituted corporal punishment. The court stated, "This contention is obviously without merit. One of the paramount purposes for which a defendant is committed to the Medical Center is that he have the benefit of receiving from trained and qualified personnel proper examination, diagnosis and all necessary available treatment."[73]

In *Peek v. Ciccone*,[74] a prisoner who was sent to the United States

Medical Center for Federal Prisoners was forcibly injected with thorazine when he refused to take the medication in oral form. His claim of cruel and unusual punishment was dismissed.

In a similar case, a prisoner who refused medication was placed in solitary confinement.[75] He claimed the medication caused chest pains and other mental defects and asked for a writ of *habeas corpus* (release from prison) because such treatment constituted cruel and unusual punishment. The court, citing the language in *Haynes v. Harris* quoted above, dismissed the case.

In *Smith v. Baker*,[76] a prisoner brought suit under the Federal Civil Rights Act claiming an injection of Prolixin given to him against his will and religious beliefs violated his civil rights. The court said, "It is well established that medical care which is administered over the objections of a prisoner does not constitute the denial of any federal rights."[77]

A prisoner in another case claimed that the treatment he received was inadequate. The court found that:

> The prisoner cannot be the ultimate judge of what medical treatment is necessary or proper for his case. See *Ayers v. Ciccone*, 300 F. Supp. 568 (W.D. Mo. 1968) *Aff'd per curiam* 413 F.2d 1049 (8 Cir. 1969). In the absence of factual allegations of obvious neglect or intentional mistreatment, the courts should place their confidence in the reports of reputable prison physicians that reasonable medical care is being rendered.[78]

Perhaps the strongest statement on this topic was made by a court in *dicta*. In *Ramsey v. Ciccone*,[79] the court said:

> Even though treatment is unusually painful, or causes unusual mental suffering, it may be administered to a prisoner without his consent if it is recognized as appropriate by recognized medical authority or authorities.[80]

In contrast, the court also stated, "[T]reatment causing unusual pain, [or] mental suffering which was not considered appropriate by any recognized branch of the healing arts" would constitute cruel and unusual punishment.[81]

This rule somewhat lessens the requirement set down two years earlier when the court found that an allegation of cruel and unusual punishment would be substantiated by showing that the nature of the treatment or medication or its administration is not sanctioned by any *"substantial* medical authority,"[82] (emphasis supplied)

From this exposition of cases one could assume that prisoners have very little to say about the medical care they receive. The apparent unanimity of these cases is readily explainable. Although they constitute the majority of cases in this area, all of these cases are from two courts—the Federal District Court of the Western District of Missouri and the Eighth Circuit Court of Appeals. The reason for this is that the United States Medical Center for Federal Prisoners is located in Missouri. As a result, there is little chance for a diversity of opinions to occur. Second, the vast majority of these cases (perhaps all) were brought by inmates without the help of counsel and were inexpertly presented. Amazingly, none of these cases cites *Schloendorff* or the line of cases that followed it. In addition, the inmates may have asked for the wrong kind of relief, *e.g.*, *habeas corpus*.

Two cases we have been able to find in other jurisdictions decide otherwise. In *Irwin v. Arrendale*,[83] a prisoner sought to recover damages for battery from a prison physician for injuries received when he was x-rayed without his consent. The court found that the relationship between a physician and a patient is a consensual one, and that physicians who treat without consent commit a battery.[84] A state may order compulsory medical examination only to protect the public health, the court stated.

The Ninth Circuit Court of Appeals also decided a case contrary to the Eighth Circuit. A prisoner alleged that a hemorrhoidectomy was performed on him without his consent and that he was denied necessary analgesics after the operation.[85] He claimed that he vigorously and repeatedly opposed any operation anf filed suit under the Federal Civil Rights Act.[86] Summary judgment was granted the defendant by the trial court and was reversed by the appeals court which stated:

> Allegations that prison medical personnel performed a major surgical procedure upon the body of an inmate, without his consent and over his known objections, that were not required to preserve his life or further a compelling interest of imprisonment or prison security, may foreshadow proof of conduct violation of rights under the 14th Amendment sufficient to justify judgment under the Civil Rights Act.
>
> A constitutionally protected right to be secure in the privacy of one's own body against invasion by the state except where necessary to support a compelling state interest has been recognized. *Roe v. Wade*, 410 U.S. 113, 153–156 (1973).[87]

The same court in a nonmedical case has found that a prisoner has a right to be free from unprovoked assaults by agents of the state while in state custody.[88]

There can be no question that these latter cases which state a prisoner must consent to his own medical care provide us with the better rule. The fact of imprisonment should not deprive a person of his capacity to decide whether or not to consent to his own health care. The right to privacy of one's body should be practically inviolable, and a competent adult, whether in prison or free-living, should be the final arbiter of what is done to his body. Fortunately, the cases that have dealt with physically invasive behavior modification techniques have adopted this rule.

Behavior Modification Cases

In *Mackey v. Procunier*,[89] a prisoner at Folsom State Prison in California was transferred, with his consent, to the California Medical Facility at Vacaville for the purpose of undergoing shock treatment. In his complaint he alleged that a drug, succinylcholine, which causes breathing to stop, resulting in enormous fright, was administered to him without his consent. As a result of this experience he claimed he suffered from frequent nightmares in which he relives the experience and wakes up unable to breathe. The sensation of fright probably cannot be overstated. The drug is given as part of an aversive therapy program in hope of developing an association between violent behavior and the consequences of the drug, which causes cessation of breathing for two minutes.[90] Dr. Arthur Nugent, the chief psychiatrist at Vacaville and a supporter of the use of the drug, has stated it "induces sensations of suffocation and drowning."[91] He is quoted as saying, "Even the toughest inmates have come to fear and hate the drug. I don't blame them, I wouldn't have one treatment myself for the world."[92]

The court found that if the use of the drug was as alleged, it could "raise serious constitutional questions respecting cruel and unusual punishment or impermissible tinkering with the mental process,"[93] and sent the case back to the lower court to be tried.

Knecht v. Gillman[94] presented a similar fact pattern. The prisoners in this case alleged they were subjected to injections of the drug apomorphine while imprisoned in the Iowa State Medical Facility (I.S.M.F.). They had not consented to the use of the drug and claimed such use without consent constituted cruel and unusual punishment. The trial court refused to issue injunctive relief and the appeals court reversed.

The court found that apomorphine was administered as part of a program of aversive stimuli in the treatment of inmates with behavior problems. The drug was administered by a nurse after an inmate violated the behavior protocol established for him. The drug was administered for such behavior as not getting up, giving cigarettes against orders, talking, swearing, or lying. Inmates or staff would observe these behaviors and report any infractions to the nurse, who would give the injection without a nurse or doctor actually observing this behavior, and without specific authorization of the doctor.

The drug is administered by taking the prisoner to a room, which contained only a water closet, where he was given an injection. He was excersised and started to vomit within fifteen minutes. The vomiting lasted from fifteen minutes to an hour. It was not clear if the initial consent of the inmate was obtained but in at least a few instances no consent was obtained. Once a consent was given, withdrawl from the program was not permitted.

Under an Iowa statute,[95] a prisoner could be transferred to the I.S.M.F. for diagnosis, evaluation, and treatment. Since the drug was clearly not used for diagnosis or evaluation it must have been used for treatment. The court found that "it is not possible to say that the use of apomorphine is a recognized and acceptable medical practice in an institution such as I.S.M.F."[96] However, it refused to prohibit use of the drug on prisoners who knowingly and intelligently consent to its use.[97]

The court also found that although the use of the drug was called treatment, without consent being obtained it actually constituted punishment. "To hold otherwise would be to ignore what each of us has learned from sad experience—that vomiting (especially in the presence of others) is a painful and debilitating experience."[98] It then went on to set forth the safeguards that must be observed prior to using the drug. First, written consent must be obtained which describes the treatment in detail. Second, consent may be revoked at any time. Third, each apomorphine injection must be individually authorized by a doctor and shall be authorized only upon personal observation by a member of the professional staff.

This case is important in two respects. It clearly establishes the proposition that aversive therapy can constitute punishment even though it is called treatment. In addition, it clearly states that prisoners are capable of consenting to be subjects in experimental programs. The applicability of this finding is somewhat limited by the fact that if this experiment was successful the prisoner would directly benefit, whereas the biomedical experimentation that was discussed earlier would not benefit the prisoner or would only indirectly benefit him.

The holding in *Knecht* is in accord with *Wolff v. McDonnell*,[99] a United States Supreme Court case which was decided after *Knecht*. *Wolff* stands for the proposition that certain procedural safeguards must be observed in prison disciplinary proceedings.[100] The *Wolff* standards were specifically adopted in another case challenging behavior modification, *Clonce v. Richardson.*[101] *Clonce* dealt with the S.T.A.R.T. (Special Treatment and Rehabilitative Training) program, a "demonstration project" located at the Medical Center for Federal Prisoners designed to treat "highly aggressive and assaultive inmates who are found in any correctional institution—federal, state, or local."[102] The program used deprivation of privileges and various status levels in an attempt to change inmate behavior. Prisoners at the lowest level had the fewest privileges and as they earned their way into higher levels, their privileges increased.

The program was involuntary. Prisoners who were selected for the program were not notified of this selection, and no hearing was held prior to placement in the program. Inmates in the program were totally segregated from other inmates. No prisoner in the program was permitted to leave the unit for the purpose of attending religious services. While at the lowest status level (orientation level) the inmate was not allowed to possess, send or use political or educational material. A prisoner was only entitled to a subscription to his hometown newspaper and a Bible of a recognized religion. As the prisoner progressed to higher levels the material he was allowed to read increased. A prisoner's actions were under constant surveillance—the ratio of correctional officers to prisoners was one to two. Commissary privileges were denied at the orientation level and were increased as the inmate progressed to higher status levels. Inmates at the orientation level were allowed to shower and change their clothes a maximum of twice weekly. The number of showers and clothing changes increased with the prisoner's status. Inmates at the orientation level were permitted two one-hour recreation periods each week.

The prisoners alleged that their transfer to S.T.A.R.T. without notice and hearings denied them due process and equal protection of law. The respondents denied this since all inmates in the S.T.A.R.T. program were in segregation prior to their transfer.

The court held that a prisoner who was transferred into the S.T.A.R.T. program, or a behavior modification program like S.T.A.R.T., "which involved a major change in the conditions of confinement is entitled, at a minimum, to the type of hearing required by the Supreme Court's opinion in *Wolff v. McDonnell.*"[103] The fact that the S.T.A.R.T. program was labeled "treatment" for the prisoner's benefit and not a form of punishment was irrelevant since it involved a major change in the conditions of the prisoner's confinement.[104]

The inmates also asked the court to find that a prisoner selected for the S.T.A.R.T. program had the right to withdraw at any time.

Unfortunately, the court refused to consider this point as the S.T.A.R.T. program had been terminated at the time of the action and the court found the issue to be moot. Elsewhere in the decision there is a puzzling statement that may indicate how the court would decide this issue. The court states:

> Forced participation in S.T.A.R.T. was obviously designed to accomplish a modification of the participant's behavior and his general motivation. He was forced to submit to procedures designed to change his mental attitudes, reactions and processes. *A prisoner may not have a constitutional right to prevent such experimentation* but procedures specifically designed and implemented to change a man's mind and therefore his behavior in a manner substantially different from the conditions to which a prisoner is subjected in segregation reflects a major change in the conditions of confinement.[105] (emphasis supplied)

It is not clear whether the court meant that the prisoner may not prevent such experimentation generally, or may not prevent such experimentation on him personally. If the latter is the case, then it would appear that the prisoner could not refuse to participate. Since this finding was not required for the court to reach its decision, and no rationale was given for it, its legal significance is minimal.

The importance of the *Clonce* case may have been substantially reduced by the recent Supreme Court case, *Meachum v. Fano.*[106] In this case the court held that a prisoner does not have to be afforded a hearing prior to transfer from one correctional institution to another, even if such a transfer results in the prisoner's being incarcerated in substantially less favorable conditions. However, *Meachum* only deals with transfer from one ordinary prison to another ordinary prison, and does not discuss transfers to experimental behavior modification programs. In any event, this case may cause future courts to focus their attention more on the nature of the specific procedures utilized and less on the method by which prisoners are chosen for participation in these programs.

In this respect the *Clonce* case does differ from *Knecht* and *Mackey* in that it did not require the use of drugs or other painful stimuli. The effects on the prisoners were considerably less outrageous than in the *Knecht* and *Mackey* cases. However, the cases are similar in that it was not the *experimental* nature of the behavior modification programs that caused the courts to regulate their use, but the apparent cruelty of the methods used.

It is highly unlikely that the *Mackey* and *Knecht* cases would have been decided differently if the use of the drugs involved were not experimental. That is to say, if there were substantial evidence that such programs did change a prisoner's behavior it would not follow that we could inject them with drugs that cause cessation of breathing or violent vomiting without their consent. The mere efficacy of a program should not lead to its use without the person's consent.

The final form of behavior modification to be discussed is the most invasive—psychosurgery. Although there are no cases involving psychosurgery conducted on prisoners, there is at least one case in which a court permitted a person about to be tried to undergo a lobotomy in an attempt to cure him of his criminal tendencies.[107]

The major case in this area, *Kaimowitz v. Department of Mental Health*,[108] involved an inmate in a state mental hospital. Louis Smith, the inmate involved, was to undergo experimental psychosurgery in a study which was to compare the efficacy of this procedure with the efficacy of certain drugs in reducing violent behavior. Smith signed a consent form and a review committee approved the procedure. Gabe Kaimowitz, an attorney, learned of the program and along with Smith filed suit to prohibit it. The court found that there was no "scientific basis" for establishing that removal or destruction of an area of the brain would have any direct therapeutic effect in controlling aggressivity.[109] The procedure was also found to be irreversible,[110] and to pose "substantial risk to the research subject."[111]

The court went on to hold that Smith, who had been involuntarily confined in the institution for seventeen years, was not capable of giving his informed consent because "the very nature of his incarceration diminishes the capacity to consent to psychosurgery."[112]

Institutionalization tends to strip the individual of the support which permits him to maintain his sense of self-worth and the value of his own physical and mental integrity. . . . The privileges of an involuntarily detained patient and the rights he exercises in the institution are within the control of institutional authorities . . . [S]uch minor things as the right to have a lamp in his room, or the right to have ground privileges to go for a picnic with his family assumed major proportions. For 17 years he lived completely under the control of the hospital. Nearly every important aspect of his life was decided without an opportunity on his part to participate in the decision-making process.

The involuntarily detained mental patient is in an inherently coercive atmosphere even though no direct pressure may be placed upon him. He finds himself stripped of customary amenities and defenses. Free movement is restricted. He becomes part of communal living subject to the control of institutional authorities.[113]

Aside from institutionalization the court found that coercion existed "when his very release from the institution may depend upon his cooperating with the institutional authorities and giving consent to experimental surgery."[114] This point is buttressed by the fact that Smith rescinded his consent to the surgery after he was released from the hospital.[115]

Whether or not the court's statements regarding the ramifications of institutionalization are accurate is open to question. However, at least one commentator has stated the same type of situation occurs in prisons.[116] He stated that considerable pressure to acquiesce to the wishes of their keepers is felt by prisoners. "The infantilizing, depersonalization, helplessness, and anonymity that occur within a prison environment force the prisoner into a state of total dependence. This is conducive to a state not unlike that found between parent and child."[117]

The court itself undercut its argument on the effect of institutionalization by relying on the experimental nature of the procedure for disallowing Smith's consent. It stated that when the psychosurgical procedure under discussion "becomes an accepted neurosurgical procedure and is no longer experimental . . . [an] involuntarily detained mental patient could consent to such an operation."[118] This conclusion is somewhat illogical in that, "The non-experimental status of this procedure may increase the prospective patient's knowledge concerning the risks and benefits involved, but it in no way counteracts the effects of institutionalization on his ability to consent in a truly informed fashion."[119] Thus the court's apparently strong feelings on this issue are considerably tempered. Assuming there is a valid psychological construct known as institutionalization, this would suggest that prisoners who have been confined for lengthy periods of time should not be asked to volunteer for either behavioral or biomedical research. It does not mean that all research must be stopped.

From an examination of the foregoing cases, one can discern the attitude courts are taking toward informed consent and behavioral research. The S.T.A.R.T. program being the least invasive of all the proposed programs of behavior modification was the least regulated by the court. The issue of consent was skirted, but the court ruled that certain due process protections regarding selection of the participants were required. The use of drugs that cause severe vomiting or fright is more invasive, and the courts set forth a requirement that informed consent must be obtained. Psychosurgery, which is the most dangerous and invasive technique, and which is the only one that is irreversible, was prohibited by the court by finding that a confined person could not consent to it. The courts seem to realize that behavior modification cannot be treated as a unitary concept. Varying behavior modification techniques have varying risks and should be regulated accordingly. But perhaps even more important than the variety of risks is that these techniques shock the conscience of the courts and offend their concepts of humane treatment to differing degrees.

However, the *Mackey* and *Knecht* cases do serve to establish one important point. Prisoners, protected by the proper safeguards, are legally capable of giving their informed consent to behavioral research even though it involves the use of procedures that cause a great deal of pain and suffering.

LEGISLATIVE AND REGULATORY RESPONSES

The previous discussion has analyzed the role of the common law (judge-made law that comes about through the resolution of specific cases) in the regulation of experimentation on prisoners. The common law can be codified or changed by statutes passed by state or federal legislatures, or regulations promulgated by administrative agencies when the agencies are given such authority by legislative mandate. As of the middle of 1976 twenty-one states have legislation or regulations which permit biomedical research and twenty-three states permit behavioral research. Eight states have chosen to ban biomedical research, one by legislation, six by regulation, and one by moratorium. Five states ban behavioral research, one by legislation, three by regulation, and one by moratorium.[120]

The legislative and regulatory responses cover the entire spectrum, from merely permitting experimentation as in Iowa,[121] Georgia,[122] and Montana,[123] to those which bar the practice altogether as in Illinois,[124] Missouri,[125] New York[126] (which has banned participation in pharmaceutical experimentation), Oregon[127] (which has banned all medical, psychiatric or psychological experimentation on prisoners), Pennsylvania,[128] and Vermont.[129] Several states that discourage or ban medical research permit research that will aid the corrections process, such as Kentucky,[130] New Jersey,[131] New York,[132] and South Carolina.[133]

In virtually all of the states that do permit any sort of experimentation, the requirement that informed consent must be obtained is explicitly set forth. In these states an implicit finding must have been made that prisoners are capable of giving informed consent even though they are incarcerated. This is specifically found to be the case by the North Carolina Attorney General.[134] Arizona law simply states that the consent of the superintendent and prison physician must be obtained that the prison physician or the investigator must disclose the dangers of participation, and that the prisoner must consent in writing.[135] On the other hand, other states have very detailed requirements regarding informed consent. California has a statute that bans the use of "organic therapy" (shock therapy; the use of drugs, electric shocks or infliction of physical pain used in a program of aversive, classical or operant conditioning; and psychosurgery, which is also regulated by a separate statute)[136] without the consent of the inmate.[137] In order to obtain informed consent the physician must explain: (1) The nature and seriousness of the illness; (2) The nature of the proposed therapy and its duration; (3) The likelihood of improvement or deterioration without the administration of the proposed organic therapy; (4) The likelihood and degree of improvement, remission or cure resulting from the therapy, and the extent of changes in and intrusion upon the person's personality and patterns of thought; (5) The likelihood, nature and duration of side effects; (6) The uncertainty of benefits or hazards because of the lack of sufficient data; (7) Reasonable alternatives to the treatment; and (8) Whether or not the treatment is considered experimental.

Massachusetts proposed policy[138] requires the prisoner to sign a consent form which explains: (1) The nature, duration and purpose of the investigation; (2) The method by which the investigation is conducted; (3) All inconveniences, hazards, discomforts and risks reasonably to be expected; (4) The effects on the subject's health; (5) A description of the benefits; (6) A disclosure of alternative procedures; (7) An offer to answer any questions; and (8) An instruction that the subject is free to withdraw at any time without affecting the conditions of his confinement. The subject must be given a copy of the form twenty-four hours prior to the time it is to be signed.

The issue of reward for participation in research is dealt with in a variety of ways. In North Carolina an attorney general's opinion states that the Department of Corrections should make no promise of pecuniary award, sentence commutation or any other kind of reward, or else coercion is intimated to the inmate.[139] In Virginia incentives are discouraged, but if approved the state has set up a rate schedule.[140] For oral medication an inmate receives 25 cents per dose with a maximum of $1.00 per day, $1.00 per injection with a $2.00 per day maximum, $1.50 for a stomach intubation, and 10 cents per urine collection.[141]

Connecticut also sets forth a fee schedule in its regulations. For studies in excess of seven days the prisoner must be paid a minimum of $25.00 and a maximum of $75.00. The specific fee is set by the Research Advisory Committee which reviews all protocols. For an initial blood drawing the prisoner is paid $10.00, for a spinal puncture he is paid $15.00, for urine and fecal samples—$1.00 each, for a unit (500 cc) of blood for research purposes—$20.00, etc.[142] Fifty percent of the total amount of all money paid to inmates in any one research project must be paid to the prison welfare fund. A direct charge of twelve percent of the total payment to prisoners is paid to the state, as well as an indirect charge of six percent. Michigan has a general statement on compensation which states that compensation may be proportionate to the discomfort or inconvenience involved, but not to the risk involved. The inducement cannot be so great that it would coerce an inmate to accept a risk beyond that which he would otherwise willingly incur. No promise concerning a recommendation to the Parole Board or prison administration may be made.[143]

Tennessee law requires payment to prisoners to be commensurate with payment for the same services to noninmates, "taking into consideration the special conditions of inmates."[144]

A number of states require the prisoners to sign a waiver, releasing the state from any liability for adverse results.[145] It can be said without question that requiring the inmate to waive his rights against the state is poor policy since it reduces the state's incentive to protect the inmate.

State regulation in this area runs from excellent to nonexistent. There is certainly no uniformity, which indicates the present state of the art in this area. However, a large number of states do permit prisoners to give informed consent to experimentation.

The federal government through the Department of the Army and the Department of Health, Education and Welfare has promulgated regulations concerning the use of prisoners as research subjects. The Army absolutely prohibits the use of prisoners of war under any circumstances.[146] Use of prisoners who are not prisoners of war is prohibited:

> Unless it has first been determined that there will be no undue inducements to such participation, taking into account such factors as whether the earnings, living conditions, medical care, quality of food, and other amenities offered to participants in the study are significantly greater than those available to non-participating prisoners.[147]

A prisoner being held in pretrial confinement may not be used as a subject unless the purpose of the experiment is to diagnose, treat or prevent a condition from which he is suffering, or it is to study the effect of confinement upon the prisoner, and involves no risk to him.[148] Finally, a senior medical officer from the U.S. Army Medical Research and Development Command Headquarters and a member of the legal staff must conduct a site visit at the prison in which the research is to be conducted.[149]

Detailed consent standards are set forth (apparently derived from proposed H.E.W. regulations) including a fair explanation of the procedures to be followed, a description of risks and discomforts, a description of benefits, disclosure of alternative procedures to be followed, an offer to answer inquiries, and an instruction that the prisoner is free to withdraw from participation at any time without prejudice to him.[150] The use of any exculpatory language is prohibited and consent must be in writing except in exceptional circumstances.[151]

The Department of Health, Education, and Welfare has proposed two sets of regulations which include guidelines for obtaining informed consent from prisoners. In the first set of proposed regulations, which were formally referred to as "a draft working document," the Organizational Review Committee was required to certify, "(1) that there will be no undue inducements to participation by prisoners as subjects in the activity, taking into account, among other factors, the sources of earnings generally available to the prisoners as compared with those offered to participants in the activity . . . and (4) that no prisoner will be offered any reduction in sentence or parole for participation in such activity which is not comparable to that offered for other activities at the facility not of a research, development demonstration or similar nature."[152] The Organizational Review Committee also sets rates of remuneration in accordance with the duration, discomfort and/or risk of the activity, but not in excess of that generally available to the inmates.[153] No person confined pending arraignment, trial, or sentencing may participate in research.[154] If a prisoner must withdraw for medical reasons, prior to the completion of the study, the Protection Committee will determine how much he is to be paid for such participation.[155] Prisons in which participation of inmates in experimentation is to occur must be accredited by H.E.W.[156]

When the second draft of the regulations was published several changes were made. In determining the absence of undue inducements the Organizational Review Committee, in addition to taking into account the earnings of the prisoners, must also take into account whether such factors as the living conditions, medical care, quality of food and amenities would be better than those generally available to the prisoner.[157] Although this broadens the Organizational Review Committee's authority to determine the presence of unfair inducements, it was done at the price of removing the Department's authority to accredit institutions.[158] The proposal to accredit institutions was criticized by a number of people "principally because of the jurisdictional problems inherent in any attempt to impose a Federal regulatory requirement on an autonomous state facility."[159] In light of the remaining regulations that control the conduct of experimentation at these autonomous state facilities, this objection seems rather anomalous. As discussed earlier in this chapter, existing conditions in a prison may act to coerce a prisoner to volunteer as a research subject. To assure that such conditions do not exist, inspection of these institutions should be required. An inherent conflict of interest exists when those responsible for prison conditions must decide whether or not those conditions are so poor as to coerce inmates into volunteering as subjects in experimental programs. By setting up accreditation standards for prison research, H.E.W. would not take control of the prisons. It would merely refuse to fund research to be conducted in those prisons which do not meet certain standards.

The second draft does not include a section prohibiting a reduction in sentence or granting of parole as a result of participation in research. Because of the inherently coercive nature of such a reduction in sentence or offer of parole, this practice should not be allowed.

In the second draft, rates of remuneration are not based on discomfort or risk, but only on the duration of the activity. However, remuneration still must not exceed that paid for other employment, and if the prisoner must withdraw for medical reasons, he must not lose any anticipated remuneration.[160]

The elements of informed consent in H.E.W.'s proposed regulations are identical to the Army regulations set out above.[161]

As in the case of a number of states, the federal regulatory scheme accepts the notion that prisoners can consent to be subjects of experimentation as long as adequate safeguards are provided.

SUMMARY AND CONCLUSION

In this chapter we have tried to set forth the barriers that might exist which would render a prisoner incapable of voluntarily consenting to biomedical and behavioral research. We have discussed the conditions that exist in prisons that might coerce or unduly influence the prisoner to participate in experiments against his will. We have also discussed the role of monetary incentives and the problem of promising prisoners early release in exchange for their participation in research. The following summarizes the discussion:

1. If a prisoner volunteers to be a research subject because conditions in the prison are abysmal, and the only way he can obtain minimally decent living conditions is to participate in research, then his participation cannot be deemed to be voluntary. For this reason we would urge the Department of Health, Education, and Welfare to reconsider its intention to accredit prisons to ensure that these conditions do not exist. Only an independent agency with no stake in either the prison conditions or the proposed research can perform this task in an objective manner.

2. As far as rewards for participation are concerned, we have established that these too can be coercive. If a prisoner must earn money to maintain his health and personal hygiene, or to obtain a minimally decent standard of living, and this money can only be earned by participating in research, then the payment of such money would constitute duress. However, where remuneration serves merely as a reward for participation in research, it would not be coercive if the reward were not so great as to cause a person to incur great personal risks that he would not otherwise take.

3. A prisoner should never be offered parole or a reduction in sentence for his participation in research as this would be inherently coercive. If a judge, when sentencing a person convicted of a crime, said, "I will sentence you to three years in prison if you do not wish to volunteer as a research subject, but only to two years in prison if you do volunteer," we could all agree that the prisoner in "volunteering" would be acting under duress. An offer of parole or sentence reduction would, in effect, produce a similar situation. We should not adopt the practice of incarcerating individuals for purposes of punishment or rehabilitation and then ask them to trade the use of their bodies in return for their freedom.

4. Not only should an offer of parole or sentence reduction be prohibited, but any action that may lead the prisoner to believe that such was the case must be guarded against. For this reason guards, wardens, and all other correctional personnel should not be permitted to ask prisoners if they wish to participate in research. As such individuals are in a "confidential relationship" with the prisoners, *i.e.*, in a position of control over them, such a request stands too great a chance of unduly influencing the prisoner's decisions.

5. The importance of the availability of an independent counselor to whom the prisoner can turn for advice cannot be overstated. As we saw in the undue influence case, the coerced confession case, and the coerced guilty plea case, the courts have given great weight to the protective role of independent counselors. This role can be played by the protection or consent committees required in the proposed fed-

eral regulations, or by a physician, lawyer or other independent person of the prisoner's choice.

6. The bodily and mental integrity of the prisoner should never be violated without his consent, as was held in the *Mackey* and *Knecht* cases. The prisoner must receive a fair explanation of the procedures to be followed, a description of risks and discomforts, a description of benefits, disclosure of alternative procedures that might be available, an offer to answer inquiries, and an instruction that he may withdraw from participation at any time without prejudice to him. The consent form should be given to him at least twenty-four hours prior to its signing, and the prisoner should receive a copy of it after it is signed. The prisoner should not be asked to waive his rights against anyone or any entity which might be liable for injuries that he may sustain. Prisons in states that have such a requirement should not be accredited for the purpose of conducting research.

This chapter does not discuss the numerous policy considerations that surround the prison research controversy. We do not discuss the ethical issues of using persons whom society has incarcerated as research subjects, or problems of the subsidization of drug companies who pay prisoners less than they would have to pay free-living individuals to participate in similar projects, or the problem of placing the burden of medical research on a very small segment of the population for the benefit of us all. Our goal was not to decide whether or not prisoners should ever be subjects of biomedical and behavioral research.

If, however, it is decided that prisoners are a proper population on which to perform biomedical and behavioral research, it is our conclusion that the law will not bar such participation, provided that the safeguards discussed in this chapter are adopted.

REFERENCES

1. United States of America v. Karl Brandt, in Katz, Experimentation with Human Beings, 305–306 (1972).

2. Pappworth, Human Guinea Pigs, 60 (1967).

3. Biomedical Experimentation on Prisoners: Review of Practices and Problems and Proposal of a New Regulatory Approach, Health Policy Program, University of California School of Medicine, San Francisco, 3 (1975).

4. Ladimer and Newman, Clinical Investigation in Medicine: Legal, Ethical and Moral Aspects, Boston University Law-Medicine Institute, 116–117 (1963).

5. Mitford, Kind and Unusual Punishment, chs. 8 and 9 (1973).

6. Official Transcript of the American Military Tribunal in the Matter of United States of America v. Karl Brandt, *et al.*, 9029, 9209 *et seq.* (1947).

7. *Id.* at 9211.

8. *Id*. at 9217.

9. *Id*. at 9218.

10. *Id*. at 9254.

11. Hodges and Bean, The Use of Prisoners for Medical Research, 202 J.A.M.A. 513, 514 (1967).

12. Ayd, Drug Studies in Prison Volunteers, 65 Southern Medical Journal 440, 441 (1972), citing Freund, Some Reflections on Consent, 98 Daedalus 314 (1968).

13. *Id*.

14. Arnold, Martin and Boyer, A Study of One Prison Population and Its Response to Medical Research, 169 Annals N.Y. Academy of Sciences, 463 (1970).

15. *Id*. at 465.

16. *Id*. at 466.

17. *Id*.

18. *Id*. at 467.

19. *Id*.

20. *Id*. at 468.

21. Martin, Arnold, Zimmerman and Richart, Human Subjects in Clinical Research—A Report of Three Studies, 279 New Eng. J. Med. 1426 (1968).

22. *Id*. at 1428.

23. *Id*. at 1429.

24. Hearings Before the Subcommittee on Health of the Committee on Labor and Public Welfare of the United States Senate, 93rd Congress, First Session (1973), at 825.

25. *Id*. at 826.

26. Mitford, *supra* note 5, at 144.

27. *Id*. at 145.

28. Williston on Contracts, §1603 (3rd ed. 1970).

29. *Id*.

30. *Id*. at §1604.

31. 227 P.2d 763 (Utah, 1951).

32. *Id*. at 764.

33. *Id*. at 765, citing 13 Words and Phrases, Perm. Ed. 643.

34. *Id*. at 766.

35. *Id*. at 764.

36. Wolf v. Marlton Corporation, 57 N.J. Super. 278, 154 A.2d 625, 629 (1959).

37. *Id*.

38. Williston, *supra* note 28, at §1624.

39. Note, Wills—Undue Influence, 50 Mich. L.R. 748, 756 (1952).

40. Note, Undue Influence—Judicial Implementation of Social Policy, Wisc. L. Rev. 569, 581 (1968).

41. *Id*. at 749.

42. Ostertag v. Donovan, 65 N.M. 6, 331 P.2d 355 (1958).

43. *Id*. at 331 P.2d 359.

44. *Id*.

45. The Collateral Consequences of a Criminal Conviction, 23 Vanderbilt L. Rev. 929, 1036-1037 (1970).

46. Bailey v. Mandel, Md. District Ct., K-74-1102, Filed Oct. 8, 1974.

47. *Supra* note 24, at 866.

48. Freedman, A Moral Theory of Informed Consent, 5 Hastings Center Report 32, 36 (August, 1975).

49. Mills and Morris, Prisoners as Laboratory Animals, 11 Society 60, 64 (July/August 1974).

50. *Id*.

51. Fox, Some Social and Cultural Factors in American Society Conducive to Medical Research on Human Subjects, Symposium on the Study of Drugs and Man, Clin. Pharm. and Therapeutics, 423, 437 (1960).

52. 136 J.A.M.A. 457 (1948).

53. *Id*. at 458.

54. *Id*.

55. *Supra* note 3, at 6.

56. *Id*. at 7.

57. Taylor v. Manson, *et al.*, U.S.D.C. Conn., #H-75-37 (Filed Jan. 29, 1975).

58. Telephone conversation with Mr. Matthew Myers, attorney for the plaintiffs (February 20, 1976).

59. 384 U.S. 436 (1966).

60. *Id*. at 448.

61. *Id*. at 455.

62. *Id*. at 467.

63. These warnings are: (1) the right to remain silent, (2) that anything the person says may be used against him, (3) that he has a right to have a lawyer present and (4) that if he cannot afford a lawyer, one will be appointed.

64. 397 U.S. 742 (1970).

65. *Id*. at 748.

66. *Id*. at 751.

67. *Id*.

68. *Id*.

69. *Id*. at 749.

70. Prosser, Law of Torts, §§9, 18 (3rd ed. 1964).

71. *See*, Bowers, Prisoners' Rights in Prison Medical Experimentation, 6 Clearinghouse Rev. 319, 327 (1972).

72. 344 F.2d 463 (8th Cir. 1965).

73. *Id*. at 465.

74. 288 F. Supp. 329 (W.D. Mo. 1968).

75. Veals v. Ciccone, 281 F. Supp. 1017 (W.D. Mo. 1968).

76, 326 F. Supp. 787 (W.D. Mo. 1970), *aff'd* 442 F.2d 928 (8th Cir. 1971).

77. *Id*. at 788.

78. Cates v. Ciccone, 422 F.2d 926, 928 (8th Cir. 1970).

79. 310 F. Supp. 600 (W.D. Mo. 1970).

80. *Id*. at 605.

81. *Id.*

82. Ayers v. Ciccone, 300 F. Supp. 568 (W.D. Mo. 1968), *aff'd per curiam* 413 F.2d 1049 (8th Cir. 1969).

83. 117 Ga. App. 1, 159 S.E.2d 719 (1967).

84. *Id.* at 724.

85. Runnels v. Rosendale, 499 F.2d 733, 734 (9th Cir. 1974).

86. 42 U.S.C. 1983.

87. *Supra* note 85, at 735.

88. Brown v. Brown 368 F.2d 992 (9th Cir. 1966).

89. 477 F.2d 877 (9th Cir. 1973).

90. Mitford, *supra* note 3, at 127.

91. *Id.* at 128.

92. *Id.*

93. *Supra* note 89, at 878.

94. 488 F.2d 1136 (8th Cir. 1973).

95. Iowa Code Ann., § 223.4.

96. *Supra* note 94, at 1138.

97. *Id.* at 1138–1139.

98. *Id.* at 1140.

99. 94 S. Ct. 2963 (1974).

100. *See*, Gobert, Psychosurgery, Conditioning, and the Prisoner's Rights to Refuse Treatment, 61 Va. L. Rev. 155, 176 (1975).

101. 379 F. Supp. 338 (W.D. Mo. 1974).

102. *Id.* at 343.

103. *Id.* at 348.

104. *Id.* at 349.

105. *Id.* at 350.

106. 44 U.S.L.W. 5053 (June 22, 1976) *See also*, Montayne v. Haymes, 44 U.S.L.W. 5051 (June 22, 1976).

107. Annas and Glantz, Psychosurgery: The Law's Response, 54 B.U.L. Rev. 249, 250 (1974).

108. Civ. No. 73-19434-AW (Cir. Ct. Wayne County, Mich., July 10, 1973). See Chapter 4, infra, for a more detailed discussion of this case.

109. *Id.* at 17.

110. *Id.* at 12.

111. *Id.* at 16.

112. *Id.* at 25.

113. *Id.* at 26–28.

114. *Id.* at 27.

115. *Id.* at 8 n.9.

116. Bach-y-Rita, The Prisoner as an Experimental Subjects, 229 J.A.M.A. 45 (July, 1974).

117. *Id.* at 45.

118. *Supra* note 108 at 40.

119. Annas and Glantz, *supra* note 106, at 263.

120. National Commission for the Protection of Human Subjects of Biomedi-

cal and Behavioral Research, Staff Paper: Prison Inmate Involvement in Biomedical and Behavioral Research in State Correctional Facilities (November 12, 1975).

121. Iowa Code Ann., §246.47.

122. Ga. Code Ann., §125-2-9-13.

123. Rev. Codes of Montana, §75-8801.

124. Dept. of Corr. Ad. Order No. 5-73 (July 5, 1973).

125. Div. of Corr. Bulletin #25 (July 7, 1975).

126. Dept. of Corr. Ad. Bulletin #120 (Nov. 4, 1974).

127. Ore. Rev. St. §421.085(b)(2).

128. Memorandum from Allyn R. Sielaff, Commissioner of Dept. of Corr. (March 19, 1975).

129. Dept. of Corr. Policy Statement (June 5, 1975).

130. Bureau of Corrections Directive #4.

131. Dept. of Institutions and Agencies Ad. Order 6:02 at III (Sept. 1, 1967).

132. *Supra* note 125.

133. Dept. of Corr. Procedures Manual. §200.13.

134. Att. Gen. Opinion (Jan. 20, 1970).

135. Ariz. Rev. Stat. §31-321.

136. Cal. Welfare and Inst. Code, §5326.3.

137. Cal. Penal Code, §2670.

138. Dept. of Corr. Order 11800.1.

139. *Supra* note 134.

140. Div. of Corr. Guidelines, Number 900 (Oct. 12, 1970).

141. Div. of Corr. Guidelines, Number 900, supplement (July 13, 1973).

142. Dept. of Corr. Guidelines 6.7 (May 20, 1974).

143. Mich. Dept. of Corr. Policy Dir. #cc-10 (Jan. 1, 1974).

144. Tennessee Code Ann., §41-2203.

145. *See, e.g.*, Ariz. Rev. St. 31-321(c); Md. Div. of Corr. Reg. #130-17 (App. 1) (March 22, 1974).

146. U.S.A.M.R.D.C. Reg. 70-25, §1-5-2.1 (Oct. 8, 1975).

147. *Id*. at 1-10-2.a.

148. *Id*. at 1-10-2.b.

149. *Id*. at 1-10-2.c.

150. *Id*. at 1-5-1.a.

151. *Id*. at 1-5-1.c and d.

152. 38 Fed. Reg. 31747, §46.44(a)(1) and (4) (Nov. 16, 1973).

153. *Id*. at §46.44(b)(3).

154. *Id*. at 31748, §46.46.

155. *Id*. at 31748, §46.47.

156. *Id*. at 31748, §46.48.

157. 39 Fed. Reg. 30654, §46.404(a)(1) (Aug. 23, 1974).

158. *Id*. at 30652.

159. *Id*.

160. *Id*. at 30655, §46.405(4).

161. 39 Fed. Reg. 18917, § 46.3(c)(1)-(6) (May 30, 1974).

Research with the Institutionalized Mentally Infirm: The Dual Problems of Incapacity and Voluntariness

The area of informed consent by institutionalized mental patients to experimentation combines the issues found in regard to prisoners and children. The problem is two-tiered, concerning both the legal capacity of the individual to consent and the issue of institutionalization. The major questions may be highlighted by reference to one of the principles of the Nuremberg Code.[1] Does an institutionalized mental patient, in general, have the legal capacity to consent? Is a particular mental patient competent so as to enable an "understanding and enlightened decision?" Is proxy consent ever valid, and, if so, under what circumstances? Does the fact of institutionalization create a situation which effectively removes the individual's ability "to exercise free power of choice?"

Institutionalized mental patients are perhaps the most isolated and underprivileged members of our society. The human and legal rights of mentally ill and retarded persons[2] have been grossly violated for centuries. The result is that they are often victims of numerous social injustices, including horrible facilities, poor or nonexistent treatment and education, indiscriminate sterilization, and deprivation of basic legal protections, including the performance of unethical and/or illegal human experimentation.

Large institutions, although outdated and often inefficient, have historically carried the responsibility for caring for the mentally deficient individual who either cannot function in the community or whose family has decided not to have him remain at home.[3] This involves a substantial number of people. There are approximately 200,000 residents in 190 public institutions for the retarded in the United States.[4] Many have spent most of their lives in institutions. In addition, one out of every ten Americans will at some time be hospitalized for mental illness.[5] There is an abundance of literature critical of mental hospitals.[6] For many individuals, institutionalization results in a worsening of their mental condition.[7] Long-term residents actually suffer deterioration and abuse.[8] Indeed, it has been estimated that the effects of institutionalization are so severe that, if a patient is not released within two years of his admission, the chances are good that he will die in the hospital.[9] Dehumanization has been amply demonstrated in such residential facilities.[10]

Institutionalized mental patients have traditionally been subjects of experiments, and not necessarily because the research has special applicability to this group.[11] Research frequently requires that a convenient, stable subject population be followed over a period of time. Thus, the institutionalized are particularly attractive to investigators because they constitute a "controlled" or "captive" community, with a relatively uniform diet, schedule of sleeping hours, and daily routine, and since they are often wards of the state, they form an inexpensive pool of experimental subjects.[12] In addition, people in institutions are often easily manipulated, either due to their own mental deficiencies or the lack of interest in their welfare demonstrated by their legal guardians and/or facility administration and staff.

For example, it has been reported that eighty mentally defective patients of the District of Columbia Training School in Laurel, Maryland were the subjects of an experiment designed to measure the blood flow in people suffering from dementia. A long needle was inserted in the femoral artery in the thigh of each individual. Then the jugular vein in the neck was treated similarly, with another needle going in just below the jaw and extending to the bulb in the vein. Finally, the patients were forced to inhale radioactive gas through a tight-fitting mask, and their blood flow was checked.[13] In another case, a meningitis vaccine was injected into mentally retarded children at the Hamburg State Home and Hospital Institution in Pennsylvania without the consent of either subject or parent, since the investigator thought that the administrator of the hospital was the legal guardian of the involved minors.[14]

A particularly outrageous example of experimentation on institutionalized mental patients involves the drug Depo-Provera, a derivative of progesterone that was approved by the FDA in 1960 for treatment of the gynecologic condition known as endometriosis, and in 1972 for treatment of carcinoma of the lining of the uterus.

The drug has been investigated for contraceptive use in human clinical and animal studies under an Investigational New Drug Application (IND) since 1963. In 1970, studies in dogs revealed that Depo-Provera produced mammary tumors, and new information received in 1972 indicated that some of these nodules were malignant.[15] Contraceptive studies with Depo-Provera under the IND were severely limited and the subjects under study were required to sign the following detailed written informed consent form.

REVISED DEPO-PROVERA WRITTEN INFORMED CONSENT FORM FOR CONTRACEPTIVE STUDIES

IMPORTANT NOTE: This is <u>NOT</u> the same informed consent form that you signed before. It has been changed to bring to your attention that breast cancers have developed in some beagle dogs undergoing long-term tests with injections of Depo-Provera. Please read it carefully.

This is to certify that I, _____, hereby agree and consent to receive an experimental drug called Depo-Provera every three months under the care and supervision of Dr. _____. I understand that this injection will be given to me in an attempt to keep me from becoming pregnant. I have been told that tests in dogs injected with this drug showed that some of them developed tumors in their breasts. Some of these tumors were cancer and spread to other organs. It is not known whether or not similar tumors or cancers will grow in my breasts after receiving the drug.

It has been explained to me that there are available other non-experimental methods of preventing pregnancy such as pills, vaginal creams, jellies, foams, diaphragms, various devices which are inserted into my womb and use of a rubber (condom) by my husband. The effectiveness of these various methods of contraception, as well as the advantages and disadvantages of each method, has been explained to me. Surgical sterilization of myself or my husband (along with its risks, advantages and disadvantages) has been explained to me as a nonreversible method of contraception. I have also been told of the effectiveness of Depo-Provera.

I have read and understand the pamphlet prepared by the American Medical Association, American College of Obstetricians and Gynecologists and the Food and Drug Administration informing users of the pill about the possible problems which a woman may encounter during its use. I understand also that Depo-Provera is similar to the pill in that I may have some of the same problems occurring that are mentioned in the pamphlet such as blood clots, tender breasts, nausea, vomiting, weight gain, weight loss, spotty darkening of the skin of the face, mental depression, elevated levels of sugar and fatty substances in the blood, dizziness, loss of hair, increase in body hair and increased or decreased sex drive.

It has been explained to me that it is quite likely that I will have un-expected vaginal bleeding, completely irregular menstrual cycles or no menstrual bleeding at all as a result of the Depo-Provera injections. I also understand that the injections may have some effect on the amount of estrogenic and adrenal hormones produced in my body and that the importances of these changes is still being investigated.

I understand, also, that after a woman stops taking Depo-Provera there may be an unpredictable and prolonged delay before she is able to become pregnant or may be unable to become pregnant at all. Because of the pos-sibility of an occasional case of permanent sterility, Depo-Provera should not be used by women who may wish to have another baby in the future.

I have tried all other kinds of birth control methods and cannot use them or I refuse to use all other kinds of birth control methods. There-fore, I hereby volunteer of my own free will to receive injections of the experimental birth control drug, Depo-Provera, with the full knowledge and understanding that it produced breast tumors and cancer in some dogs and it is not known whether similar tumors or cancers will develop in my breasts.

I understand that I may withdraw from this investigational study of the use of Depo-Provera for contraception at any time.[16]

Although Depo-Provera is an experimental drug for the purpose of birth control, it was considered by the authorities of the Arling-ton Hospital and School, a facility for the mentally retarded in Tennessee, as a viable and valuable contraceptive method since it is highly effective, temporarily halts the patient's menstrual cycle, and need only be administered through an injection once every three months. Beginning in 1970, almost 200 female child-bearing age residents of the institution were receiving Depo-Provera.[17] However, in contrast to the elaborate consent form presented to the "normal" subjects using Depo-Provera, the following form was employed to obtain the consent of the parents or guardian of the institutional-ized individuals to the administration of the drug.

PERMIT FOR DEPO PROVERA PROGRAM

I, _____ , (father, mother or legal guardian) of _____
_____ , now a resident of Arlington Hospital and School, give my permission to enter her into the program designed at Arlington Hospital and School to use depo provera.

This drug is to be injected every three months for the purposes of pre-venting menstruation, thereby making the resident more comfortable and to lessen nursing care. A second purpose is that of preventing pregnancy in the event of exposure.[18]

Indeed, based on the statements by Dr. James S. Brown, super-intendent of the facility, before Senator Kennedy's 1973 Hearings on Human Experimentation, the institutional authorities were either unaware of or had little concern for the experimental nature of the drug.

> *Dr. Brown:* I would like to clarify a couple things, at least in terminol-ogy, as I listened to the hearings this morning. We keep referring to Depo-Provera as an experimental drug. It has never been our understanding that it is an experimental drug, and our use of Depo-Provera has not been within the context or the framework of the way we would go about doing an experimental study if we did one.

> *Senator Kennedy:* Just to clarify our terms. Dr. Edwards (Commissioner of Food and Drugs, Department of Health, Education, and Welfare) indi-cates Depo-Provera is an experimental drug for the purpose of birth control.

> *Dr. Brown:* What is an experimental drug? If you have a drug such as Depo-Provera that is licensed for human use at a certain dose, and for cer-tain indications, is it experimental?

> This is the question in my mind. Is it experimental again for another in-dication that you are using it for in human beings?

> *Senator Kennedy:* Dr. Brown, Dr. Edwards just said this morning it is not to be used for birth control purposes.

> *Dr. Brown:* He said the FDA has not licensed it for birth control pur-poses.

> *Senator Kennedy:* That is right.

> *Dr. Brown:* Senator, I am not an expert on Depo-Provera. As a pedia-trician and as an administrator I would like to tell you about our prob-lem and what we did and how we went about it.[19]

Dr. Brown went on to indicate that the major reason for adminis-tration of the drug was to provide an effective means of preventing pregnancy and menstruation, two conditions which present problems to the efficient functioning of an institution. Indeed, the testimony continued as follows:

> *Dr. Brown:* Senator, I do not think that anyone has given you any in-formation on the unsafety of the drug for human use. We do not have it either. If we could get it, we would stop the drug today.

> *Senator Kennedy:* The Food and Drug Administration, which is the pres-ent regulatory agency, which has the resources—financial and research re-sources—to make these judgments, has indicated that it has not approved this for this purpose.

Your consultants have reached other conclusions. What we must determine is whether we are going to have individual doctors using these various drugs, or State agencies in effect substituting their judgment for the judgment of the Food and Drug Administration.

Should that be permitted?

Dr. Brown: Well, certainly, if there is any question about its safety and the FDA had not told me what it is, my consultants would certainly find out and advise us, and we would take our people off the drug. I think we still have not quite established this, Senator Kennedy.

Senator Kennedy: You what?

Dr. Brown: I am not sure we have established what this is, at least so far as communicating is concerned.

Senator Kennedy: Do you think physicians should independently be able to decide whether or not a drug is safe?

Dr. Brown: No, I do not. I certainly do not.

Senator Kennedy: Is this not really what has happened here?

Dr. Brown: Well, I do not think the FDA has said it was unsafe.

Senatory Kennedy: Unresolved questions of safety? You say there is a significant doubt, a serious doubt.

Dr. Brown: That is correct.

Senator Kennedy: That doubt on the part of the Food and Drug Administration is in no way reflected in your consent form, is it?

Dr. Brown: No, it is not.[20]

It seems clear that the administrator of an institution for the mentally retarded failed to understand the significance of the fact that the method chosen by the facility to achieve a particular purpose was experimental, and that accordingly different factors enter into the determination as to its use and the parameters of the informed consent required before its employment.

CAPACITY TO CONSENT

In general, "every human being of adult years and sound mind has a right to determine what shall be done with his own body."[21] Thus, the competent adult has the right to choose the course of his care and to be apprised of the facts necessary to make that choice.[22] This is true even though the reason for a particular medical decision may seem irrational when viewed objectively. For example, in *Palm Springs General Hospital v. Martinez*,[23] the court determined that a conscious adult patient who was mentally competent had the right to refuse medical treatment involving surgery and blood transfusions, although medical opinion deemed the procedures necessary to save her life.[24]

Institutionalization in a facility for the mentally deficient and legal incompetence are not necessarily synonymous.[25] Thus, the institutionalized individual is often deemed to have the same legal ability to exercise his rights as a free-living person.[26]

This principle has been recognized by court action in a number of states.[27] In the recent case of *Horacek v. Exon*,[28] it was determined that all mentally retarded persons in Nebraska, including those institutionalized, have the same rights as all other persons in that state. The court in *McAuliffe v. Carlson*[29] ruled that the Connecticut statute which provided for the appointment of the state Commissioner of Finance as conservator for the funds of residents of mental institutions was unconstitutional because the conservator was appointed without any hearing to determine that the resident was incompetent to manage his own affairs. A somewhat similar process for state management of patient finances was struck down in *Vecchione v. Wohlgemuth*,[30] based on the court's determination that the fact of institutionalization does not in and of itself create a status of incompetency. Furthermore, courts have held that the sole fact of residence in an institution for the retarded does not render a person ineligible to register to vote.[31]

This principle is applicable to the ability of an institutionalized patient to give or withhold consent to medical treatment. In the case of *In re Yetter*,[32] a sixty-year-old involuntarily committed mental patient declined to consent to a recommended surgical breast biopsy. Her fears were based on the death of an aunt following such surgery (although the court was presented evidence indicating that the aunt had died fifteen years following the surgery from unrelated causes), as well as the concern that the operation would interfere with her genital system, affecting her ability to have babies, and would prohibit a movie career. Although her reasoning was becoming somewhat delusional, the court found that at the time the patient made her initial decision not to have the surgery, she was lucid, rational, and had the ability to understand the recommended procedure and the possible consequences of her refusal, including the risk of death. Even though it indicated that the patient's decision in this situation might be "irrational and foolish," the court nevertheless determined that Yetter was competent to reach this conclusion, and therefore declined to appoint a guardian for her for the purpose of consenting to the surgery. The court stated that the mere commitment of an individual to a state facility does not destroy the person's competency nor require the appointment of a guardian.

Several states, such as California,[33] Minnesota,[34] Michigan,[35] Massachusetts,[36] New York,[37] Oklahoma,[38] South Carolina,[39] South Dakota,[40] and Tennessee,[41] have statutes which specify that institutionalization is not automatically equivalent to incompetency. Other state statutes deal with the question on an issue-by-issue basis, determining whether institutionalization renders an individual incompetent for a particular purpose. Thus, for example, mental patients are specifically given the right to vote in South Carolina,[42] South Dakota,[43] New Mexico,[44] Louisiana,[45] Kentucky,[46] Alaska,[47] Georgia,[48] Maryland,[49] and New York,[50] the right to contract in South Carolina,[51] Louisiana,[52] Kentucky,[53] and Alaska,[54] the right to marry in South Carolina,[55] and the right to make a will in South Carolina[56] and Georgia.[57]

However, the laws in a number of states still envision the mental patient as one who is and will continue to be devoid of all ability to comprehend or exercise any rights.[58] A number of states have blanket restrictions on the right to marry, vote, contract, drive, or conduct one's affairs, giving little regard to the particular individual's capacities to exercise those rights.[59] For example, a West Virginia law provides that "[t]he entry of an order ordering hospitalization for an indeterminate period shall relieve the patient of legal capacity,"[60] while a Wisconsin law provides that "[h]ospitalization under this chapter, whether by voluntary admission or commitment . . . raises a rebuttable or disputable presumption of incompetency while the patient is under the jurisdiction of hospital authorities."[61] The rights to vote, make a will, contract, or marry are restricted in Alabama, Arkansas,[63] Maine,[64] and New Jersey.[65]

Overall, the state of the law in this area may be summarized as follows:

The effect in law of a hospitalization order on the competency status of a patient varies from state to state. In a few states the hospitalization order is also an adjudication of incompetency; in others, it results in at least a presumptive incapacity; and in still others, there is a complete separation of hospitalization and incompetency. . . . In many states the effect of a hospitalization order on competency cannot be determined from the written law, [but] the trend in legislation during the last 15 years has been toward a complete separation of hospitalization and incompetency.[66]

It may reasonably be concluded that mental patients are not presumptively incompetent in *most* jurisdictions.

In general, therefore, as concerns a therapeutic[67] biomedical or behavioral procedure, informed consent is needed prior to its performance. This consent is to be obtained from the patient, unless he is a minor or has been judicially declared an incompetent, in which case the requisite consent is obtained from his parent or legal guardian, respectively. This substitute consent is valid since, by definition, a therapeutic procedure is for the benefit of the individual.[68] Thus, if an incompetent mental patient needed an appendectomy, the substitute consent of his guardian would be sufficient.[69] In regard to nontherapeutic procedures, while informed consent is still a prerequisite, this consent may only be secured from a competent patient himself. Since the procedure is not for the patient's benefit, proxy consent is not sufficient.

BARRIERS TO CAPACITY

Effects of "Institutionalization"
The problem of whether an institutionalized individual is competent to consent is complicated by various factors. In the first place, the very fact that the individual is institutionalized may have a practical effect on the issue of competency. This is due to the results of a process termed "institutionalization." People who are cordoned off from the outside world are often effectively stripped of their concept of "self," a perception which is vital in order to satisfy the demands of informed consent. Erving Goffman, in his book *Asylums*,[70] discusses the effects of "total institutions."

> In total institutions there is a basic split between a large managed group, conveniently called inmates, and a small supervisory staff. Inmates typically live in the institution and have restricted contact with the world outside the walls; staff often operate on an eight-hour day and are socially integrated into the outside world. Each grouping tends to conceive of the other in terms of narrow hostile stereotypes, staff often seeing inmates as bitter, secretive, and untrustworthy, while inmates often see staff as condescending, high-handed, and mean. Staff tends to feel superior and righteous; inmates tend, in some ways at least, to feel inferior, weak, blameworthy, and guilty.[71]

This may result not only in lowered self-esteem, but in a diminution of decision-making power as well.[72] The total effects of this can be devastating. For example, a report by the Michigan Auditor General on the Caro Residential Center for the Mentally Retarded found at least five people in that facility who were not retarded but had been institutionalized for so long that the Center felt that they would not be capable of living in the outside world.[73]

Further complicating this situation is the element of duress present within the institution whenever an attempt is made to obtain consent. Physicians are often able to "engineer" consent from their patients/subjects by manipulation of their "fiduciary" relationship. In addition, a patient will often be swayed by hopes of influence with institutional authorities or release from an indeterminate commitment—even if these things were never promised nor even mentioned by the physician in his discussions with the individual. The supreme inducement to consent is the hope of obtaining freedom. This is revealed in the words of a former mental patient, "I played the game of patient .to wits end, as the only means of escape."[74] The institutional setting makes it difficult for one not to feel some sort of coercion or encouragement to consent merely in being approached for the particular procedure. This is particularly true for those individuals who see little or no hope of their eventual release, but who are assured that this particular treatment may make this possible.

This was the situation under consideration in *Kaimowitz v. Department of Mental Health.*[75] The controversy arose with a proposal for a research project designed to compare the effectiveness of psychosurgery and drug therapy for stopping uncontrollable agression in chronically violent wards of the state. The chemical method involved the administration of cyproterone acetate, a drug which renders the patient impotent as well as docile. The surgical procedure was to have consisted of measuring waves on an electroencephalogram to determine whether the patient's brain manifested a disturbance that could be charted. If so, electrodes would have been inserted into his brain to determine if the condition was generalized or localized. If generalized, no further action would have been taken; if localized, the amygdala would have been removed by electrocoagulation, a sophisticated form of surgery involving the burning out rather than the cutting out of the alleged affected parts.[76]

The original program outline was to include twenty-four patients. The subjects were all to be non-psychotic brain damaged males who had not responded to traditional treatment and who were deemed to be capable of understanding and deciding whether they wanted to undergo the treatment. The first subject chosen was thirty-six-year-old Louis Smith, a criminal sexual psychopath who had been in state institutions for the criminally insane for seventeen years after confessing to murder and rape. Both Smith and his parents signed the following detailed consent form.

Since conventional treatment efforts over a period of several years have not enabled me to control my outbursts of rage and anti-social behavior, I submit an application to be a subject in a research project which may offer me a form of effective therapy. This therapy is based upon the idea that episodes of anti-social rage and sexuality might be triggered by a disturbance in certain portions of my brain. I understand that in order to be certain that a significant brain disturbance exists, which might relate to my anti-social behavior, an initial operation will have to be performed. This procedure consists of placing fine wires into my brain, which will record the electrical activity from those structures which play a part in anger and sexuality. These electrical waves can then be studied to determine the presence of an abnormality.

In addition electrical stimulation with weak currents passed through these wires will be done in order to find out if one or several points in the brain can trigger my episodes of violence or unlawful sexuality. In other words this stimulation may cause me to want to commit an aggressive or sexual act, but every effort will be made to have a sufficient number of people present to control me. If the brain disturbance is limited to a small area, I understand that the investigators will destroy this part of my brain with an electrical current. If the abnormality comes from a larger part of my brain, I agree that it should be surgically removed, if the doctors determine that it can be done so, without risk of side effects. Should the electrical activity from the parts of my brain into which the wires have been placed reveal that there is no significant abnormality the wires will simply be withdrawn.

I realize that any operation on the brain carries a number of risks which may be slight, but could be potentially serious. These risks include infection, bleeding, temporary or permanent weakness or paralysis of one or more of my legs or arms, difficulties with speech and thinking, as well as the ability to feel, touch, pain and temperature. Under extraordinary circumstances, it is also possible that I might not survive the operation.

Fully aware of the risks detailed in the paragraphs above, I authorize the physicians of Lafayette Clinic and Providence Hospital to perform the procedures as outlined above.[77]

Conventional therapies had been considered to be ineffective for treatment of Smith's condition. Therefore, although he was later released from the institution on the basis of the court's conclusion that he could be safely returned to society,[78] the psychosurgery appeared at the time to be the only possible hope for securing his freedom.

The court adopted the Nuremberg Code as a guide in its determinations.[79] Therefore, it concluded that, in order for the informed consent of an individual to be valid, the three necessary components —competency, voluntariness, and knowledge—must be present.[80]

In its consideration of competence, the court did not maintain that a mental patient is automatically legally incompetent. Instead, the court found that the process of institutionalization and the dependency which often accompanies residence in a mental hospital lead to an atrophying of a patient's decision-making powers, rendering him incapable of making decisions as serious and complex as whether to undergo experimental psychosurgery. As concerns voluntariness, the court considered the issue in relation to the institutional setting. If perceived that a captive person unavoidably views any cooperation with his keepers as a potential key to release.[81] Even in the absence of direct pressure from institutional authorities, the realities of confinement and total institutional control over every minute detail of a patient's life[82] create an inherently coercive environment. In this setting, the potential subject is not "able to exercise free power of choice, without the intervention of force . . . or other ulterior form of constraint or coercion."[83] The fact that Smith, upon his release from the institution, revoked his consent to the psychosurgery, adds credence to the court's point of view.[84] With respect to the knowledge factor, the court considered expert testimony about the complexity of the brain, and evidenced concern about the lack of extensive animal and human experimentation in determining and studying brain function. It viewed the risks and benefits of psychosurgery as profoundly uncertain, and held that "lack of knowledge on the subject makes a knowledgeable consent to psychosurgery literally impossible."[85]

There are various problems with the court's reasoning. To begin with, if institutionalization leads to the deterioration of decision-making abilities, thereby rendering a patient incompetent to consent to experimental psychosurgery, it would seem that this same condition would render the person incompetent to make other important and complex decisions. Yet any extension of this concept beyond the specific facts of the case would be unacceptable because it would practically resurrect the notion that mental patient status *per se* establishes legal incompetence (at least as to those patients who have been institutionalized for a long period of time) —a notion that is rapidly losing credence in the law.

Similarly, the court's conception of coercion has disturbing possible ramifications. If the chance for release is the coercive element behind consent to psychosurgery, then it may also be viewed as such in relation to other, more generally accepted forms of therapy. Involuntary commitment could therefore be considered to coerce all decisions to engage in therapy, thereby making all such decisions invalid.

In its discussion of knowledge, the court, as noted earlier, found that the lack of knowledge about experimental brain surgery makes knowledgeable consent to experimental psychosurgery impossible to obtain. However, the consent form signed by the patient was extremely detailed, listing numerous serious risks, including the possibility of death. It may be argued that such a complete form adequately notifies the patient of the potential risks involved in psychosurgery, since it is practically impossible to inform a subject of hazards which are unknown to the medical profession generally when a proposed treatment involves innovative procedures. This interpretation of the knowledge element of informed consent is unprecedented, and has yet to be followed by another court.

Furthermore, the court concluded that, when psychosurgery is no longer considered experimental but becomes an accepted neurosurgical practice, an involuntarily committed mental patient can give legally binding informed consent to its performance. However, this seems to weaken the court's earlier discussion of the effect of institutionalization on the elements of competence and voluntariness. The presence of added knowledge concerning psychosurgery and its possible risks and benefits should have no effect on whether the patient can give voluntary and competent consent to the procedure.[86]

Ultimately, the decision of the court may be seen as a condemnation of choices, the consequences of which it deems unacceptable. Thus, choices considered beneficial typically are sustained despite the presence of many of those same elements which negated the effectiveness of the patient's consent in the present case. If the conditions of the entire situation are regarded as reasonable, the consent will not usually be legally condemned. Thus, psychosurgery, because it is experimental, drastic, and irreversible, with no known lasting benefits and many possible unknown side effects, is at present considered by this court to be an inappropriate and impermissible treatment or research choice for involuntarily confined patients. It is reasonable for patients to submit to generally accepted therapy, but it is unreasonable for them to submit to no-benefit or low-benefit, high-risk experimentation.

Ability to "Comprehend"
Another troubling factor influencing the issue of competency is the fact that there are numerous levels of mental retardation and mental illness, ranging from rather mild to severe, found within

each facility. It is estimated, for example, that eighteen percent of the mentally retarded residents of institutions are either mildly or borderline retarded, while another twenty-two percent are moderately retarded.[87] These individuals are capable of a relatively independent life, as opposed to the severely and profoundly retarded, who range from those who may function under sheltered conditions to those who are completely helpless. The same holds true for the difference in the level of functions of the various groups of mentally ill. The severely mentally ill constitute only about one percent of the total hospital population.[88] Many forms of mental illness have a highly specific impact, leaving the decision-making capacity and reasoning of the involved individuals largely unimpaired.[89] In addition, while the condition of the mentally retarded, which is often due to deficiencies from infancy, can usually be improved with programs of care and rehabilitation, it is a relatively stable and constant condition, not subject to the same possibility for rapid, frequent, and complete change in mental capacity as is the case with mental illness. A mentally ill patient may be competent to consent one day and yet become incompetent the next. An acute onslaught of particular forms of mental illness are often possible, so that a patient's condition can change dramatically in a very short period of time.

Finally, it is not always easy to distinguish competency from incompetency. Although a particular patient may not have been judicially determined to be incompetent, from a practical viewpoint it may be impossible to gain adequate consent from him. For example, how does one obtain consent from a severely ill catatonic schizophrenic who sits and stares at a blank wall all day, refusing to speak to anyone? Certainly if a patient is psychotic or hallucinating and cannot assimilate information about a proposed procedure, he does not have the capacity to reach a decision about the matter in question. Some mental patients are incapable of evaluating information in what most people would call a rational manner. A treatment decision might ordinarily be based on considerations of perceived personal objectives, or long-term versus short-term risks and benefits. But there are patients whose acceptance or rejection of a treatment is not made in relation to any "factual" information. To add to this dilemma, while a mental patient may refuse to give his consent to a procedure, his refusal may only be a manifestation of his illness, having little resemblance to his actual desires.

A possible solution to this problem has been offered by one commentator, who suggested that persons incapable of giving consent should be treated with the least intrusive therapies until they learn "to appreciate the value of treatment and those who offer it."[90]

Another possibility would be to bring all people falling within this category to court for a competency hearing. If found incompetent, a guardian could then be appointed. Problems with this approach include the fact that the procedure would be burdensome and time-consuming. In addition, it may be an instance of "overkill." Does one really want to subject the patient to the stigma of the incompetency label, as well as the removal of many of his rights, under these circumstances? Beyond that, many of these individuals would probably not meet the standards necessary for declaring someone legally incompetent. Persons who are mentally handicapped may have impaired functioning in some areas but be perfectly functional and competent in others.

Another way of approaching the predicament would be to, on a procedure-by-procedure basis, classify legally competent patients who are potential subjects into two groups: those having the capacity to give consent and those not having that capacity either because of an inability to communicate or because of their illness. Those in the second group would be subjects in the experiment if a neutral decision-maker decided it was in their best interest.

In determining which patients are members of which category, one could define the requisite competency in a number of ways. For example, one could require the reviewer to determine whether the patient's decision was one which a reasonably competent person would have made.[91] Competency could be defined as the capacity to understand the nature of the procedure, to weigh the risks and benefits, and to reach a decision for rational reasons.[92] The reviewer could be obliged to honor the patient's decision so long as he had a sufficient understanding of the nature of the procedure, its risks and benefits, and the possible alternatives.[93] Alternatively, competency could simply be defined as the ability to understand and knowingly act upon the information provided.[94]

The goal in choosing a standard of competency is to enhance self-autonomy and guard against paternalism, while simultaneously providing for added protection in determining the best interest of the patient when necessary. Any determination of what personalities and traits are considered worthy of protection is highly subjective. Unfortunately, too little attention has been focused on this problem to date.

PROXY CONSENT

Individuals who are legally incompetent are precluded from making legally binding determinations concerning medical care. The fact that the person has not reached the age of majority is usually taken to mean that he does not have the intelligence and capability to comprehend fully the nature and purpose of a procedure or to engage in the weighing of risks and benefits which is involved in the decision-making process. The same holds true for someone who, as the result of a judicial hearing, has been declared legally incompetent to manage his own affairs, and has therefore had a guardian appointed for him. Thus is created a situation in which other parties, the parents for the child and the court-appointed guardian for the adjudicated mentally incompetent adult, assume this function for him. The purpose of this is the protection of the incompetent individual from harm that might result from either his own lack of knowledge or from coercive methods used to obtain his consent. However, under the common law, guardian consent on behalf of an incompetent may only be granted or withheld on the sole basis of the incompetent's welfare. Indeed, the judgment of the guardian regarding the incompetent's best interests is not always conclusive, and the courts will intervene to protect the welfare of the incompetent.[95] Therefore, the state, exercising its ultimate responsibility for the welfare of the mentally deficient under the doctrine of *parens patriae*, which provides that the state has the duty to care for those individuals who are not able to do so themselves, will intervene when the question arises as to whether the guardian has acted in the best interest of his ward.[96] A more detailed discussion of proxy consent may be found in the earlier chapter of this book dealing with children.[97] The general conclusions in that analysis are applicable to the area of mental patients as well.

However, the proxy consent scheme runs into a number of serious problems when one considers it in relation to institutionalized mentally ill and mentally retarded persons. For example, there is the question as to whether the parent/guardian has both the motivation and capability to represent the best interests of the institutionalized incompetent. Implicit in the guardianship status is the belief that there is an identity or, at least, compatibility of interest between the guardian and incompetent. In addition, it is assumed that the guardian has the ability to care for and deal with the incompetent and represent him in his dealings with society in general and the institution in particular.[98]

There may be a conflict of interest between the guardian and ward so as to preclude adequate representation of the institutionalized person's interests. Thus, the parent/guardian may have been the individual who originally "voluntarily" placed a minor/incompetent in the facility. There are many societal pressures that operate to induce this, including mental and physical frustration, economic stress, hostility toward the individual stemming from added pressures, and perceived stigma of mental deficiency.[99] Often, the individual is institutionalized less for his own benefit than for the comfort of others. Similarly, the guardian may have been the initiator of involuntary commitment proceedings against the incompetent. In general, the fact of institutionalization affords the guardian the opportunity to "distance" himself from his ward and to deal with the situation in an abstract manner, thereby absolving himself from responsibility because the incompetent is entrusted to an institution.

Additionally, the particular guardian may be unable to deal effectively with the public and private institutional providers of service due to the disparity in leverage and sophistication that normally exists between guardian and institution. The guardian may be hesitant to counter the requests of the institution because the person in the facility is constantly subject to the threat of subtle, or not so subtle, retaliation. Moreover, the guardian may worry that if he disturbs the institutional authorities, the incompetent may, under certain circumstances, be released and perhaps thereby become a direct burden on the guardian.

Accordingly, in making provisions for the application of proxy consent on behalf of an institutionalized mental patient, one should always be aware of these potential conflicts. Particularly as regards consent to experimentation, consent by proxy should be viewed with suspicion, and should not be accepted as valid and legally adequate until it has been critically reviewed to assure that it serves its original purpose, *i.e.*, the protection of the interests of the individual subject.

THERAPEUTIC EXPERIMENTATION

Biomedical Procedures

There is little statutory or case law dealing specifically with experimentation on institutionalized mental patients. Therefore, it is necessary to analogize to the factors involved in the nonexperimental situation. While this is worthwhile, it is also potentially dangerous. One must always keep in mind that, theoretically at least, in the nonexperimental situation the physician's only concern is the patient's well-being. With an experiment, not only are there usually more uncertainties and greater risks, but the physician who contemplates the procedure is motivated in part or entirely by a search for scientific knowledge of general applicability. The physician-patient relationship is altered by the broadened objectives of the physician-researcher, who may no longer be sufficiently disinterested to be an objective participant. Thus, it is likely that, with informed consent, the law will be stricter and more protective of the subject's rights in its analysis of the experimental situation. The main codes of ethics which guide researchers in their work with human subjects—the Nuremberg Code (1948), the American Medical Association Code (1946 and 1966), and the Declaration of Helsinki (1964)[100]—all base their protections ultimately on the adequacy of informed consent.[101]

As stated earlier,[102] in general, informed consent is necessary before the performance of a therapeutic medical procedure. This consent may take the form of an assent by a competent patient or an assent by a guardian for an incompetent patient.

A number of states have passed statutes which specifically limit the performance of certain medical procedures, usually surgery, without the consent of the patient.[103] However, several statutes also provide for proxy consent to such medical procedures, seemingly regardless of whether the patient is deemed to be legally incompetent. For example, Tennessee provides that surgery may be performed if the consent of either the patient, parent, guardian, or next-of-kin is obtained.[104] Several states allow substitute consent when the patient is incompetent or of "unsound mind" to give consent, but most do not go on to define incompetent so as to indicate whether it is confined to those situations in which the patient has been adjudicated incompetent.[105] In Alaska, the head of the hospital makes the competency determination, and on this basis may substitute the consent of a parent, spouse, or guardian for that of the patient.[106] As can be seen, not only is proxy consent permitted under these questionable circumstances, but the person given this authority is expanding beyond the confines of a legal guardian to include parents of children who have reached majority, spouses, and even just the next-of-kin. Indeed, in New Jersey, the head of the institution can consent to physician-prescribed medical, surgical and dental treatment for the inmates of the facility.[107]

The problem of developing procedures for the resolution of treatment decisions for incompetent mental patients is presently being considered by the Massachusetts Supreme Judicial Court. It involves the review of an order by the Probate Court for Hampshire County which prohibited the administration of chemotherapy to Joseph Saikewicz, a profoundly retarded sixty-seven-year-old man who had resided in a state institution for approximately fifty years. He had an I.Q. of 10 and a mental age equivalent to a child aged two years and eight months, and therefore could not consent to medical treatment. It had recently been discovered that Saikewicz was suffering from acute myeloblastic monocytic leukemia, a terminal illness for which the only known treatment is the use of chemotherapy.[108]

The director of the institution petitioned the court for permission to have Saikewicz treated. A guardian *ad litem* and the treating physicians recommended against treatment. They argued that, because of his age and his inability to cooperate with the treatment, Saikewicz would have only a thirty to fifty percent chance of achieving a two to thirteen-month remission. In addition, the treatments would cause great pain and suffering.[109] The state argued that it had an obligation to protect life and treat the patient, especially given the testimony that the large majority of competent individuals would choose treatment.[110] However, the court ruled that Saikewicz should not be given chemotherapy.[111]

On appeal to the state's highest court, the state not only filed a brief in favor of treatment, but also gained permission to file one against treatment, an occurrence which was unprecedented in Massachusetts legal history.[112] In its "con" position, the state said that, although the court is expected to act in the best interest of an incompetent person, there may be circumstances under which the interests of an incompetent are best served by withholding treatment. It argued that the Saikewicz situation came within this category, since it maintained that the record of the case established the "net disutility" of treatment for the patient.[113]

The Supreme Judicial Court unanimously ruled that the Probate Court had the power to make the treatment decision for Saikewicz. In a split decision, the court decided that the lower court had ruled correctly in ordering treatment withheld.[114]

The court has asked for further briefs on the question of how it might establish guidelines for deciding such cases in the future.[115] The court is considering a suggestion by plaintiffs that decisions regarding medical treatment for incompetent persons in state institutions generally be made by medical personnel through the use of a Medical Ethics Committee reviewing the recommendation of a temporary guardian.[116] The Civil Rights and Liberties Division of the State Attorney General's office, which had previously filed the "con" brief, maintains that decisions regarding the treatment of incompetent individuals who have terminal diseases, or who have illnesses for which the proposed treatment is experimental or has severe toxic side effects, should be made by the judiciary in a formal adversary procedure. It would then be the responsibility of the court to decide, based on its obligation to protect the best interest of the patient, whether or not to approve treatment for the patient.[117] The written opinion in the case, which will help resolve the dilemma in this area, was not available as of this writing.

There is evidence that certain therapeutic procedures may be given separate and different consideration by the law. For example, let us consider the case of sterilization.

It is possible that the sterilization of an incompetent individual may be deemed to be "therapeutic," or in his best interests. For those incompetents who do not have the requisite mental capacity to adequately use alternative forms of birth control, sterilization may be the only viable option for preventing pregnancy. There may be medical reasons preventing the adoption of other birth control options, as well as social and psychological information which contraindicate these methods.

Regardless of this, the court in *Relf v. Weinberger*[118] decided that the consent of a representative of a mentally incompetent individual cannot impute voluntariness to a person actually undergoing irreversible sterilization.[119] This finding was based on the determination that, at least when important human rights are at stake, there is a requirement that "the individual have at his disposal the information necessary to make his decision and the mental competence to appreciate the significance of that information."[120] Therefore, since the federal statute under consideration only permitted federally-assisted family planning sterilizations on a voluntary basis, the court held that they cannot be performed on any person incompetent to personally consent to the procedure. Thus, proxy consent to sterilization was found not to be voluntary consent, seemingly regardless of whether the particular sterilization was considered therapeutic or not. In a further development in this case, the court in *Relf v. Mathews*[121] rejected proposed modifications of its previous judgment. The court noted that it intended to implement its decision that federal funds be available for sterilizations only for persons having the necessary capacity to decide voluntarily and free of coercion, and that the modifications were designed to substitute a universal federal standard of voluntariness which would permit sterilization of persons eighteen years of age and older even where such persons were otherwise incompetent in fact because of age or mental condition under state standards. Similarly, the sterilization guidelines of the New York Health and Hospitals Corporation absolutely prohibit sterilization of women who are legally incompetent.[122]

In *Wyatt v. Aderholt*,[123] a three-judge federal court declared that the Alabama involuntary sterilization statute is unconstitutional. In addition, it promulgated guidelines for the voluntary sterilization of institutionalized mental patients. Initially, the court determined that, not only must the sterilization be in the "best interest" of the resident, but it also may not be performed without the consent of the person to be sterilized if he is competent to consent. If the individual is incompetent, the court does not allow guardian/proxy consent, even though the procedure must be, according to the guidelines, in the best interest of the ward, and therefore traditionally within the scope of authority of a guardian. Instead, the court provides that sterilization may not be performed under these circumstances unless it is approved by the director of the institution, a review committee, *and* a court of competent jurisdiction.[124]

This principle of protecting the incompetent's interests by requiring court review was followed by the court in *In re Anderson*.[125] In this case, the father and guardian of a mentally retarded woman petitioned the court for an order authorizing him to consent to her sterilization. In denying the petition, the court stated that sterilization may only be performed when it is in the person's best interest, and that, regardless of this, the authorization to sterilize may not come from the guardian but only from a court after a full evidentiary hearing.

Thus, there is authority for the performance of serious therapeutic medical procedures upon a mental patient without his consent. However, there is also authority for the proposition that certain medical procedures are by their very nature so important and intrusive that either proxy consent will not be found valid at all, or it will only be allowed in the context of stringent procedural safeguards. While this has been found to be the case with irreversible sterilization, it is unclear exactly which other procedures would be included in this category. However, it seems clear that, the more drastic the procedure and its possible effect upon the patient and the exercise of his rights, the more likely that the stricter standards will apply.

Behavior Modification

The problem of consent becomes even more complex when one considers behavior modification procedures. The term behavior modification at one time had a precise and narrowly defined meaning.[126] Its underlying principle was that behavior is primarily influenced by its consequences, so that in order to change behavior, it is necessary to alter the consequences of that behavior. However, in recent years it has come to mean *all* of the ways in which human behavior is modified, changed, or influenced, and that is the definition which will be used for purposes of this book. Therefore, behavior modification may include milieu therapy, psychotherapy, positive reinforcement, token economy programs, aversive conditioning, as well as electroconvulsive therapy, injection of psychoactive drugs, and psychosurgery.[127] In this sense, behavior modification is used to refer only to the end product of the process—a change in behavior.

Initially, one may begin with the assumption that the analysis made earlier is valid here,[128] *i.e.*, a mental patient has the power to consent or withhold consent to behavior modification, unless he is legally incompetent, in which case a guardian can consent to those procedures which are for his benefit.

Thus, in *Winters v. Miller,*[129] an involuntarily committed mental patient alleged that her rights had been violated due to the imposition of forced medication, mostly in the form of tranquilizers. Although the court based its decision on First Amendment grounds, in that the patient was a Christian Scientist who was refusing to consent to the treatment on religious grounds, the court nevertheless emphasized the fact that, although Winters was involuntarily committed, she had never been legally determined to be incompetent, and therefore retained the ability to make her own choice concerning consent to treatment. Similarly, the court in *Belger v. Arnot*[130] found that the consent of the husband to the care and treatment of his wife's mental condition was not valid and did not bar an assault and battery action against the treating physician. Since the woman had never been declared legally incompetent, it was her consent which was essential.

However, the situation is complicated by consideration of the purpose behind institutionalization of mental patients.[131] The majority of hospitalized mental patients in the United States are involuntarily confined.[132] The statutory standards governing involuntary commitment vary greatly from state to state.[133] About thirty-five states provide for commitment of those people found to be "in need of care and treatment." This *parens patriae* theory has traditionally been held a proper state purpose.[134] Since 1845,[135] both courts and legislatures have generally assumed that the *parens patriae* power justifies the involuntary commitment of the mentally deficient for care and treatment and protection from harm.[136] Thus, under this rationale, an individual may be committed when he lacks the capacity to make a rational decision concerning hospitalization, and the treatment available would be sufficiently beneficial to outweigh the deprivations which commitment would impose. There is legal authority for the proposition that inherent in this exercise of the state's *parens patriae* power is the decision that the patient can be forced to accept treatments found to be in his best interest. Thus, under these circumstances, the concept of consent by the institutionalized individual becomes meaningless.

> It is widely assumed that the commitment of a person to a mental hospital . . . confers on the hospital administrators the authority to "treat" him in whatever manner they deem appropriate.[137]

The case of *Whitree v. State*[138] seems to support this view. The court held that a state hospital must provide treatment to a mental patient even if the patient will not consent to treatment. In its decision, the court stated:

> We find that he [Whitree] was not treated with any of the modern tranquilizing drugs or any of their less effective antecedents during his entire stay in the hospital. We find that the reason for not using such drugs was that Whitree refused them. We consider such reason to be illogical, unprofessional and not consonant with prevailing medical standards.[139]

If the above principle is accepted, the question follows whether this is applicable to all treatment offered under the *parens patriae* authority of the state, *i.e.*, in an attempt to treat the patient's mental condition, or whether it only applies to those procedures generally recognized and accepted as treatment modalities. The problem here is that the arts of rehabilitation and treatment are in a fairly primitive state.[140] For example, even trained personnel cannot accurately determine the most effective treatment in each instance.[141] Indeed, there is a growing skepticism of the mental health profession's ability to diagnose, treat, or even define various forms of mental illness.[142] There is also the predicament of the patient with a condition which is found not to be responsive to any of the traditional techniques. Thus, the range of available treatment will often be presented in the context of what may be considered experimental treatment and rehabilitation techniques.

However, some states allow involuntary commitment only if the individual is dangerous to himself or to others. The trend seems to be in the direction of requiring this standard as the prerequisite to involuntary commitment.[143] It would seem that such patients would maintain the ability to make treatment decisions.[144]

Moreover, what is the situation of the *voluntary* mental patient? It may be argued that such a patient has the legal right to make his own decisions concerning treatment. If he refuses to consent to recommended therapy, the facility may simply expel him unless the legal standards for an involuntary commitment proceeding can be met. The practical application of this principle may be difficult, since for many institutionalized mental patients the option of release is not a valid alternative, so they may often be as "forced" to give their consent to a procedure as an involuntary patient. Nevertheless, this does not change the premise that the ability to give or withhold consent is theirs.

Another view of this situation holds that, when a person is voluntarily committed, he cedes to his custodians all decisions concerning treatment during that confinement.[145] There are numerous difficulties with this. Again, the question arises as to whether this only is meant to include treatment within the bounds of generally accepted procedures, or whether experimental therapies are also encompassed. Next is the problem of withdrawal of consent. Does not the right to consent always imply the right to revoke? Although the patient may have impliedly consented to treatment upon commitment, can he not reverse his decision when later confronted with a particular therapy? Yet permitting this may result in no effective treatment at all, thereby frustrating the purpose of voluntary commitment. Finally, most voluntary commitments are voluntary only in that a parent or guardian (usually in these cases a state agency) volunteers his child or ward to be institutionalized.[146] Therefore, the actual patient has not chosen to be placed in the facility, and cannot be said to have personally consented to treatment. However, this situation appears to be changing, as several cases have held that minors may not be "voluntarily" committed to an institution without due process guidelines being observed.[147]

Indeed, the entire distinction between voluntary and involuntary hsopitalization is often murky. The majority of voluntary admittees enter "voluntarily" only under the threat of involuntary commitment, so that the situation actually involves substantial elements of coercion.[148] For example, in Massachusetts, most voluntary patients in institutions for the mentally ill are admitted as "conditional voluntary" patients.[149] This means that the patient must give three days notice to the superintendent of his intention to withdraw from the facility. However, if, during this time, the superintendent petitions the court to order the patient's involuntary commitment, the patient will remain institutionalized until a hearing on the matter is held.[150]

There have been some attempts to abolish the differentiation between voluntary and involuntary mental patients. For example, in *In re Buttonow*,[151] an inmate who had signed a contract to become a voluntary patient was held to be entitled to the safeguards which were given to involuntary patients. Some state mental health legislation specifically provide that a voluntary patient is entitled to the same rights and privileges as an involuntary patient.[152]

Yet there are indications that, for the more severe and intrusive behavior modification techniques, more protective consent mechanisms are legally required, regardless of whether the institution views the procedure as therapeutic and beneficial for the patient. The more the procedure is drastic and violative of self-determination, controversial and experimental, and seems akin to punishment, the more likely it is that these special requirements will arise.

In *Kaimowitz*,[153] the court held that the performance of psychosurgery on an involuntarily committed mental patient would violate his constitutional rights. The court noted that psychosurgery is "irreversible and intrusive, often leads to the blunting of emotions . . . and limits the ability to generate new ideas." In addition, the court noted that the surgery was experimental, posed unknown risks, and was not even known to be beneficial. Under these circumstances, although the surgery was recommended as the only available alternative which could possibly control the patient's hostility and aggressiveness, thereby giving him what was considered his only possibility of release from the facility, it was found that the procedure could not be performed in that the patient's consent was a necessary prerequisite.

In *Mackey v. Procunier*,[154] the plaintiff, a prisoner, alleged that he consented to electroshock therapy as a behavior modification technique. Instead of receiving this therapy, he was given succinylcholine, a drug generally used as an adjunct to electroshock and given while the patient is unconscious. Succinycholine is a terrifying drug that stops the patient's breathing and produces feelings of imminent death. The administration of the drug was part of an experimental design to test aversive therapy. The court held that proof of the administration of this particular experimental process without the patient's consent could "raise serious constitutional questions respecting cruel and unusual punishment or impermissible tinkering with the mental processes."[155]

Knecht v. Gillman[156] deals with the administration of the drug apomorphine to two prisoner-residents of the Iowa Security Medical Facility. The vomit-inducing drug was used on unconsenting patients as part of an aversive conditioning program for individuals with minor behavioral problems. Administration of apomorphine without informed consent was found to violate the patients' constitutional rights, and its administration was enjoined except with the written consent from the participant which could be withdrawn at any time.

The court in the recent case of *Scott v. Plante*[157] found that there are numerous constitutional deprivations which may accompany the administration, without his consent and against his will, of psychotherapeutic substances to a patient confined in a state mental institution. First, the involuntary administration of drugs which affect the mental processes could amount, under an appropriate set of facts, to an interference with the patient's rights under the First Amendment. Furthermore, although the patient under consideration may have been properly commitable, he had never been adjudicated an incompetent who would be incapable of giving informed consent to medical treatment. Therefore, due process would require, in the absence of an emergency, that some form of notice and opportunity to be heard be given to the patient or to someone standing *in loco parentis* to him before he could be subjected to such treatment. In addition, under certain conditions, such a claim could raise an Eighth Amendment issue respecting cruel and unusual punishment. Finally, a fourth possible constitutional deprivation might be an invasion of the patient's right to bodily privacy. Accordingly, the court held that the forced administration of drugs states a valid cause of action.

Similarly, the case of *New York Health and Hospitals Corporation v. Stein*[158] concerned an involuntarily committed mental patient's refusal to consent to electroshock therapy. The New York City Health and Hospitals Corporation and the director of the institution applied to the court for permission to administer the therapy without the patient's consent. Although the court took note of the possibility that, without this treatment, the patient's condition might become irreversible, the court seemed even more concerned with the fact that electroshock therapy is "the subject of great controversy within the psychiatric profession, both as to its efficacy, and as to its dangers."[159] The court concluded that, while the patient was sufficiently mentally ill to require further retention, she still had the requisite ability to consent or withhold consent to electroshock therapy, regardless of whether the court or others viewing the situation objectively would agree with her decision. Therefore, the application was denied. The requirement of patient consent prior to the provision of shock therapy has also been found by courts in *Mitchell v. Robinson*,[160] *Wilson v. Lehman*,[161] and *Aiken v. Clary*.[162]

Recently, a number of states have decided to deal with this situation by passing applicable statutes which require consent before the administration of particularly intrusive procedures. The most frequently regulated procedures are psychosurgery and electroconvulsive therapy.[163] Some states require informed consent prior to the administration of experimental drugs and other experimental procedures.[164]

However, many of those states which specifically require consent to these procedures also make allowances for the application of proxy consent by relatives, a guardian, or a court.[165] while others even allow these consent requirements to be overridden by the director of the mental institution. For example, Massachusetts requires the patient's consent to electroconvulsive therapy unless the superintendent determines that there is "good cause" for the therapy and the patient's guardian or nearest relative consents.[166]

In 1974, California passed a statute which specified the conditions under which psychosurgery and shock treatment could be performed.[167] Under its provisions, a patient had an absolute right to refuse psychosurgery. If he wanted the procedure to be performed, he had to have the capacity to consent and had to sign a written consent form. The physician was required to explain to the patient and a responsible relative, guardian or conservator the procedures used in the treatment, the benefits, risks, side effects, and their degree of uncertainty, the nature and seriousness of the patient's disorder, and the right of the patient to withdraw consent at any time. In addition, the physician was required to document his opinion that the treatment was critically needed, specifying his reasons for the procedures, and noting that all appropriate treatment modalities had been exhausted. The bill further established a review committee of three physicians which had to unanimously agree that the procedure was indicated and that the patient had the capacity to consent.[168] The provisions governing the use of shock treatment were similar, except that if the review committee determined that the patient did not have the capacity to give informed consent, documentation of the physician and approval by the review committee were sufficient to authorize treatment.[169] Thus, for the more intrusive and experimental procedure, psychosurgery, the state recognized only patient consent as valid, while for the less serious or dangerous treatment, shock therapy, the statute allowed proxy consent, although only following the application of certain safeguards.

Two mental patients and three physicians challenged the statute in court. Although finding that the regulation of such intrusive medical procedures is properly within the state's police power, the court in *Aden v. Younger*[170] held that the statute was unconstitutionally vague as concerns the treatment criterion, "critically needed for the welfare of the patient,"[171] and that the failure to provide for adequate notice of hearing was a denial of due process.[172]

The court spent considerable time in its analysis of informed consent. It considered the purpose of the law to be the protection of the right to refuse treatment and the prevention of unnecessary administration of hazardous and intrusive treatments.[173] It felt that the requirement of informing a relative concerning the treatment did nothing to accomplish this objective. Under the statute, the relative had no standing to further the rights of the patient, and was in no way directly involved in the consent decision. Therefore, the provision was found to be an invasion of the patient's right to privacy and confidentiality.[174]

However, the court had more trouble with the committee review requirement of the legislation. It was determined that the state's interest in protecting patients from the unconsented-to and unnecessary administration of psychosurgery justified a review procedure to insure the competence of the patient and the voluntary nature of his consent. Because incompetent patients cannot consent to the treatment, the review process was considered a valid means of protecting them from such procedures.[175] The proceeding was also upheld as concerns involuntary patients, since the voluntariness of the consent of this category of patients "can never be adequately confirmed."[176] Although the court expressed concern over the application of the section to competent, voluntary patients, it concluded that "the hazardous, experimental nature of psychosurgery" justified this regulation of its use.[177] The seriousness of psychosurgery's consequences and the fact that its effects may be so intrusive and irreversible, coupled with the importance of assuring that consent to the procedure is voluntarily given by informed, competent patients, led the court to find the review valid.[178]

However, the court reached a different conclusion as concerns the review of patient consent to shock treatment. As applied to involuntary patients, the court determined that the review was constitutional, again because of the difficulty in acquiring voluntary consent from this particular population.[179] The court also approved the proceeding in the case of incompetent patients, thereby permitting the use of shock therapy on patients who do not consent for themselves, but rather have the assent of the physician and review committee substituted for them.[180] Yet it found the review process unconstitutional as concerns competent and voluntary patients. It stated that, once the competency of a voluntary patient and the voluntary nature of his consent is determined, there is no longer any justification for such review. The court concluded that, since shock treatment is not experimental, nor is it as hazardous as psychosurgery, there was no reason for infringing upon the patient's right to privacy in making treatment decisions.[181]

Even though only certain sections of the statute were found to be unconstitutional, the impossibility of effectively severing the legislation led the court to declare the entire bill invalid.[182] However, this does not disturb the court's recognition that the requirement of specific procedures to safeguard the consent of certain mental patients to particularly intrusive treatments is a valid exercise of the state police power. Beyond that, the hazardous and experimental nature of psychosurgery enabled the court to approve the absolute requirement of patient consent to the procedure. On the other hand, the court's decision also approved the substitute of consent to shock treatment by a physician review committee for a patient who has not been judicially-declared incompetent. Indeed, the court had so little trouble with this particular provision that it actually did not discuss it in any detail.

The California legislature recently passed a new piece of legislation to replace the statute considered in *Aden*.[183] It answers many of the problems of the previous bill. As concerns consent, the provisions pertaining to psychosurgery remain the same. In dealing with shock therapy, patients are classified according to whether they were committed voluntarily or involuntarily. For an involuntary patient, a review committee similar to that in the previous statute must unanimously approve of the treatment.[184] If any of the legal representatives of the patient or the treatment physician doubt the patient's capacity to consent, he is entitled to a judicial hearing. If he is adjudicated as being incapable of giving consent, the right to do so passes to a legal guardian.[185] A voluntary patient could be given shock therapy if he consents and a physician other than the attending one verifies that the patient is competent and actually gave informed consent.[186] For those voluntary patients who do not have the capacity to give informed consent, the committee and judicial review requirements as they pertain to involuntary patients must also be met.[187] Thus, although it is still possible for a patient to be given shock treatment without his consent, the circumstances under which this is possible are more stringently regulated than before.

Beyond these statutory considerations, there are a few cases which permit proxy consent as well. Thus, in *Farber v. Olkon*,[188] the court found that the consent of the parent of an institutionalized adult child to shock therapy was legally sufficient. Again, in *Anonymous v. State*,[189] the consent of the father to shock therapy on his institutionalized child was upheld, even though the patient was thirty-four years old and had never been adjudged incompetent. Even the consent to shock treatment of one spouse for another who had not been declared legally incompetent has been found to be valid.[190]

The recent decision in *Price v. Sheppard*[191] takes a more complex view of the issue of consent than that exhibited in the previous cases. In this case, a minor was involuntarily committed to a mental institution, where his condition was diagnosed as simple schizophrenia. He was treated with tranquilizing and antidepressant medications, but apparently failed to respond and was instead aggressive and assaultive to the staff and other patients. His physician at the facility prescribed electroshock therapy, and sought the consent of the patient's mother to the procedure. Although the mother refused to give her consent, a series of twenty electroshock treatments was administered to the patient. An action was filed claiming that the administration of shock therapy to an involuntarily committed minor patient without the consent of the minor's guardian violated his right to be free from cruel and unusual punishment and his right of privacy. The court quickly dismissed the Eighth Amendment ground, stating that the electroshock therapy served the legitimate purpose of treatment, rather than being used as a deterrent or to reprimand the individual, so that the cruel and unusual punishment clause was inapplicable.

However, the court had more trouble with the issue of the right of privacy. Defining the concept as the right to conduct one's life free from governmental intrusion, it nevertheless stated that this was not an absolute right, and must therefore give way to certain legitimate and important state interests. The balancing process involved here was seen as turning on "the impact of the decision on the life of the individual. As the impact increases, so must the importance of the state's interest."[192] In addition, the means utilized in serving this interest must, in light of the alternatives, be the least intrusive.[193] In applying this principle to the situation under consideration, the court determined that the impact of the decision as to whether the patient will undergo psychiatric treatment is enormous, since the result may be the alteration of the patient's personality. The state's interest involved in assuming the decision is in the performance of its *parens patriae* function, or the fulfilling of its duty to protect the well-being of its citizens "who are incapable of so acting for themselves."[194] The court concluded that, if this state interest is sufficiently important to allow it to deprive an individual of his physical liberty, it followed that it would be important enough for the state to assume the treatment decision, as long as the means chosen was necessary and reasonable under the circumstances of a particular patient's case.

Yet while the court upheld the right of the state to administer treatment to an involuntarily committed mental patient without the consent of the patient or his guardian, it nevertheless declined to leave this decision solely within the discretion of institutional personnel when it involved the imposition of the more intrusive forms of treatment. Therefore, the court mandated that, in future cases, if the patient is incompetent to give consent or refuses consent or his guardian refuses to consent, before more intrusive forms of treatment may be utilized, the medical director of the institution must petition the court for an order authorizing treatment. A guardian *ad litem* is to be appointed to represent the interests of the patient, and during an adversary proceeding, the court is to determine the necessity and reasonableness of the prescribed treatment. In making this determination, the decision stated that the patient's need for treatment should be balanced against the intrusiveness of the procedure, and included a list of six factors to be considered in this determination:

(1) The extent and duration of changes in behavior patterns and mental activity effected by the treatment.

(2) The risks of adverse side effects.

(3) The experimental nature of the treatment.

(4) Its acceptance by the medical community of the state.

(5) The extent of intrusion into the patient's body and the pain connected with the treatment.

(6) The patient's ability to competently determine for himself whether the treatment is desirable.[195]

The court did not clearly establish how one would determine which forms of treatment are so intrusive as to require this procedural hearing. It did, however, state that the use of mild tranquilizers or those therapies requiring the cooperation of the patient would certainly not fall within this category, while psychosurgery and electroshock therapy would definitely be included.

Therefore, even though the court in *Price* permits the administration of electroshock therapy without the patient's consent, it nevertheless requires a detailed and elaborate system of review, and authorizes the use of this procedure only with the proxy consent of a court. Significantly, in making its authorization decision, one of the elements to be considered by a court is the *experimental* nature of the procedure. Accordingly, it seems that the more experimental the proposed treatment, the more likely it is that the individual's privacy right will outweigh the state's interest in providing treatment, so that the state, or court, would not have the authority to authorize its administration.

The court in *Wyatt v. Stickney*[196] attempted to resolve the dilemma in this area. This important case dealt with a class action on be-half of patients involuntarily confined in institutions for the mentally ill and mentally retarded. The court found that these individuals have a constitutional right to treatment, and furthermore that conditions in the respective institutions were such as to deprive the patients of this right. Accordingly, the court issued sets of minimum constitu-tional standards for the adequate treatment of both the mentally ill and mentally retarded.

Included in these standards were provisions which state that patients of institutions for the mentally ill have "a right not to be subjected to treatment procedures such as lobotomy, electroconvul-sive treatment, adversive reinforcement conditioning or other un-usual or hazardous treatment procedures without their express and informed consent after consultation with counsel or interested party of the patient's choice."[197] In addition, patients have "a right not to be subjected to experimental research without the express and informed consent of the patient, if the patient is able to give such consent, and of his guardian or next-of-kin, after opportunities for consultation with independent specialists and with legal coun-sel."[198] It is also necessary for the proposed research to have first been reviewed and approved by the institution's Human Rights Committee. It is unclear from the court's opinion whether this provision refers to therapeutic as well as nontherapeutic experi-mentation.

In regard to the institutionalized mentally retarded, the court formulated slightly different standards. Behavior modification pro-grams involving the use of noxious or adversive stimuli are to be reviewed and approved by the institution's Human Rights Com-mittee and are to be conducted only with the express and informed consent of the resident, if he is able to give such consent, and of his guardian or next-of-kin, after opportunities for consultation with independent specialists and legal counsel. The same procedure must be followed for unusual or hazardous treatment procedures. Elec-tric shock treatment is considered a research technique and is allowed only "in extraordinary circumstances to prevent self-mutilation . . . and only after alternative techniques have failed."[199] The pro-vision regarding experimental research is the same as for the men-tally ill.

Thus, the court in *Wyatt* recognized that certain behavior modifi-cation procedures may be deemed so offensive, frightening, or risky that their use should be restricted by requiring the patient's informed consent.[200] Although there are some provisions for proxy consent, the court nevertheless took steps to provide added layers of protection by requiring the opportunity for outside, independent consultation, as well as the involvement of a Human Rights Committee.

It seems that the cost of some therapies is considered too great, while others are considered acceptable. The problem comes in determining the boundaries of the two.[201] In deciding whether a particular procedure is so intrusive or coercive as to require these added protections, one commentator has suggested the following guidelines:

1. The extent and duration of changes in behavior patterns and mental activity effected by the therapy—the degree of change in personality.
2. The side effects associated with the therapy.
3. The extent to which the therapy requires physical intrusion into the inmate's body.
4. The degree of pain, if any, associated with the therapy.
5. The extent to which an uncooperative inmate can avoid the effcts of the therapy.[202]

Thus, informed consent is not a unitary concept. It will vary depending on the nature of the procedure for which it is requested. The more potentially harmful, intrusive, or experimental the procedure, the stricter and more numerous must be the safeguards to protect the individual. Thus, there is precedent for the scrutiny of potentially hazardous or intrusive "treatments" and for an attempt to delimit the conditions under which informed consent is obtained. Since each state has differing statutes and case law concerning the use of behavioral techniques, it is impossible to generalize as to the limitations which may be imposed. However, it is clear that there is a trend toward increased regulation and imposition of protection in this area.

In general, in order to protect a patient involved in an experimental procedure, there should be a review of his consent. This would ensure the competent and voluntary character of the consent. The closer that the institution came to meeting the constitutional minimum standard of *Wyatt v. Stickney*, the more likely it would be that, as concerns the effect of institutionalization on a patient's competence and voluntariness, the consent would be found to be valid. For an adjudicatively-found incompetent patient, this would review the best interest determination made by his guardian in his proxy consent decision. For the practically-incompetent patient, this would consist, not of a review of a consent decision by the patient or guardian, but of an original determination of the best interest of the patient. The categorizing of the patient as a member of this group could be made either at this level or, as an added means of protection, by an earlier determination by a separate review mechanism.

These review mechanisms may take several different forms. The director or superintendent of the facility could perform this function. However, there may be a possible conflict of interest problem here.

> A problem may also be presented by the possibility of role conflict aris-
> ing from the entrusting of the notice and explanation of right function
> to the same agency which undertakes to perform the therapeutic func-
> tion.[203]

Instead, a committee structure could be used, either totally independent of the institution or one composed partly of institutional administration and staff and partly of independent people. The committee could be patterned after the Human Rights Committee provided for in *Wyatt*. Alternatively, this review could be done by an agency specially created to protect mental patients' rights. Finally, there could be court review of the adequacy of these procedures. However, this last procedure might prove very costly and cumbersome, so that it might be best to reserve it for those cases in which particularly coercive or intrusive experiments are being considered.

NONTHERAPEUTIC EXPERIMENTATION

The earlier analysis of capacity to consent provides the basis for a discussion of nontherapeutic experimentation.[204] To briefly summarize, since nontherapeutic experimentation is, by definition, not for the benefit of the subject, no proxy consent is theoretically permissible. Therefore, unless the particular patient is legally competent to give informed consent, it would seem that there could be no nontherapeutic experimentation on institutionalized mental patients.

Thus, in *Frazier v. Levi*,[205] a mother, acting as guardian, sought a sterilization for her adult pregnant daughter, who had a mental age of six years, was sexually permissive, and had two retarded illegitimate children. Although the mother maintained that she was no longer financially and emotionally able to support any more of her daughter's children and that the operation would therefore be to everyone's benefit, she admitted that the operation was not medically necessary. The court refused to authorize the procedure and held that the daughter lacked the mental capacity to consent to the operation and that, without consent, she could not be deprived of her legal rights.[206]

The case of *A.L. v. G.R.H.*[207] involved a petition by a mother to receive authorization to order the sterilization of her son. The fifteen-year-old child had suffered brain damage as the result of being struck by an automobile during early childhood, and presently had an I.Q. of 83, which is considered to be within the "dull" or "borderline" area. However, the boy appeared capable of further improvement. Indeed, it seemed that he would eventually be capable of earning his own living either in specially supervised work or in entry-level jobs in the general marketplace. His mental disability would not be transmittable to his offspring, nor did he exhibit a propensity to force his attentions on others, although he had shown interest in social activity with girls. Expert testimony indicated that he was sufficiently intelligent to understand what was involved in sterilization and to participate in the decision-making process.[208]

The court decided that the facts of the case did not bring it within the legal principles which either permit parents to consent on behalf of their child to necessary medical services, or allow state intervention over the parents' wishes to rescue the child from parental neglect or to save his life. It maintained that the desirability of sterilization did not emanate from any life-saving necessities, but rather had as its sole purpose the prevention of the capability of fathering children. Thus, the court held that parents do not have the power to consent to sterilization of their children even though they believe that it would benefit the child, and accordingly affirmed the trial court's denial of the request.[209]

Similarly, in *In re Richardson*,[210] an action was brought by the parents of a minor retarded child to permit the donation of one of the child's kidneys for transplantation into the child's older sister. The mother, father, and older sister all consented to the procedure, but the mentally retarded child, having a mental age of a three- or four-year old, was not capable of giving legal consent. The court defined its duties to be the protection and promotion of the ultimate best interest of the child. In particular, it determined that the minor had a right to be free from bodily intrusion to the extent of the loss of an organ unless it was specifically found that the removal of the kidney was in the child's best interest. Rejecting a claim that the child would benefit by a successful operation because, when his mother and father die, his older sister would, be able to take care of him, the majority found that the operation would clearly be, against the child's best interest, and that therefore neither his parents nor the courts could authorize the surgery.[211]

However, there are circumstances under which nontherapeutic

procedures are performed on incompetents. These situations also involve the transplantation of organs and sterilization.

In *Strunk v. Strunk*,[212] the mother of an incompetent ward of the state petitioned the court of equity to permit the removal of one of his kidneys for transplantation into his twenty-eight-year-old brother. The potential donor was twenty-seven years of age, but had a mental age of approximately six years and had been previously committed to a state institution for the feeble-minded. All other members of the family and the Department of Mental Health had consented to the operation, but the donor was considered incompetent to give legally valid consent. A guardian *ad litem* had been appointed to contest the state's authority to allow the operation at every stage of the proceeding.

The court placed controlling emphasis on the psychiatric testimony. A psychiatrist who examined the incompetent determined that, in his opinion, the death of the brother would have "an extremely traumatic effect" on the potential donor. It was also argued that, while mental incompetents have difficulty establishing a sense of identity with other people, they nevertheless have a need for close intimacy, so that the donor's identification with his brother, who was his family tie, made it vital to the incompetent's improvement that his brother survive.

Even though the transplant, from the donor's point of view, was physically nonbeneficial, the Kentucky Court of Appeals implicitly and summarily equated benefit in the constitutional sense with a vague showing that possible psychological detriment might be avoided. The court concluded that, while a parent did not have the authority to consent to such an operation, except when the life of the incompetent himself was in danger, the court did have the ability to do so by exercising its equitable powers under the doctrine of *parens patriae*.[213]

Another case following this mold is *Howard v. Fulton-Dekalb Hospital Authority*.[214] In this case, a mother was suffering from chronic renal disease and the only person medically suitable for transplant purposes was her fifteen-year-old "moderately retarded" daughter. Both mother and daughter consented to the operation. However, the court found that, due to her minority and mental retardation, the daughter's consent was not legally valid. It also recognized the duty of the court, through its function as *parens patriae*, to independently review the circumstances of the case to assure that the best interests of the child were being protected, regardless of the existence of the mother's consent. However, this court also paid special attention to the psychiatric testimony, and decided that the kidney transplant should be allowed to proceed so as to protect the daughter from "the physical deprivation and emotional shock" which would result from the loss of her mother.

However, the factors involved in this type of situation, including the fact that a specific life will be saved in exchange for the imposition of a minimal risk on the incompetent donor, as well as the concept of family unity in making determinations of this type, make this line of cases somewhat inapplicable to other instances of nontherapeutic procedures on incompetents.[215]

Analogy can also be made to the compulsory sterilization of incompetents for nontherapeutic purposes. At present, twenty-three states have laws providing for some form of sterilization of persons suffering from mental disorders.[216] All of these laws provide for sterilization of persons in state institutions. The statutes vary in their provisions. Most permit the superintendent of the institution in which the individual is confined to begin the proceeding. Some also permit relatives, guardians, physicians, state welfare boards or others to initiate the proceeding. Most of the statutes provide for notice to the person who is to be sterilized and usually to his relatives, as well as for a hearing before an administrative agency or a court. Some states (Montana, Connecticut, Maine, Minnesota, North Carolina, and West Virginia) have "modernized" their compulsory sterilization laws by introducing new procedural safeguards. Some of these states have added a requirement that the candidate for sterilization, or his relatives or guardian, consent in writing to the procedure; others guarantee that the person to be sterilized have a hearing, with the right to counsel at all stages of the proceedings.[217] None of the new laws, however, provide for a review committee.

The validity of such statutes was upheld by the Supreme Court in *Buck v. Bell*.[218] The issue was the constitutionality of a Virginia statute authorizing the sterilization of patients in state institutions who were afflicted with hereditary forms of mental illness and mental retardation. The statute was premised on the assumption that the state was supporting in institutions "many defective persons who if . . . discharged would become a menace but if incapable of procreating might be discharged with safety and become self-supporting with benefit to themselves and to society."[219] The Court accepted the trial court's finding that "Carrie Buck 'is the probable potential parent of socially inadequate offspring.' "[220] Analogizing sterilization to compulsory vaccination, the Court held that the means chosen were reasonably related to a permissible state purpose, preventing society from being "swamped with incompetence."[221] In the closing words of Justice Holmes: "Three generations of imbeciles are enough."[222] The *Buck* case has never been specifically overturned, so that it is still the law today. However, recent developments in both law and genetics leads one to view the decision and its reasoning with suspicion.[223] Recent Supreme Court decisions have extended protection to the rights of a married or single person to be free from unwarranted governmental intrusion into matters so fundamentally effecting an individual as the decision whether or not to have a child.[224] Stricter equal protection and due process standards have developed in the areas of marriage and procreation since the *Buck* decision, with courts imposing heavy burdens on the state to prove that legislation curtailing these rights is needed. Furthermore, recent advances in medical science have dispelled the theory that all mentally retarded individuals reproduce mental defectives while normal people do not, thereby reducing the degree of "threat" which such reproduction poses for society.[225]

Yet the *Buck v. Bell* case served as the major basis for the recent upholding of the North Carolina involuntary sterilization statute. *In re Moore*[226] concerned the filing of a petition by the director of the county Department of Social Services, requesting that the court enter an order authorizing the sterilization of a minor, Joseph Lee Moore. Moore was functioning at a moderately retarded level, with an I.Q. of under 40. The petitioner contended that the child was a proper subject for sterilization because of the likelihood that, unless sterilized, he would procreate children who would probably have serious physical, mental, or nervous disease or deficiencies. Although he and his mother originally consented to the procedure, Moore later changed his mind, objected to the petition, and requested a hearing, at which he alleged that the controlling statute was unconstitutional. Both the District and Superior Courts agreed, but the state Supreme Court reversed, considering the issues of procedural and substantive due process, equal protection, and cruel and unusual punishment.

Relying in large part on *Buck*, the court maintained that the state has a right to sterilize retarded or insane persons. In analyzing the provisions of the statute, which provide for notice, a hearing, if requested, the right to appeal, and counsel at every stage of the proceeding, the court reached the conclusion that the legislation far exceeds the minimum requirements of procedural due process.[227]

In its discussion of substantive due process, the court was concerned with the individual's right of privacy, which it considered as including the right to procreate. However, it determined that this right is not absolute, but rather is open to a certain degree of state regulation. Since the right of privacy is considered "fundamental," such a limitation would only be justified by a compelling state interest. It considered the welfare of the parent and the future life and health of the unborn child to be the chief concerns of North Carolina in the authorization of sterilization of individuals under certain circumstances. The interest of the unborn child was considered sufficient to warrant sterilization of a mentally retarded person, as was the right of the state to prevent the procreation of children who will become public burdens. Again referring to *Buck*, the court stated that the welfare of all citizens should take precedence over the rights of individuals to procreate.[228] Beyond that, the court maintained that the sterilization of a mentally ill or mentally retarded person, at certain times, may be in the individual's best interest.[229] The person may not be able to determine his inability to cope with children, or may be capable of functioning in society and caring for his own needs, but unable to handle the additional responsibility of children. This type of individual might not be able to practice other forms of birth control, so that sterilization is the only available option. Accordingly, the state may be providing for the welfare of the individual when he is unable to do so himself. These considerations were found by the court to rise to the level of a compelling state interest, so that the statutory sterilization was held to be a valid and reasonable exercise of the state's police power.[230]

In its equal protection analysis, the court stated that the constitutional provision requires that any legislative classification be based on differences which are reasonably related to the statute's purposes. Considering that the object of the sterilization statute is to prevent the procreation of children by mentally deficient individuals who would probably be unable to care for their offspring or whose children would probably be similarly deficient, the court concluded that the statute classification was reasonable.[231]

The court quickly dispensed with the cruel and unusual argument. Since the proceeding in question is not a criminal proceeding, and the cruel and unusual punishment clause refers to those persons convicted of a crime, the court concluded that Moore's contention had no basis.[232]

The court mentioned that it could not find any case which held that a state does not have the right to sterilize a mentally ill or mentally retarded person if notice and hearing are provided by a statute which applies equally to all persons and is not prescribed as punishment for a crime.[233] Accordingly, the court declared that the sterilization statute is constitutional.

In the only other sterilization case heard by the Supreme Court since *Buck*, *Skinner v. Oklahoma*,[234] procreation was determined to be a fundamental interest. Therefore, in order to justify the sterilization statutes, a state interest of sufficient importance to subordinate the individual's interest must be found. Two legitimate state interests are generally considered to be furthered by such legislation. The first is eugenic, or the interest of the state in avoiding another generation of mentally deficient people and, more generally, in improving the gene pool of the population,[235] although, as mentioned above, this justification is becoming viewed with suspicion among the scientific community. The second is the state's interest in providing children with fit and capable parents.[236]

In the case of *Cook v. Oregon*,[237] the plaintiff appealed from a sterilization order by the State Board of Social Protection. The court determined that the seventeen-year-old girl in question, who was both mentally ill and mentally retarded, would not be able to provide the parental guidance and judgment which a child requires. Inability of an individual to provide a proper environment for a child was considered to be an adequate reason for the state to require sterilization. Therefore, on that basis, the court affirmed the sterilization order.[238]

Similarly, the case of *In re Sallmaier*[239] involved the application of a mother for an order authorizing her to consent to a sterilization procedure on behalf of her adult, mentally retarded daughter. The twenty-three year old woman had suffered a seizure at the age of two which resulted in brain damage. Although diagnosed by a court-appointed psychiatrist as suffering from severe mental retardation with marked infantile thinking, behavior and attitudes, her condition, while irreversible, was not congenital. She was sexually mature, but had an I.Q. of 62 and functioned at a six or seven-year-old age level. Unable to understand abstract concepts, she did not know the difference between a man and a woman. In addition, she refused all medication, had numerous phobias, and had her personal hygiene and menstrual cycle handled by her mother. As a result, the court concluded that the mentally retarded woman did not have the capacity to knowingly consent or withhold consent to the sterilization procedure.[249]

Although New York does not have a statute authorizing the sterilization of individuals, the court based its jurisdiction in this matter on the common law *parens patriae* concept, stating that it could order compulsory medical treatment for a person if it is determined to be in his best interest. In deciding whether sterilization would be in the woman's best interest, the court gave great weight to the testimony of the court-appointed psychiatrist, who recommended sterilization because, in his opinion, pregnancy would have a substantial likelihood of causing a psychotic reaction in her. Therefore, the court concluded that it would be in the woman's best interest to be sterilized, and accordingly granted the application.[241]

Thus, there may be situations in which a procedure that is admittedly nontherapeutic may be carried out, without the consent of a competent institutionalized individual and regardless of the common law inability to obtain valid consent on behalf of an incompetent. However, this exception is limited to those circumstances in which a valid state interest sufficiently outweighs the rights of the individual so as to justify use of the police power in this manner. Thus, its application is admittedly narrow.

The most notorious case of nontherapeutic experimentation on institutionalized individuals took place in New York's Willowbrook State School.[242] The facility, the world's largest institution for the mentally retarded, has become infamous for its deplorable conditions.[243]

Built in 1941 to house 3,000 residents, Willowbrook at one time had a population of 5,200. At least three-quarters of the patients are classified as "profoundly" or "severely" retarded.[244] The facility is grim, with the stench of sweat, feces, and urine everywhere. For most residents it is a warehouse, providing only shelter and the barest essentials. Conditions have been described as hazardous to the health, safety, and sanity of the residents, contributing to the deterioration of the patients through overcrowded conditions and shortage of adequately trained personnel. Indeed, it has been said that Willowbrook is "an atrocity, a massive regressive machine."[245] Charges have been made that ninety percent of the school's mortalities have as their underlying cause "neglect, deprivation, and malnutrition. You can see it in the kids' skin condition, loss of hair, slow hearing."[246] There have been tales of maggot-infested wounds, assembly-line bathing, inadequate medical care, inadequate clothing, and cruel and inappropriate use of restraints.[247]

Beyond that, Willowbrook has been called a dangerous place. "It breeds disease and battered children," with a mortality rate of three to four preventable deaths a week.[248] There are many bruised and beaten children, with the loss of an eye, the breaking of teeth, the loss of part of an ear bitten off by another resident, and frequent scalp wounds, being typical of the dangers facing residents. Much serious injury often results from assaults by other patients, who are bored, frustrated, and angry at their environment.

In addition, infectious diseases, such as hepatitis and shigella, are rampant in the wards. An infected patient is loaded up with numerous antibiotics, so that the staph there is almost completely resistant.[249]

The crowding and unsanitary conditions of the facility, coupled with the poor personal hygiene of residents, caused an epidemic of fecally-borne infectious hepatitis. Hepatitis is frequently protracted and debilitating and sometimes fatal to the victim. Nearly everyone at the school was infected, so that new arrivals would probably have contracted the virus within six months.[250]

Beginning in 1956, physicians at the institution worked at finding a vaccine for this particular strain of infectious hepatitis.[251] They isolated strains of the virus, and, with parental consent, infected several retarded children newly admitted to the school. Many of the children became quite ill. All of them risked serious illness. However, as a result of these efforts, a vaccine for the Willowbrook virus was developed. An expert in the field of mental retardation, Dr. Richard Koch, has noted that the immunization work is "probably the only good thing that's ever come out of the institution."[252]

The physicians involved in the study felt it was justified for numerous reasons. First, the residents were bound to be exposed to the same strains under the natural conditions in the facility anyway. Second, if they were admitted to the special hepatitis unit, they would be protected from the risk of multiple infections which were prevalent in the remainder of the institution. Finally, it was hoped that the residents, following a subclinical infection, would have an immunity to the particular hepatitis virus.[253] In addition, it was maintained that, under circumstances in which active individuals are in constant contact with each other and with fecal matter, a vaccine is the best protection against infectious disease.[254]

There were many criticisms of the Willowbrook experiment. For example, children were infected with the virus, but had protective doses of gamma-globulin withheld from them. This was at a time when other residents not in the study, as well as staff, were receiving the gamma-globulin.[255] By entering the study, a child increased his risk of contracting chronic liver disease while at the institution.[256] Moreover, it was argued that the research money should have been spent on cleaning up the institution as a better means of eradicating this disease.[257] It is documented that the incidence of clinical hepatitis is very low at small, well-staffed institutions. Highly-susceptible Down's Syndrome children admitted to small, private institutions showed only a one and one-half percent prevalence of a particular strain of hepatitis, while similar children admitted to large state institutions showed a thirty percent rate.[258]

A particularly controversial aspect of the program involved the means by which parental consent was obtained. In late 1964, Willow-brook was closed to all new admissions because of overcrowding. Parents seeking admission for their children were informed of this and placed on a waiting list. However, the hepatitis study, occupying its own space in the institution, continued to admit new patients. For a period of time, letters were sent to the parents informing them that there were a few vacancies in the hepatitis research unit if they cared to consider volunteering their child for that.[259] Many parents felt that this situation coerced them into consenting to have their children participate.[260]

The hepatitis experiment was one of the factors which, combined with the general horrible conditions of the facility, led to the filing of the suit in *New York State Association for Retarded Children v. Carey.*[261] The court found that voluntarily institutionalized mentally retarded individuals have a constitutional right to protection from harm. This is similar to the right to treatment found by the court in *Wyatt v. Stickney.*[262] Appropriately, the court approved a detailed consent decree which set up standards and procedures, similar to those in *Wyatt*, which would serve to ensure the recognition of the residents' right to protection from harm. This was felt to be neces-sary because "harm can result not only from neglect but from con-ditions which cause regression or which prevent development of an individual's capabilities."[263] Significantly, the decree absolutely forbids medical experimentation. In addition, it creates three boards with important functions. The Review Panel will oversee the imple-mentation of standards and procedures mandated in the consent decree, the Consumer Advisory Board will evaluate alleged dehu-manizing practices and violations of individual and legal rights, and a Professional Advisory Board will give advice on professional pro-grams and plans, budget requests, and objectives, as well as investi-gate alleged violations.

Presently pending in Michigan is a case which may decide many of the issues in this area. *Jobes v. Michigan Department of Mental Health*[264] involves a suit brought to prevent a study which hypothe-sizes zinc deficiency as a cause of behavior and intellectual problems. This experiment was to be carried out on minor residents of a state mental institution. Plaintiffs allege that parental or court consent is valid only if there is a direct therapeutic benefit to the child-subject, which is absent in the study under consideration. Thus, the case is concerned with, under what circumstances and from whom, one may obtain legally binding informed consent to nontherapeutic experimentation on an incompetent mental patient.

In August 1975, the Michigan Department of Mental Health pro-

mulgated administrative rules, on an emergency basis, which prohibited persons under 18 years of age from participating in medical
research and experimentation not directly for their benefit if they
were recipients of mental health services. Those rules have expired,
and the legislature is seeking the assistance of the National Commission for the Protection of Human Subjects of Biomedical and Behavioral Research before promulgating new rules. Counsel for the
plaintiffs has indicated that he will wait for publication of the new
rules before deciding whether to proceed to trial.

CONCLUSIONS AND RECOMMENDATIONS

1. Recognizing the problems pertaining specifically to institutionalized mental patients, the law has scrutinized consent with special care, but in general has permitted either resident or substitute
consent to procedures after ascertaining that reasonable efforts have
been undertaken to ensure capacity and voluntariness.

2. Consent is even more carefully analyzed and protected when
the procedure to be employed is particularly hazardous or intrusive.
Yet sound public policy dictates that standards for consent be
formulated which balance the threats to the obtaining of informed
consent against the equally serious threat of paternalism.

3. There seems to be no legal reason for precluding institutionalized mental patients from participating in therapeutic experimentation.[265] A competent patient could consent for his own
treatment, while proxy consent by a guardian would be appropriate
for an incompetent individual.

4. Unless the illness is serious and any conventional or less intrusive or less hazardous treatments have either already been exhausted
or are not likely to help, the risks should not be great.

5. It is difficult at this time to make a definitive rule about nontherapeutic experimentation based on the law. In general, competent
patients may consent to participation.

6. When the need for the information is great, and the risk to the
individual participant minimal, this type of research should probably
be permitted with incompetent patients as well, assuming that proxy
consent has been obtained. Examples of procedures included in this
category are the taking of blood and the collection of urine specimens. However, the refusal of an incompetent person to involvement
in the experiment should be binding, regardless of either his reasons
for the decision or the wishes of the patient's guardian.

7. Nontherapeutic research is justified only when the condition

under investigation is related to mental disability and the information sought cannot be obtained from noninstitutionalized subjects.

8. A system needs to be developed for dealing with those patients who are incompetent in a *practical* sense, but who have not been *legally* declared to be incompetent.[266] An appropriate mechanism could be designed along the lines of those procedures suggested earlier.[267]

9. Institutions often seem to impute constraints on the rights of patients which are simply not found in the law. Therefore, in that the institutional setting always carries a serious potential for abuse of the rights of residents, a system of review should be developed to make sure that the above guidelines are being followed.[268]

REFERENCES

1. *See*, ch. 1, *supra* at 6-7.

2. This chapter is concerned with the problem of informed consent to experimentation by those institutionalized individuals considered mentally infirm, including the mentally ill, the mentally retarded, the emotionally disturbed, the psychotic, and the senile. However, the important issues are common to all of these categories, and since the majority of the law in this area deals specifically with the mentally ill and/or the mentally retarded, we will throughout the section refer to these particular groups.

3. *See*, Silent Minority, President's Committee on Mental Retardation, DHEW Pub. No. (OHD) 74-21002, at 10.

4. Mental Retardation Source Book, Department of Health, Education and Welfare, 15, 19 (1973).

5. Ennis and Siegel, The Rights of Mental Patients, 11 (1973).

6. *See, e.g.*, Dybwad, Challenges in Mental Retardation, 21 (1964); Herr, Civil Rights, Uncivil Asylums and the Retarded, 43 Cinn. L. Rev. 679 (1974).

7. *See*, Comment, Civil Restraint, Mental Illness, and the Right to Treatment, 77 Yale L.J. 87,88 (1967).

8. *See, e.g.*, Harter, Mental Age, IQ and Motivational Factors in the Discrimination Learning Set Performance of Normal and Retarded Children, 5 J. Experimental Child Psych. 123 (1967); Iscoe and McCann, The Perception of an Emotional Continuum by Older and Younger Mental Retardates, 1 J. Personality & Social Psych. 383 (1965); Lyle, The Effect of an Institutional Environment upon the Verbal Development of Imbecile Children, 3 J. Mental Deficiency Research 122 (1959).

9. Bloomberg, A Proposal for a Community Based Hospital as a Branch of a State Hospital, 116 Am. J. Psych. 814 (1960).

10. *E.g.*, Blatt and Kaplan, Christmas in Purgatory: A Photographic Essay on Mental Retardation (1966).

11. Comment, Behavior Modification and Other Legal Imbroglios of Human Experimentation, 52 J. Urban L. 155, 157 (1974).

12. *See,* Ritts, A Physician's View of Informed Consent in Human Experimentation, 36 Fordham L. Rev. 631 (1968).

13. Experimentation, The Real Paper, Aug. 7, 1974, at 6.

14. Wecht, Medical, Legal, and Moral Considerations in Human Experiments Involving Minors and Incompetent Adults, J. Legal Med., Feb. 1976, at 27, 30.

15. Hearings on Quality of Health Care—Human Experimentation Before the Subcomm. on Health of the Senate Comm. on Labor & Public Welfare, 93d Cong., 1st Sess., pt. 1, at 42–44 (1973).

16. *Id.* at 111–113.

17. *Id.* at 66, 94–98.

18. *Id.* at 109.

19. *Id.* at 94.

20. *Id.* at 99–100.

21. Schloendorff v. Society of N.Y. Hosp., 211 N.Y. 125, 105 N.E. 92, 93 (1914). *See,* Prosser, Law of Torts 34 (4th ed. 1971).

22. *E.g.,* Natanson v. Kline, 186 Kan. 393, 350 P.2d 1093 (1960); Bang v. Charles T. Miller Hosp., 251 Minn. 427, 88 N.W.2d 186 (1958).

23. Dade Co., 11th Circuit Ct., Fla., No. 71-12687 (July 2, 1971).

24. *Accord* Erickson v. Dilgard, 44 Misc. 2d 27, 252 N.Y.S.2d 705 (Sup. Ct. 1962). *See,* Cantor, A Patient's Decision to Decline Life-Saving Medical Treatment: Bodily Integrity versus the Preservation of Life, 26 Rutgers L. Rev. 228 (1973); Note, Compulsory Medical Treatment: The State's Interest Re-evaluated, 51 Minn. L. Rev. 293 (1966); Note, Informed Consent and the Dying Patient, 83 Yale L.J. 1632 (1974).

25. Shapiro, Legislating the Control of Behavior Control: Autonomy and the Coercive Use of Organic Therapies, 47 So. Calif. L. Rev. 237, 308–309 (1974).

26. Schoenfeld, Human Rights for the Mentally Retarded: Their Recognition by the Providers of Service, 4 Human Rights 31 (1974), in which he discusses the 1971 United Nations Declaration of General and Special Rights of the Mentally Retarded, in which the international community recognized the principle that the mentally retarded have the same rights as other citizens of the same country and age.

27. *See,* Wyatt v. Stickney, 344 F. Supp. 373, 387, 399 (M.D. Ala. 1972), *aff'd sub nom.* Wyatt v. Aderholt, 503 F.2d 1305 (5th Cir. 1974): "No person shall be presumed mentally incompetent solely by reason of his admission or commitment to the institution." *See, also* Davis v. Watkins, 384 F. Supp. 1196, 1206 (N.D. Ohio 1974).

28. Dist. Ct. Neb., Civil No. 72-C-299 (Aug. 6, 1975), consent order approved by court (Oct. 3, 1975). (Preliminary order, 357 F. Supp. 71 (D. Ct. Neb. 1973)).

29. 377 F. Supp. 896 (D. Conn. 1974), supplemental decision, 386 F. Supp. 1245 (D. Conn. 1975). This case was later reversed by the Second Circuit, 520 F.2d 1305 (2d Cir. 1975), but for reasons which do not conflict with the analysis of the lower court as to the effect of institutionalization on the status of mental patients. In essence, the higher court decided that a mental patient's claim in federal district court for restitution of funds appropriated by the Commissioner of Finance under subsequently invalidated Connecticut statutes is

indistinguishable from an award of damages against the state and is barred by the Eleventh Amendment. Furthermore, the assumption by the Commissioner of fiduciary duties toward the patients did not impliedly waive the Eleventh Amendment immunity. On June 30, 1976, the Supreme Court denied *certiorari* in this case.

30. 377 F. Supp. 1361 (E.D. Pa. 1974).

31. Boyd v. Board of Registrars of Voters, No. 75-141 (Sup. Jud. Ct. Mass., Sept. 30, 1975); Carroll v. Cobb, No. A-669-74 and A-1044-74 (Sup. Ct. N.J., App. Div., Feb. 23, 1976).

32. 62 Penn. Dist. & Cty. Rpts. 2d 619 (1972).

33. Cal. Welfare and Inst. Code §5331 (West Supp. 1974).

34. Minn. Stat. Ann. §253A.18.1 (1971).

35. Mich. Stat. Ann. §14-800 (702) (1974).

36. Mass. Gen. Laws Ann. ch. 123 §25 (Supp. 1972).

37. N.Y. Mental Hygiene Law §29.03 (McKinney Supp. 1973).

38. Okla Stats. Ann. ch. 43A §64.

39. S.C. Code art. 5 §32-997.

40. S.D. Stats. ch. 27-12-15.

41. Tenn. Code Ann. §33-306(3) (Cum. Supp. 1975).

42. S.C. Code art. 5 §32-997.

43. S.D. Stats. ch. 27-4-22.1.

44. N.M. Stats. Ann. art. VI §3-6-3.

45. La. Rev. Stat. 28:171.

46. Kent. Stat. ch. 202.272.

47. Alaska Stat. §47.30.150 (Cum. Supp. 1970).

48. Ga. Code Ann. §88-502.7 (1971).

49. Ann. Code Md. art. 59 §§50–51 (1972).

50. N.Y. Mental Hygiene Law §15.01 (McKinney Supp. 1973).

51. S.C. Code art. 5 §32-997.

52. La. Rev. Stat. 28:171.

53. Kent. Stat. ch. 202.272.

54. Alaska Stat. §47.30.150 (Cum. Supp. 1970).

55. S.C. Code art. 5 §32-997.

56. *Id.*

57. Ga. Code Ann. §113–201, 202 (1971).

58. Morris, Institutionalizing the Rights of Mental Patients: Committing the Legislature, 62 Calif. L. Rev. 957, 967 (1974).

59. *See, generally* Allen, Ferster and Weihoffen, Mental Impairment and Legal Incompetency (1968).

60. W. Va. Code §27-5-4 (Supp. 1973).

61. Wis. Stat. §51.005(2) (1957).

62. Ala. Code tit. 17 §15; tit. 1 §1–2; tit. 9 §43.

63. Ark. Stat. tit. 3 §101.

64. Maine Rev. Stat. Ann. tit. 19 §32 (1965).

65. N.J. Stats. Ann. ch. 19 §4-1; ch. 3A §3-1.

66. Allen, Ferster and Weihoffen, *supra* note 59, at 46–49.

67. It should be emphasized that, throughout this section, the term "thera-

peutic" experimentation is used according to the manner in which it was defined in ch. 1, *supra* at 2. Therefore, although it designates procedures that may be of direct benefit to the subject, the intent of the investigator is not always controlling. Where the risks to the subject are very great, the procedure is considered nontherapeutic regardless of the motivation of the researcher and the subject.

68. *See*, discussion of proxy consent, text accompanying notes 95-99 *infra*.

69. *Id.*

70. Goffman, Asylums, Essays on the Social Situation of Mental Patients and Other Inmates (1962).

71. *Id.* at 7. *See*, Kramer, The Subtle Subversion of Patients' Rights by Hospital Staff Members, 25 Hosp. & Community Psychiat. 475 (1974).

72. Fletcher, Human Experimentation—Ethics in the Consent Situation, in Medical Progress and the Law 75-76 (C. Havighurst ed. 1969).

73. Kaimowitz, Patient or Victim, 11 Trial, Nov./Dec. 1975, at 14, 15.

74. A Report on Involuntary Commitment, Citizens Commission on Human Rights 2 (1975).

75. Civ. No. 73-19434-AW (Cir. Ct. Wayne County, Mich., July 10, 1973).

76. Amended Petition and Complaint for the Petitioners—Plaintiffs, Kaimowitz v. Department of Mental Health, at 7 (1973).

77. Kaimowitz v. Department of Mental Health, at 4 n.5.

78. *Id.* at 6.

79. *Id.* at 23. For a discussion of the Nuremberg Code and its legal standing, *see*, ch. 1, *supra* at 6. For the entire text of the Nuremberg Code, *see*, Appendix I, *infra*.

80. There are two unreported cases on psychosurgery which have also considered the issue of informed consent. Medical News, 225 J.A.M.A. 1035, 1036, 1044 (1973). In Virginia, the parents of a patient who engaged in acts of self-mutilation consented to the use of psychosurgery. However, upon learning of the proposed procedure, the Virginia Attorney General's office intervened on behalf of the patient. The court stayed the surgery on the ground of the patient's inability to give consent. The second case was settled before trial. The plaintiff, who had been blinded as a result of a psychosurgical procedure, recovered a settlement on the ground that she was inadequately informed of the risk in the procedure.

81. Kaimowitz v. Department of Mental Health at 27.

82. *Id.* at 27-29.

83. *Id.* at 27.

84. *Id.* at 29.

85. *Id.* at 27.

86. Annas and Glantz, Psychosurgery: The Law's Response, 54 B.U.L. Rev. 249, 263 (1974).

87. Changing Patterns in Residential Services for the Mentally Retarded 20 (Kugel and Wolfensberger eds. 1969).

88. Bomstein, The Forcible Administration of Drugs to Prisoners and Mental Patients, Clearinghouse Rev., Oct. 1975, at 379, 380.

89. *See, e.g.*, Dershowitz, Psychiatry in the Legal Process: A Knife That Cuts

Both Ways, 4 Trial, Feb./March, 1968, at 2932; Siegel, The Justifications for Medical Commitment—Real or Illusory, 6 Wake Forest Intra. L. Rev. 21, 31–33 (1969).

90. Katz, The Right to Treatment—An Enchanting Legal Fiction, 36 U. Chi. L. Rev. 755, 773 (1969).

91. Note, Civil Commitment of the Mentally Ill: Theories and Procedures, 79 Harv. L. Rev. 1288 (1966).

92. *See, e.g.,* Postel, Civil Commitment: A Functional Analysis, 38 Brooklyn L. Rev. 1 (1971).

93. *See,* Note, Informed Consent and the Dying Patient, *supra,* note 24.

94. Friedman, Legal Regulation of Applied Behavior Analysis in Mental Institutions and Prisons, 17 Arizona L. Rev. 39, 99 (1975).

95. From Roman law comes the idea that in some circumstances the state should relate to the citizen as the parent to his child. Known as the doctrine of parens patriae, this concept is firmly recognized in Anglo-American law. It gives the sovereign both the right and the duty to protect the persons and property of those who are unable to care for themselves because of minority or mental illness. Ross, Commitment of the Mentally Ill: Problems of Law and Policy, 57 Mich. L. Rev. 945, 956–957 (1959).

96. *See,* Hawaii v. Standard Oil Co., 405 U.S. 251, 257 (1972) *quoting* W. Blackstone, Commentaries 47.

97. *See,* ch. 2, *supra* at 87.

98. *See,* Allen, Legal Rights of the Disabled and Disadvantaged 23 (1969).

99. Allen, The Retarded Citizen: Victim of Legal and Mental Deficiency, 2 U. Md. L.F. 4 (1971). *Cf.,* Lewis, McCollum, Schwartz and Grunt, Informed Consent in Pediatric Research, 16 Children 143, 144–145 (1969).

100. For the text of each of these codes, *see,* Appendix I (Nuremberg), Appendix II (Helsinki), and Appendix III (A.M.A.), *infra.*

101. *See,* Comment, Behavior Modification and Other Legal Imbroglios of Human Experimentation, *supra* note 11, at 167.

102. *See,* text accompanying notes 21–69 *supra.*

103. *See,* Alaska Stat. §47.30.130 (Cum. Supp. 1970) (consent required for surgery and psychiatric therapies); Conn. Gen. Stat. Ann. §17-206d (Cum. Supp. 1975) (no medical or surgical procedures, including electroshock therapy, may be performed without consent); Mich. Stat. Ann. §14.800(716) (1974) (consent required for nonemergency surgery and electroshock therapy); N.Y. Mental Hygiene Law §15.03(b)(4) (McKinney Supp. 1974-1975) (consent required for surgery and shock treatment); N.C. Gen. Stat. §122-55.6 (1974) (informed consent required for nonemergency surgery and electroshock treatment); Vt. Stat. Ann. tit. 18 §7708 (1968) (consent required for surgery); Wash. Rev. Code Ann. §71.05.370(7) (Supp. 1974) (involuntarily detained patient has right to refuse shock treatment and nonemergency surgery).

104. Tenn. Code Ann. §33-307 (Cum. Supp. 1974).

105. *E.g.,* Ark. Stat. tit. 82 §363; Conn. Gen. Stat. Ann. §17-206d (Cum. Supp. 1975); Fla. Stats. Ann. ch. 394.459.

106. Alaska stat. §47.30.130 (Cum. Supp. 1970).

107. N.J. Stats. Ann. ch. 30 §4-7 (Supp. 1974).

108. Colen, The Legal Right to Medical Treatment, Washington Post, Aug. 2, 1976, at A1, A2.

109. *Id.*

110. *Id.*

111. Brief *Amicus Curiae* of the Civil Rights and Liberties Division of the Department of the Attorney General on Behalf of the Defendant-Appellee, Jones v. Saikewicz, S.J.C.—No. 711, at 4 (June 30, 1976) [hereinafter cited as *Amicus Curiae* Brief].

112. Colen, *supra* note 108.

113. *Amicus Curiae* Brief at 13.

114. Jones v. Saikewicz, 4 M.L.W. 583 (July 19, 1976).

115. The court's decision on this issue will have no effect on the present case, since Mr. Saikewicz died on September 4, 1976. Supplemental Brief *Amicus Curiae* of the Civil Rights and Liberties Division of the Department of the Attorney General on Behalf of the Defendant-Appellee, Jones v. Saikewicz, S.J.C. —No. 711, at 3.

116. *Id.* at 14.

117. *Id.* at 10–13.

118. 372 F. Supp. 1196 (D.D.C. 1974).

119. *Id.* at 1202.

120. *Id.*

121. 403 F. Supp. 1235 (D.D.C. 1975).

122. Kaiser, Against Sterilization Policy Here, N.Y. Times, Jan. 12, 1976, at 29, col. 2.

123. 368 F. Supp. 1382 (M.D. Ala. 1973); District Court Order, Jan. 8, 1974.

124. *Id.* at 1384.

125. Dane Cty. Ct., Branch I, Wis. (Nov. 1974). *Cf.*, Wade v. Bethesda Hosp., 337 F. Supp. 671 (S.D. Ohio 1971); In re M.K.R., 515 S.W.2d 467 (Mo. 1974); In re Kemp, 118 Cal. Rep. 64 (Ct. App. 1974); Holmes v. Powers, 439 S.W.2d 579 (Ky. 1969).

126. *See*, Krasner and Ullmann, Case Studies in Behavior Modification 1–2 (1965).

127. *See*, Ayllon, Behavior Modification in Institutional Settings, 17 Ariz. L. Rev. 3 (1975); Kassirer, Behavior Modification for Patients and Prisoners: Constitutional Ramifications of Enforced Therapy, 2 J. Psychiatry & L. 245 (1974).

128. *See*, text accompanying notes 21–69 *supra*.

129. 306 F. Supp. 1158 (E.D.N.Y. 1969), *rev'd on other grounds*, 446 F.2d 65 (2d Cir. 1971), *cert. denied*, 404 U.S. 985 (1971).

130. 344 Mass. 679, 183 N.E.2d 866 (1962) (*dicta*).

131. Many of the issues presented in this chapter are currently being considered in an action pending in Massachusetts. Rogers v. Macht, Civil Action No. 75-1610T.

132. Bomstein, *supra* note 88, at 383.

133. *See*, Schwartz, In the Name of Treatment: Autonomy, Civil Commitment, and the Right to Refuse Treatment, 50 Notre Dame Lawyer 808, 817 (1975).

134. Jackson v. Indiana, 406 U.S. 715, 737 (1972).

135. In re Oakes, 8 Law Rep. 122 (Mass. 1845).

136. *See*, Comment, Wyatt v. Stickney and The Right of Civilly Committed Mental Patients to Adequate Treatment, 86 Harv. L. Rev. 1282, 1289 (1973); Note, The Nascent Right to Treatment, 53 Va. L. Rev. 1134 (1967).

137. Brooks, Law, Psychiatry and the Mental Health System 877 (1974).

138. 56 Misc. 2d 693, 290 N.Y.S.2d 486 (Ct. Cl. 1968).

139. *Id.* at 699, 290 N.Y.S.2d at 501.

140. *See*, Schwitzgebel, The Right to Effective Mental Treatment, 62 Calif. L. Rev. 936 (1974).

141. Crinker, Emerging Concepts of Mental Illness and Models of Treatment: The Medical Point of View, 125 Am. J. Psychiatry 865, 866 (1969).

142. *See, e.g.*, Rosenham, On Being Sane in Insane Places, 179 Science 250 (1973), reprinted in 13 Santa Clara Lawyer 379 (1973).

143. *E.g.*, Suzuki v. Quisenberry, 44 U.S.L.W. 2422 (D. Haw. Feb. 24, 1976); Cal. Welfare & Inst. Code §§5008(h), 5300-6, 5350-68 (West 1972); Mass. Gen. Laws Ann. ch. 123 §§1-37 (Supp. 1974); N.C. Gen. Stat. §§122-58.1-.8 (1974).

144. Developments in the Law—Civil Commitment of the Mentally Ill, 87 Harv. L. Rev. 1190, 1351 (1974).

145. *Cf.*, O'Donoghue v. Riggs, 73 Wash. 2d 814, 820 n.2, 440 P.2d 823, 828 n.2 (1968): "One who enters a hospital as a mentally ill person . . . impliedly consents to the use of such force as may be reasonably necessary to the proper care of the patient."

146. *See* Ellis, Volunteering Children: Parental Commitment of Minors to Mental Institutions, 3 Calif. L. Rev. 840 (1974).

147. J.L. v. Parham, 44 U.S.L.W. 2421 (M.D. Ga. Feb. 26, 1976); Saville v. Treadway, C.A. No. 6969 (U.S.D.C., M.D. Tenn., Order of April 18, 1974); Bartley v. Kremens, 402 F. Supp. 1039 (E.D. Pa. 1975). The United States Supreme Court has agreed to review the *Bartley* case. Its decision should help clarify this area.

148. Gilboy and Schmidt, Voluntary Hospitalization of the Mentally Ill, 66 Nw. U.L. Rev. 429 (1971).

149. Materials for Civil Rights Officers, Proposed Draft, Mass. Dept. of Mental Health 7.

150. Mass. Gen. Laws Ann. ch. 123 §§10-11 (Supp. 1972).

151. 23 N.Y.2d 385, 244 N.E.2d 677, 297 N.Y.S.2d 97 (1968). *See generally* Breggin, Coercion of Voluntary Patients in an Open Hospital, 10 Arch. Gen. Psychiat. 173 (1964).

152. *See, e.g.*, Wash. Rev. Code Ann. §71.05.380 (Supp. 1974): "All persons voluntarily entering or remaining in any facility, institution, or hospital providing evaluation and treatment for mental disorder shall have no less than all rights secured to involuntarily detained persons."

153. Kaimowitz v. Department of Mental Health, Wayne Co., Civil No. 73-19434-AW (July 10, 1973).

154. 477 F.2d 877 (9th Cir. 1973). This case is discussed in more detail in the chapter on prisoners. *See* ch. 3, *supra* at 122.

155. *Id.*
156. 488 F.2d 1136 (8th Cir. 1973). This case is discussed in more detail in the chapter on prisoners. *See* ch. 3, *supra* at 122.
157. Scott v. Plante, 44 U.S.L.W. 2480 (3d Cir. March 29, 1976).
158. 70 Misc. 2d 944, 335 N.Y.S.2d 461 (1972).
159. *Id.* at 464.
160. 334 S.W.2d 11 (Mo. 1960).
161. 379 S.W.2d 478 (Ct. App. Ky. 1964).
162. 396 S.W.2d 668 (Mo. 1965).
163. *See, e.g.,* statutes included in note 103 *supra. See also* Ch. 616 [1973 Ore. Reg. Sess.] (S. Bill 298), *amending* Ore. Rev. Stat. 677.190 (1971).
164. *See,* Ga. Code Ann. §88-502.3(a) (1971) (unless consent is given, no treatment which is not recognized as standard psychiatric treatment shall be given); N.Y. Mental Hygiene Law §15.03(b)(4) (McKinney Supp. 1974-1975) (consent required for experimental drugs or procedures); N.C. Gen. Stat. §122.55.6 (1974) (treatment involving experimental drugs or procedures shall not be given without informed consent).
165. *See, e.g.,* Ga. Code Ann. §88-502.3(a) (1971); N.J. Stat. Ann.§§30:4-7.1-7.2 (Supp. 1974); N.C. Gen. Stat. §122-55.6 (1974).
166. Mass. Gen. Laws Ann. ch. 123 §23 (Supp. 1972). *See,* ch. 173 §24 (1973), Idaho Code 379.
167. Cal. Welfare & Inst. Code §§5325-5326.4 (West. Supp. 1974).
168. *Id.* §§5325-5326.3.
169. *Id.* §5326.4.
170. 129 Cal. Rptr. 535 (4th Dist. App. 1976). *See* the discussion of this case in the chapter on psychosurgery, *infra.*
171. *Id.* at 545.
172. *Id.* at 550.
173. *Id.* at 547.
174. *Id.*
175. *Id.* at 548.
176. *Id.*
177. *Id.* at 549.
178. *Id.*
179. *Id.*
180. *Id.*
181. *Id.* at 549.
182. *Id.* at 550-51.
183. Assembly Bill No. 1032 (1976). *See generally* Note, Legislative Control of Shock Treatment, 9 U. San Fran. L. Rev. 738 (1975).
184. AB 1032 §5326.7 (b).
185. *Id.* §§5326.7 (f), (g).
186. *Id.* §5326.75 (b).
187. *Id.* §5326.75 (c).
188. 40 Cal. 2d 546, 254 P.2d 520 (1953).
189. 17 A.D.2d 495, 236 N.Y.S.2d 88 (1963).
190. Maben v. Rankin, 358 P.2d 681 (Calif. 1961) (husband consenting for

wife); Lester v. Aetna Casualty & Surety Co., 240 F.2d 676 (5th Cir. 1957) (wife consenting for husband).

191. 239 N.W.2d 905 (Minn. 1976).

192. *Id*. at 910.

193. *Id*.

194. *Id*. at 911.

195. *Id*. at 913.

196. 344 F. Supp. 373 and 387 (M.D. Ala. 1972), *aff'd sub nom*. Wyatt v. Aderholt, 503 F.2d 1305 (5th Cir. 1974).

197. *Id*. at 380.

198. *Id*.

199. *Id*. at 387, 401.

200. *See, generally*, Wexler, Token and Taboo: Behavior Modification, Token Economies, and the Law, 61 Calif. L. Rev. 81 (1973).

201. Friedman, Legal Regulation of Applied Behavior Analysis in Mental Institutions and Prisons, 17 Ariz. L. Rev. 39, 90 (1975).

202. Note, Conditioning and Other Technologies Used to "Treat?" "Rehabilitate?" "Demolish?" Prisoners and Mental Patients, 45 So. Calif. L. Rev. 616, 659 (1972). *See*, Note, Advances in Mental Health: A Case for the Right to Refuse Treatment, 48 Temple L.Q. 354, 363 (1975).

203. Thorn v. Superior Court, 1 Cal. 3d 666, 675, 462 P.2d 56, 62, 83 Cal. Rptr. 600, 606 (1970).

204. *See*, text accompanying notes 21–69 *supra*.

205. 440 S.W.2d 393 (Tex. Ct. Civ. App. 1969).

206. *Accord* In re M.K.R., 515 S.W.2d 467 (Mo. 1974). *Cf*., Wade v. Bethesda Hosp., 337 F. Supp. 671 (S.D. Ohio 1971).

207. 325 N.E.2d 501 (3d Dist. Ct. App. Ind. 1975). The United States Supreme Court has declined to review the decision in this case. A.L. v. G.R.H., 44 U.S.L.W. 3593 (Apr. 20, 1976).

208. *Id*. at 502.

209. *Id*. *Accord* In re Kemp's Estate, 43 Cal. App. 3d 758, 118 Cal. Rptr. 64 (1974). *See*, Holmes v. Powers, 439 S.W.2d 579 (Ky. 1968).

210. 284 So. 2d 185 (La. App. 1973).

211. *Accord* In re Pescinski, 67 Wis. 2d 4, 226 N.W.2d 180 (1975).

212. 445 S.W.2d 145 (Ky. 1969). This case is discussed in more detail in the chapter on children. *See* ch. 2., *supra* at 81.

213. *See*, Baron, Botsford and Cole, Live Organ and Tissue Transplants from Minor Donors in Massachusetts, 55 B.U.L. Rev. 159, 179 (1975); Comment, Spare Parts From Incompetents: A Problem of Consent, 9 J. Family L. 309 (1969).

214. 42 U.S.L.W. 2322 (Ga. Sup. Ct., Fulton Cty. Nov. 29, 1975).

215. For further discussion of this point, *see*, ch. 2., *supra* at 86.

216. Arizona, Arkansas, California, Connecticut, Delaware, Georgia, Idaho, Iowa, Maine, Michigan, Minnesota, Mississippi, Montana, New Hampshire, North Carolina, Oklahoma, Oregon, South Carolina, Utah, Vermont, Virginia, West Virginia, and Wisconsin. *See*, Pate and Plant, Sterilization of Mental Defectives, 3 Cumberland-Samford L. Rev. 458 (1972).

217. Paul, The Sterilization of Mentally Retarded Persons: The Issues and Conflicts, 3 Family Planning/Population Rep. 96, 97 (1974).

218. 274 U.S. 200 (1927).

219. *Id.* at 205–206.

220. *Id.* at 207.

221. *Id.*

222. *Id.*

223. Baron, Voluntary Sterilization of the Mentally Retarded, in Genetics and the Law 267 (Milunsky and Annas eds. 1976).

224. *See* Eisenstadt v. Baird, 405 U.S. 438 (1972); Roe v. Wade, 93 S. Ct. 705 (1973).

225. Am. Neurological Ass'n., Comm. for the Investigation of Eugenical Sterilization, Report (1936); Ferster, Eliminating the Unfit—Is Sterilization the Answer?, 27 Ohio St. L.J. 591 (1966). *See* In re Cavitt, 182 Neb. 712, 157 N.W.2d 171 (1968).

226. 221 S.E.2d 307 (N.C. 1976).

227. *Id.* at 311.

228. *Id.* at 312.

229. *Id.*

230. *Id.* at 313.

231. *Id.*

232. *Id.* at 315.

233. *Id.* at 309.

234. 316 U.S. 535 (1942).

235. *See* Silent Minority, *supra* note 3, at 33; Kittrie, The Right to Be Different: Deviance and Enforced Therapy 298 (1971).

236. *See* Murdock, Sterilization of the Retarded: A Problem or a Solution?, 62 Calif. L. Rev. 917, 924–932 (1974).

237. 9 Ore App. 224, 495 P.2d 768 (1972).

238. *See* In re Moore, 44 U.S.L.W. 2385 (N.C. Sup. Ct. Jan. 29, 1976); In re Cavitt, 182 Neb. 712, 157 N.W.2d 171; 183 Neb. 243, 159 N.W.2d 566 (1968).

239. 378 N.Y.S.2d 989 (N.Y. Sup. Ct., Jan. 26, 1976).

240. *Id.* at 990.

241. *Id.* at 991.

242. Krugman, Ward, Giles & Jacobs, Infectious Hepatitis: Studies on the Effect of Gamma Globulin on the Incidence of Inapparent Infection, 174 J.A.M.A. 823 (1960); Krugman, Giles & Hammond, Viral Hepatitis, Type B (MS-2 Strain), 218 J.A.M.A. 1665 (1971); Krugman & Giles, Viral Hepatitis, Type B (MS-2-Strain), 288 J.A.M.A. 755 (1973).

243. For some description of conditions at Willowbrook, *see*, Rivera, Willowbrook: A Report on How It Is and Why It Doesn't Have to Be That Way (1972); Ramsey, The Patient As Person 47-58 (1970); N.Y.U. Medical Center, Proceedings of the Symposium on Ethical Issues in Human Experimentation: The Case of Willowbrook State Hospital Research (Urban Health Affairs Program, N.Y.U. Medical Center, May 4, 1972).

244. *See* Bedlam in 1972—Retarded Care at Willowbrook, Med. World News, Jan. 28, 1972, at 15.

245. *Id.* (quoting Dr. William G. Bronston).

246. *Id.* at 16 (quoting Dr. William G. Bronston).

247. *See* Note, Voluntarily Confined Mental Retardates: The Right to Treatment vs. The Right to Protection from Harm, 23 Catholic U.L. Rev. 787, 791 (1974).

248. Bedlam in 1972—Retarded Care at Willowbrook, *supra* note 244 (quoting Dr. Michael S. Wilkins).

249. *Id.* at 16.

250. Experimentation, Real Paper, Aug. 7, 1974, at 6.

251. Ratnoff, Who Shall Decide When Doctors Disagree? A Review of the Legal Development of Informed Consent and the Implications of Proposed Lay Review of Human Experimentation, 25 Case Western Res. L. Rev. 472, 489 (1975).

252. Bedlam in 1972—Retarded Care at Willowbrook, *supra* note 244, at 17. *See*, Ingelfinger, Ethics of Experiments on Children, 288 N. Eng. J. Med. 791 (1973); Ratnoff, *supra* note 251, at 489-491.

253. Krugman, Experiments at the Willowbrook State School, 1 Lancet 966, 967 (1971).

254. Bedlam in 1972—Retarded Care at Willowbrook, *supra* note 244, at 17.

255. *See* Beecher, Research and the Individual 119 (1970); Katz, Experimentation with Human Beings 1007 (1972).

256. Willowbrook, Hepatitis and Dr. Saul Krugman 2 (N.Y.C. Med. Comm. for Human Rts.).

257. Bedlam in 1972—Retarded Care at Willowbrook, *supra* note 244, at 17.

258. Willowbrook, Hepatitis and Dr. Saul Krugman, *supra* note 256, at 1.

259. Studies with Children Backed on Medical, Ethical Grounds, 8 Med. Tribune 1, 23 (1967). *See* Krugman & Giles, Viral Hepatitis—New Light on an Old Disease, 212 J.A.M.A. 1019, 1020 (1970).

260. Ratnoff, *supra* note 251, at 490.

261. 393 F. Supp. 715 (E.D.N.Y. 1975), 357 F. Supp. 752 (E.D.N.Y. 1973).

262. *See*, text accompanying notes, 196-200 *supra*.

263. 393 F. Supp. at 718.

264. Civil No. 74-004-130 DC (Cir. Ct., Wayne Cty., Mich.) (filed Feb. 19, 1975).

265. *See*, note 67 *supra*.

266. *See*, text accompanying notes 87-89.

267. *See*, text accompanying notes 90-94.

268. *See*, text accompanying notes 202-203.

Chapter 6

Fetal Research: The Limited Role of Informed Consent in Protecting the Unborn

Of all research discussed in this book, experimentation with fetuses is perhaps the most controversial. Indeed, the National Research Act[1] required the National Commission for the Protection of Human Subjects of Biomedical and Behavioral Research to report on fetal research before dealing with any other topic.

The recent controversy has been stirred by a number of factors. Primary among these is probably the United States Supreme Court decision of *Roe v. Wade*[2] that liberalized all abortion laws in the United States. By increasing the number of abortions, this decision also increased the number of fetuses and the amount of fetal material that would be available for research. At the same time, the medical profession has shown a heightened interest in prenatal and perinatal diagnosis and treatment, thereby necessitating additional fetal research.

Only a small portion of the controversy surrounding fetal research is directly related to the issue of informed consent. Most of the debate focuses on the ethics of such research, the morality of abortion, and whether or not the fetus is "human" and therefore deserving of protection. However, there has been a good deal of legislative action[3] and scholarly examination[4] on the subject of the legal control of experimentation with fetuses as will be discussed in this chapter.

TYPES OF FETAL RESEARCH

Professor Maurice Mahoney has conducted an extensive literature review of over three thousand articles dealing with fetal research.[5] He has classified fetal research into the four areas discussed below.

Growth and Development in Utero

The purpose of this type of research is to obtain information concerning the normal physiological and metabolic development of the fetus. Anatomic studies are usually performed on extrauterine dead fetuses. Such studies utilize a variety of chemical, histological, and x-ray procedures, and are conducted on dead fetuses from both spontaneous and induced abortions. In some studies, however, such as studies of brain tissue, in which specimens must be obtained very quickly after death, fetuses resulting only from induced abortions (after hysterotomies) are used.

The majority of physiologic and metabolic studies also utilize tissues from dead fetuses, although some of these studies are commenced prior to the abortion itself. In such studies, a chemical is usually given to the mother a few hours before the abortion or caesarian section, and, following the procedure, metabolic products are analyzed from fetal blood.

Fetal behavior is investigated in a number of ways. Ultra-sound is used to study fetal breathing, fetal hearing is documented by using a sound stimulus given through the maternal abdomen, with a response determined by a change in fetal heart-rate, and fetal vision is inferred from changes in fetal heart-rate when a light is shined transabdominally. Previable fetuses which are the products of a hysterotomy are used to document swallowing movements in a twelve-week fetus, and response to touch is demonstrated in a seven-week fetus.[6]

Diagnosis of Fetal Disease or Abnormality

Since 1966, 800 papers have been published dealing with the detection of genetic defects. Techniques used are (1) amniocentesis, (2) radiologic procedures, (3) ultrasound, (4) the identification of fetal cells in maternal blood, (5) the detection of fetal metabolites in maternal urine, and (6) direct observation of the fetus using a fetoscopy. In several cases, therapy of some sort is instituted after the discovery of a fetal abnormality. Such techniques are also used as an aid in genetic counseling.

A number of studies have been done on lung maturation. Included in this area are studies in which corticosteroids are introduced into the amniotic fluid to increase the rate of maturation in the hope of saving the lives of prematurely born infants. The effect of the substance on other developing organ systems is, however, presently unknown.[7]

Fetal Therapy and Pharmacology

According to Professor Mahoney's study, very little, if any, research has been performed for the sole purpose of determining the effect of a drug on a fetus. The vast majority of the studies deal with the effect drugs have on a fetus when taken by the mother for therapeutic purposes.

All studies done to determine the effect of drug ingestion in early pregnancy have been performed in a retrospective manner. The drugs in question were used by the mother for her own reasons (such as birth control pills or heroin), and the effects on the fetus were later observed.

There are other studies that attempted to determine the effects of antibiotics, hormones, anticonvulsants, and other substances that the mother would take to treat an illness during pregnancy. Similar to these are studies that determine the effect on the fetus of drugs used to facilitate labor, such as analgesics and anesthetics.

Studies have been done to determine whether or not live virus vaccines, following administration to the mother, would cross the placenta and invade the fetus. In a study of rubella vaccine, women who requested an abortion were asked to take the vaccine and to postpone the abortion procedure for three to four weeks. These studies showed that the vaccine did affect the fetus.[8]

Research on Previable Fetuses
Outside the Uterus

Of the 3,000 articles found through the literature research, only fourteen dealt with studies of previable *ex utero* fetuses. Such research can encompass a broad spectrum of manipulation, from merely observing the fetus, to mild manipulations associated with measuring the fetus, to monitoring fetuses with instruments such as an electroencephalogram, to collection of samples of urine, hair and blood, to collection of tissues through biopsies of skin or brain, or removal of whole organs.

Some of the interventions are even more extreme. One study which seems particularly gruesome, and which is commonly cited by opponents of fetal research,[9] involved measuring the ability of the fetal brain to utilize substances other than glucose for fuel. To perform this study, the researchers removed the heads of eight fetuses of twelve to seventeen weeks gestation, and passed solutions of these substances through the isolated heads.

A few studies have been done in an attempt to discover ways in which to keep fetuses alive. A number of fetuses survived up to twenty-two hours by the use of a variety of medical techniques.[10]

ETHICAL ISSUES

Perhaps more has been written on the topic of the ethics of fetal research than on any other area of this subject matter. The morality of abortion, the use (or exploitation, depending on your point of view) of these uncomprehending subjects, the issue of the "humanness" of the fetus, and the interests of society have been repeatedly argued and discussed.

Joseph Fletcher,[11] a proponent of fetal research, believes that the core issue which must be addressed is whether or not the fetus is a person. He readily agrees that a fetus is biologically part of the human species, but argues that this fact does not mean that a fetus must be given the status of a person. Fletcher also believes that it is specious to maintain that one must protect the fetus because it has the potential to become a human, since this view fails to differentiate between what is and what is yet to be. In addition, he feels that a fetus is precious or "has value" only when its potentiality is wanted by its progenitors. Indeed, it is Fletcher's position that not to perform fetal research on "nonpersons" is immoral because such research would not only help avert or treat fetal disorders in fetuses that are wanted, but can also teach us how to prevent spontaneous abortions and how to help maintain the health of pregnant women.

Paul Ramsey merely states that it is "obvious that fetal research is human experimentation."[12] He goes on to draw analogies between certain classes of human beings and fetuses. For example, he likens fetuses to a newborn infant, to an unconscious patient, to a dying patient (spontaneous abortion), and to a condemned person (induced abortion).[13] However, Ramsey is not opposed to all fetal research, and would permit such research if it were for the fetus' benefit or would not entail risk to the fetus.[14]

The issue of "risk" to the fetus is another essential aspect of the ethical arguments concerning fetal research. Thus, if a fetus is about to be legally aborted, and the abortion will lead to death, does research on such a fetus constitute any risk of harm? What does the fetus lose by being subjected to such research? Perhaps the most in depth analysis of this issue has been performed by Sissela Bok,[15] who has analyzed the interests of various parties who might be involved in fetal research.

First, Dr. Bok analyzes the interest society has in protecting human life as follows:

a. For the victim, harm and/or killing:

1) if anticipated, causes intense anguish, fear, and a sense of loss of all that can be experienced and valued in life,

2) Can cause great suffering,

3) Can unjustly deprive those who have begun to experience life of their continued experience thereof.

b. For the agent, killing and harming others can be brutalizing and criminalizing. It is not only destructive to the agent, therefore, but a threat to others.

c. For the family of the victim and others who care there can be deep grief and loss. They may be tied to the victim by affection or economic dependence; they may have given of themselves in the relationship so that its severance causes deep suffering.

d. All society, as a result, has a stake in the protection of life. Permitting killing and harm sets patterns for victims, agents, and others, that are threatening and ultimately harmful to all.[16]

Dr. Bok then suggests that, as long as only fetuses which are less than eighteen weeks of gestational age and less than 300 grams in weight are used for research, the dangers listed above can be avoided.[17] Such young fetuses cannot feel pain or fear death, are not conscious of the interruption of their lives and are not tied by bonds of affection to others. An abortion or research with such fetuses will not cause grief to the parents of a nature similar to the death of a child, nor will it be brutalizing to the person performing it.[18]

Because there is no semblance of human form, no conscious life or capability to live independently, no knowledge of death, no sense of pain, words such as "harm" or "deprive" cannot be meaningfully used in the context of early abortion and fetal research.[19]

Of course, the very issue of abortion is often interjected into the debate regarding fetal research. On the one hand, one may ask:

Ought one to make experimental use of the products of an abortion system, when one would object on ethical grounds to many or most of the abortions performed within that system?[20]

No matter how one answers these questions, it only resolves the issue as it relates to one class of fetuses on whom experiments may be performed.

On the other hand, it is argued that, since we as a society condone abortion through our laws, any experiment that might be done would be considerably less of an assault against a fetus than the abortion itself.[21] This is a much broader approach because it states that a societal lack of concern for all fetuses should permit one to perform all sorts of research on a variety of fetuses.

The very nature of this type of ethical analysis points to the fact that the ethical issues are unresolvable. Moral "facts" can neither be proved nor disproved. What we do know is that fetal research has been done, and continues to be done, and that ultimately any protection the fetus will receive will be from the law.

THE FETUS AND THE LAW

For the most part, the law follows Fletcher's previously stated theory that one must differentiate between what will be and what is. Traditionally, the fetus *in utero* had virtually no vested rights at all, but had inchoate rights that would vest at birth. Thus, for example, the killing of a fetus *in utero* has never been found to be homicide. Homicide requires the killing of a "person," and no person exists prior to birth. Generally, birth requires complete expulsion from the mother, breathing, and independent circulation.[22] A 1970 California Supreme Court case upheld the theory that, in the absence of a specific feticide statute, the intentional killing of a viable fetus *in utero* (thirty-one to thirty-six weeks gestational age) does not constitute homicide.[23]

In the area of tort law, the older cases found that one could not be held responsible for injuring a fetus *in utero*. The earliest case, *Dietrich v. Northampton Hospital*,[24] involved a four-to-five month pregnant woman who slipped on a highway due to a defect in the road. Justice Holmes, then sitting on the Massachusetts Supreme Judicial Court, found that, since a fetus is not a person in being, no one could owe it a duty of care, and therefore no one could be held liable for any injury caused to it. He added that this ruling would not be affected by the age of the fetus.

In 1946, this approach began to change with the case of *Bonbrest v. Kotz*,[25] in which a child injured during delivery sued a physician for malpractice. Unlike the *Dietrich* case, this court found that the injury was actually done to a viable child who was born alive. The court stated that, if it held that the child could not sue for damages, the child would be compelled to live a life with the heavy burden of infirmity, which it incurred due to no fault of its own, but rather due to the fault of another. As a matter of natural justice, the court held that the child should be compensated for the damage done to it. Since 1946, a number of courts have held that a fetus may recover for injuries done to it *in utero* as long as the injuries were sustained after viability and the child was born alive. The trend seems clear, however, that if a fetus is injured any time during a pregnancy and is later born alive, it may collect damages for that injury.

The requirement of live birth seems to demonstrate that courts are not concerned with the protection of the fetus, per se, but with the protection of the living child. After a child is born alive it will need special medical care, schooling and a variety of other assistance even if it received its injuries while *in utero*. The courts have been finding that the person who caused this *child's* injuries should be responsible for making its existence as comfortable and normal as possible.

A growing number of states also permit recovery if the fetus is born dead as a result of some individual's wrongdoing.[26] These suits are brought as actions for "wrongful death," which are entirely matters of statutory law and not based on common-law or constitutional rights. Indeed, such cases truly compensate potential parents for loss of the child they would have had had it not been for the wrongful actions of some individual, and do not involve the protection of fetal rights.

In a separate area of the law, fetuses cannot own or inherit property. Should property be left to a fetus, its right to that properly only vests after live birth.[27]

Roe v. Wade

Certainly the most important judicial statement regarding fetal rights is the 1973 Supreme Court decision of *Roe v. Wade*,[28] which had the effect of liberalizing all United States abortion laws. Because of the many misconceptions about this case, and because the issue of fetal research and abortion are often bound together, it is worthwhile to examine this case in some detail.

Roe involved a pregnant unmarried woman who wished to have an abortion. A resident of Texas, she was unable to procure an abortion because Texas law permitted a woman to have an abortion only if the procedure were required to save her life. The woman involved did not fall into this category, and claimed that the statute was unconstitutional. In its lengthy opinion, the Court examined various aspects of fetal rights and the history of abortion.

First, the Court found that present day attitudes and laws concerning abortion are of fairly recent vintage. Neither the ancient Greeks or Romans seriously disapproved of the practice of abortion. At common law, an abortion performed before quickening (the first recognizable movement of the fetus *in utero*) was not an indictable offense.[29] After quickening, abortion was probably not a felony, but a lesser offense.[30]

The first American statute regarding abortion was adopted in Connecticut in 1821 and outlawed abortion after quickening. Abortion before quickening was made a crime in that state in 1860.[31] In the middle and late 19th century, most states adopted abortion laws which did not draw distinctions on the basis of quickening and which increased the degree of the offense, and the penalties associated with it. By the end of the 1950s almost all states had laws banning abortion unless it was performed to preserve the life of the mother. Thus, the Court found that abortion had historically been looked upon with less disfavor than during recent times.

According to the Court, there were three possible reasons for the adoption of restrictive abortion laws in the 19th century—discouragement of illicit sexual conduct, regulation of a medical procedure dangerous to the mother's health, and protection of fetal life. First, the Court found that no one today would argue that society should adopt abortion laws to discourage certain sexual conduct, and if that were the rationale, the law would have to be deemed to be unconstitutional.[32]

Second, the Court found that when most criminal abortion laws were enacted, the procedure was hazardous to the mother. However, modern abortion techniques were found to be relatively safe, indeed as safe or safer than normal childbirth, especially when the procedure is performed early in the pregnancy.[33] As a result of this fact, the state interest in the protection of the woman from a hazardous procedure has virtually disappeared. However, the state can regulate abortion, as it does all other medical procedures, in order to ensure that it is performed in medically safe circumstances.

The third contention, that the state has an interest in protecting fetal life, is the one the Court addressed most seriously. At the outset, the Court found that the constitutional right to privacy encompassed a woman's decision concerning termination of her pregnancy,[34] and that this right is "fundamental," which means that a state must demonstrate a "compelling state interest" before it can be invaded.[35]

In weighing the interests of the state against the right to privacy of the woman, the Court held that a fetus has never been found to be a "person" within the meaning of the Fourteenth Amendment of the

Constitution, and therefore is not entitled to constitutional protection.[36] Additionally, as discussed previously, neither tort nor criminal law has protected the fetus.[37] However, it was found that the woman's right to privacy is not absolute, and that the state's interest becomes more compelling as the length of time the woman is pregnant increases. Therefore, at about the end of the first trimester, the abortion procedure becomes more hazardous to the mother and the state may regulate it to the extent that the regulations reasonably relate to the protection of maternal health.[38] The state interest in protecting the life of the fetus becomes valid after viability, because it is at this point that the fetus "has the capability of meaningful life outside the mother's womb."[39] The state may at this point proscribe abortion altogether, except when it is necessary to preserve the life or health of the mother.[40]

With all that has been said and argued regarding this decision's impact on the rights of fetuses, one may see from this analysis that it really says very little about what the state can do to protect fetuses. The holding of this case is that, up to the point of viability, the woman's right to privacy is greater than the state's interest in protecting fetal life. It is concerned with the right of the woman to make a decision concerning the continuation of her pregnancy. It does not say that a state cannot pass a feticide statute, or allow a child to recover for damages done to it when it was a fetus *in utero*, or regulate fetal research. It does not say that the state has no interest in fetal life or health, but only that its interest is not sufficient to override a woman's right not to continue her pregnancy.

Thus, after *Roe*, it is as difficult as ever to actually determine what legal control a woman has over her fetus other than the decision to have it removed from her body. For example, in a pre-*Roe* case, a pregnant woman refused to undergo transfusions that were necessary to sustain the life of her fetus.[41] In this case, the court found that the "unborn child" had a right to the law's protection, and a transfusion was ordered. After *Roe*, the mother could argue that, since she has a right to abort the child, she has a right not to undergo the transfusion necessary to protect its life or health. The state could argue that, as long as she doesn't terminate her pregnancy, there is always the possibility (perhaps the probability, depending on the circumstances) that the child will be born, and the state has a right to ensure that the children of the state are healthy.[42] In effect, the right to be free from pregnancy may not be equivalent to the right to injure the fetus as long as the pregnancy continues.

There is an issue in the regulation of fetal research which is directly related to a woman's right to terminate her pregnancy. In Massachusetts the fetal research statute states that no research may be conducted on a fetus that is "the subject of a planned abortion."[43] This means that a woman who intends to exercise a constitutional right is prevented from participating in an activity in which one who does not intend to exercise this right is permitted to engage. In effect, a "penalty" exists for the exercise of a constitutional right. It has been suggested by one legal commentator that such a provision might be an unconstitutional invasion of a "woman's right to decide about what medical steps are in her own best interests."[44] Whether or not this is the case is not clear. *Roe v. Wade*, as we have seen, did not say a woman can do anything she wants with her body. It states that the right to privacy extends to the decision whether or not to continue a pregnancy. Under the fetal research statute, a woman would not be prevented from receiving an abortion under any circumstances. Unless one can argue that she has a right to volunteer her fetus to be a research subject, it is difficult to perceive how this statute interferes with any right she might have.

It is true that the state, through this statute, does differentiate between women who intend to have an abortion and those who do not. But the state does have certain interests that it might put forth to justify this distinction. It might argue, for example, that it does have an interest in fetal well-being, and that a woman who intends to abort is less likely to protect the fetus than one who does not desire to abort. (This is further discussed in the next section). Alternatively, it may state that its interest is in maternal well-being. That is to say, if a woman submits her fetus to a procedure that might injure the fetus, the woman in fact loses the ability to later change her mind in regard to the decision to terminate her pregnancy. By drawing this distinction, the state helps to preserve the woman's free choice. Unless a woman has a fundamental right to volunteer her fetus to be a research subject, it would be surprising to have a court strike down these reasons as being irrational.

Consent
The issue of who can consent to research on the fetus is one of the most hotly debated questions in the fetal research area. In discussing this problem, it will be necessary to break down fetal research into different types and discuss each one individually.

The Dead Fetus
This is the easiest category to discuss since one need not be concerned with protecting this class of fetus from harm. Proxy consent to experiment on a dead fetus should be no different from proxy

consent to experiment on a dead person. In such cases, one is actually concerned with protecting the sensibilities or rights of the survivors, and therefore it is their consent that is required. The Uniform Anatomical Gift Act specifically permits guardians to donate the body of a decedent for purposes of medical research.[45] The term decedent encompasses "stillborn infant" and "fetus."[46]

Therapeutic Research

For purposes of therapeutic research either *in utero* or *ex utero*, there once again appears to be little difficulty in permitting a parent to consent on behalf of a fetus. Indeed, by consenting to research that might benefit the fetus, the parent demonstrates a desire to further the best interests of her potential child, and to protect it from harm. If we permit proxy consent in order to protect the uncomprehending subject, it would seem that the prospective parent would be qualified to give proxy consent to therapeutic research on the fetus.

Nontherapeutic Research

Nontherapeutic research on a fetus which has been or is about to be aborted presents us with the most difficult problem. On the one hand, there is the argument that, since a woman can consent to an abortion which terminates the fetus' life, she should be able to consent to virtually any other act that affects the fetus. As has been dis discussed above, the right to have an abortion involves the right of the woman to be free from pregnancy, and not the right to do anything she chooses to the fetus.

On the other hand, there are those who argue that parents lose the right to consent to research on a fetus when they agree to an elective abortion. It is argued that we allow parents to consent to experimentation on their children because they care about their children's best interests, will protect their children from harm, and have a personal, including financial interest in the future health of their child. In other words, they have a direct personal stake in protecting their child from harm. However, one who chooses to have an abortion when it is not medically required demonstrates a lack of concern for that fetus' future, has no personal stake in that fetus, and thus will not serve to protect that fetus from harm which might result from research.[47] Ramsey summarizes this point of view by stating that it would be "morally outrageous . . . to designate women who elect abortions for comparatively trivial reasons, or for social convenience or economic betterment,"[48] to decide whether or not a fetus will be the subject of an experiment.

The assumption that a majority or even a substantial minority of women who have abortions have them for "trivial reasons" is the basis for any argument against the acceptability of maternal consent. Without further proof, this argument must be deemed specious. The decision to terminate one's pregnancy is often an agonizingly difficult one for a woman to make. The fact that an abortion is not required to save the life or health of the mother does not mean that the decision is easily reached. There are certainly psychological ties between the mother and the fetus even when the mother decides to abort her pregnancy.[49] It may also be argued that a fetus will probably be better protected by its mother than by a judge or some other state official.[50]

As a matter of law, consent to experiment on a fetus may not be required at all. If one returns to Sissela Bok's analysis described earlier, there may be no interest in young fetuses that needs to be protected by the use of consent. Of course, the consent of the mother to *in utero* research would still be required as her body is being invaded. If the state chooses to require consent to fetal research, it could do so along the lines of research on children, especially after the fetus becomes viable. Thus, consent could be given only to non-therapeutic research that presents either no risk of "harm" or a risk of minimal "harm" to the fetus.[57] Of course, the concept of "harm" might change depending on the development of the fetus. For example, a very young fetus may not be able to experience pain, whereas a more mature fetus may be capable of doing so. In addition, the use of an ethical review panel could be used to further protect the fetus. Laws and regulations promulgated for this purpose are discussed in the following section.

Laws and Regulations

At lease fifteen states have enacted legislation regarding fetal experimentation. More legislation has been passed concerning fetal research than any other type of research. Both the number of statutes, as well as their generally poor quality, demonstrate the emotional aspect of this issue. Virtually all these statutes were passed within the two years following the *Roe v. Wade* decision.

One of the most interesting aspects of this legislation is that very little, if anything, is said about consent. The only statute that directly addresses the maternal consent issue states in its entirety:

Experimentation with fetuses without written consent of the woman shall be prohibited.[52]

If this provision changes the law at all it makes it more liberal. No distinction is drawn between therapeutic and nontherapeutic research, or between *in utero* or *ex utero* research.

The Kentucky statute indirectly discusses the consent issue. It states:

> Whoever shall sell, transfer, distribute or give away any live or viable aborted child or permits such child to be used for any form of experimentation shall be imprisoned in the penitentiary for a term of not less than ten (10) nor more than twenty (20) years.[53]

This statute would penalize any person who consented to research on a fetus, although not the person who actually conducted the research. In this state, the crime is the consent itself. It does not apply to fetuses *in utero*, nor does it appear to permit therapeutic research.

Perhaps the most detailed statute, the Massachusetts law, does not even mention the consent issue as it pertains to live fetuses.[54] The statute commences by stating a general prohibition against all research on live human fetuses, whether before or after expulsion from the womb. The remainder of the statute states exceptions to this general rule. One may study a fetus *in utero* if such a procedure does not "substantially jeopardize" the life or health of the fetus and provided the fetus is not the subject of a planned abortion. The mother is given the authority to consent to research on a dead fetus.[55]

Perhaps the most blatant example of overreaction to this issue is found in Louisiana, where the law states that:

> Human experimentation is the use of any live born human being, without the consent of that live born human being . . . for any scientific or laboratory research or any other kind of experimentation or study except to protect or preserve the life and health of said live born human being, or the conduct on a human embryo or fetus in utero, of any experimentation or study except to preserve the life or to improve the health of said embryo or fetus.[56]

The "crime of human experimentation" is punishable by imprisonment at hard labor for not less than five nor more than twenty years, or a fine of not more than ten thousand dollars, or both.

This statute outlaws all research on children, some institutionalized mentally ill persons, some prisoners, and anyone else who cannot given consent for themselves, since they are all "live born." Also, any person who experiments on an individual who has not given adequate consent may be imprisoned for a long period of time. The problem is exacerbated by the fact that the term "consent" is not defined in the statute.

A similar problem, perhaps in an even more extreme form, exists in Maine, which outlaws the use of "any product of conception considered live born . . . for any form of experimentation," and subjects violators to a fine and imprisonment.[57] As every person in existence is a "live born product of conception," this statute may ban all research on human beings in that state.

Other statutes deal with the issue in a nonuniform and haphazard manner. Utah prohibits all research on "live unborn children," but says nothing about *ex utero* research.[58] Ohio prohibits research on the "product of human conception which is aborted," but says nothing about *in utero* research.[59] Illinois outlaws the "exploitation or experimentation" of "aborted tissue"[60]

The examination of fetal research laws demonstrates a hodgepodge of regulation and prohibition, with little consistency among the various jurisdictions. It is instructive to note, however, that informed consent plays a very small role in any of the regulatory schemes, which may indicate that, when a legislature truly desires to control research, informed consent is not a sufficient mechanism.

. The federal government has also become involved in regulating research with fetuses. After a number of drafts,[61] H.E.W. promulgated final regulations following receipt of recommendations from the National Commission for the Protection of Subjects of Biomedical and Behavioral Research.[62]

Under these regulations, two Ethical Advisory Boards are to be created by the Secretary of H.E.W. One is to advise the Public Health Service and its components, and the other is to advise all other agencies within H.E.W. concerning application for research on fetuses and pregnant women.

Additional duties are also imposed on individual Institutional Review Boards.[63] In connection with research on fetuses and pregnant women, they must determine that adequate consideration has been given to the manner in which potential subjects will be selected, and must make sure that an adequate mechanism exists for monitoring "the actual informed consent process."[64]

The regulations provide general limitations on fetal research which state:

a. No activity to which this subpart is applicable may be undertaken unless:

1) Appropriate studies on animals and nonpregnant individuals have been completed;

2) Except where the purpose of the activity is to meet the health needs of the mother or the particular fetus, the risk to the fetus is minimal and, in all cases, is the least possible risk for achieving the objectives of the activity.

3) Individuals engaged in the activity will have no part in: (i) Any decisions as to the timing, method, and procedures used to terminate the pregnancy, and (ii) determining the viability of the fetus at the termination of the pregnancy; and

4) No procedural changes which may cause greater than minimal risk to the fetus or the pregnant woman will be introduced into the procedure for terminating the pregnancy solely in the interest of the activity.

b. No inducements, monetary or otherwise, may be offered to terminate pregnancy for the purpose of the activity.[65]

The regulations specifically permit *in utero* therapeutic research, and allow *in utero* nontherapeutic research as long as the risk to the fetus is minimal and the purpose of the research is the development of "important biomedical knowledge which cannot be obtained by other means."[66] Prior to conducting fetal research, the consent of both parents is required, except that the father's consent need not be secured if his identity or whereabouts cannot reasonably be ascertained, he is not reasonably available, or the pregnancy resulted from rape.[67]

Prior to conducting research with *ex utero* fetuses, a person not involved with the research must determine if the *ex utero* fetus is viable.[68] This determination need not be made prior to conducting the research if there is "no added risk" to the fetus as a result of the research and it is for the development of important biomedical knowledge that cannot be obtained by other means. If an *ex utero* fetus is determined to be viable, it is subject to the regulations, yet to be promulgated, that control research with children.[69] As a general rule, vital function of the nonviable *ex utero* fetus may not be artificially maintained. This may be done where the purpose of the research is to develop new methods for enabling fetuses to survive to the point of viability.[70] This is true even though the fetus-subject will not benefit from this research. Under no circumstances do the regulations permit activities that would cause termination of fetal heartbeat or respiration. Finally, any nontherapeutic research that is done must be for the purpose of developing important biomedical knowledge that cannot be obtained by other means.[71] The consent requirement by the mother and father is the same as for *in utero* research.

Thus, the federal regulations do permit a variety of nontherapeutic and therapeutic research, both *in utero* and *ex utero*, to be conducted when it is the only way to acquire a certain body of important biomedical knowledge. Although informed consent of the parents does play a role here, the truly regulatory aspects of the H.E.W. regulations go directly to the type of research permitted and prohibited.

BRITISH GUIDELINES

The H.E.W. regulations, which were adopted pursuant to recommendations made by the National Commission, are similar in many respects to guidelines adopted in Great Britain in 1972, and differ in other respects. The British guidelines were developed by an expert advisory group appointed by the government, and their final product is known as the "Peel Report" after the chairman, Sir John Peel.[72] The guidelines in this report are rather straightforward, and in some places extremely specific.

1. *In utero* research is only permissible if its purpose is to benefit the mother or the fetus. Any other *in utero* research is impermissible even if the mother intends to have an abortion.[73]
2. Only procedures that are performed to promote the life of the fetus are permissible on viable fetuses after delivery. According to the Peel Report evidence of a period of gestation of twenty weeks (approximately 400–500 grams) should be regarded as prima facie proof of viability.[74]
3. Virtually any procedure may be performed on a previable *ex utero* fetus as long as it is found by the hospital ethics committee that the research is "valid," that the sought after information cannot be obtained any other way, and that investigators have the necessary facilities and skills. However, to ensure an extra margin of safety, only fetuses weighing 300 grams may be used for such research.[75]
4. The issue of consent is treated very differently in the British guidelines than in the United States guidelines. The Peel Report finds that when the fetus is viable, the parent's consent to procedures that promote and preserve the fetus' life can be "inferred." In the H.E.W. guidelines consent is never inferred. When the procedure will neither benefit nor harm the fetus, the Peel Report requires the consent of one parent.[76]
5. All fetal research must be approved by an "ethical committee" within the institution in which the research is to be conducted. These committees are to consist of only physicians.[77]

CONCLUSION

Regulation of research on fetuses is perhaps the most complex and emotional issue discussed in this book. Such regulation is made more complex in that, unlike the other subjects we have discussed, the term "fetus" encompasses a number of different types of "subjects." It can be previable, or viable, *in utero* or *ex utero*, and the way we regulate this type of research may depend on which categories the particular fetus falls into.

The emotional nature of the issue is spurred by the feeling of some individuals that the fetus is the most unprotected of all subjects. It is the smallest, totally unable to protect itself, and often without someone willing to protect it.

Additionally, it is also the only subject of research whose very "personhood" is questioned. It is claimed by some that a previable fetus is nothing more than a piece of unwanted tissue, while others argue that from the moment of conception a fetus must be treated like any other member of the human race.

The confusion over these issues has led a number of legislatures to rush and try to regulate or prohibit research on fetuses. This legislation is almost totally ineffectual, and often irrational.

Fortunately, H.E.W. with the assistance of the National Commission has attempted to deal with these issues, and has promulgated regulations that, while not perfect, do try to solve some of these problems in a rational manner. The only thing that can be said with certainty about the fetal research issue, is that a great deal of uncertainty will exist for quite some time. Regulations and laws will be written and rewritten in an attempt to balance the interests society has in medical advances, with any interests the fetus may have in being left alone.

REFERENCES

1. P.L. 93–348 §202(b).
2. 410 U.S. 179 (1973).
3. *See* pp. 206, *infra*.
4. *See, e.g.*, Reback, Fetal Experimentation: Moral, Legal and Medical Implications, 26 Stanford L. Rev. 1191 (1974); Munson, Fetal Research: A view from Right to Life to Wrongful Death, 52 Chicago-Kent L. Rev. 133 (1975); Martin, Ethical Standards for Fetal Experimentation, 43 Fordham L. Rev. 547 (1975).
5. *Research On the Fetus*, Report and Recommendations of the National

Commission for the Protection of Human Subjects of Biomedical and Behavioral Research, Appendix at 1-1. (Hereinafter "Appendix")

6. *Id*. at 1-2—1-5.

7. *Id*. at 1-5—1-14.

8. *Id*. at 1-14—1-22.

9. *See, e.g.*, Tiefel, The Cost of Fetal Research: Ethical Considerations, 294 New England Journal of Medicine 85, 85 (Jan. 8, 1976).

10. *Supra* note 5 at 1-22—1-25.

11. Fetal Research: An Ethical Appraisal, Appendix 3-1.

12. Ramsey, *The Ethics of Fetal Research* 28 (Yale University Press, 1975).

13. *Id*. at 28-29.

14. Ramsey, Moral Issues in Fetal Research, Appendix 6-1 at 6-7.

15. Bok, Fetal Research and the Value of Life, Appendix 2-1.

16. *Id*. at 2-6.

17. *Id*. at 2-12.

18. *Id*. at 2-7.

19. *Id*.

20. Walters, Ethical Issues in Experimentation on the Human Fetus, 2 J. of Religious Ethics 33 (Spring 1974), cited in Ramsey, *supra* note 12 at 30.

21. Gaylin and Lappe, Fetal Politics: The Debate on Experimenting with the Unborn, unpublished manuscript, cited in Ramsey, *supra* note 12 at 41.

22. 159 ALR 523 (1945). *See generally*, Comment, The Nonconsensual Killing of an Unborn Infant: A Criminal Act, 20 Buffalo Law Rev. 563 (1970-71).

23. Keeler v. Superior Ct., 87 Cal. Rpt. 481, 470 P.2d 617 (1970).

24. 138 Mass. 14 (1884).

25. 65 F. Supp. 138 (D.D.C. 1946).

26. *See*, Chrisafogeorgis v. Brandenburg, 55 Ill. 2d 368, 304 N.W.2d 88 (1973); Note, Damages for the Wrongful Death of a Fetus—Proof of Fetal Viability, 51 Chicago-Kent L. Rev. 1 (1974); Note, Wrongful Death-Recovery for Death of a Viable Unborn Child, 39 Mo. Law Rev. 665 (1974).

27. Roe v. Wade, 410 U.S. 113, 162 (1973); Matter of Peabody, 5 N.Y.2d 541, 158 N.E.2d 841 (1959).

28. 410 U.S. 113 (1973).

29. *Id*. at 132.

30. *Id*. at 133.

31. *Id*. at 138.

32. *Id*. at 148.

33. *Id*. at 149.

34. *Id*. at 153.

35. *Id*. at 155.

36. *Id*. at 158.

37. *Id*. at 161-2.

38. *Id*. at 163.

39. *Id*.

40. *Id*. at 164.

41. Raleigh Fitkin-Paul Memorial Hospital v. Anderson, 42 N.J. 421, 201 A.2d 53 (1964), cert. den. 377 U.S. 95 (1964).

42. *See, e.g.*, In re Sampson, 317 N.Y.S. 641 (1970); In re Clark, 185 N.E.2d 128 (Ohio, 1962).

43. Mass. Gen. Laws Ch. 112 §12J.

44. Capron, The Law Relating to Experimentation with the Fetus, Appendix 13-1, 13-30.

45. *See, e.g.*, Mass. Gen. Laws Ch. 113 §8(b) and 9.

46. Mass. Gen. Laws Ch. 113 §7(b).

47. *See* Ramsey, *supra* note 12 at 93-96.

48. *Id.* at 95.

49. Toulmin, Fetal Experimentation: Moral Issues and Institutional Controls, Appendix 10-1, 10-18, and Capron, *supra* note 44 at 13-19.

50. Capron, *supra* note 44 at 10-19.

51. *See* Chapter 3 on Research with Children.

52. South Dakota Code 34-23A-17.

53. Kentucky Rev. St. 436.026.

54. Mass. Gen. Laws Ch. 112 §12J.

55. For a discussion of how the Massachusetts statute was adopted *see*, Culliton, Fetal Research: The Case History of a Massachusetts Law, 187 Science 237 (Jan. 24, 1975) and Culliton, Fetal Research (II): The Nature of a Massachusetts Law, 187 Science 411 (Feb. 7, 1975).

56. La. Rev. St. Title 14 §87.2.

57. Maine Rev. Statutes, Title 22 §1574.

58. Utah Crim. Code 76-7-316.

59. 1974 Laws of Ohio, Am. Sub. House Bill 989.

60. Ill. Crim. Law and Proc. Ch. 38 §81-18.

61. 38 Fed. Reg. 31747 §46.31 (Nov. 16, 1973); 39 Fed. Reg. 30653 §46.301 (August 23, 1974).

62. 40 Fed. Reg. 33526 (Aug. 8, 1975). The report of the Commission may be found on pages 33530-33551 in the same volume.

63. 40 Fed. Reg. 11855 §46.7(b).

64. 40 Fed. Reg. §3529 §46.205 (August 8, 1975).

65. *Id.* at 46.206. Paragraph (a)(2) appears as amended by 40 Fed. Reg. 51638 (Nov. 6, 1975).

66. *Id.* at 46.208(a)(2).

67. *Id.* at 46.209(b).

68. *Id.* at 46.206(3)(ii), 46.209(g).

69. *Id.* at 46.203(d) and 46.209(c).

70. *Id.* at 46.209(b)(1).

71. *Id.* at 46.209(b)(3).

72. The Use of Fetuses and Fetal Material for Research, Report of the Advisory Group, Chaired by Sir John Peel (London, 1972), Appendix 19-1.

73. *Id.* at 19-6, paragraph 26.

74. *Id.* at 19-7—19-8, paragraphs 28-31.

75. *Id.* at 19-8—19-9, paragraphs 32-35.

76. *Id.* at 19-10, paragraphs 41-42.

77. *Id.* at 19-12, paragraphs 47-48.

※ *Chapter 7*

Psychosurgery: The Regulation of
Surgical Innovation

Psychosurgery has been a focal point in the debate over human experimentation and the role of informed consent and institutional review committees. Only psychosurgery and fetal experimentation were, for example, singled out for special consideration by the Congress in the National Research Act of 1974 (P.L. 93-348). Because of the extensive discussion it has received, and because of the issues it illustrates concerning informed consent to surgical experimentation and the role of review committees in approving and monitoring consent procedures, we are devoting a separate chapter to psychosurgery. In doing this some of the points made in other chapters will of necessity be repeated, and an effort has been made to cross-reference material where appropriate.

Participants in the psychosurgery controversy generally espouse one of three competing points of view. First, there are the surgeons who argue that psychosurgical procedures have developed beyond the experimental stage to the point where they may be considered therapeutic for certain types of patients.[1] Second, there are those who support further research in the area in the hope of developing genuinely therapeutic procedures, but who recognize the importance of safeguarding against potential abuses in the course of this development.[2] Finally, there are the antipsychosurgeons, who argue for the total prohibition of psychosurgery on ethical, spiritual, or political grounds independent of its characterization as experimental or therapeutic.[3] While definitions vary, for the purposes of this discussion, the term "psychosurgery" will be used to mean any procedure that destroys brain tissue for the primary purpose of modifying behavior.[4]

TRADITIONAL MECHANISMS OF LEGAL REGULATION

Historical Overview

The first procedure fitting this definition was the prefrontal lobotomy developed by Egas Moniz in 1935.[5] It was first performed in the United States in 1936, by Drs. Walter Freeman and James Watts of George Washington University.[6] Schizophrenic patients who had been habitually hospitalized and who were irritable and helpless became "quiet, more cooperative, clean, able to eat by themselves, capable of working in the hospital, and could even be sent home to their families."[7] In addition, these patients lost their ability to solve simple problems, to reason abstractly, and to relate to their family members.[8] It was the side effect of extreme passivity,[9] however, that eventually brought the procedure to the attention of a criminal court.

In 1945, Millard Wright was arrested for ten house-breaking and robberies in Pittsburgh, Pennsylvania. Six weeks after his arrest, he refused to eat or converse, seemed confused and apparently attempted suicide. He was therefore transferred to a hospital for the criminally insane until he was placed on trial in 1947. At that time both Wright's lawyer and the local district attorney requested that the defendant be lobotomized in an attempt to cure him of his criminal tendencies. The judge agreed, but upon Wright's return to court two months after his lobotomy a different judge was presiding. Both the surgeon and the defendant were eager to have an opportunity to test the efficacy of the procedure, but the new judge was not convinced that Wright should be allowed to go free. However, because of Wright's demonstrable desire to help medical science, he received a comparatively light sentence of 2 to 12 years instead of the possible 40 years to life. Wright later committed suicide while in prison.[10]

In 1949, the Stanford Law Review discussed the problems involved in drafting a statute to regulate the use of lobotomy and concluded that "the greater good will be achieved by avoiding legislative fetters and relying for protection on the high standards of the medical profession and the individuals who compose it."[11] The Soviet Union demonstrated its disagreement with this conclusion by its prohibition of the performance of lobotomy in 1951.[12] As N.I. Oserezki, a Soviet psychiatrist, told the World Federation of Mental Health, the procedure is "an antiphysiological method that violates the principles of humanity [and] makes the patient an intellectual invalid. . . ." Through lobotomy, he argued, "an insane person is changed into an idiot."[13] Arguing the contrary position in the United States, Drs. Freeman and Watts wrote "(i)t is better for the patient to have a simplified intellect capable of elementary acts, than an intellect where there reigns the disorder of subtle synthesis. Society can accommodate itself to the most humble laborer, but it justifiably distrusts the mad thinker."[14] Thus, Freeman was satisfied when he could reflect upon his operations and comment "[o]n the whole, lobotomized patients make rather good citizens."[15]

Throughout the 1950s and 1960s, psychosurgery was ignored by the legal community. During this time, however, there existed and continued to develop a general system of regulation over medical practice. This system provides the context for current proposals to further regulate psychosurgery. As will be demonstrated, informed consent played almost no role as a potential control mechanism until the 1970s.

Private Actions

As with other medical procedures, the best known course of action available to a dissatisfied patient is the malpractice suit.[16] A psychosurgical patient might successfully sue for malpractice on any one of the following three grounds: (1) the performance of the procedure was negligent; (2) the patient did not give informed consent to the procedure; or (3) the method of review constituted negligence.

Negligent Performance of the Procedure. A claim that the performance of a psychosurgical procedure was negligent may actually involve one or more of three individual questions: (1) what procedure was used; (2) what were the qualifications of the person performing the procedure; and (3) was the chosen procedure performed without negligence. Doctors have a legal duty to perform on at least the level of the "average practitioner"[17] or, if they are specialists, on the level of the "average specialist."[18] If violation of this duty results in injury to the patient, he is entitled to compensation. Certainly this duty requires, at a minimum, that the physician not employ discredited procedures. The classical lobotomy, as exemplified by the techniques of Dr. Walter Freeman, involved the insertion of a device shaped like an ice pick into the patient's orbital cavity while the patient was anesthetized through electroshock treatment. This device was moved around within the cranial cavity to grossly cut tissue.[19] In view of the general agreement among contemporary

surgeons that the performance of the classical lobotomy is unjustifiable, it would seem that any patient subjected to such a procedure
should be successful in a malpractice suit. Dr. Bertram Brown, Director of the National Institute of Mental Health, said: "I think I can
state unequivocally that no responsible scientist today would condone a classical lobotomy operation."[20]

Generally, of course, there is the question of whether the performance of any psychosurgical procedure is justified. Apart from the
controversy over the therapeutic value of psychosurgery, there is the
further consideration that the United States has an oversupply of
neurosurgeons. Thus, there is tremendous pressure on each neurosurgeon to justify his specialization, a phenomenon that may lead to
the performance of unnecessary surgery.[22] Indeed, psychosurgery
has been performed to treat homosexuality,[23] violent behavior,[24]
and marijuana use[25]—although performing surgery for these latter
indications may have more to do with one's view on deviance rather
than with one's avarice.

Another avenue of attack relates to the psychosurgeon's professional qualifications. States license doctors to practice medicine,[26]
but do not directly oversee their work. Thus, if a licensed doctor
can obtain an operating room, he may perform whatever form of
surgery he desires even if he has had no surgical training. Two-thirds
of all the surgeons practicing in the United States today are either
certified by the American Board of Surgery or by a subspecialty
surgical board, or are currently in training leading to such certification.[27] The remaining one-third, however, are self-designated surgeons. Dr. Walter Freeman, for example, was a psychiatrist.[28] He
disagreed with the view of his colleague Dr. James Watts "that any
procedure involving cutting of brain tissue is a major operation and
should remain in the hands of the neurological surgeon."[29] Freeman's view notwithstanding, it would seem that the performance
of psychosurgery by any physician lacking either certification to
perform neurosurgery or equivalent training should constitute malpractice.

A psychosurgeon may also be negligent in the performance of the
procedure. A case in Kentucky, for example, involved a surgeon who
missed the temporal lobe connections and destroyed the patient's
optic nerve instead. A settlement was reached out of court for a substantial but undisclosed amount.[30]

The Absence of Informed Consent. As has been discussed in
more detail in the first chapter, the concept of informed consent is
presently being redefined by the courts.[31] This redefinition is de-

signed to give the patient more power and to thereby equalize the doctor-patient relationship; a development consistent with judicial innovation in the landlord-tenant,[32] seller-buyer,[33] employer-employee,[34] creditor-debtor,[35] warden-prisoner[36] and police-suspect[37] areas. Medical treatment in the absence of consent has traditionally been regarded as a battery; a touching by the doctor not consented to by the patient.[38] More recently, the courts have begun to find an affirmative duty on the part of the physician to inform the patient of the risks involved in a suggested procedure and the available alternatives. A breach of this duty may form the basis of a suit for negligence.[39]

Since 1972, certain courts have gone even further by holding that expert testimony is not required to define the duty of disclosure. The emphasis, instead, is on the patient's perception of his situation.[40] In the words of one court, "the patient's right of self-decision is the measure of the physician's duty to reveal . . . [and] the test for determining whether a potential peril must be divulged is its materiality to the patient's decision."[41] Employing this perspective, a leading case has held a doctor liable for not disclosing to the patient that laminectomy carries a one percent risk of paralysis.[42] There seems to be almost uniform agreement that the risks of psychosurgery are not fully known and that they are therefore unquantifiable.[43] Thus, a patient's consent to psychosurgery could not be informed unless he were at least made aware of the dangers that have been documented, the fact that serious and permanent unknown side effects may develop, and the possibility of death.

Additional problems are introduced when the patient's competency is questioned. Arguably, no patient who can be considered a candidate for psychosurgery is capable of giving informed consent to the procedure because, in the physician's view, his brain is either damaged or malfunctioning. In such cases, the law usually gives the patient's legal guardian the power to consent to treatment,[44] but recent cases have made it clear that there are limits to the exercise of proxy consent. For example, as discussed in the chapter on children, parents have been required to obtain court approval for their consent to kidney[45] and bone marrow[46] transplants involving healthy, minor siblings who act as donors.

Dr. Peter Breggin, perhaps this country's most ardent opponent of psychosurgery, claims that psychosurgery is no more "a medical procedure . . . than the mutilation of an arm as punishment of a crime is a medical procedure."[47] This argument has legal implications because neither individuals nor their legal guardians may consent to a procedure that may be considered a maim or mutilation.[48]

The ancient rationale for this rule was the king's right to be the aid of his subjects. The rule survives, however, due to the state's interest in maintaining the health of its citizens. Maiming is therefore analogous to murder in that consent on the part of the victim is not a valid defense.[49] In the case of *State v. Bass*,[50] for example, a doctor was convicted as an accessory before the fact to the crime of mayhem for anesthetizing the fingers of an individual who desired to amputate them to obtain insurance proceeds. The actual amputation was performed by the individual when the doctor refused to perform the procedure himself.

The argument could be made that psychosurgery, like the amputation in the *Bass* case, involves the removal of nonpathologic tissue and thus constitutes the common law crime of mayhem. The counterargument would be that psychosurgery may be performed for the sound medical purpose of alleviating aberrant behavior. However, there are more direct ways to modify behavior. Should the result have been different in the *Bass* case if the patient sought the removal of his fingers to render himself incapable of using a gun during periods of violence? Alternatively, should the result have been different if, instead of aiding the amputation of the patient's fingers, the defendant has paralyzed them using a neurologic procedure?

The paralysis or removal of portions of an individual's brain in an antiseptic and highly sophisticated operating room has seemed so far removed from the early mayhem cases that the analogy has rarely been mentioned.[51] Although this mayhem argument would not apply to those psychosurgical operations that involve an underlying brain pathology, it would cover the removal or destruction of healthy brain tissue for the sole purpose of modifying behavior. Whether or not liability should follow directly from this analogy, it is certainly compelling enough to indicate that stringent safeguards must be instituted to protect patients before psychosurgical procedures are performed. The current emphasis on such protective procedures suggests yet another ground for a malpractice action.

Negligence in the Method of Review.   A successful suit for negligence must rest on the breach of a duty owed by the defendant to the plaintiff. Such duties are often based on the standard of the reasonable person which, in turn, often refers to what is the "usual and customary conduct of others under similar circumstances. . . ."[52] The current absence of psychosurgery review committees in almost all hospitals does not, however, mean that a review committee is not legally required. Indeed, as Judge Learned Hand wrote in the leading case of The T.J. Hooper:[53]

(I)n most cases reasonable prudence is in fact common prudence; but strictly it is never its measure; a whole calling may have unduly lagged in the adoption of new and available devices. It never may set its own tests, however persuasive be its usages. Courts must in the end say what is required; there are precautions so imperative that even their universal disregard will not excuse their omission.[54]

Thus, a tugboat company was held negligent for not having radio communications aboard even though it was acting in conformance with the prevailing standards within the industry. This rationale has also been employed to hold a hospital liable for its failure to ensure that a general practitioner call in an orthopedic consultant in a particular case, although such supervision was not customary and to hold opthamologists liable for failure to routinely test for glaucoma, even though such testing was not generally performed by other specialists.[55] In light of the known dangers involved in psychosurgical practice, courts would be justified in improsing upon hospitals where psychosurgery is performed, a duty to provide exhaustive scientific and lay review even though such procedures are not as yet customary.[56]

In addition, if there is an established review committee, it may be liable for negligence in the performance of its duties.[57] If it could be demonstrated that a committee breached a duty to protect the interests of prospective psychosurgical candidates by allowing the operation to be performed on inappropriate subjects, the committee itself as well as the hospital may be liable under traditional negligence theory.

The first reported court case involving psychosurgery, *Kaimowitz v. Department of Mental Health*,[58] may provide a specific illustration of negligence on the part of review committee members. One member of the review committee in that case failed to attend any of the meetings relating to the proposed surgery on the plaintiff. It was his view that:

As a layman I am unqualified to comment on any of the technical aspects which are involved in the project. Therefore we must all trust the good intentions and technical competence of the Hospital Medical Committee, psychologist, psychiatrists, neurologists, etc., who have reviewed and evaluated John Doe's case.[59]

If it was clear to this committee member what his responsibilities were, then such evasion of them would be morally unjustifiable. And if, as appears necessary for responsible action on their part, a duty to protect the patient is imposed on such committees, such inaction would constitute its breach of this duty.[60]

Public Actions

Before a new drug is put on the market, the manufacturer is required to demonstrate to the satisfaction of the Food and Drug Administration that it is both safe and effective.[61] If one wishes to experiment with a new surgical technique, however, no prior approval from any governmental or professional agency is generally needed before its use is promoted. The history of heart transplants illustrates the absence of regulation over surgical innovation. The first human heart transplant was performed in South Africa on December 3, 1967.[62] In a race to match this performance, more than 100 transplants were performed within the following year.[63] The fad ended rather quickly, however, because of the operation's high cost and low success rate. Both the initiation of the craze and its demise were governed solely by the actions of individual surgeons.

The growth of psychosurgical practice has taken place in much the same fashion. Psychosurgeons reporting their own results on their own scales have claimed amazing rates of success.[64] Although these self-evaluated "before and after" studies reveal some of the dangers involved, their anecdotal nature destroys their utility for the purpose of determining whether psychosurgery is a therapeutic medical procedure. A review of the medical literature reveals only two well-designed retrospectively controlled studies of psychosurgery. They conclude that lobotomy does not improve one's chances of leaving a mental institution.[65] The only prospective case-controlled studies that exist support the efficacy of psychosurgery in only the most limited of ways.[66] Finally, there are no controlled studies of the more modern forms of psychosurgery, such as amygdalectomy and cingulotomy.[67] Studies done in 1976 under contract to the National Commission for the Protection of Human Subjects of Biomedical and Behavioral Research are extremely limited, and are discussed in detail later in this chapter.

Dr. Henry Beecher has demonstrated the importance of controlled studies in the evaluation of surgical techniques.[68] His research presents convincing evidence that there is a placebo effect in surgery comparable to that in drug therapy. In a prospectively controlled study of ligation of the mammary artery to relieve angina, for example, it was discovered that those receiving placebo surgery— that is, an incision was made, the artery was located but not ligated, and then the incision was closed—improved in clinical and objective terms as much as those receiving the actual mammary ligation. Also citing other studies of surgical treatments now in disrepute, Beecher was able to suggest that the placebo effect in surgery is approximately 35 percent.

Beecher also discovered other relevant variables affecting the "success" of placebo operations. These variables included the patient's frame of mind, usually one of stress due to pain or illness, and the relative enthusiasm of the surgeon for the procedure. Thus, in a study of gastroenterostomies for the treatment of duodenal ulcers, for example, skeptical surgeons obtained only half as many cures and 20 times as many marginal ulcers as did the enthusiasts.

These studies are particularly relevant to the debate over the efficacy of psychosurgical procedures. First, the candidate for psychosurgery is likely to be strongly motivated toward recovery. Second, the surgeons currently performing psychosurgery are enthusiasts who strongly believe in the ability of their procedures to allevaite symptoms.[69] Finally, the placebo effect is particularly prevalent when subjective psychologic states rather than pathologic entities are being treated. Thus, when Dr. Orlando Andy estimates his own success rate at 19 percent,[70] the efficacy of his procedures is called into serious question, because one might anticipate even better results on the basis of the placebo effect alone. Nor are "success" rates in the area of 50 percent very persuasive.

The absence of reliable medical data suggests that independent review of psychosurgical practice is required. Under present government policy, psychosurgeons' protocols are reviewed only when they are funded by grants or contracts from the National Institutes of Health (NIH) or when the facility in which their studies are being conducted receive such funds.[71] Although these categories may seem rather inclusive, most psychosurgeons in the United States operate on patients outside the framework of an experimental design.[72] Thus, for example, until 1975 Dr. Thomas Ballantine of the Massachusetts General Hospital regularly performed cingulotomies for depression, anxiety cases, obsessional neurosis, and intractable pain without independent review of either his surgical protocols or his consent procedures.[73] Dr. Orlando Andy also operated without committee review, until the summer of 1973 when the University of Mississippi Medical Center, though its Human Investigation Committee, decided that his surgery was basically investigative and experimental. Accordingly, a moratorium was imposed upon his performance of psychosurgery until an acceptable research protocol was submitted to the committee.[74]

Even this limited form of institutional review is a relatively new development. It was not until 1966 that NIH first promulgated a policy requiring such review for the purpose of determining whether (1) the rights and welfare of individual patients were protected; (2) informed consent was procured; and (3) the potential medical benefits either to the patient or to society outweighed the risks of the suggested procedure.[75] However, since the required review committees could be composed solely of physicians,[76] NIH policy promoted merely another form of peer review, a mechanism of control that has generally proven ineffective.[77]

CURRENT LEGAL RESPONSES TO PSYCHOSURGERY

Judicial Action

Only two reported cases to date have dealt directly with psychosurgical procedures outside of the malpractice area. The first, *Kaimowitz v. Dept. of Mental Health*, is a lower court opinion written by three judges that has no binding precedential effect in Detroit, Michigan or any other jurisdiction. Nevertheless, because it was the first case on the issue, it is important as the only case that existed for a number of years. While it is discussed for specific purposes in both the chapter on Prisoners and the chapter on Mental Patients, the case is important enough to review some of the facts again with emphasis on those that illustrate the court's view of psychosurgery itself, and the safeguards that should be instituted to protect psychosurgery candidates.

In 1972, two psychiatrists at the Lafayette Clinic sought and obtained state funds to study the effects of amygdalotomy and cyproterone acetate (an antiandrogen) on male aggression in institutional settings. The study protocol was approved both by a scientific review committee and by a multidisciplinary "human rights committee." Twenty-four candidates were originally sought, but only one, Louis Smith, was considered suitable. For 17 years he had been confined in a Michigan state hospital as a criminal sexual psychopath after being charged with murder and rape. The researchers presented Smith and his parents a detailed consent form, which they all signed.[79]

However, before the researchers were able to proceed with the implantation of electrodes, the Medical Committee on Human Rights filed a petition on behalf of Smith and similarly situated patients challenging the proposed research. It was ultimately discovered that Smith was being held unconstitutionally, and he was therefore ordered to be released.[80] In addition, publicity resulting from the case led Michigan's Department of Mental Health to withdraw its approval of the project. Nevertheless, a three-judge panel decided that the question involved was likely to arise again and proceeded to determine whether involuntarily confined individuals could ever legally consent to experimental brain surgery designed to ameliorate aggressive behavior.

After evaluating the risks and potential benefits of the proposed procedure with the help of expert testimony, the court concluded:

> [t]here is no scientific basis for establishing that the removal or destruction of an area of limbic brain would have any direct therapeutic effect in controlling aggressivity or improving tormenting personal behavior, absent the showing of a well-defined clinical syndrome such as epilepsy.[81]

On the other hand, however, the known risks to the physical and mental condition of the patient were great, including loss of reasoning ability, memory, and general apathy.[82] In light of this evidence, the court felt that psychosurgery must be regarded as highly experimental.

Proceeding to the question of consent, the court cited the entire text of the Nuremberg Code,[83] and concluded that the inherently coercive atmosphere of lengthy institutionalization so greatly diminishes an individual's capacity to make a reasoned and voluntary decision about an experimental and irreversible surgical procedure that it is impossible to give legally valid consent in such circumstances.[84]

Although the case was an important victory for proponents of the regulation of psychosurgery, the court's reasoning seems contradictory. The court emphasized the effects of institutionalization on the capacity of the patient to give informed and voluntary consent, and yet limited its holding to experimental situations. If amygdalotomy were to be considered an accepted neurosurgical practice, the involuntarily detained mental patient could, in the court's view, give legally adequate consent to the performance of the procedure on his brain.[85] The nonexperimental status of a procedure may increase the prospective patient's knowledge concerning the risks and benefits involved, but it in no way counteracts the effects of institutionalization on his ability to give competent and voluntary consent. The court could have avoided this difficulty by treating the effect of institutionalization on voluntariness and competence as a fact question to be determined in each case, rather than as a matter of law.

The case also raises serious questions concerning the efficacy of both scientific and human rights review committees. In the *Kaimowitz* case, such committees approved the protocol, but failed to maintain sufficient supervision to cancel the study when only one appropriate subject could be found. At least one member of the multidisciplinary committee personally interviewed Smith to determine the voluntariness and competency of his consent. Smith did, in fact, assure that member of his willingness to participate in the experiment, but upon his release from custody he withdrew his previously given consent.[86] It is therefore questionable whether well-meaning human rights committees can adequately evaluate the coercive effect of institutionalization on prospective candidates for controversial procedures. The promotion of such mechanisms of review in this context may only provide false comfort to our consciences.[87]

The second case, *Aden v. Younger*, also mentioned in the chapter on Mental Patients, involved a challenge to an initial attempt by the state of California to regulate psychosurgical procedures by statute.[88] The challenged statute provided that patients involuntarily detained and persons voluntarily admitted to state hospitals, private mental institutions, county psychiatric hospitals, and certain mentally retarded persons, had a right to refuse psychosurgery. It provided further that no such patient who *wanted* psychosurgery could have it unless he met the following conditions:

(a) The patient must give written informed consent, dated, witnessed and entered in his record. The consent may be withdrawn at any time. An oral explanation by the doctor is necessary.

(b) The patient must have the capacity to consent.

(c) A relative, guardian or conservator has been given a thorough oral explanation.

(d) The reasons for the surgery must be in the patient's record, other treatments must be exhausted and surgery must be critically needed.

(e) Three appointed physicians (two board-certified psychiatrists or neurosurgeons), must examine the patient and unanimously agree with the treating physician's determinations and that the patient has capacity to consent. There must be a 72-hour wait after the patient's written consent before surgery.[89]

This statute was challenged as unconstitutional by a patient who wanted a "multiple target procedure" type of psychosurgery and her physician. The court, citing the *Kaimowitz* decision, found that psychosurgical procedures are "destructive" of brain tissue and "experimental" in nature, and presented "undisputed dangers" to the patient.[90] While the court found generally that the state could properly regulate psychosurgery as a legitimate exercise of the state's inherent police power, it found certain portions of the statute unconstitutional. It found specifically, for example, that the term "critically needed" was "so imprecise" as to be "impermissibly vague," since the term "provides no guide to the degree of need required."[91] The court asks rhetorically, "If all other forms of appropriate therapies have been attempted has a critical need for ECT or psychosurgery been established?"[92] It concludes that this and other questions are ones that the statutory language is incapable of answering.

The other major objection the court found to the statute was the requirement of notifying a "relative, guardian or conservator" of the elements of informed consent before the treatment could be administered. The court agreed with the plaintiffs that this requirement constituted an impermissable invasion of the patient's right to privacy and confidentiality, and served no legitimate state purpose since no standing was given to the relative to assert the patient's individual rights.[93] As important as these two holdings of the case are, perhaps the most noteworthy aspect of the court's decision is its *approval* of the review committee procedure.

The court notes that such a review is justified for incompetent patients or patients whose competence is suspect in order to promote "the state's interest in protecting patients from unconsented-to and unnecessary psychosurgery"—and that such a review can insure that the patient is competent and the consent voluntary.[94] The court further approves such review for involuntarily committed patients whose voluntary consent can "never be adequately confirmed," as the only alternative to an outright prohibition of psychosurgery on this population.[95] The court finds the most difficulty with requiring the review procedure for competent and voluntary patients, but approves it, explaining:

> There are sound reasons why the treating physician's assessment of his patient's competency and voluntariness may not always be objective, and he may not necessarily be the best or most objective judge of how appropriate an experimental procedure would be. Because the consequences to the patient are so serious, and the effects he may suffer are so intrusive and irreversible, tort damages are totally inadequate. The need for some form of restraint is a sufficiently compelling state interest to justify the

attendant invasion of the patient's right to privacy. The right is not absolute and must give way to appropriate regulation.[96]

The court also and significantly approved the requirement that the three physicians be unanimous in their decision saying, "Requiring unanimity by the review committee insures each approved treatment is an appropriate use of an experimental procedure."[97] While the great majority of the statute on psychosurgery was thus approved (the portion of the statute on ECT was also discussed by the court and disapproved because ECT was seen as a less intrusive and dangerous procedure), the court declared the entire statute unconstitutional since the legislature had shown no intent to make its provisions severable.

Nonetheless, the court's approval of a review committee mechanism to help insure that informed, voluntary and competent consent was actually obtained is an extremely important decision since this mechanism is perhaps the most controversial proposal to be considered as a supplement to informed consent. As will be discussed in the following section, it is currently law in only one other state, and in another state controversy over a similar proposal has thus far prevented psychosurgery regulations from being adopted.

In the fall of 1976 the Governor of the State of California, Gerald Brown, signed a revised statute designed to meet the court's objections.[98] It retained the provisions for unanimous review by three physicians, but made the notification of a "responsible relative" optional with the patient. The statute also contains extremely explicit language on the subject of informed consent and the manner in which it is to be obtained.[99]

Legislative Action

Other than the California statute just discussed, Oregon is the only state to attempt to regulate psychosurgery formally. Their statute provides that psychosurgery may be performed only with the affirmative vote of at least six members of a statewide nine-member review board. The function of this panel is to determine, according to statutory guidelines, whether the consent of the patient or his legal guardian is "informed" and "voluntary" and whether the proposed procedure is "appropriate treatment for the specific patient."[100]

The provisions of the statute are, however, insensitive to certain problems raised by psychosurgery. At least a majority and as many as seven members of the nine-member board, may be physicians. Only one must be an attorney and only one is designated as a "member of the general public." The board is thus heavily biased toward the scientific research community and may approve the performance of psychosurgery even in the face of a dissent by all the public and "lay" members.

Another problem with the statute relates to the nature of the hearing. If the patient has a legal guardian, the board is required to review only the consent of the guardian and the appropriateness of the proposed procedure. The patient himself need not testify, and the board may approve the procedure even if the prospective patient specifically opposes it. Unlike *Kaimowitz*, then, the statute can be read to sanction the performance of psychosurgery on a nonconsenting, involuntarily committed mental patient under guardianship so long as six of the nine board members approve. It seems certain that the sponsors of the statute were responding to the emerging concept of the "right to treatment" in allowing this result. As *Wyatt v. Stickney*[101] made clear, however, involuntarily committed mental patients are entitled to "a *realistic* opportunity to be cured or to improve (their) mental condition."[102] Moreover, that court specifically addressed the problem of psychosurgery in the following manner:

> Patients have a right not to be subjected to treatment procedures such as lobotomy, electroconvulsive treatment, adversive reinforcement conditioning or other unusual or hazardous treatment procedures without their express and informed consent after consultation with counsel or interested party of the patient's choice.[103]

In its attempt to establish a unified approach to psychosurgery, the Oregon legislature oversimplified the problems of consent by failing to make any distinctions among voluntarily or involuntarily confined mental patients, prisoners, children, or competent adults. Finally, a lawyer need not be appointed for any class of patients unless one is affirmatively requested. This choice or oversight could substantially weaken the protection for the mentally-disabled provided by the statute.

Nevertheless, even with these limitations and the additional difficulty experienced in obtaining an appropriation for legal and secretarial assistance, the Board's brief history is one of being an effective safeguard of patient rights. As of this writing, the Board has reviewed five cases. Three have been rejected and two are pending. It is instructive to review briefly the first four cases handled by the Board, all involving the same neurosurgeon.

Case 1:   This case involved a 22 year old housewife who had been diagnosed as psychotic or severely depressed with a "strong, chronic schizoid component." The application was returned for insufficient documentation and later withdrawn when the patient developed what her referring psychiatrist described as "some ambivalence toward the procedure."

Case 2:   This case involved a 34 year old male "obsessional accountant who had been treated with tranquilizers, antidepressives, phenothiazines, and ECT. After his physicians were notified of their failure to comply with the statutory requirements, the petition was abandoned. A member of the Board was later informed that the petition was withdrawn because "the patient had recovered while waiting for a hearing."

Case 3:   This case involved an obese middle-aged woman who had been treated for at least 25 years by her family physician with a wide variety of drugs. She had been institutionalized voluntarily, but repeatedly left and upon returning home called to demand that something be done for her. A number of psychiatric diagnoses were suggested, but the Board determined that from the history and data presented they could not determine whether she was suffering from an anxiety reaction or from multiple pulmonary emboli. During the hearing, the patient became acutely ambivalent, and only consented to reconsider the operation when assured she could withdraw her consent at any time. The Board determined that a complete and comprehensive psychiatric evaluation and treatment history had to be submitted before further proceedings were held. Several months later the petition was withdrawn when her attending physician wrote stating that she had died of a pulmonary embolus.

Case 4:   This case involved a 30 year old male inmate of the Oregon State Hospital who had been in and out of state institutions since he was nine years old. He was committed to the Hospital by a court after having been found dangerous but not guilty of murder by reason of insanity. He had a history of repeated assaults on guards and prisoners, including the killing of a prison guard, and a wide variety of therapies had been tried on him, including ECT which had to be given at least once a week to achieve noticeable results.

During the first hearing the patient sat in front of the committee and drooled, unresponsive to his environment, and obviously unable to give his consent. At a second hearing, several weeks later, he was "100% improved" and able to respond to questions in a "child-like fashion" but was unable to recall if the operation had already been performed or not. Diagnosis was anti-social personality, and passive-aggressive personality, explosive type. The Board advised the petitioners that a disinterested party would have to be appointed guardian and the guardian provided with legal counsel before the hearing could proceed.

The state hospital dropped the petition for awhile, then named themselves as guardian. The Board questioned the propriety of this action, and went to court to have it rescinded, which the judge did. Efforts are continuing to have an appropriate guardian selected.[104]

The fifth case is described as one that is "superbly documented" and one in which the consent hearing has been successfully completed. The Board found the patient capable of giving his informed consent, but ordered additional tests. After these were completed, and after doing some reading about psychosurgery, the patient has requested that the application be suspended, primarily due to a marked improvement in his condition.[105]

These cases illustrate at least two things: (1) some psychosurgery is done (or at least attempted to be done) with little medical rationale, a poor or faulty diagnosis, and an inadequate medical history; and (2) a consent committee that personally interviews the patient can be a powerful tool both in determining the competency and knowledgeability of the patient, and helping the patient make an informed decision. It performs this latter function by acting as a neutral and authoritative entity with which the patient can communicate his or her questions and concerns. The fact that three of the first five patients changed their minds after petitions were filed also illustrates the great danger in rushing ahead too fast with this form of surgery, and the importance of requiring a time lag of at least 72 hours between the signing of a consent form and the operative procedure.[106]

In Massachusetts, the Commissioner of Mental Health appointed a volunteer Task Force to develop proposed regulations on psychosurgery performed in the state. After a year of study the 14 member Commission issued a Report suggesting, among other things, review of the consent of the patient by a patient interview conducted by a multidisciplinary committee.[107] The Commission split 8 to 6, with the minority, all physicians, vigorously objecting to the review as an interference with the doctor-patient relationship and an encouragement of breaches of privacy.[108] The Massachusetts Medical Society hired a law firm to draft a position paper against the proposal and had it published in the *New England Journal of Medicine*.[109] The proposed Regulations had a public hearing at which they were attacked by the medical profession and some patients, and defended by one of the authors (GJA, a Commission member) and the state Attorney General's office.[110] After more than a year of closed door negotiations and rewriting, and the departure of the Commissioners of both Mental Health and Public Health, the regulations are in their eighth draft, with little prospect of adoption with the majority's review recommendations.

It is somewhat ironic that the issue of multidisciplinary review would doom these regulations in Massachusetts, since one of the state's only three neurosurgeon's performing psychosurgery had employed this method of review for more than a year prior to the appointment of the Task Force. Two of the authors (GJA and LHG) were members of that Boston City Hospital Committee which consisted of a physician, a psychiatrist, two lawyers, a political scientist, a minister, a medical student, a sociologist, a research biogeneticist, and two representatives from the local community. All members were chosen by the Chairman, Dr. David Allen, who himself was appointed by the Board of Trustees of the Hospital.

The Committee reviewed two cases in depth. Although both involved temporal lobe epilepsy, and are thus not the type of psychosurgery usually subject to either controversy or regulations,[111] review if appropriate for epilepsy is *a fortiori* appropriate for other modes of psychosurgery (except for intractible pain). In one case the Committee met with the patient, who was suffering from temporal lobe epilepsy, and his family a number of times over a period of approximately eight months. The committee determined, and the patient confirmed, that it was the adult patient's parents who were desirous of the operation and not the patient. Six months after this decision the patient returned to the surgeon and the committee with another request for "something to be done" about his seizures. Meetings were held with both the surgeon and the committee. After extended discussion with both the patient and his parents, the committee again concluded that the patient did not want surgery, and surgery was not performed.

In another case, involving a minor who was suffering from severe temporal lobe epilepsy, the committee met with the patient and her parents approximately three times over a two week period. The final session was videotaped. Consent was obtained and approved by the committee to an experimental psychosurgical procedure. Weeks after the procedure was performed the father of the patient contacted the committee chairman to express his appreciation for the thoughtfulness and completeness which characterized the committee's work. He concluded that he, his child, and his wife all felt they understood the alternatives, the risks, and the possibilities of success of the surgery in a way they could not have if the committee had not discussed these issues with them.

The experiences with patients at the Boston City Hospital, while limited, were all positive, and no patient or family member interviewed ever objected to the procedure or raised the issue of "breach of privacy" or confidentiality.

It should be noted in conclusion that regardless of their position on review committees personally interviewing the patient, all 14 members of the Massachusetts Department of Mental Health Task Force agreed that the following elements concerning informed consent should be set out on a written document signed by the patient before any psychosurgical procedure was performed:

How the procedure is performed.
It is the duty of the physician responsible for performing the procedure to explain to the subject, in lay terms, how the procedure is performed. The physician must also make himself available to answer any questions that the subject may have.

The risks involved in the procedure.
Risks of death or serious disability (e.g., paralysis, blindness, deafness, impotence, etc.) must be disclosed even if the probability of their occurring is minimal. Any risk that is expected to occur with more than 1% frequency must be disclosed even though it may not be considered serious (e.g., headache, temporary loss of memory, etc.). Any probability of the procedure making the problem for which surgery is being recommended worse, must also be fully disclosed.

The benefits to be derived from the procedure.
The subject must be told how successful or unsuccessful this particular procedure has been in the past with other patients as well as the probability for a successful outcome in his particular case. The subject must understand that success is not guaranteed, and what success means to the physician.

Available alternative modes of treatment.
The subject must understand what, if any, alternative modes of treatment are available. The risks, benefits, and probabilities of success of these treatments must be explained to the subject.

An understanding that a procedure is experimental or investigational, if it is, and what these terms mean. This should include the number of times the procedure has been performed and the outcomes.

The ability to rescind his consent at any time.
The subject must understand that he will not suffer in any way by withdrawing his consent and that alternative modes of therapy will be made available. The subject should also understand that if he decides not to undergo the procedure at this time, he may change his mind at a later date and the procedure will be performed at that time.[112]

Administrative Action

Much activity has recently taken place on the federal level in the

Department of Health, Education and Welfare. In 1974, HEW promulgated regulations that required all institutional review committees to be composed of "not less than five persons with varying backgrounds."[113] Also in 1974 Congress enacted the "National Research Act" which, among other things, set up the National Commission for the Protection of Human Subjects of Biomedical and Behavioral Research.[114] The Act charged this committee to review biomedical and behavioral research in general, but to give specific attention to two areas: fetal research and psychosurgery. Concerning psychosurgery the Commission was charged to:

". . . conduct an investigation and study of the use of psychosurgery in the United States during the five-year period ending December 31, 1972. The Commission shall determine the appropriateness of its use, evaluate the need for it, and recommend to the Secretary policies defining the circumstances (if any) under which its use may be appropriate."[115]

To fulfill this mandate the Commission had three studies performed. The first involved a literature review by Professor Elliot Valenstein.[116] From an extensive review, he concluded that:

1. Approximately 140 neurosurgeons in the U.S. performed from 400 to 500 psychosurgical operations annually in the years 1971, 1972 and 1973, after which the rates probably declined. 25% of these are performed by surgeons doing three or fewer operations a year, while four surgeons were responsible for 48% of all procedures reported in 1973.[117]

2. The most common diagnostic categories into which these patients fell were severe depression, obsessive-compulsives, phobia, and hypochondriacs.

3. Between 60 and 90% of patients (depending on diagnostic category) experience a significant reduction of their most troublesome symptoms.

4. There is no reliable evidence of any minority group being used in psychosurgery, and published data reveals only 7 cases of operations on children under 15 since 1970 in the U.S.

5. The published literature on psychosurgery is judged to be "quite low in scientific merit. For example, 56% of the articles published in the U.S. mentioned *no* objective test data."[118] Very few articles contain adequate information on patients, adequate experimental controls, or report the use of reliable test instruments. Because of the above considerations, the possibility that such factors as patient-selection bias, the patients' anticipation of favorable results (the "placebo effect"), and improved postoperative care and treatment can account for a sub-

stantial amount of the reported success of psychosurgery cannot be ruled out.

6. The rationale supporting psychosurgery has not advanced very much in the past 30 years.[119]

The second study involved a review of patient records and interviews with selected patients operated on by three surgeons. The surgeons were volunteers. The study was conducted by Dr. Allan F. Mirsky and Dr. Maressa Orzack.[120] Each surgeon studied specializes in a particular type of psychosurgery: one does only orbital undercuttings that sever fibers in the inferior surface of the frontal lobe; another performs multitarget bilateral, sterotaxic, radio frequency (or other) lesions aimed at 4-6 targets; and the third performs only prefrontal sonic lesions. From these three surgeons, a total of twenty-seven patients was individually examined. Based on two independent interviews patients were put into two classifications, "very favorable outcome" and "less favorable outcome." Fourteen were given the first classification and thirteen the latter. Classification was primarily based on the patient's own perception of degree of relief, current status, and willingness to undergo the operation again.[121]

From this study the researchers concluded:

1. The large majority of patients had adequate explanations of risks and benefits before surgery;

2. There was no significant evidence of neurological deficit attributable to the operation;

3. Depression may be especially amenable to psychosurgery; and

4. Retrospective research on psychosurgery is feasible, and "further study may help to illuminate the question of which patients may receive benefit from psychosurgical intervention."[122]

While the study may bear the weight assigned to it by its authors, it cannot be generalized to any other population. The major reasons are potential bias in the sample of surgeons, the subjective measures of success, and the use of both intractable pain subjects and subjects who had had a previous psychosurgical procedure in the sample. For example, if all pain patients[123] and all patients with a previous psychosurgical procedure had been eliminated, only thirteen patients would remain. This is hardly a sample group large enough to draw conclusions from, although the "success rate" in it would increase to almost 70 percent. On the other hand, if the first operation in patients having more than one was counted as a "failure," the success rate reported in this study would drop to approximately 38 percent—about the same as the placebo effect postulated by Beecher.[124] Thus, using three plausible measures, the success rate could vary from 38 to 70 percent. Likewise, the measure of "success" was so subjective and ill-defined as to be incapable of generalization. For example, the following case, as described by the authors, was one of the "very favorable outcomes:"

> This 54 year old white woman with a Ph.D. in mathematics and a history of severe depression and tension dating back 17 years to a postpartum depression after the birth of her second child. She was given anti-depressant medication but with limited effect. With ECT she improved somewhat but became depressed again. She was unable to obtain a job in the small midwestern town where her husband taught mathematics. This may have contributed to her feelings of depression and rejection.
>
> In 1970 she underwent psychosurgery. She made the decision herself with no disagreement from the family. She has no regrets and would do it again.
>
> Since surgery she has lost her depressive feelings. She is taking further training while in Boston for a year in order to have special qualifications for a job. Her performance on the IQ and Memory tests were superior although there was a considerable discrepancy between the verbal and performance scores. She was able to perform the Wisconsin Card Sorting and Benton Visual Retention Tests with minimal errors.[125]

One does not have to be a psychologist to find this case history ambiguous on many points, including alternatives to psychosurgery and quality of outcome. While it is shorter than most of the others, it is not otherwise unrepresentative.

The third study involved the review of thirty-four cases of cingulotomies performed by one neurosurgeon in Boston. The cases were reviewed by a team at the Massachusetts Institute of Technology headed by Hans-Lukas Teuber.[126] Eighteen of the thirty-four cases were seen and tested both before and after surgery. Sixteen of the thirty-four were deemed to have had "successful" surgery. However, eleven of these cases involved intractable pain (a procedure which Valenotein notes in his report is *not* psychosurgery) with nine successes in this category. If this group is eliminated, the "success rate" in this group drops to seven of twenty-three, or approximately 30 percent—somewhat less than would have been expected from the placebo effect alone. Further, if the first procedure in those that had two and the first two in those that had three are counted as failures, the success rate for the nonpain patients drops to less than 20 percent—much worse than one would have predicted based on the placebo effect alone. These figures are especially significant in this group of patients because the surgeon involved is strongly committed to his procedure, has tremendous faith in its efficacy, and has the ability (apparently) to impart this faith to his patients. He also operates in a community in Massachusetts where, as discussed previously, psychosurgery has been under scrutiny for a number of years. Again, an illustration of a "success" may prove enlightening:

A rather heavy-set unmarried country girl of 26, coming from a highly religious Catholic farm family in the Middle West who gives a history of having had a "breakdown" in her second year in college. Had multiple hospitalizations, has been on various mood-elevating drugs, received over 100 ECT when barely 20 years old. Called a severe unipolar depression in most of her medical records. Possibly first mood disorder in early teens (12 years old). Many religious preoccupations; during six to seven hospitalizations diagnosis of depression sometimes replaced by schizo-affective psychosis. Was considered resistant to all other treatments till (sic) she received her cingulotomy in July 1975. She describes outcome as "fantastic", relates it to interviewers in strongly religious terms, as a rebirth. Apparently had arguments with a priest beforehand who opposed surgery—now she wants to crusade for it. Works since the early postoperative period in a somewhat protected employment as a file clerk in a record room. Thinks her religious feelings have been deepened, but also claims to react more naturally than before to people around her; has her first boyfriend. Apparently in full remission for 3/4 year, should be followed for a longer period.[127]

As with the case illustration from the Mirsky study, this one raises more questions than it answers. However, also as with Professor Mirsky, Professor Teuber's conclusions from this "pilot" study are relatively modest. In his words:

Contrary to our expectations when this survey was begun, the cingulotomy procedure by itself did not visibly impair the patients' capacity to perform a wide range of tasks in the laboratory or in real life . . . The undeniable therapeutic effects that were seen in some cases, *most convincingly in those patients who had complained of persistent pain*, and least in the predominantly obsessional and compulsive patients may well represent a mixture, in unknown proportions, of placebo effects, and perhaps (relatively non-specific) neurochemical alterations, not necessarily at the point of surgical attack, but in areas to which the cingulum and adjacent fiber bundles project. Sprouting of injured fibers, and shifts in neurotransmitter balance, or even the development of some denervation supersensitivity might all play a role. (emphasis supplied)[128]

The writers conclude their report by proposing animal experiments on the implantation of brain tissue instead of its destruction as a possible method of modifying function by addition rather than destruction.[129]

On the basis of these limited studies the Commission made some rather remarkable initial recommendations in August of 1976. The first was that HEW "encourage" and financially "support" research on psychosurgical procedures.[130] This recommendation was based almost exclusively on the Mirsky and Teuber studies, summarized above, which the Commission found:

> provided evidence that (1) more than half of the patients improved significantly following psychosurgery . . . and (2) none of the patients experienced significant neurological or psychological impairment attributable to the surgery . . . *The presumption that all forms of psychosurgery are unsafe and ineffective was thus rebutted by research teams* . . . (emphasis supplied)[131]

Such a conclusion can only be made by both redefining the term psychosurgery as used in the legislation and giving the study results their most favorable interpretation. Specifically, Congress did *not* include intractable pain in its definition of psychosurgery.[132] If the fifteen patients with this diagnosis in the two studies are eliminated, the total sample drops from sixty-one to forty-six, the number of "successes" drops from thirty-one to twenty, the percentage of successes drops from 51 to about 43 percent—closing in on the "placebo effect" range. Further, if the first and second procedures involved in patients who had more than one are counted as failures (not an unreasonable thing to do), the success rate per nonpain operation drops to less than 30 percent, making the entire procedure immediatley suspect rather than immediately appealing. Moreover, the "lack of significant impairment" attributable to the surgery is also questionable. Of the sample group studied, one lost her job following surgery, another began to experience irregular menstrual cycles, another was permanently hospitalized, four began to have seizures, one became drug resistant, and at least three experienced significant weight gain.[133] Although it must be emphasized that the limitations of the study design make it impossible to draw meaningful conclusions about the significance of these impairments or their relationship to surgery.

The recommendation was not only unsupported by the data available to the Commission, it also goes in the opposite direction of current trends in legislation, judicial action, and administrative decision-making. The former two have been dealt with. As to administrative decision making, it was only two years ago when the Law Enforcement Assistance Administration decided to discontinue its funding of studies related to doing psychosurgery for violence. It was this type of experimentation that created the furor which brought the psychosurgery debate into the legislation that founded the Commission. The Commission did *no* study of amygdalotomy or any other type of psychosurgery for violence, yet apparently recommended further research in this area. Moreover, although its own studies leave much to be desired (each is being continued to attempt to obtain more data), the Commission felt itself on strong enough grounds to condemn the only legal decision in this area, the *Kaimowitz* case. It argued that if the court had had the data before it that the Commission had, it would not have prohibited the psychosurgical study in question.[134]

Many of these shortcomings were recognized, and at their meetings in September and December of 1976 the Commission decided to rewrite its August recommendations. Its final report on psychosurgery was released March 14, 1977. Unfortunately, it did not attempt to deal with the following three critical questions: (1) Under what circumstances, if any, should psychosurgery be permitted to be performed on individuals who cannot give their own informed consent if and when its effectiveness to modify behavior is demonstrated? A corollary to this question is, should the federal government place a high priority on trying to develop this capacity, or are its potentials for abuse such that its development should not be encouraged?; (2) Is there a constitutional right to be the subject of an experimental psychosurgical operation?; and (3) Should surgical innovation be treated like drug innovation, with strict controls applied until safety and efficacy are proven?

The first question is the one which really underlies the entire psychosurgery debate—rather than the question of safety as the Commission initially presumed. As the Commission's studies make clear, the decrease in morbidity and mortality from psychosurgery is the result of better operating techniques and better management of operating rooms, *not* a better understanding of what the surgeon is doing. As illustrated by their studies of four surgeons doing four completely different operations on different parts of the brain for essentially the same indications, no one knows why or how it "works," only that it sometimes does. But given that it is relatively "safe," the question of effectiveness still remains. Currently it is essentially unpredictable, even using the Commission's figures, in cases involving diagnoses other than pain. When it becomes wholly predictable, should this be viewed as a major scientific breakthrough or tragedy? Is the specter of a prison-free, *Clockwork Orange* society a realistic or foolishly naive view of our future? This issue demands systematic thought and concentrating on pain alleviation rather than neutralizing the violent prisoner or the political dissident purposely avoids it.

The second issue, the "right to be experimented on," is one the Commission currently seems somewhat uncertain about. Its prose introduction to its final March 1977 recommendations suggests that both prohibiting proxy consent to psychosurgery and prohibiting its use on prisoners "may be" unconstitutional,[135] as a violation of the patient's right to privacy. This is a highly dubious proposition, but one that is susceptible to constitutional analysis. The Commission did not attempt this, but has apparently assumed, on the basis of two cases which held the opposite, that such a right might exist.[136] What is probably at stake, although not well articulated, is the view of some Commissioners that individuals should not be "denied the potential benefits of a new therapy." That, of course, is exactly what regulation of human experimentation is about—the denial of "potential" benefits to the majority, until a favorable risk/benefit ratio and other relevant factors have been demonstrated. Courts have consistently rejected any notion that there is a constitutional right to take illicit drugs, and courts have traditionally upheld certain safeguards of individuals even though they may impinge with individual rights. Examples like maiming, dueling, and motor cycle helmets are discussed elsewhere in this book.[137]

The Commission also seems to be uncertain on the issue of patient confidentiality. Its final March 1977 Report, for example, attempts to keep members of the IRB from personally interviewing candidates for psychosurgery. Physicians, are, however, permitted to review individual patients apparently on the erroneous view that such conversations and examinations are "covered by the physician-patient privilege."[138] The final report does, however, permit complete IRB review at the patients' option, with a court review mandated if the patient refused and his capacity to give informed consent was questionable. Such a procedure, of course, merely substitutes a public forum for a private one, and can hardly be seen as protective of confidentiality. A more rational result would have been to require full committee interviews—by a special review committee set up for this purpose rather than an IRB—as a prerequisite to surgery.

Third, although the Commission's final report on psychosurgery consistently uses the terms "safe and effective," the Commission did not examine the critical question of whether it is either appropriate or possible to regulate surgical innovation in the same way drug innovation is currently regulated.[139] This important question deserved at least discussion in the psychosurgery report since it is the only one the Commission will do on surgical innovation.

All this is a rather lengthy, but we believe necessary, introduction to the Commission's final recommendations concerning the informed consent and review procedures to be employed in research involving psychosurgery. Essentially the Commission recommended that such research only be done in institutions that have an Institutional Review Board (IRB) formed and approved specifically to review proposed psychosurgery, and then only after the IRB has made a determination that:

a. the surgeon has the competence to perform the procedure;
b. it is appropriate, based upon sufficient assessment of the patient, to perform the procedure on that patient;
c. adequate pre- and post-operative evaluations will be performed; and
d. the patient has given informed consent.[140]

In their commentary to this recommendation the Commission state regarding informed consent:

The consent by each patient should be reviewed by the IRB as a whole to assure that the patient's rights are protected. This review should focus on procedures or forms employed in the *consent process*, as well as the *circumstances of the actual consent* given by each patient. The IRB *may* require that a *third person*, unaffiliated with the surgical team or the patient's referring physician, observe or participate in the consent process. The IRB may also require that an examination by appropriate consultants or a hearing before the IRB be conducted to determine the patient's ability to give informed consent to psychosurgery.[141] (emphasis supplied)

This paragraph is followed by language that makes it clear that this "third person" participation is optional with the IRB, and is to be preferred to interviewing the patient before the entire IRB. It is submitted that such "third person" participation in the consent process is grossly inferior to complete IRB participation, and is likely to place the IRB in the position of being a "rubber stamp." If the IRB is to take into account the actual "consent process," as the commission suggested, it is submitted that this is impossible unless they have been personally involved in it and discussed it with the patient. This is especially vital in psychosurgery where many other things have been tried and failed, and surgery looks like an "easy" out for the patient, and the surgeon involved is generally a "true believer."

where many other things have been tried and failed, and surgery looks like an "easy" out for the patient, and the surgeon involved is generally a "true believer."

All of the evidence we have (admittedly not much, but it is unequivocal) from Massachusetts and Oregon indicates that such full committee review is extremely important in determining patient competency to consent and understanding of the proposed treatment.[142] It is to be hoped that their final report will include committee consent review, with mandatory subject appearance before a committee specifically designed for this review function.

Even more surprising, however, was the Commission's proposal for psychosurgery research on children and prisoners. The rationale here is that we shouldn't "deny children the possible advantages of a new therapy." In using the word "new" here, and in the prisoner section, instead of the word "experimental," they are doing what one of their staff members warned against—substituting a positive value-laden word for a neutral or negative-laden one.[143] The use of courts as the decision-makers regarding these populations is also somewhat troublesome. The Commission, unable to come to grips with the issues involved, and unsatisfied with the way the *Kaimowitz* court dealt with them after months of court hearings and deliberations, proposed that courts be the one to make the ultimate decision on whether or not to proceed with a psychosurgical procedure on children or prisoners. It is respectfully suggested that it is unlikely that a court will be better able to decide this issue than either the National Commission or an IRB,[144] and the courts themselves are attempting to get decisions involving individual treatments made at the hospital level rather than in court.[145]

Imputing motives is generally an unfruitful exercise. It is, however, worth speculating why the Commission, which was set up to protect human subjects, would, at least initially, decide to promote instead the rights of psychosurgeons. We would postulate three reasons. The first is that the Commissioners had a "Cuckoo's Nest" view of psychosurgery, and were genuinely surprised that the Boston University and M.I.T. studies did not unearth many persons permanently locked away in the back wards as a result of psychosurgery.[146] The second is that they had a sometimes mistaken and often oversimplified view of the law.[147] And the third is that they did not initially view psychosurgery as an especially important issue.[148] It is to be hoped that H.E.W.'s ultimate regulations on this subject will be issued only after a complete consideration of all the difficult issues involved.

CONCLUSIONS ON REVIEW COMMITTEES FOR PSYCHOSURGERY

Dr. Franz Ingelfinger has argued that informed consent is not meaningful in the hospital setting because of the control doctors exercise over their patients. In his view, "the subject's only real protection . . . depends on the conscience and compassion of the investigator and his peers."[149] Although our society has been willing to rely on this form of protection in the past, recent developments in medical technology and an increasing awareness of past abuses have made the establishment of more stringent safeguards imperative. Community sensibilities will no longer allow, for example, the unregulated research of scientists who respond to suggestions concerning the special nature of the human brain as opposed to other organs with the argument that "[t]he inviolability of the brain is only a social construct, like nudity."[150]

We believe this book in general, and this chapter in particular, have amply demonstrated both the utility and limits of the doctrine of informed consent in the experimental setting. Because of these limits, especially when dealing with experimental procedures on potentially incompetent or involuntary subjects, more protections are called for. One such protection that merits additional experimentation itself is the involvement of community representatives and nonmedical professionals in the decision-making process. The problems posed by psychosurgery and many other medical procedures are not capable of resolution merely on the basis of medical considerations. It is for this reason, and because of the tendency of peer review committees to act as rubber stamps for the research protocols of members of their own profession, that significant nonmedical representation on review committees should be assured.

Our experience with multidisciplinary committees, however, is so limited that we must guard against their becoming a mechanism which merely serves a legitimizing function on the basis of inadequate consideration. The criteria they employ and the decisions they reach should receive constant scrutiny to assure that the rights of patients are being protected. IRB's should probably not interview individual patients, since this has never been their function and there is no indication that they can do it well. A multidisciplinary committee should, however, be specially formed to this purpose. In addition, certain procedural safeguards should be built into the review process. First, a prospective patient should always be represented by legal counsel during committee proceedings, and should have the right to cross-examine witnesses and challenge documents presented. Second, the committees should follow written standards for review of voluntariness, competency, information, knowledgeability of the patient, and appropriateness of the procedure, keep minutes of their meetings, and record individual votes for every decision. The keeping of detailed minutes and the recording of votes should act as a safeguard against the diffusion of personal responsibility.[151] If the research proposal and the consent of the patient are reviewed and approved according to such procedures, individuals legally competent to give their informed consent should be allowed to undergo psychosurgical operations.

Certain classes of prospective patients, however, require more stringent protection. The confinement or status of prisoners, institutionalized mental patients, and children makes them especially vulnerable. Thus, in addition to committee review and approval, there should be established a presumption, rebuttable only in a court of law, that psychosurgery cannot be performed on them. To rebut this presumption, the proponent of psychosurgery should be required to demonstrate beyond a reasonable doubt that the patient's consent is both voluntary and knowledgeable, and that there is a reasonable probability that the procedure will produce the desired effect. Although this proposal may amount to a *de facto* ban on the performance of psychosurgery on members of these groups, it would permit such operations under extremely compelling circumstances.

It is much too early in our experience with the mechanism of multidisciplinary review to reach any final conclusions with respect to its ability to regulate potentially abusive medical procedures. It is clear, however, that the current system of regulation is not only woefully inadequate, but almost nonexistent. For the present the establishment of review committees along the lines suggested above offers a regulatory approach that permits the medical community to proceed with research on the human brain without sacrificing the individual rights of patients.

Finally, we would urge the creation of some federal agency to begin to examine the question of which technologies or surgical procedures *should* be developed. At some point procedures, like drugs and devices, have a life of their own and regulation becomes difficult if not impossible. The question of whether or not we should control human behavior by brain manipulation should be answered before the question of how we conduct research in this area is viewed as the only relevant one.[152]

REFERENCES

1. Mark & Ervin, Violence and the Brain (1970); Hearings on S. 974, S. 878 and S.J. Res. 71 Before the Subcomm. on Health of the Senate Comm. on Labor and Public Welfare, 93d Cong., 1st Sess., pt. 2, at 348-57, 363-68 (remarks of Drs. Orlando Andy and Robert Heath).

2. Hearings, *supra* note 1, at 338-47 (remarks of Dr. Bertram Brown, Director of the National Institute of Mental Health).

3. *Id.* at 357-63 (remarks of Dr. Peter Breggin, presently Director of the Center for the Study of Psychiatry).

4. Other definitions of psychosurgery follow:

> Psychosurgery can best be defined as a surgical removal or destruction of brain tissue of the cutting of brain tissue to disconnect one part of the brain from another, with the intent of altering behavior, even though there may be no direct evidence of structural disease or damage in the brain.

Id. at 339 (remarks of Dr. Bertram Brown).

> Psychosurgery is a term which has been loosely used to identify brain operations performed for the treatment of behavioral and related neurological disorders.

Id. at 348 (remarks of Dr. Orlando Andy).

> The definition of psychosurgery is to destroy normal brain tissue to control the emotions or behavior or, a diseased tissue when the disease has nothing to do with behavior . . . the man is trying to control.

Id. at 359 (remarks of Dr. Peter Breggin).

> "Psychosurgery" means any operation designed to irreversibly lesion or destroy brain tissue for the primary purpose of altering thoughts, emotions or behavior of a human being. "Psychosurgery" does not include procedures which may irreversibly lesion or destroy brain tissues when undertaken to cure well-defined disease such as brain tumor, epileptic foci and certain chronic pain syndromes.

Ch. 616, §1(6) [1973 Ore. Reg. Sess.] (S. Bill 298), amending Ore. Rev. Stat. 677. 190 (1971).

> The term "psychosurgery" means those operations currently referred to as lobotomy, psychiatric surgery, and behavioral surgery and all other forms of brain surgery if the surgery is performed for the purpose of—
> (a) modification of thoughts, feelings, actions, or behavior rather than the treatment of a known and diagnosed physical disease of the brain; (b) modification of normal brain function or normal brain tissue in order to control thoughts, feelings, action, or behavior; or (c) treatment of abnormal brain function or abnormal brain tissue in order to modify

thoughts, feelings, actions, or behavior when the abnormality is not an established cause for those thoughts, feelings, actions, or behavior. Such terms does not include electroshock treatment, the electrical stimulation of the brain, or drug therapy, except when substances are injected or inserted directly into brain tissue. H.R. 5371, 93d Cong., 1st Sess. §1 (1973).

"Psychosurgery means brain surgery on (1) normal brain tissue of an individual who does not suffer from any physical disease, for the purpose of changing or controlling the behavior or emotions of such individual, or (2) diseased brain tissue of an individual, if the sole object of the performance of such surgery is to control, change, or affect any behavioral or emotional disturbance of such individual. Such term does not include brain surgery designed to cure or ameliorate the effects of epilepsy and electric shock treatment." National Research Act of 1974, P.L. 93-348.

"Psychosurgery is defined as those operations currently referred to as lobotomy, psychiatric surgery, and behavioral surgery and all other forms of brain surgery if the surgery is performed for the purpose of the following: (1) Modification of control of thoughts, feelings, actions, or behavior rather than the treatment of a known and diagnosed physical disease of the brain; (2) Modification of normal brain function or normal brain tissue in order to control thoughts, feelings, action, or behavior; or (3) Treatment of abnormal brain function or abnormal brain tissue in order to modify thoughts, feelings, actions or behavior when the abnormality is not an established cause for those thoughts, feelings, action or behavior. Psychosurgery does not include prefrontal sonic treatment wherein there is no destruction of brain tissue." California A.B. 1032 (1976).

For a discussion of the various types of psychosurgical procedures *see* Andy, Neurosurgical Treatment of Abnormal Behavior, 252 Am. J. Med. Sci. 232 (1966), reprinted in Hearings, *supra* note 1, at 417. For another definition of psychosurgery *see* Stedman's Medical Dictionary 1040 (22d ed. 1972).

5. Szasz (ed.) The Age of Madness 157 (1973), reprinting in part Moniz, How I Came to Perform Prefrontal Leucotomy, in Congress of Psychosurgery 7 (Lisboa: Edicoes Atica 1948).

6. Freeman, Frontal lobotomy in early schizophrenia long follow-up in 415 cases, 119 Brit. J. Psychiat. 621 (1971).

7. Goldstein, Prefrontal lobotomy: Analysis and warning, Scientific Am. 44 (1950).

8. *Id.* at 46-47; Holden et al., Prefrontal lobotomy: Steppingstone or pitfall?, 127 Am. J. Psychiat. 591 (1970).

9. Goldstein, *supra* note 7, at 46-47.

10. The case is discussed in Mayer, Prefrontal Lobotomy in the Courts, 38 J. Crim. L.C. & P.S. 576 (1948). *See also* Silbermann & Ransohoff, Medico-

legal problems in psychosurgery, 110 Am. J. Psychiat. 801, 806 n.4 (1954); Time, July 14, 1947, at 53, col. 3.

11. Note, Lobotomy: Surgery for the insane, 1 Stan. L. Rev. 463, 474 (1949).

12. Trotter, A clockwork orange in a California prison,101 Sci. News 174, 175 (1972).

13. Scientific Am., Oct. 1953, at 60. It is well-known, however, that the Soviet Union continues to treat political dissidents as if they were insane. *See*, *e.g.*, Chorover, Big brother and psychotechnology, Psychology Today 43, 44 (1973).

14. Brown, et al., Psychosurgery: Perspective on a current issue 3 DHEW Pub. No. HSM 73-9119 (1973).

15. Silbermann & Ransohoff, *supra* note 10, at 808.

16. Although doctors argue that malpractice suits have reached crisis proportions, the most recent statistics reveal that one suit is filed for every 226,000 doctor-patient encounters. Report of the Secretary's Comm. on Medical Malpractice, 12 DHEW Pub. No. OS 73-88 (1973). *See also* Dietz, Baird & Berul, The Medical Malpractice Legal System 97 (Appendix to DHEW Pub. No. OS 73-88, 1973).

17. Harney, Medical Malpractice 91 (1973).

18. *Id.* at 116. *See also* Brune v. Belinkoff, 354 Mass. 102, 235 N.E. 2d 793 (1968); McCoid, The care required of medical practitioners, 12 Vand. L. Rev. 549 (1959); Note, The standard of care in malpractice cases, 4 Osgoode Hall L. J. 222 (1966).

19. Freeman estimated that he had lobotomized more than 3,500 persons. Freeman, *supra* note 6, at 622; *see* Freeman, W. & Watts. J., Psychosurgery 51–57 (2d ed 1950).

20. Hearings, *supra* note 1, at 340. According to the National Institute of Mental Health, some lobotomized patients showed improvement, but the classical lobotomy was a "therapy of desperation." Brown et al., *supra* note 14, at 2. *See also* Scoville, Psychosurgery and other lesions of the brain affecting human behavior, in Psychosurgery 5, 8 (Hitchcock, E., Laitinen, L. & Vaernet, K. eds. 1972); Sweet, Treatment of medically intractable mental diseases by limited frontal leucotomy—justifiable?, 289 N. Eng. J. Med. 1117 (1973).

21. *See* Bergland, Neurosurgery may die. 288 N. Eng. J. Med. 1043 (1973). The average neurosurgeon in 1970 in the United States performed an average of only five or six major operations per month. *Id.* at 1045, quoting Odom, Neurological surgery in our changing times: The 1972 AANS Presidential Address, 37 J. Neurosurg. 255 (1972).

22. *See* Gonzales v. Nork (Super. Ct., Sacramento County, Cal., Nov. 19, 1973) (awarding $1.7 million in compensatory and $2 million in punitive damages against a doctor who performed an unnecessary laminectomy); Bunker, Surgical manpower: A comparison of operations and surgeons in the United States and in England and Wales, 282 N. Eng. J. Med. 135 (1970); Lewis, Variations in the Incidence of Surgery, 281 N. Eng. J. Med. 880 (1969); Vayda, A

comparison of operations and surgeons in the United States and England and Wales, 289 N. Eng. J. Med. 1124 (1973); Comment, Unnecessary surgery: Doctor and hospital liability, 61 Geo. L. J. 807 (1973).

23. Shoemaker, Operation to relieve perversion, 97 Sci. News 50 (1970).

24. Mark & Ervin, *supra* note 1, at 69-91.

25. Hearings, *supra* note 1, at 368; Trotter, Psychosurgery, the courts and congress, 103 Sci. News 310, 311 (1973).

26. *See* Curran & Shapiro, Law, Medicine, and Forensic Science 522 (2d ed. 1970); *see, e.g.,* Mass. Gen. Laws Ann. ch. 112, §§ 2 et seq.

27. Child, Surgical intervention, Scientific Am. 98 (1973). There are presently 1,500 certified neurosurgeons and 600 in specialty training in neurosurgery. Bergland, *supra* note 21, at 1044. Prior to taking the Board examination, an applicant must have completed one year's training in general surgery, a minimum of four years graduate study in neurologic surgery and two years of independent practice in neurologic surgery. In Director of Medical Specialists (15th ed. Marquis 1972 at 603).

28. *See* Trotter, *supra* note 12, at 174; cf. Freeman & Watts, *supra* note 19.

29. *Id.*

30. Hearings, *supra* note 1, at 384. cf. Chase v. Groff, 410 F. Supp. 602 (D.C. Pa., 1976).

31. *See* Karchmer, Informed consent: A plaintiff's medical malpractice "Wonder Drug," 31 Mo. L. Rev. 29 (1966); Oppenheim, Informed consent to medical treatment, 11 Clev. L. Mar. 249 (1962); Waltz & Scheuneman, Informed consent to therapy, 64 Nw. U.L. Rev. 628 (1970): Note, Restructuring informed consent: Legal therapy for the doctor-patient relationship, 79 Yale L.J. 1533 (1970); Comment, Informed consent in medical malpractice, 55 Calif. L. Rev. 1396 (1967).

32. *See, e.g.,* Boston Housing Authority v. Hemingway, 293 N.E. 2d 831 (Mass. 1973).

33. *See, e.g.,* Henningsen v. Bloomfield Motors, Inc., 32 N.J. 358, 161 A.2d 69 (1960).

34. *See, e.g.,* Bunting v. Oregon, 243 U.S. 426 (1917); Labor-Management Relations Act of 1947, 29 U.S.C. §§ 141 et seq. (1970).

35. *See, e.g.,* Unico v. Owen, 50 N.J. 101, 232 A.2d 405 (1967).

36. *See* Rudovsky, The Rights of Prisoners (1973).

37. *See, e.g.,* Miranda v. Arizona, 384 U.S. 436 (1966).

38. Prosser, The Law of Torts § 32 (4th ed. 1971 at 165).

39. Harney, *supra* note 17, at 83; Prosser, *supra* note 38. *See, e.g.,* Wilkenson v. Vesey, 110 R. I. 606, 295 A.2d 676 (1972).

40. Canterbury v. Spence, 464 F.2d 772 (D.C. Cir.), cert. denied, 409 U.S. 1064 (1972); Cobbs v. Grant, 8 Cal. 3d 229, 502 P.2d 1, 104 Cal. Rptr. 505 (1972); Fogal v. Genesee Hosp., 41 App. Div. 2d 468, 344 N.Y.S.2d 552 (1973); Wilkenson v. Vesey, 110 R.I. 606, 295 A.2d 676 (1972); Trogun v. Fruchtman, 58 Wis. 2d 569, 207 N.W.2d 297 (1973). But *see* Tatro v. Lukin, 512 P.2d 529 (Kan. 1973).

41. Cobbs v. Grant, 8 3d 229, 245, 502 P.2d 1, 11, 104 Cal. Rptr. 505, 515 (Cal. 1972), citing Canterbury v. Spence, 464 F.2d 772 (D.C. Cir.), cert. denied, 409 U.S. 1064 (1972).

42. Canterbury v. Spence, 464 F.2d 772 (D.C. Cir.), cert. denied, 409 U.S. 1064 (1972). Accord, Wilson v. Scott, 412 S.W. 2d 299 (Tex. 1967) failure to disclose one percent risk of loss of hearing in a stapedectomy). *See also* Sterling Drug, Inc. v. Cornish, 370 F.2d 82 (8th Cir. 1966) (duty of drug manufacturer to warn doctors of the possibility of serious side effects in a small percentage of patients); Stromsodt v. Parke-Davis & Co., 257 F. Supp. 991 (D.M.D. 1966), aff'd, 411 F.2d 1390 1390 (8th Cir. 1969) (duty of drug manufacturer to give adequate warning of small percentage of risk in case involving first reported incidence of injury).

43. *See* Kaimowtiz v. Department of Mental Health, Civil No. 73-19434-AW, slip op. at 16 (Cir. Ct., Wayne County, Mich., July 10, 1973); Edson, The psyche and the surgeon, N.Y. Times, Sept. 30, 1973 §6, pt. 1 (magazine), at 14, 88–89. In one series, however, Dr. Walter Freeman reported eight deaths in 415 patients, or a two percent mortality rate. Freeman, *supra* note 6, at 622. But *see* discussion of National Commission's report in this chapter, infra.

44. *See* Waltz & Inbau, Medical Jurisprudence (Macmillan 1971 at 172).

45. *See* Hart v. Brown, 29 Conn. Super. 368, 289 A.2d 386 (1972); Howard v. Fulton-DeKalb Hosp. Authority, 42 U.S.L.W. 2322 (Ga. Super. Ct., Nov. 29, 1973); Strunk v. Strunk, 445 S.W. 2d 145 (Ky. 1969). Three unreported Massachusetts decisions are discussed in Curran, A problem of consent kidney transplantation in minors, 34 N.Y.U.L. Rev. 891 (1959).

46. *See* Smith v. Smith, Eq. No. 43919 (Md. Cir. Ct., July 14, 1972); Camitta v. Fager, Eq. No. 73-171 (Mass., Sept. 5, 1973).

47. Hearings, *supra* note 1, at 359.

48. *See* 4 Blackstone, Commentaries *205; Annot., 86 A.L.R. 2d 268 (1962).

49. *See* State v. Bass, 255 N.C. 42, 46–47, 120 S.E. 2d 580, 583 (1961). Cf. Physical Manipulation of the Brain, Hastings Center Report 7 (Special Supp., May 1973) (remarks of Dr. Robert Michels);

> Does a person have the right to informedly consent to anything that might be done to him? Suicide raises the question most clearly. Does the individual have the moral, legal, ethical, or social right to kill himself if he fully understands the nature and the meaning of his act and weighs the consequences thereof? Our law says no. Well, if you can't kill yourself, can you cut out 98 percent of your brain? Or 97 percent? Or 0.38 percent? Whre is the line? If you can't kill yourself to relieve pain, can you destroy your essential humanity to relieve pain? What are the limits of essential humanity? Are there any? Does the concept mean anything?

50. 255 N.C. 42, 120 S.E. 2d 580 (1961).

51. *See* Kidd, Limits of the right of a person to consent to experimentation on himself, 117 Science 211, 212 (1953); Note, Experimentation on human

beings, 20 Stan. L. Rev. 99, 116 (1967); And *see* more detail discussion in chapter one.

52. Prosser, *supra* note 38, §33, at 166.

53. 60 F.2d 737 (2d Cir.), cert. denied, 287 U.S. 662 (1932).

54. *Id.* at 740.

55. Darling v. Charleston Community Memorial Hosp., 33 2d 326, 211 N.E. 2d 253 (Ill. 1965), cert. denied, 383 U.S. 946 (1966); Helling v. Carey, 83 Wash. 2d 514, 519 P.2d 981 (1974).

56. A federal court has imposed sterilization guidelines on Alabama state-run institutions. Included in the guidelines is the requirement of approval of the procedures by a sterilization review committee which must include a patient from the institution, a doctor, a lawyer, at least two women, and two minority group members. Med. World News, Feb. 1, 1974, at 4. The authors are aware of the existence of only two psychosurgery review committees. One has been established in Oregon under stautory mandate, *see* text accompanying note 88 infra, and the other has been established at the request of the Board of Trustees at Boston City Hospital. *See* infra. However, the medical community is familiar with the use of review committees in other contexts. *See* Dagi, The ethical tribunal in medicine, 54 B.U.L. Rev. 268 (1974); Kayes, Selection of recipients and donors for renal transplantation, 123 Arch. Inter. Med. 511 (1969); Mishkin, Multidisciplinary review for the protection of human subjects in biomedical research: Past and prospective HEW policy, 54 B.U.L. Rev. 278 (1974); Packer & Gampell, Therapeutic abortion: A problem in law and medicine, 11 Stan. L. Rev. 417 (1959); Rostenberg, The ethics and sociology of peer review, 27 J. Am. Med. Women's Ass'n 318 (1972); Slee Streamlining the tissue committee, 44 Bull. Am. College of Surgeons 518 (1959); Teel, The Physician's Dilemma: A doctor's view: What the law should be, 27 Baylor L. Rev. 6 (1975).

57. Cf. Purcell v. Zimbelman, 18 App. 75, 500 P.2d 335 (Ariz. 1972).

58. Civil No. 73-19434-AW (Cir. Ct., Wayne County, Mich., July 10, 1973).

59. Letter from Frank Moran, Complaint, exhibit F. Kaimowitz v. Department of Mental Health, Civil No. 73-19434-AW (Cir. Ct., Wayne County, Mich., July 10, 1973).

60. The committee's duty would be derived from its purpose of protecting the prospective patient. It could be established by legislation, judicial declaration, hospital policy, the promulgation of regulations, or standards of professional organizations. To encourage their active participation, committee members should be reimbursed for their expenses and should receive some compensation for their time.

61. For a detailed discussion of the law in this area see Toulmin, A Treatise on the Law of Foods, Drugs & Cosmetics (2d *ed.* W.H. Anderson Co. 1963).

62. Thompson, Hearts 278 (1971).

63. *Id.* at 278-90.

64. In one study, Freeman and Watts reported that 45 percent of their patients had good results, 33 percent were fair and 19 percent were poor. Freeman & Watts, *supra* note 19, at 494. In a later study, Freeman reported that 87 percent of the patients were able to leave the hospital. Sixty-five percent of this group were considered successes because of their ability to be employed or

keep house. The other 22 percent live in a "state of idle dependency" either at home or in a nursing institution. Freeman, *supra* note 6, at 623. For a discussion of other studies showing high success rates, *see* Sweet, *supra* note 20.

65. McKenzie & Kaczanowski, Prefrontal leukotomy: A five-year controlled study, 91 Can. Med. Assoc. J. 1193 (1964); Robin, A controlled study of the effects of leucotomy, 21 J. Neurol. Neurosurg. Psychiat. 262 (1958).

66. Marks et al, Modified leucotomy in severe agoraphobia: A controlled serial inquiry, 112 Brit. J. Psychiat. 757 (1966); Tan et al, Bimedial leucotomy in obessive-compulsive neurosis: A controlled serial enquiry, 118 Brit. J. Psychiat. 115 (1971). Dr. William H. Sweet has argued that one "carefully designed and executed" prospective study of lobotomy revealed significant beneficial results. Sweet, *supra* note 20, at 1118, citing Ball et al., The Veterans Administration study of prefrontal lobotomy, 20 J. Clin. Exp. Psychopathol. Q. Rev. Psychiat. Neurol. 205 (1959). However, Sweet neglects to point out the following: (1) the study disclosed no significant differences between the two groups in years one, two, three, and five, *id.* at 208; (2) the lobotomized patients were more compliant, submissive, and self-deprecating than the controls, *id.;* (3) almost half of the 373 patients were lost during the five-year evaluation period, *id.;* (4) the method used to match the controls was not discussed; (5) all conclusions relating to discharged patients were made on the basis of only 27 lobotomized patients and 18 controls, *id;* and (6) the researchers evaluating the results were aware of which patients had been lobotomized and which had not, *id.* at 214.

67. Sweet, *supra* note 20.

68. Beecher, Surgery as placebo, 176 J.A.M.A. 1102 (1961). *See* Beecher, Evidence for increased effectiveness of placebos with increased stress, 187 Am. J. Physiol. 163 (1956); Cobb et al, An evaluation of internal-mammary-artery ligation by a double-blind technic, 260 N. Eng. J. Med. 1115 (1959); Dimond et al. Comparison of internal mammary artery ligation and sham operation for angina pectoris, 5 Am. J. Cardiol. 483 (1960). But *see* Livingston, Cingulate cortex isolation for the treatment of psychoses and psychoneurosis, 31 Psychiatric Treatment: Proceedings of the Association for Research on Nervous and Mental Diseases, 374, 377 (1953) (reports four placebo cigulumotomies that had no effect upon patient behavior).

69. *See, e.g.,* Psychosurgery (Hitchcock et al, eds. 1972).

70. National Broadcasting Co., Should Man Play God? (Educational Enterprises Documentary Film, 1973).

71. U.S. Dep't of Health, Education & Welfare, Institutional Guide to DHEW Policy on Protection of Human Subjects 1 (1971). As of March 31, 1973, however, the federal government is no longer funding any clinical psychosurgery. Hearings, *supra* note 1, at 344 (remarks of Dr. Bertram Brown, Director of the National Institute of Mental Health). *See also* N.Y. Times, Feb. 15, 1974, at 54 col. 1.

72. Cf. Hearings, *supra* note 1, at 345.

73. Ballantine et al, Frontal Cingulumotomy for Mood Disturbance, in Psychosurgery, *supra*, note 69, at 221. In 1974 Dr. Ballantine's patients were evaluated by a psychiatrist and a neurologist, usually the day before surgery is

scheduled to be performed. *See* infra. for a discussion of current review procedures.

74. Memorandum from Dr. Albert Breland, Chairman, to the Committee on Surgical Therapy of Behavioral Disorders, Aug. 27, 1973 (on file at Center for Law and Health Sciences, Boston University Schools of Law and Medicine).

75. Curran, Governmental regulation of the use of human subjects in medical research: The approach of two federal agencies, 98 Daedalus 542, 578 (1969). Cf. U.S. Dep't of Health, Education & Welfare, *supra* note 71, at 5-8.

76. U.S. Dep't of Health, Education & Welfare, *supra* note 71, at 4.

77. Compare *id.* with U.S. Dep't of Health, Education & Welfare, National Institutes of Health, Protection of Human subjects, policies and procedures, 38 Fed. Reg. 31738, 31741 (1973).

78. Civil No. 73-19434-AW (Cir. Ct., Wayne County, Mich., July 10, 1973). The case is discussed in greater detail in Comment, Kaimowitz v. Department of Mental Health: A right to be free from experimental psychosurgery?, 54 B.U.L. Rev. 301 (1974).

79. The form is set forth at p. 149 of this book.

80. Civil No. 73-19434-AW, slip. op. at 4 n. 5 (Cir. Ct., Wayne County, Mich., July 10, 1973) at 6.

81. *Id.* at 17-18.

82. *Id.* at 17.

83. *Id.* at 23-24.

84. *Id.* at 31.

85. *Id.* at 40.

86. *Id.* at 29-30 n. 23.

87. Annas, In re Quinlan: Legal Comfort for Doctors, The Hastings Center Report, June, 1976, at 29.

88. 129 Cal. Rptr. 535 (Ct. App. 4th Dist., Div. 1, 1976).

89. *Id.* at 539.

90. *Id.* at 541.

91. *Id.* at 545.

92. *Id.*

93. *Id.* at 547.

94. *Id.* at 549.

95. *Id.* at 548.

96. *Id.* at 549.

97. *Id.*

98. California A.B. 1032 (1976).

99. To constitute voluntary informed consent, the following information shall be given to the patient in a clear and explicit manner: (a) the reason for treatment, that is, the nature and seriousness of the patient's illness, disorder or defect; (b) the nature of the procedures to be used in the proposed treatment, including its probable frequency and duration; (c) the probable degree and duration (temporary or permanent) of improvement or remission, expected with or without such treatment; (d) the nature, degree, duration, and the probability of the side effects and significant risks, commonly known by the medical profession, of such treatment, including its adjuvants, especially noting the degree and duration of memory loss (including its irreversibility) and how and to

what extent they may be controlled, if at all; (e) that there exists a divison of opinion as to the efficacy of the proposed treatment, why and how it works and its commonly known risks and side effects; (f) the reasonable alternative treatments, and why the physician is recommending this particular treatment; (g) that the patient has the right to accept or refuse the proposed treatment, and that if he or she consents, has the right to revoke his or her consent for any reason, at any time prior to or between treatments.

100. Ch. 616 [1973 Ore. Reg. Sess.], (S. Bill 298), amending Ore. Rev. Stat. 677.190 (1971). The entire statute is reprinted as an appendix to Atkins & Lauriat, Psychosurgery and the role of legislation, 54 B.U.L. Rev. 288 (1974).

101. The developments in this case are reported at 325 F. Supp. 781 (M.D. Ala. 1971); 334 F. Supp. 1341 (1971); 344 F. Supp. 373 (1972).

102. 325 F. Supp. at 784 (emphasis added).

103. 344 F. Supp. at 380.

104. Kjaer, The Psychosurgery Board of Review for Oregon, 1973-1976, paper presnted at the 1976 meeting of the Northwest Society of Neurology and Psychiatry, Victoria, B.C., Canada, April 8, 1976. Summaries of cases appear at pages 5-7.

105. Personal correspondence with Dr. Donald S. Rushmer, Chairman of the Oregon Review Committee, October 18, 1976 and letter by Dr. Rushmer to the National Commission dated Nov. 3, 1976 (correspondence in files at the Center for Law and Health Sciences, Boston University School of Law). We are indebted to Dr. Rushmer for supplying us with information concerning the workings of the Oregon committee.

106. This specific requirement appears in the California statute, *supra.*, note 98.

107. Stone et al, Psychosurgery in Massachusetts: A Task Force Report, 5 Mass. Journal of Mental Health 26 (Spring, 1975).

108. *Id.* at 34; Boston Globe, Sept. 1, 1974, p. 15.

109. Psychosurgery Regulations 293 New Eng. J. Med 875 (1975).

110. Boston Globe, Sept. 11, 1975, p. 3.

111. See note 4, *supra.*

112. Stone, *supra* note 107, at 30-31, and 37-38.

113. Protection of Human Subjects, 45 C.F.R. §46.101 et. seq. (source: 40 FR 11854, March 13, 1975. Redesignated at 40 FR 33528, August 8, 1975).

114. P.L. 93-348.

115. *Id.* Sec. 202(c). The definition appears at note 4, *supra.*

116. Professor of Psychology at the University of Michigan and author of *Brain Control* (1973). His study was based on an examination of 700 English language articles published after 1970. 152 of these dealt with direct patient contacts, twenty-six referring to procedures performed in the U.S. The Report is entitled: The Practice of Psychosurgery: A Survey of the Literature (1971-1976).

117. Based on a survey of the active members of the American Association of Neurological Surgeons and the American Congress of Neurological Surgeons conducted by John Donnelly, M.D. for the Commission.

118. Using a rating scale from one to six (in which a rating of one represents the best scientific design and use of data, and a rating of six represents a

report presenting only descriptive information and lacking comparison groups) almost 90 percent of the United States articles (i.e. all but three) received a rating of four or higher, and 41 percent received a rating of six.

119. Valenstein, *supra* note 116 at 95-96.

120. Both researchers are psychologists at Boston University School of Medicine. Their report is entitled Final Report on Psychosurgery Pilot Study and is dated August 6, 1976.

121. *Id.* at 15.

122. *Id.* at 36-37.

123. See definitions of psychosurgery set forth in note 4, *supra.*

124. See *supra* note 68.

125. *Supra*, note 120 at 67, Case History No. 224.

126. Hans-Lukas Teuber, Suzanne Corkin, Thomas E. Twitchell, A Study of Cingulotomy in Man, Psychophysiological Laboratory, Dept. of Psychology and Brain Science, and Clinical Research Center, Massachusetts Institute of Technology (undated).

127. *Id.* Appendix, at 11, D7.

128. *Id.* at 76-77.

129. *Id.* at 77.

130. Draft Report and Recommendation: Psychosurgery, November 4, 1976, at 55. And see Culliton, Psychosurgery: National Commission Issues Surprisingly Favorable Report, 194 Science 299 (October 15, 1976) and Chavkin, Congress Endorses Psychosurgery, The Nation, October 25, 1976 at 398.

131. *Id.*

132. See *supra* note 4.

133. Taken from the individual histories appended to each study.

134. *Supra*, note 130 at 20, 21, and 64, and *infra* note 135 at 66.

135. Report on Psychosurgery, March 14, 1977 at 22.

136. See *supra* discussion of *Kaimowitz* and *Alden* cases at pages 224-228.

137. See pages 51-53 *supra.*

138. *Supra* note 135 at 16. The doctor-patient privilege, of course, only applies when there is a doctor-patient relationship, and even then it is subject to many exceptions. See generally, Annas, The Rights of Hospital Patients (1975) 121-129.

139. See discussion on this issue, *supra* page 222.

140. *Supra* note 135 at 56.

141. *Id.* at 59-60.

142. See discussion on the Oregon and Massachusetts experience, *supra* pages 228-233.

143. See, e.g., Gray, Human Subjects in Medical Experimentation (1975) at 109-110.

144. See discussion in chapters on Children, and Mental Patients.

145. *Id.* and see In re Quinlan, 355 A.2d 647 (N.J. 1976).

146. E.g., Statement of the Chairman of the Commission Dr. J. Kenneth Ryan, "We looked at the data and saw that they did not support our prejudices. I, for one, did not expect to come out in favor of psychosurgery. But we saw that some very sick people had been helped by it, and that it did not destroy

their intelligence or rob them of feelings. Their marriages were intact. They were also able to work. The operation shouldn't be banned." Quoted by Culliton, *supra* note 130 at 299.

147. See discussion at 239–141 *supra*.

148. This is purely speculation. See Annas, G.J., Psychosurgery: The Commission's Procedural Safeguards, *Hastings Center Report*, April 1977.

149. Ingelfinger, Informed (but uneducated) consent, 287 N. Eng. J. Med. 465 (1972).

150. Physical manipulation of the brain, *supra* note 49 (remarks of Dr. Jose Delgado).

151. Stanley Milgram's experiments have demonstrated that the fragmentation of responsibility may lead average individuals to commit inhuman acts. Milgrim, The Perils of Obedience, Harper's Dec. 1973 at 62. *See also* Milgram, Obedience to Authority (1974). Thus, the proliferation of committees proposed by NIH may prove self-defeating. *See* text accompanying notes 140–143.

152. The entire question of psychosurgery regulation and research may be an appropriate one to use in a pilot study on the concept of a "Science Court." *See, e.g.*, Kantrowitz et al., The Science Court Experiment: An Interior Report, 193 SCIENCE 653 (Aug. 20, 1976), and Casper, Technology Policy and Democracy, 194 SCIENCE 29 (October 1, 1976).

※ *Chapter 8*

Compensation for Harm: An Additional Protection for Human Subjects

A major unanswered question in the area of human experimentation is how to compensate subjects who are injured in the course of an experiment.[1] Liability of this type is not mentioned in the Nuremberg Code nor in any of the other codes governing conduct of experiments. Precedents in the law for compensation of injured parties are generally limited to those instances in which the damage can be demonstrated to be due to negligence on the part of the experimenter.[2] The only practical recourse today is the finding of liability in a personal injury suit for damages.[3] Yet even here there is a lack of pertinent statutes and cases.[4] In the area of experimentation, it is difficult for the plaintiff to establish a standard by which the conduct of the defendant is to be judged to determine the issue of negligence.[5]

Beyond that, in a carefully conceived and developed experiment, it is more likely that an adverse result would be due to an unanticipated accident rather than to negligence. What of the subject who is unintentionally injured in an experiment in which there has been no mistake or error? Even if all reasonable precautions have been taken to protect the subject from physical damage as well as from unethical practices, there may still remain the possibility of injury.

It has been postulated that the informed consent of the subject should operate as a bar to recovery for nonnegligent injuries which are the result of experimentation.[6] However, this view confuses the effect of consent in the normal physician-patient relationship with its role in the experimentation area. In the former, permitting the patient to assume the costs of nonnegligent damages which resulted from treatment for which the patient had given his consent is a logical extension of the notion that costs should flow in the same direction as benefits. It is more difficult to justify this allocation in the experimental setting. Under these circumstances, most of the benefit does not go directly to the subject, but rather is ultimately achieved by society.[7] The purpose of consent is not to force the subject to assume the risk of injury within the context of the experiment, nor to shift the cost-bearing element of the situation to the subject.

Beyond that, the fact that most subjects in experiments are not informed prior to participation that they will not be compensated for any resulting nonnegligent injuries or losses raises the entire concept of informed consent into question in this situation. If subjects willingly participated with this information, it would be more reasonable to argue that consent should shift this burden onto the individual subject, since it could be maintained that this responsibility was knowingly assumed. However, under present conditions, without the knowledge that he is bearing the financial as well as physical injury, the subject's informed consent does not meet the level required to justify imposing these risks on an individual for the benefit of others.[8]

On the other hand, consent alone is not a sufficient means of protecting the subject in the experimental setting. There must be other, more direct ways of reflecting societal choices and societal goals when risks are taken for the common good. One important way to achieve this is through a system of indemnification.[9] Society has permitted the experimenter to expose the subject to a risk of harm for its own benefit, not for the benefit of the individual. This gives rise to the feeling that, since the purpose is public benefit, the costs of participation should not fall upon the subject, regardless of their cause. As Lasagna has said, "Patients must not seek court settlements capriciously; neither must they silently suffer pain, injury, or death in the course of research. The problem is both subtle and complex and deserves an honest and equitable solution."[10]

EXAMPLES OF INDEMNIFICATION PROBLEMS

In order to gain a practical awareness of the area and its complexities, it is helpful to briefly examine a few examples of problems in the field of indemnification. One of the earliest attempts at compensation of subjects injured during the course of an experiment was a crude scheme devised in the early 1900's by Dr. Walter Reed. Dr. Reed directed a series of studies in Cuba to investigate the cause of yellow fever and to recommend methods for preventing it. American soldiers and Spanish volunteers were subjected to living in the soiled bedclothes and bedding of people who had died from yellow fever, as well as exposed to the bites of mosquitoes. Each of the volunteers was paid $100 in gold to participate in the experiment. In addition, if a subject actually contracted yellow fever, he was provided another $100. No provision was made for extra compensation in the event of a volunteer's death.[11]

In 1972, the so-called Tuskegee Study was exposed to public view. In this thirty-year study by the United States Public Health Service, 400 poor black men, diagnosed as having syphilis, were examined periodically to determine the nature and course of the disease. They were reportedly induced through cash payments and other promises to remain in the study and entrust their treatment to the physicians working on the project.[12]

In the 1930s, the known treatments for the disease were only marginally effective. However, by 1945 penicillin had become available as a safe and extremely effective cure for syphilis. Yet such treatment was withheld from the study group.[13] An estimated 107 subjects died from the effects of the disease.[14]

After termination of the study, the federal government arranged to pay for whatever medical services the survivors of the experiment required, whether provided by government doctors or private physicians chosen by the subjects themselves.[15] However, this measure was merely the initial provision of compensation for the subjects injured by the Tuskegee study. Further compensation for the injured parties, and the manner by which it would be supplied, was a significant governmental concern, as evidenced by the exchange between Senator Edward Kennedy and Dr. Henry Simmons, Deputy Assistant Secretary for Health and Scientific Affairs, before the 1973 Hearings on Human Experimentation.

Senator Kennedy: Is one of the questions going to be compensation of these victims?

Dr. Simmons: I believe that is being taken up right now with the study done by the National Institutes of Health.

• • •

Senator Kennedy: Is there any compensation? . . . Maybe they are sick and tired of the Public Health Service and the Federal Government. They might want to make their own arrangements. Would you blame them?

Dr. Simmons: We not only would not blame them, but we are allowing them to do that.

Senator Kennedy: Maybe they would like to get some money to be able to do it. . . .

. . .

Senator Kennedy: What do you think any of these people would be able to get in malpractice suits?

Dr. Simmons: I do not know, Mr. Chairman.

. . .

Senator Kennedy: I am wondering in your charge to the people at NIH about whether you might provide some compensation to these families. Are you considering at all what they would possibly be able to get in a malpractice suit against the Government, when they were denied drugs when the drugs were already in existence? What do you think a jury would do on that?

Dr. Simmons: I could never predict.[16]

It seems that the federal government, like Dr. Simmons, decided not to try to predict what a jury would award the subjects of the Tuskegee experiment as compensation, and instead settled out-of-court on what was to have been the first day of trial in a class action filed on behalf of all the participants, both syphilitic group members and nonsyphilitic control group members in the study.[17] The civil suit, filed in federal district court by forty of the survivors, led to a settlement which provided for individual monetary awards not only for the syphilitic participants or their estates, but also for members of the control group. The settlement of the $1.8 million damage suit awarded $37,500 to each living participant, $15,000 to control subjects, $15,000 to families of deceased subjects who had syphilis, and $5,000 to survivors of deceased participants who did not have the disease.[18] This compensation works out to about $2.40 a day for syphilitic survivors of the study.[19] It is interesting to note that the settlement for the control group must have been based solely on the failure to obtain their informed consent, since they generally received only benefits, such as free medical care, from their participation. This is the first time in which informed consent served as the basis of recovery in the experimentation setting.[20]

An analogous problem of indemnification is involved in the situation of mass immunization, as pointed out by the recent controversy surrounding the issue of indemnification of vaccine manufacturers and vaccine providers for lawsuits stemming from the administration of swine-influenza vaccine.[21] In order to resolve this dilemma, it has been proposed that an industry-government fund be developed to compensate people who suffer adverse reactions in mass vaccination programs.[22] Manufacturers, medical providers, and the government would participate in the compensatory fund. Therefore, a pool of insurers would set up the fund, with government appropriations for administration and for payments beyond those initially expected. The fund would not provide automatic compensation, but rather the injured party would have to show that a permanent or protracted disability was related to a recommended vaccine administered to him as a suitable recipient. However, he would not be required to prove negligence or fault. This approach was partially modeled on the scheme for federal coverage for catastrophic nuclear accidents. The rationale for the provision of such a fund is the notion that individuals vaccinated in programs for the benefit of their communities serve on behalf of others as well as themselves.[23]

LIABILITY WITHOUT FAULT

The fact that an individual volunteers to participate in an experiment, whether for the general good or exclusively for personal advantage, does not mean that any hazard, even if seemingly accepted, may be imposed. This is true even though, as a society, we approve of and encourage such participation for the benefit of the human race. It is at this point that a third party enters into the field of research activity. The investigator and the subject are not the only concerned parties. The public, in some instances represented by the federal government, has an interest, and a responsibility, in the proceedings.[24] In this sense, it is no longer logical to speak in terms of person-to-person liability as concerns negligence, but rather becomes necessary to discuss social responsibility.[25] As the ultimate beneficiary and implied endorser of experimentation, society may be expected to assume certain burdens.

It is significant that, in 1973, the Report of the Secretary's Commission on Medical Malpractice recommended that:

> Whenever a grant or other funding is provided by the Federal Government for medical research involving human subjects, the grant should include a sum sufficient to provide compensation to any human subject who may be impaired in the course of the research . . . The Commission recommends that whenever research involving human subjects is conducted by the private sector that insurance be provided to protect against mishaps, injury or illness directly arising out of that research.[26]

> Similarly, the HEW Secretary's Task Force on the Compensation of Injured Research Subjects suggested:

> Human subjects who suffer physical, psychological, or social injury in the course of research conducted or supported by the Public Health Service should be compensated if (1) the injury is proximately caused by such research, and (2) the injury on balance exceeds that reasonably associated

with such illness from which the subject may be suffering, as well as with treatment usually associated with such illness.[27]

In the field of torts law, many activities are permitted which are known to cost lives since it has been determined that to make these activities safer or to abstain totally from them would cost too much. Much of the control over the taking of human life is determined by the "market system," in which human beings are given a money value, the activities which injure people pay the victims, and society coldly decides whether it is cheaper to make the activity safer or to pay the cost of injuries. Thus, the control mechanism takes into account both the value of lives taken as well as the cost of saving them.[28]

The medical experimentation area, on the other hand, is concerned with risking lives in order to save other ones, not in order to save money. However, there presently is no control system analogous to that in the accident field which allows a sufficient balancing of present against future lives.[29] This could be accomplished by setting up a mechanism by which subjects injured in experiments are compensated without regard to fault.

The idea of nonfault liability is not new.[30] Indeed, some human experimentation already takes place under a similar system. Research performed on government employees in programs directly supervised by a government agency comes within the purview of the Federal Employees Compensation Act. When the subject is injured in the line of duty, he may recover against the government without having to prove a breach of duty.[31] Nonfault liability, in a very broad sense, encompasses any compensation system that uses criteria other than fault to determine benefits coverage. This relatively large category may be further subdivided into two groups.

The first group is classified generally as "no-fault insurance." A system of this type has certain basic principles. Benefits, paid to recipients without regard to fault, are arranged through private-enterprise insurers. In addition, these payments are the principal source of compensation for individuals who sustain injuries within the scope of the insurance contracts. On the basis of this, there is a partial or total exemption from negligence-based liability.[32] No-fault automobile and no-fault medical malpractice insurance are two examples of this system.

The other group uses a social security system as the major source of compensation. In essence, such a mechanism has government management and funding, and uses a criteria for compensation that is often more closely related to the need for benefits than to the causes of the need.[33] Worker's compensation is generally considered a special system of social security,[34] and the federal government plan for compensation of victims of nuclear power accidents under the Price-Anderson Act also falls within this category.

It should be noted that this classification of systems seems to make precise distinctions in a field in which that is not always possible. Often a particular system will have some characteristics of the group other than the one in which it has been designated. However, this classification can nevertheless aid in the analysis of the area.

Automobile Accident Insurance

In the area of compensation for automobile accidents, the Keeton-O'Connell plan allows the injured party to recover up to a certain predetermined amount in damages, expenses, loss of wages, etc., without inquiry into fault. Recovery for pain and suffering would still require a lawsuit demonstrating proof of the defendant's fault. In other words, the scheme provides the individual the security of prompt and certain recovery to a fixed amount of his out-of-pocket expenses, in return for which he surrenders his right to recover in tort to the extent he is eligible for personal injury protection benefits.

For example, under the Massachusetts system,[35] as the expenses covered accrue, personal injury protection benefits are paid by the insurer to the insured, members of his household, authorized operators or passengers of his automobile, and any pedestrians struck by him, regardless of fault in the causation of the accident. The benefits are limited in amount to $2,000, and cover medical expenses and a percentage of the actual lost wages of the injured party. If the victim was unemployed, he receives the same percentage of wages he can prove he would have received from work he would have had had he not been injured. The injured party retains his common law action against the potential defendant for any elements of damage not recovered as personal injury protection benefits. However, recovery of damages for pain and suffering is eliminated unless the medical expenses incurred by the plaintiff in treatment of his injuries exceeded $500, or the plaintiff's injury was of the type which necessarily entails considerable pain and suffering. This has been defined to encompass a fracture, injury causing death, injury consisting in whole or in part of loss of a body member, permanent and serious disfigurement, and injury resulting in loss of sight or hearing.

During the first six months of operation of this system in Massachusetts, the number of incurred claims and the average paid claim cost each fell more than fifty percent below the level of the comparable period one year earlier.[36] The law has been upheld by the state's Supreme Judicial Court.[37] However, care must be taken in the drafting of this kind of legislation so as to avoid successful challenges such as the recent decision which found unconstitutional a provision in the Michigan bill which distinguished damage to a motorist's vehicle from other types of property damage.[36]

No-fault automobile statutes were drafted to reduce insurance rates, help clear clogged court calendars of motor vehicle accident cases, and to cure the inequities of the fault-based scheme for compensating victims. The tort liability system allocated benefits unevenly among the limited number of victims it purported to serve. There were long delays in getting financial aid to the injured party, who was confronted with medical and subsistence bills during a period of possible limited or no employment. The time spent in investigation and required for proof of negligence, coupled with common exaggeration of claims and possibilities of perjured testimony, underlie the no-fault system in this area.[39]

Medical Malpractice Insurance

A similar approach has been suggested in the medical malpractice field.[40] Conventional automobile insurance and medical malpractice insurance are alike in a number of ways. For instance, coverage is provided for injuries which may be severe and incapacitating. Litigation is required to determine blame and compensation, and this process is long, costly, and serves to crowd the court system. Finally, the insurance is carried by someone other than the injured party.[41]

The outline of most no-fault plans in this field is also similar to that found in the automobile area. Medical expenses and at least partial compensation for lost earnings of injured patients are paid by the insurance carrier without regard to fault, with the right to sue curtailed. Some schemes call for the health care provider to purchase the insurance, while in others it is procured by the patient.[42] The benefits anticipated from this system are similar to those considered under no-fault automobile insurance.[43]

However, the major problem in applying the no-fault concept to medical malpractice lies in the means of defining the compensable event. In the automobile insurance area, it is relatively easy to determine when a compensable event has occurred, since it is fairly obvious when a car collides with another vehicle, or hits a tree, or strikes a pedestrian. However, in the health care area, it is difficult to define the event so clearly. The purpose of the system would be to cover only iatrogenic complications, or those which were caused by the medical intervention, without regard to the existence of fault. Yet a progression or complication of the patient's disease could mistakenly be diagnosed as an iatrogenic complication. Thus, it is necessary to develop a method for verifying with a reasonable degree of certainty whether a complication was actually caused by the medical treatment. This has yet to be satisfactorily done.

However, one proposed no-fault medical malpractice scheme attempts to avoid this problem.[44] Proponents of this method argue that, for most medical procedures, the risks have been precisely identified. Under this system, the health care provider would choose certain procedures that he does for which the adverse results can be predicted. For these results a specific amount would be paid without question. There would be no necessity of determining whether the results were caused by a preexisting condition of the patient, the inevitable risk of the procedure, or the negligence of the provider. The physician or health care institution would not be required to substitute no-fault for all risks, but would be permitted to choose those for which the decision was made to do so. Whenever the provider elected to pay for injuries on a no-fault basis, the patient would be precluded from bringing a malpractice lawsuit.

Worker's Compensation

Worker's compensation preempted the entire field of liability of employers for injuries to employees. Over sixty years experience has given this form of compensation an accepted place in American society. The employee is automatically covered when he suffers harm by accident arising out of the course of his employment. Issues of negligence and fault are considered immaterial. When an injury is covered by worker's compensation, this is the employee's sole remedy. Recovery at common law in a lawsuit is barred. Thus, the remedy is somewhat of a compromise. The worker accepts limited compensation, which is usually smaller than he would have received had he proceeded to trial, in exchange for extended liability of the employer. The benefits provided include wage-loss, medical, and rehabilitation benefits.

Regulation of worker's compensation is left entirely to the states. A minority of jurisdictions have "monopolistic" state insurance funds which are responsible for benefits and to which all nonexempt employers must contribute the amount estimated to cover their risk. Other states, however, allow the covered employer to insure his compensation liability with a private insurance company writing worker's compensation insurance, with some jurisdictions providing state compensation insurance funds as an alternative.[45]

The worker's compensation system finds its basis more on a theory of social insurance than on a theory of liability. Yet it is like tort in that its operative procedure is unilateral employer liability without contribution by the state or the employee. Although social in character, it is private in structure, in that it is a matter between the employer, employee, and insurance company.

Benefits are based on a social theory of providing support and preventing destitution. The underlying basis is the desire to provide the financial benefits which society would feel obligated to provide in any case in some other form.[46] In this way, the mechanism is not quite a true social security system, since actual need is not the measure of compensation. Rather, it involves a compromise between actual loss and arbitrary presumption of amount needed.

At the base of this framework is the notion that payment should be allocated to the most appropriate source, the consumer of the product. The cost is not placed on society in general, but rather on a particular category of consumers. It follows that the hazards of the industry are reflected in the cost of the product. Thus, the ultimate objective of worker's compensation is to provide a fund for injured workers while passing on the cost to the consuming public.[47]

The Price-Anderson Act

The purpose of the Price-Anderson Act of 1957[48] was to establish a mechanism for compensating members of the public who might sustain injury as the result of a serious nuclear accident as well as to avoid the possibility that a serious accident might result in enormous, uninsurable liability which would bankrupt the utilities and industrial concerns.[49] The Act required that each construction permit and operating license issued by the Atomic Energy Commission (AEC) have as a condition the requirement that the licensee have and maintain financial protection to cover public liability claims. It further provided that, whenever financial protection was required, the licensee must enter into an indemnity agreement with the AEC. This agreement served to indemnify not only the licensee but also any other person liable for damages caused by a nuclear accident. The nuclear power industry was thus insulated from financial liability since no liability was imposed which was not covered under the insurance or indemnity arrangements.[50]

Under the original terms of the Act, the indemnity was available only when the claimant established that legal liability existed under applicable state law. However, in September 1966, the Act was amended to provide strict liability for nuclear accidents. This was accomplished through a provision for waiver of certain defenses by persons indemnified and their insurers. This waiver is applicable only when the accident is an "extraordinary nuclear occurrence," or an incident causing dispersal of radioactive material that the AEC determines has resulted, or will probably result, in substantial off-site damage. Otherwise, the defendants may still use the defenses.

It is difficult to argue against a public policy which provides a guarantee that individual members of society who are injured due to a major disaster receive financial aid from the federal government. It makes sense for the government to devise a scheme of insurance whereby prompt, certain, and sufficient financial compensation for damages resulting from a catastrophic event is provided. However, it seems likely that nuclear energy was singled out for this unique treatment by the government for a reason other than providing this compensation in an area for which adequate insurance was not available.[51]

There was a national policy commitment to bringing about the rapid development and employment of nuclear power, and to rely upon private industry to achieve this goal. The primary purpose of the Act, therefore, was to free the nuclear industry from the threat of potential massive liability, thereby eliminating a major obstacle to the industry's growth. In a sense it could be viewed as a government subsidy of the nuclear industry.[52]

A business will only invest funds in projects for which it is estimated that the investment will yield a profit. In estimating costs to determine how they compare to revenues, the cost of potential liability must be considered. This will be analyzed by a consideration of the aggregate liability that might occur, discounted by the probability of the event taking place. The obtaining of liability insurance permits the shifting of the risk of liability to insurance companies. The premiums charged for this coverage represent the determination of the insurance companies as to the magnitude of potential liability. If the insurance rates are too high compared to the anticipated revenues, investment will be discouraged. If adequate insurance is not available, investment will again be deterred. Thus, the liability mechanism serves to regulate and discourage extrahazardous activity.

The effect of the Price-Anderson Act, therefore, was to overcome this deterrent effect. It encouraged business to make determinations based on technological and economic considerations without reckoning with the full social costs. The overall effect of the Act was to externalize these costs.[53]

An important policy issue raised in this context concerns the degree of risk that society will be compelled to accept in the name of technological progress.[54] It raises the question whether there is any level of potential disaster which may result from the development and employment of a technology which society will consider unacceptable, regardless of the fact that the technology will yield substantial benefits. The Act permitted business to use a highly hazardous technology, and forced the public to accept the hazard because it was deemed vital to the public interest. The public was made to bear this risk which the industry itself was not prepared to bear, and in return was offered a fund to compensate losses sustained if an accident in fact occurred.

AN INDEMNIFICATION PROPOSAL

In the field of experimentation, it might be possible to develop an indemnification system based on the no-fault automobile and medical malpractice insurance schemes.[55] Under such a plan, compensation could be due, without inquiry into fault, for expenses and loss of wages up to a certain set figure, such as $10,000. Recovery for losses beyond this amount or for pain and suffering would necessitate a lawsuit involving proof of the experimenter's fault. A variation of this might require proof of "gross" fault under these circumstances, in order to discourage speculative claims while retaining a deterrent against recklessness.[56]

The question then would be raised as to which party should bear the responsibility for locating and obtaining this no-fault insurance. Should it be the investigater, the subject, the institution in which the experiment is being conducted, the funding agency, etc.?[57]

An analogy may be made to the situation concerning the donation of live organs from minor donors.[58] The insurance could be considered part of the medical care costs of the transplant recipient, and accordingly paid by his medical insurer, or the parents of the donor might be required to procure the premiums. However, it would seem that the hospital in which the procedure is to be performed has the best opportunity for negotiating comprehensive coverage with insurance companies. Some recent cases have supported this view. For example, in the Massachusetts case of *Nathan v. Farinelli*,[59] the court ordered the hospital, its counsel, and the guardian *ad litem* to take reasonable steps to obtain such insurance before the performance of the procedure. Unfortunately, an acceptable policy at a reasonable cost was not able to be obtained prior to the necessity of going forward with the operation.

Similarly, there may be some difficulty in obtaining private insurance to cover the expenses in the experimentation area.[60] For example, UCLA has institutional insurance that will pay the medical cost of injury from experiments, but not lost earnings and pain and suffering. An informal poll of ten Wisconsin insurance companies revealed that none of them was willing to cover experiment-related injuries.[61]

The only encouraging sign in this area is the policy provided by the Aetna Insurance Company for the University of Washington. This insurance coverage protects subjects of human experimentation from nonnegligently caused injuries for several years at a cost of $.50 per experimental subject. The coverage is a rider to the University's professional malpractice coverage and has a total cost of $17,500 per year for 35,000 experimental subjects.[62]

However, there are two characteristics of the experimentation model which stand out as important factors in structuring a compensation system. One is the fact that a subject is injured as a result of an activity which was designed to benefit society, and therefore there is a feeling that a system should be devised that places the costs on those who benefit. This is similar to the principle underlying worker's compensation schemes.[63] A comparison of these two areas reveals certain similarities.[64] For example, each area involves activities which society considers essential, and yet which may give rise to a certain number of unavoidable injuries. In order to avoid this, society would be forced to eliminate all dangerous activities, such as the use of complicated machinery at the workplace which allows for increased production, and the use of human beings in experiments which may lead to a cure for cancer. In addition, the use of common law remedies in each area to compensate injured individuals has severe problems. Before the passage of worker's compensation legislation, the requirement that the employer be found solely responsible for the worker's injury had the practical result of preventing most injured workers from recovering under their common law remedies. Similarly, requiring a finding of negligence on the part of the experimenter blocks a substantial number of those injured by an experiment from being compensated.

However, there is a major difference between these two fields. Under worker's compensation, since there would be times during which a worker who had been injured due to his own "fault" would be compensated, a balance was achieved so that, although work-related injuries were compensated regardless of fault, the type of injury covered and the measure and amount of damages were narrowly specified. In that the interest being protected by the scheme was the worker's ability to produce, in general only those injuries which impair earning ability were covered, thereby eliminating the need to permit recovery for pain and suffering as well as for injuries which would not interfere with work.[65]

Yet this analysis is not applicable to the area of human experimentation, where subject injuries will rarely result from his own "fault." Therefore, this aspect of the indemnification problem more closely resembles the situation dealt with by the Price-Anderson Act, which compensates victims of nuclear energy accidents who in no way could be considered as having contributed to the damage.[66] In addition, the Price-Anderson area also involves the notion of individual sacrifice for the benefit of society in general which underlies both the worker's compensation and human experimentation fields. Therefore, it seems reasonable to suggest that a nonfault mechanism based on a social security principle, combining facets of both the worker's compensation system and the 1957 Price-Anderson Act, be developed to compensate injured subjects of human experimentation.

First, indemnification should be made from a federal compensation fund, as was originally done under the Price-Anderson Act. Otherwise, there might be situations in which both the experimenter and sponsoring institution lacked sufficient resources to adequately compensate an injured subject. Additionally, since the system is based on a "non-fault" premise, the researcher and institution are blameless, and imposing financial responsibility on them could make them unwilling to accept the risk of liability, thereby curtailing the amount of research done.

Beyond this, the federal government, through its direct and indirect support of research, has encouraged experimentation with human subjects. The benefits of experimentation accrue to our society as a whole, and not to an individual component within it, be that component an institution or a state. In addition, compensation is a critical matter of national concern, and should therefore be dealt with by a uniform federal policy, not subjected to the whims of individual states.

To finance this fund, one could require the payment of premiums from experimenters or research institutions, or surcharge the medical bills of the sick. In the alternative, one could provide the necessary money through general revenues. Since the taxing structure available to the federal government provides the most efficient means of allocating the costs to society, and since the results of experimentation benefit all of society, it is logical to distribute the burden of costs through the use of general revenues.[67] A similar approach had been taken by the federal government under the Price-Anderson Act.

Costs should be covered for injuries incurred through participation in an experiment. It would be irrelevant whether the cause of the damage was fault on the part of the experimenter or a nonnegligent accident. However, it is often difficult to determine when a subject's injury is truly attributable to his participation in the experiment. If the subject is a healthy volunteer, any injury might be fairly assumed to be the result of the experiment. Yet most subjects of experiments do not necessarily fall within this category, and therefore the question remains whether the injury is attributable to the subject's prior state of health. This is essentially the same problem faced by proponents of no-fault medical malpractice insurance, who are running into serious difficulty in developing a scheme for determining the compensable event.

However, since the underlying rationale for indemnification of human subjects is different than that forming the basis for compensating patients injured by medical malpractice in the course of ordinary therapy, in that the subject's participation in the experiment is for the ultimate benefit of society, the solution to this problem in the experimentation area should perhaps not create the same obstacle to implementation of the program. Since it would necessitate a large expenditure of administrative funds to determine the compensable event, it might be preferable to add those resources to the money allocated for direct compensation. Even though certain subjects may benefit from a windfall, it would be better to avoid the entire causation dilemma. Thus, compensation should be available in all instances in which the injury is not clearly unrelated to participation in the experiment. Eligibility would therefore depend only on a showing of participation in an experiment coupled with minimal proof of injury.[68] Since participation benefits all of society, the plan should favor compensation of the subject.

The next inquiry is whether subjects of both therapeutic and nontherapeutic experimentation should be covered by the system. Obviously, a subject in a nontherapeutic experiment is exposing himself to risk for the public interest, and is therefore deserving of indemnification for injuries. This would include not only a healthy subject who volunteers to participate in research, but also a diseased subject who submits to an experiment which is not directly related to his own illness.

But what of a participant in a therapeutic experiment? As discussed earlier, the distinction between these two categories of experiments is often a tenuous one at best.[69] Therefore, it should not be used as the basis for determining who is to be compensated. Beyond that, even if a distinction of this type could be made, the subject injured as a result of therapeutic research is nevertheless in a position to not directly share the benefits which his role as a subject has conferred on society. Thus, if those receiving the benefits, the general public, should bear the burden of producing them, it becomes inconsistent with distributive concerns to refuse to compensate the injured therapeutic subject.[70] Rather, all subjects of experimental research should be included within the compensating mechanism.

What should be separated out from possible compensation is innovative treatment, not therapeutic experimentation. The difficulty lies in distinguishing between the two. It has been suggested that the following factors may give a reasonable indication as to whether the procedure is innovative therapy:

(1) What are the number of patients involved in similar treatment?
(2) What is the outside funding involvement, if any?
(3) What is the intent of the physician concerning publication of the findings of the case?
(4) What collegial involvement is there?
(5) What is the degree of variance from standard practice?[71]

In general, a basic presumption can be made that, when the therapy involves only one physician and one patient, their relationship is not of an experimental nature so as to include it within the compensation scheme. The claimant would then have to overcome this presumption with proof indicating otherwise in order to be compensated. However, when it is unclear into which category a particular activity falls, the system should favor inclusion within the compensation plan so as to avoid the chance that a subject has been used by society without being indemnified for his contribution.

Another possible way of determining whether the injured individual was a subject of an experiment or a patient involved in innovative therapy could be on the basis of whether the person's own physician, who is presumably responsible only for the welfare of his patient and not for the general advancement of knowledge, would have recommended such a course of treatment.[72] This is premised on the physician having the same information possessed by the experimenters. In addition, this determination may be made not only at the start of the procedure, but at any time throughout the course of the "experiment."

One of the most difficult problems is determining the amount of compensation which a subject will receive. The fund should cover the cost of medical expenses and loss of earnings, but should this be individualized, depending on the actual losses sustained and requiring a rather extensive hearing on the matter, or should it be provided by a schedule, as in worker's compensation. It would seem that, in an area in which fault determinations have been rejected, a schedule of payments related to average costs does not seem an unreasonable way to fairly fulfill society's obligation. However, one must keep in mind an additional problem when dealing with lost wages.[73] If the schedule of payments is kept at a relatively low minimum level, this would have the practical effect of having most experiments draw a large percentage of their subjects from a low income population, which would in turn often turn out to be institutionalized populations. As a societal goal, this should be avoided.

Finally, there is the question as to whether the compensation should extend to the cost of pain and suffering. A large percentage of subjects of experiments are already sick. Unless the compensatory nature of the program is to prove a farce for these people, "aggravated" pain and suffering should be compensated.[74] Therefore, all subjects should receive indemnification for any pain and suffering which results from the untoward consequences of participation, measured as it is under tort law. However, compensation should not be available for anticipated pain and suffering about which the subject had previously been informed, since one can assume that he consented to it.[75] In the alternative, if it is decided not to include indemnification for pain and suffering, it would be appropriate to preserve the subject's right to bring a personal negligence cause of action for recovery of pain and suffering.[76]

One potential problem with a program of federal government indemnification should be noted. There is a danger there will be a lack of a financial incentive on the part of researchers which would otherwise have prevented them from pursuing risky and hazardous experiments. This issue was discussed in connection with the Price-Anderson Act. By analogy, one way of determining whether there is enough confidence in a proposed experiment is to assume payment for the people who may be injured by the procedure. If there is not, it is reasonable to assume that the particular experiment is too risky. Thus, requiring compensation of injured subjects by the experimenters would cause the full cost of human research to be placed on the parties carrying out the experiment. A decision to proceed with the procedure would require a conscious consideration of the risks, converted into money, forcing a determination of whether the experiment was worth it, and whether there was a safer, alternate way of achieving the same results.[77]

However, this controversy appears to be resolvable. Institutional review committees at individual facilities could become more active in determining which experiments are unjustified. In addition, the indemnification system could be set up so that institutions with much higher than average rates of compensable subjects would pay losses directly, eliminating the institution's eligibility to participate in the program. This would serve to reinforce the activities of the review committee.[78]

SUMMARY AND CONCLUSIONS

1. Subjects injured as a result of participation in experimentation have suffered a loss while performing a socially useful function.

2. Because of this, some measure of indemnification seems justified and appropriate.

3. Existing common law remedies are inadequate, particularly as concerns those subjects injured in nonnegligent situations. If the subject has not given valid consent, or if his injury was caused by negligence, he has a cause of action against the experimenter, but recovery depends upon proof of fault and is subject to the delays of litigation. For those subjects who gave valid consent and were involved in nonnegligent procedures, there is no reliable method of indemnification at all.

4. In response to this, a system of recovery based on nonfault liability would serve to fairly allocate risks and benefits between the individual subject and the general public.

5. Such a system may follow the design of no-fault insurance schemes, as has been developed in the automobile accident and medical malpractice areas.

6. A more workable mechanism would be one which uses as its model a social security system, such as the worker's compensation system and the procedure developed under the 1957 Price-Anderson Act for compensating victims of nuclear power accidents.

7. This system should provide for indemnification from a federal compensation fund.

8. Compensation would be made for any injury received as a result of participation in an experiment, whether therapeutic or nontherapeutic, without the necessity of determining fault or negligence.

REFERENCES

1. An initial inquiry is the determination of the incidence of research-related injuries. A survey conducted by the HEW Secretary's Task Force on the Compensation of Injured Research Subjects suggested that the risks of participation in nontherapeutic research may be no greater than those of everyday life, while those involved in therapeutic research are no greater than those of treatment in other settings. Cardon, Dommel, & Trumble, Injuries to Research Subjects: A Survey of Investigators, 295 N. Eng. J. Med. 650 (1976). If this is true, then it should serve to alleviate one of the problems of critics of any movement to compensate injured research subjects, i.e., if so few injuries and subjects are involved, the cost of such a system should be minimal.

2. *See* Miller & Rockwell, The Use of Human Subjects in Human Factors Research, 14 Human Factors 35, 36–38 (1972).

3. W. Prosser, Law of Torts 161-65 (4th ed. 1971).

4. Grad, Regulation of Clinical Research By the State, 169 Ann. N.Y. Acad. Sci. 533 (1970).

5. *See* ch. 1, text and accompanying footnotes 40-45, *supra.*

6. Freund, Legal Frameworks for Human Experimentation, 98 Daedalus 314, 321 (1969). *See* Graham v. Doctor Pratt Inst., 163 Ill. App. 91 (1911); Note, 40 Calif. L. Rev. 159 (1952). *But see*, Task Force Report, *infra*, note 27, at vi-5. *Cf.* Note, Experimentation on Human Beings, 20 Stan. L. Rev. 99, 114 (1967).

7. Adams & Shea-Stonum, Toward a Theory of Control of Medical Experimentation With Human Subjects: The Role of Compensation, 25 Case Western Res. L. Rev. 604, 609 (1975).

8. For a fuller treatment of this question, see Robertson, Compensating Injured Research Subjects: II. The Law, 6 Hastings Center Rep., Dec. 1976, at 29.

9. Calabresi, Reflections on Medical Experimentation in Humans, 98 Daedalus 387, 403-04 (1969).

10. L. Lasagna, The Doctors' Dilemmas 203 (1962).

11. Bean, Walter Reed: A Biographical Sketch, 134 Arch. Intern. Med. 871, 876 (1974).

12. Adams & Shea-Stonum, *supra* note 7, at 605, n. 2.

13. Barber, The Ethics of Experimentation with Human Subjects, 234 Sci. Am. 25, 26 (1976); N.Y. Times, July 26, 1972, §1, at 1, col. 1.

14. N.Y. Times, Sept. 12, 1972, §1, at 23, col. 1.

15. Hearings on Quality of Health Care—Human Experimentation Before the Subcomm. on Health of the Senate Comm. on Labor & Public Welfare, 93d Cong., 1st Sess., pt. 4, at 1191-93 (1973).

16. *Id.* at 1199-1200.

17. N.Y. Times, Dec. 18, 1974, §2, at 56, col. 4.

18. Medical News, Proposed Compensation for Tuskegee Study Men, 231 J.A.M.A. 233 (1975).

19. *Id.*

20. Adams & Shea-Stonum, *supra* note 7, at 616-17.

21. Public Law No. 94-380 (Aug. 1976).

22. N.Y. Times, Oct. 3, 1976, at 51, col. 1.

23. *Id.* at col. 3-4.

24. Schreiner & Bogdonoff, Limbo to Limb—The Moral and Legal Entanglements of the Clinical Investigator, 11 Clinical Research 127 (1963).

25. Ladimer, Protecting Participants in Human Studies, 169 Ann. N.Y. Acad. Sci. 564 (1970).

26. Medical Malpractice: Report of the Secretary's Commission on Medical Malpractice, DHEW Pub. No. S 73-88, Jan. 16, 1974, at 79.

27. Report of HEW's Secretary's Task Force on the Compensation of Injured Research Subjects, DHEW Pub. No. OS-77-003, Jan. 1977, at II-2.

28. Calabresi, *supra* note 9, at 389.

29. *Id.* at 393.

30. *See* Beecher, Human Studies, 164 Science 1256 (1969); Havighurst, Compensating Persons Injured in Human Experimentation, 169 Science 153 (1970); Comment, Legal Implications of Psychological Research with Human Subjects, 1960 Duke L.J. 265, 274.

31. *See* Note, Medical Experiment Insurance, 70 Colum. L. Rev. 965, 969 (1970); Note, Experimentation on Human Beings, *supra* note 6, at 115.

32. Keeton, Compensation for Medical Accidents, 121 U. Pa. L. Rev. 590, 600-01 (1973).

33. *Id*.

34. Riesenfeld, Contemporary Trends in Compensation for Industrial Accidents Here and Abroad, 42 Calif. L. Rev. 531, 532 (1954).

35. Mass. Gen. Laws Ann., ch. 90, § 34A (Supp. 1976).

36. Sabbagh, Memorandum to Commissioner of Insurance, Commonwealth of Mass., July 27, 1971.

37. Pinnick v. Cleary, 271 N.E.2d 592 (Mass. 1971).

38. Shavers v. Attorney General, 237 N.W.2d 325 (Mich. Ct. App. 1975).

39. *See* Pinnick v. Cleary, 271 N.E.2d 592 (Mass. 1971).

40. *See* J. O'Connell, Ending Insult to Injury (1975); Dornett, Medical Injury Insurance—A Possible Remedy for the Malpractice Problem, 78 Case & Comment 25 (Sept.-Oct. 1973).

41. Dorentte, Medical Injury Insurance—A Possible Remedy for the Malpractice Problem, *supra* note 40, at 28.

42. *Id*. at 29.

43. Hitchings, The Malpractice Insurance Miasma: A Way Out—I, Med. World News, Feb. 1, 1974, at 52, 53.

44. *See* O'Connell, Proposed: "No-Fault" Insurance to Stem Malpractice Suits, *supra* note 40.

45. Risenfeld, *supra* note 34, at 557.

46. Note, Nature and Origins of Workman's Compensation, 37 Cornell L.Q. 206, 210 (1952).

47. *Id*. at 218.

48. 42 U.S.C. § 2210 (1970). The 1975 amendment of the Atomic Energy Act of 1954 modified the Price-Anderson Act to amend the Atomic Energy Act, H.R. 8631. The 1975 law seeks to phase out governmental indemnity as a source of funds for public remuneration in the event of a nuclear incident and provides for a payment pool of all licensees through retroactive payments where the amounts needed exceed the insurance available. However, this change in the present law does not invalidate the analysis of the original indemnification plan under the Act as a possible model for a compensation system for human experimentation.

49. Cong. Rec., S 14594 (Aug. 8, 1974).

50. Green, The Insurance Umbrella, 10 Trial 29 (Jan.-Feb. 1974).

51. Green, Nuclear Power: Risk, Liability and Indemnity, Mich. L. Rev. (1973).

52. H. Green & A. Rosenthal, Government of the Atom: The Integration of Powers, 146-49 (1963).

53. *Cf*. Katz, The Function of Tort Liability in Technology Assessment, 38 U. Cin. L. Rev. 587 (1969).

54. Green, *supra* note 51.

55. *See* Miller & Rockwell, *supra* note 2, at 39.

56. Beecher, *supra* note 23.

57. *See* Casebeer, Injured Research Subjects: What Do We Owe Them?, 2 Kennedy Inst. Q. Rep. 5, 6 (1976).

58. *See* Baron, Botsford & Cole, Live Organ and Tissue Transplants from Minor Donors in Massachusetts, 55 B.U.L. Rev. 159 (1975).

59. Nathan v. Farinelli, S.J.C. Civ. Act 74-87 (1974).

60. Note, Medical Experiment Insurance, *supra* note 31, at 971. *But see* Task Force, *supra.*, note 27, at III-5.

61. Robertson, *supra* note 8, at 30.

62. Letter from Diana McCann, Director of Research Services, University of Washington, Seattle, to Garrick Cole, July 2, 1974 (on file at Boston University Center for Law and Health Sciences).

63. *See* sec. on Worker's Compensation, *supra.*

64. Adams & Shea-Stonum, *supra* note 7, at 637. *See generally* A. Larson, The Law of Workmen's Compensation §§4.10-.40 (1972).

65. A. Larson, *supra* note 64, §2.50.

66. *See* sec. on The Price-Anderson Act, *supra.*

67. Adams & Shea-Stonum, *supra* note 7, at 641.

68. Casebeer, *supra* note 57.

69. *See* ch. 1, *supra* at 3. *See also* H. Beecher, Research and the Individual 88-90 (1970); Moore, Therapeutic Innovation: Ethical Boundaries in Initial Clinical Trials of New Drugs and Surgical Procedures, 98 Daedalus 502 (1969).

70. Robertson, *supra* note 8, at 30. *See* Task Force, *supra* note 27, at VI-9.

71. Note, Medical Experiment Insurance, *supra* note 31, at 977.

72. Calabresi, *supra* note 9, at 396.

73. Casebeer, *supra* note 57, at 7-8.

74. Adams & Shea-Stonum, *supra* note 7, at 645.

75. *Id.* at 646.

76. Note, Medical Experiment Insurance, *supra* note 31, at 973.

77. Calabresi, *supra* note 9, at 398.

78. Casebeer, *supra* note 57, at 8.

The Nuremberg Code

1. The voluntary consent of the human subject is absolutely essential. This means that the person involved should have legal capacity to give consent: should be so situated as to be able to exercise free power of choice without the intervention of any element of force, fraud, deceit, duress, over reaching, or other ulterior form of constraint or coercion and should have sufficient knowledge and comprehension of the elements of the subject matter involved as to enable him to make an understanding and enlightened decision. This latter element requires that before the acceptance of an affirmative decision by the experimental subject there should be made known to him the nature, duration, and purpose of the experiment; the method and means by which it is to be conducted; all inconveniences and hazards reasonably to be expected; and the effects upon his health or person which may possibly come from his participation in the experiment.

The duty and responsibility for ascertaining the quality of the consent rests upon each individual who initiates, directs, or engages in the experiment. It is a personal duty and responsibility which may not be delegated to another with impunity.

2. The experiment should be such as to yield fruitful results for the good of society, unprocurable by other methods or means of study, and not random and unnecessary in nature.

3. The experiment should be so designed and based on the results of animal experimentation and a knowledge of the natural history of the disease or other problem under study that the anticipated results will justify the performance of the experiment.

4.   The experiment should be so conducted as to avoid all unnecessary physical and mental suffering and injury.

5.   No experiment should be conducted where there is an *a priori* reason to believe that death or disabling injury will occur; except, perhaps in those experiments where the experimental physicians also serve as subject.

6. The degree of risk to be taken should never exceed that determined by the humanitarian importance of the problem to be solved by the experiment.

7.   Proper preparations should be made and adequate facilities provided to protect the experimental subject against even remote possibilities of injury, disability, or death.

8.   The experiment should be conducted only by scientifically qualified persons. The highest degree of skill and care should be required through all stages of the experiment of those who conduct or engage in the experiment.

9.   During the course of the experiment the human subject should be at liberty to bring the experiment to an end if he has reached the physical or mental state where continuation of the experiment seems to him to be impossible.

10.   During the course of the experiment the scientist in charge must be prepared to terminate the experiment at any stage, if he has probable cause to believe, in the exercise of the good faith, superior skill, and careful judgment required of him, that a continuation of the experiment is likely to result in injury, disability, or death to the experimental subject.

Appendix II

Declaration of Helsinki

Recommendations Guiding Doctors in Clinical Research

INTRODUCTION

It is the mission of the doctor to safeguard the health of the people. His knowledge and conscience are dedicated to the fulfillment of this mission.

The Declaration of Geneva of The World Medical Association binds the doctor with the words: "The health of my patient will be my first consideration" and the International Code of Medical Ethics which declares that "Any act or advice which could weaken physical or mental resistance of a human being may be used only in his interest."

Because it is essential that the results of laboratory experiments be applied to human beings to further scientific knowledge and to help suffering humanity, The World Medical Association has prepared the following recommendations as a guide to each doctor in clinical research. It must be stressed that the standards as drafted are only a guide to physicians all over the world. Doctors are not relieved from criminal, civil and ethical responsibilities under the laws of their own countries.

In the field of clinical research a fundamental distinction must be recognized between clinical research in which the aim is essentially therapeutic for a patient, and the clinical research, the essential object of which is purely scientific and without therapeutic value to the person subjected to the research.

I. BASIC PRINCIPLES

1. Clinical research must conform to the moral and scientific principles that justify medical research and should be based on on laboratory and animal experiments or other scientifically established facts.
2. Clinical research should be conducted only by scientifically qualified persons and under the supervision of a qualified medical man.
3. Clinical research cannot legitimately be carried out unless the importance of the objective is in proportion to the inherent risk to the subject.
4. Every clinical research project should be preceded by careful assessment of inherent risks in comparison to foreseeable benefits to the subject or to others.
5. Special caution should be exercised by the doctor in performing clinical research in which the personality of the subject is liable to be altered by drugs or experimental procedure.

II. CLINICAL RESEARCH COMBINED WITH PROFESSIONAL CARE

1. In the treatment of the sick person, the doctor must be free to use a new therapeutic measure, if in his judgment it offers hope of saving life, reestablishing health, or alleviating suffering.

   If at all possible, consistent with patient psychology, the doctor should obtain the patient's freely given consent after the patient has been given a full explanation. In case of legal incapacity, consent should also be procured from the legal guardian; in case of physical incapacity the permission of the legal guardian replaces that of the patient.
2. The doctor can combine clinical research with professional care, the objective being the acquisition of new medical knowledge, only to the extent that clinical research is justified by its therapeutic value for the patient.

III. NON-THERAPEUTIC CLINICAL RESEARCH

1. In the purely scientific application of clinical research carried out on a human being, it is the duty of the doctor to remain the protector of the life and health of that person on whom clinical research is being carried out.

2. The nature, the purpose and the risk of clinical research must be explained to the subject by the doctor.
3a. Clinical research on a human being cannot be undertaken without his free consent after he has been informed; if he is legally incompetent, the consent of the legal guardian should be procured.
3b. The subject of clinical research should be in such a mental, physical and legal state as to be able to exercise fully his power of choice.
3c. Consent should, as a rule, be obtained in writing. However, the responsibility for clinical research always remains with the research worker; it never falls on the subject even after consent is obtained.
4a. The investigator must respect the right of each individual to safeguard his personal integrity, especially if the subject is in a dependent relationship to the investigator.
4b. At any time during the course of clinical research the subject or his guardian should be free to withdraw permission for research to be continued.

    The investigator or the investigating team should discontinue the research if in his or their judgment, it may, if continued, be harmful to the individual.

AMA Ethical Guidelines for Clinical Investigation

(Adopted by House of Delegates, American
Medical Association, Nov. 30, 1966)

At the 1966 Annual Convention of its House of Delegates, the American Medical Association endorsed the ethical principles set forth in the 1964 *Declaration of Helsinki* of the World Medical Association concerning human experimentation. These principles conform to and express fundamental concepts already embodied in the *Principles of Medical Ethics* of the American Medical Association.

The following guidelines, enlarging on these fundamental concepts, are intended to aid physicians in fulfilling their ethical responsibilities when they engage in the clinical investigation of new drugs and procedures.

1. A physician may participate in clinical investigation only to the extent that his activities are a part of a systematic program competently designed, under accepted standards of scientific research, to produce data which is scientifically valid and significant.

2. In conducting clinical investigation, the investigator should demonstrate the same concern and caution for the welfare, safety and comfort of the person involved as is required of a physician who is furnishing medical care to a patient independent of any clinical investigation.

3. In clinical investigation *primarily for treatment*—
   A. The physician must recognize that the physician-patient rela-

tionship exists and that he is expected to exercise his professional judgment and skill in the best interest of the patient.

B. Voluntary consent must be obtained from the patient, or from his legally authorized representative if the patient lacks the capacity to consent, following: (1) disclosure that the physician intends to use an investigational drug or experimental procedure, (b) a reasonable explanation of the nature of the drug or procedure to be used, risks to be expected, and possible therapeutic benefits, (c) an offer to answer any inquiries concerning the drug or procedure, and (d) a disclosure of alternative drugs or procedures that may be available.

   i. In exceptional circumstances and to the extent that disclosure of information concerning the nature of the drug or experimental procedure or risks would be expected to materially affect the health of the patient and would be detrimental to his best interests, such information may be withheld from the patient. In such circumstances such information shall be disclosed to a responsible relative or friend of the patient where possible.

   ii. Ordinarily, consent should be in writing, except where the physician deems it necessary to rely upon consent in other than written form because of the physical or emotional state of the patient.

   iii. Where emergency treatment is necessary and the patient is incapable of giving consent and no one is available who has authority to act on his behalf, consent is assumed.

4. In clinical investigation *primarily for the accumulation of scientific knowledge—*

A. Adequate safeguards must be provided for the welfare, safety and comfort of the subject.

B. Consent, in writing, should be obtained from the subject, or from his legally authorized representative if the subject lacks the capacity to consent, following: (a) a disclosure of the fact that an investigational drug or procedure is to be used, (b) a reasonable explanation of the nature of the procedure to be used and risks to be expected, and (c) an offer to answer any inquiries concerning the drug or procedure.

C. Minors or mentally incompetent persons may be used as subjects only if:

   i. The nature of the investigation is such that mentally competent adults would not be suitable subjects.

   ii. Consent, in writing, is given by a legally authorized representative of the subject under circumstances in which an informed and prudent adult would reasonably be expected to volunteer himself or his child as a subject.

D. No person may be used as a subject against his will. (emphasis in original)

Appendix IV

H.E.W. Regulations on the Protection of Human Subjects

APPENDIX IV
45 Code of Federal Regulations, Title 46

PART 46—PROTECTION OF HUMAN SUBJECTS

Subpart A
Sec.
46.101 Applicability.
46.102 Policy.
46.103 Definitions.
46.104 Submission of assurances.
46.105 Types of assurances.
46.106 Minimum requirements for general assurances.
46.107 Minimum requirements for special assurances.
46.108 Evaluation and disposition of assurances.
Sec.
46.109 Obligation to obtain informed consent; prohibition of exculpatory clauses.
46.110 Documentation of informed consent.
46.111 Submission and certification of applications and proposals, general assurances.
46.112 Submission and certification of applications and proposals, special assurances.

46.113 Applications and proposals lacking definite plans for involvement of human subjects.
46.114 Applications and proposals submitted with the intent of not involving human subjects.
46.115 Evaluation and disposition of applications and proposals.
46.116 Cooperative activities.
46.117 Investigational new drug 30-day delay requirement.
46.118 Institution's executive responsibility.
46.119 Institution's records; confidentiality.
46.120 Reports.
46.121 Early termination of awards; evaluation of subsequent applications and proposals.
46.122 Conditions.

Subpart B—Additional Protection Pertaining to Research, Development, and Related Activities Involving Fetuses, Pregnant Women, and Human in Vitro Fertilization
46.201 Applicability.
46.202 Purpose.
46.203 Definitions.

46.204 Ethical Advisory Boards.
46.205 Additional duties of the Institutional Review Boards in connection with activities involving fetuses, pregnant women, or human in vitro fertilization.
46.206 General limitations.
46.207 Activities directed toward pregnant women as subjects.
46.208 Activities directed toward fetuses in utero as subjects.
46.209 Activities directed toward fetuses ex utero, including nonviable fetuses, as subjects.
46.210 Activities involving the dead fetus, fetal material, or the placenta.
46.211 Modification or waiver of specific requirements.

Subpart C—General Provisions
46.301 Activities conducted by Department employees.
Authority: 5 U.S.C. 301; sec. 474 (a), 88 Stat. 352 (42 U.S.C. 2891–3(a)) unless otherwise noted.

Subpart A
Source: 40 FR 11854, Mar. 13, 1975. Redesignated at 40 FR 33528, Aug. 8, 1975.

§46.101 Applicability.
(a) The regulations in this part are applicable to all Department of Health, Education, and Welfare grants and contracts supporting research, development, and related activities in which human subjects are involved.

(b) The Secretary may, from time to time, determine in advance whether specific programs, methods, or procedues to which this past is applicable place subjects at risk, as defined in §46.3(b). Such determinations will be published as notices in the Federal Register and will be included in an appendix to this part.

§46.102 Policy.
(a) Safeguarding the rights and welfare of subjects at risk in activities supported under grants and contracts from DHEW is primarily the responsibility of the institution which receives or is accountable to DHEW for the funds awarded for the support of the activity. In order to provide for the adequate discharge of this institutional responsibility, it is the policy of DHEW that no activity involving human subjects to be supported by DHEW grants or contracts shall be undertaken unless an Institutional Review Board has reviewed and approved such activity, and the institution has submitted to DHEW a certification of such review and approval, in accordance with the requirements of this part.

(b) This review shall determine whether these subjects will be placed at risk, and, if risk is involved, whether:

(1) The risks to the subject are so outweighed by the sum of the benefit to the subject and the importance of the knowledge to be gained as to warrant a decision to allow the subject to accept these risks;

(2) The rights and welfare of any such subjects will be adequately protected; and

(3) Legally effective informed consent will be obtained by adequate and appropriate methods in accordance with the provisions of this part.

(c) Unless the activity is covered by Subpart B of this Part, if it involves as subjects women who could become pregnant, the Board shall also determine as part of its review that adequate steps will be taken in the conduct of the activity to avoid involvement of women who are in fact pregnant, when such activity would involve risk to a fetus.

(d) Where the Board finds risk is involved under paragraph (b) of this section, it shall review the conduct of the activity at timely intervals.

(e) No grant or contract involving human subjects at risk shall be made to an individual unless he is affiliated with or sponsored by an institution which can and does assume responsibility for the subjects involved. [40 FR 11854, Mar. 13, 1975. Redesignated and amended at 40 FR 38528, Aug. 8, 1975]

§46.103 Definitions.

(a) "Institution" means any public or private institution or agency (including Federal, State, and local government agencies).

(b) "Subject at risk" means any individual who may be exposed to the possibility of injury, including physical, psychological, or social injury, as a consequence of participation as a subject in any research, development, or related activity which departs from the application of those established and accepted methods necessary to meet his needs, or which increases the ordinary risks of daily life, including the recognized risks inherent in a chosen occupation or field of service.

(c) "Informed consent" means the knowing consent of an individual or his legally authorized representative, so situated as to be able to exercise free power of choice without undue inducement or any element of force, fraud, deceit, duress, or other form of constraint or coercion. The basic elements of information necessary to such consent include:

(1) A fair explanation of the procedures to be followed, and their purposes, including identification of any procedures which are experimental;

(2) A description of any attendant discomforts and risks reasonably to be expected;

(3) A description of any benefits reasonably to be expected;

(4) A disclosure of any appropriate alternative procedures that might be advantageous for the subject;

(5) An offer to answer any inquiries concerning the procedures; and

(6) An instruction that the person is free to withdraw his consent and to discontinue participation in the project or activity at any time without prejudice to the subject.

(d) "Secretary" means the Secretary of Health, Education, and Welfare or any other officer or employee of the Department of Health, Education, and Welfare to whom authority has been delegated.

(e) "DHEW" means the Department of Health, Education, and Welfare.

(f) "Approved assurance" means a document that fulfills the requirements of this part and is approved by the Secretary.

(g) "Certification" means the official institutional notification to DHEW in accordance with the requirements of this part that a project or activity involving human subjects at risk has been reviewed and approved by the institution in accordance with the "approved assurance" on file at DHEW.

(h) "Legally authorized representative" means an individual or judicial or other body authorized under applicable law to consent on behalf of a prospective subject to such subject's participation in the particular activity or procedure.

§46.104 Submission of Assurances.

(a) Recipients or prospective recipients of DHEW support under a grant or contract involving subjects at risk shall provide written assurance acceptable to DHEW that they will comply with DHEW policy as set forth in this part. Each assurance shall embody a statement of compliance with DHEW requirements for initial and continuing Institutional Review Board review of the supported activities; a set of implementing guidelines, including identification of the Board and a description of its review procedures; or, in the case of special assurances concerned with single activities or projects, a report of initial findings of the Board and of its proposed continuing review procedures.

(b) Such assurance shall be executed by an individual authorized to act for the institution and to assume on behalf of the institution the obligations imposed by this part, and shall be filed in such form and manner as the Secretary may require.

§46.150 Types of Assurances.

(a) *General assurances.* A general assurance describes the review and implementation procedures applicable to all DHEW-supported activities conducted by an institution regardless of the number, location, or types of its components or field activities. General assurances will be required from institutions having a significant number of concurrent DHEW-supported projects or activities involving human subjects.

(b) *Speical assurances.* A special assurance will, as a rule, describe those review and implementation procedures applicable to a single activity or project. A special assurance will not be solicited or accepted from an institution which has on file with DHEW an approved general assurance.

§46.106 Minimum Requirements for General Assurances.

General assurances shall be submitted in such form and manner as the Secretary may require. The institution must include, as part of its general assurance, implementing guidelines that specifically provide for:

(a) A statement of principles which will govern the institution in the discharge of its responsibilities for protecting the rights and welfare of subjects. This may include appropriate existing codes or declarations, or statements formulated by the institution itself. It is to be understood that no such principles supersede DHEW policy or applicable law.

(b) An Institutional Review Board or Board structure which will conduct initial and continuing reviews in accordance with the policy outlines in §46.2. Such Board structure or Board shall meet the following requirements:

(1) The Board must be composed of not less than five persons with varying backgrounds to assure complete and adequate review of activities commonly conducted by the institution. The Board must be sufficiently qualified through the maturity, experience, and expertise of its members and diversity of its membership to insure respect for its advice and counsel for safeguarding the rights and welfare of human subjects. In addition to possessing the professional competence necessary to review specific activities, the Board must be able to ascertain the acceptability of applications and proposals in terms of institutional commitments and regulations, applicable law, standards of professional conduct and practice, and community attitudes. The Board must therefore include persons whose concerns are in these areas.

(2) The Board members shall be identified to DHEW by name; earned degrees, if any; position or occupation; representative capacity; and by other pertinent indications of experience such as board certification, licenses, etc., sufficient to describe each member's chief anticipated contributions to Board deliberations. Any employment or other relationship between each member and the institution shall be identified, i.e., full-time employee, part-time employee, member of governing panel or board, paid consultant, unpaid consultant. Changes in Board membership shall be reported to DHEW in such form and at such times as the Secretary may require.

(3) No member of a Board shall be involved in either the initial or continuing review of an activity in which he has a conflicting interest, except to provide information requested by the Board.

(4) No Board shall consist entirely of persons who are officers, employees, or agents, of, or are otherwise associated with the institution, apart from their membership on the Board.

(5) No Board shall consist entirely of members of a single professional group.

(6) The quorum of the Board shall be defined, but may in no event be less than a majority of the total membership duly convened to carry out the Board's responsibilities under the terms of the assurance.

(c) Procedures which the institution will follow in its initial and continuing review of applications, proposals, and activities.

(d) Procedures which the Board will follow (1) to provide advice and counsel to activity directors and investigators with regard to the Board's actions, (2) to insure prompt reporting to the Board of proposed changes in an activity and of unanticipated problems involving risk to subjects or others, and (3) to insure that any such problems, including adverse reactions to biologicals, drugs, radioisotope labelled drugs, or to medical devices, are promptly reported to DHEW.

(e) Procedures which the institution will follow to maintain an active and effective Board and to implement its recommendations.

§46.107 Minimum Requirements for Special Assurances.

Special assurances shall be submitted in such form and manner as the Secretary may require. An acceptable special assurance shall:

(a) Identify the specific grant or contract involved by its full title; and by the name of the activity or project director, principal investigator, fellow, or other person immediately responsible for the conduct of the activity.

(b) Include a statement, executed by an appropriate institutional official, indicating that the institution has established an Institutional Review Board

satisfying the requirements of §46.6 (b).

(c) Describe the makeup of the Board and the training, experience, and background of its members, as required by §46.6(b)(2).

(d) Describe in general terms the risks to subjects that the Board recognizes as inherent in the activity, and justify its decision that these risks are so outweighed by the sum of the benefit to the subject and the importance of the knowledge to be gained as to warrant the Board's decision to permit the subject to accept these risks.

(e) Describe the informed consent procedures to be used and attach documentation as required by §46.10.

(f) Describe procedures which the Board will follow to insure prompt reporting to the Board of proposed changes in the activity and of any unanticipated problems, involving risks to subjects or others and to insure that any such problems, including adverse reactions to biologicals, drugs, radioisotope labelled drugs, or to medical devices are promptly reported to DHEW.

(g) Indicate at what time intervals the Board will meet to provide for continuing review. Such review must occur no less than annually.

(h) Be signed by the individual members of the Board and be endorsed by an appropriate institutional official.

§46.108 Evaluation and Disposition of Assurances.

(a) All assurances submitted in accordance with §§46.6 and 46.7 shall be evaluated by the Secretary through such officers and employees of DHEW and such experts or consultants engaged for this purpose as he determines to be appropriate. The Secretary's evaluation shall take into consideration, among other pertinent factors, the adequacy of the proposed Institutional Review Board in the light of the anticipated scope of the applicant institution's activities and the types of subject populations likely to be involved, the appropriateness of the proposed initial and continuing review procedures in the light of the probable risks, and the size and complexity of the institution.

(b) On the basis of his evaluation of an assurance pursuant to paragraph (a) of this section, the Secretary shall (1) approve, (2) enter into negotiations to develop a more satisfactory assurance, or (3) disapprôve. With respect to approved assurances, the Secretary may determine the period during which any particular assurance or class of assurances shall remain effective or otherwise condition or restrict his approval. With respect to negotiations, the Secretary may, pending completion of negotiations for a general assurance, require an institution otherwise eligible for such an assurance, to submit special assurances.

§46.109 Obligation to Obtain Informed Consent; Prohibition of Exculpatory Clauses.

Any institution proposing to place any subject at risk is obligated to obtain and document legally effective informed consent. No such informed consent, oral or written, obtained under an assurance provided pursuant to this part shall include any exculpatory language through which the subject is made to waive, or to appear to waive, any of his legal rights, including any release of the institution or its agents from liability for negligence.

§46.110 Documentation of Informed Consent.

The actual procedure utilized in obtaining legally effective informed consent and the basis for Institutional Review Board determinations that the procedures are adequate and appropriate shall be fully documented. The documentation of consent will employ one of the following three forms:

(a) Provision of a written consent document embodying all of the basic elements of informed consent. This may be read to the subject or to his legally authorized representative, but in any event he or his legally authorized representative must be given adequate opportunity to read it. This document is to be signed by the subject or his legally authorized representative. Sample copies of the consent form as approved by the Board are to be retained in its records.

(b) Provision of a "short form" written consent document indicating that the basic elements of informed consent have been presented orally to the subject or his legally authorized representative. Written summaries of what is to be said to the patient are to be approved by the Board. The short form is to be signed by the subject or his legally authorized representative and by an auditor witness to the oral presentation and to the subject's signature. A copy of the approved summary, annotated to show any additions, is to be signed by the persons officially obtaining the consent and by the auditor witness. Sample copies of the consent form and of the summaries as approved by the Board are to be retained in its records.

(c) Modification of either of the primary procedures outlined in paragraphs (a) and (b) of this section. Granting of permission to use modified procedures imposes additional responsibility upon the Board and the institution to establish: (1) That the risk to any subject is minimal, (2) that use of either of the primary procedures for obtaining informed consent would surely invalidate objectives of considerable immediate importance, and (3) that any reasonable alternative means for attaining these objectives would be less advantageous to the subjects. The Board's reasons for permitting the use of modified procedures must be individually and specifically documented in the minutes and in reports of Board actions to the files of the institution. All such modifications should be regularly reconsidered as a function of continuing review and as required for annual review, with documentation of reaffirmation, revision, or discontinuation, as appropriate.

§46.111 Submission and Certification of Applications and Proposals, General Assurances.

(a) *Timely review.* Any institution having an approved general assurance shall indicate in each application or proposal for support of activities covered by this part (or in a separate document submitted with such application or proposal) that it has on file with DHEW such an assurance. In addition, unless the Secretary otherwise provides, each such application or proposal must be given review and, when found to involve subjects at risk, approval, prior to submission to DHEW. In the event the Secretary provides for the performance of institutional review of an application or proposal after its submission to DHEW, processing of such application or proposal by DHEW will under no circumstances be completed until such institutional review and approval has been certified. Except where the institution determines that human subjects are not involved, the application or proposal should be appropriately certified in the spaces provided on forms, or one of the following certifications, as appropriate, should be typed on the lower or right hand margin of the page bearing the name of an official authorized to sign or execute applications or proposals for the institution.

Human Subjects: Reviewed, Not at Risk.

- -

(Date)

Human Subjects: Reviewed, At Risk, Approved

- -

(Date)

(b) *Applications and proposals not certified.* Applications and proposals not properly certified, or submitted as not involving human subjects and

found by the operating agency to involve human subjects, will be returned to the institution concerned.

§46.112 Submission and Certification of Applications and Proposals, Special Assurances.

(a) Except as provided in paragraph (b) of this section, institutions not having an approved general assurance shall submit in or with each application or proposal for support of activities covered by this part a separate special assurance and certification of its review and approval.

(b) If the Secretary so provides, the assurance which must be submitted in or with the application or proposal under paragraph (a) of this section need satisfy only the requirements of §§46.7(a) and 46.7(b). Under such circumstances, processing of such application or proposal by DHEW will not be completed until a further assurance satisfying the remaining requirements of §46.7 has been submitted to DHEW.

(c) An assurance and certification prepared in accordance with this part and approved by DHEW shall be considered to have met the requirement for certification for the initial grant or contract period concerned. If the terms of the grant or contract recommend additional support periods, each application or proposal for continuation or renewal of support must satisfy the requirements of this section or §46.11 whichever is applicable at the time of its submission.

§46.113 Applications and Proposals Lacking Definite Plans for Involvement of Human Subjects.

Certain types of applications or proposals are submitted with the knowledge that subjects are to be involved within the support period, but definite plans for this involvement would not normally be set forth in the application or proposal. These include such activities as (a) institutional type grants where selection of projects is the responsibility of the institution, (b) training grants where training projects remain to be selected, and (c) research, pilot, or developmental studies in which involvement depends upon such things as the completion of instruments, or of prior animal studies, or upon the purification of compounds. Such applications or proposals shall be reviewed and certified in the same manner as more definitive applications or proposals. The initial certification indicates institutional approval of the applications or proposals as submitted, and commits the institution to later review of the plans when completed. Such later review and certification to DHEW should be completed prior to the beginning of the budget period during which actual involvement of human subjects is to begin. Review and certification to DHEW must in any event be completed prior to involvement of human subjects.

§46.114 Applications and Proposals Submitted with the Intent of Not Involving Human Subjects.

If an application or proposal does not anticipate involving or intend to involve human subjects, no certification should be included with the initial submission of the application or proposal. In those instances, however, when later it becomes appropriate to use all or part of awarded funds for one or more activities which will involve subjects, each such activity shall be reviewed and approved in accordance with the assurance of the institution prior to the involvement of subjects. In addition, no such activity shall be undertaken until the institution has submitted to DHEW. (a) A certification that the activity has been reviewed and approved in accordance with this part, and (b) a detailed description of the proposed activity (including any protocol or similar document). Also, where support is provided by project grants or contracts, subjects shall not be involved prior to

certification and institutional receipt of DHEW approval and, in the case of contracts, prior to negotiation and approval of an amended contract description of work.

§46.115 Evaluation and Disposition of Applications and Proposals.

(a) Notwithstanding any prior review, approval, and certification by the institution all applications or proposals involving human subjects at risk submitted to DHEW shall be evaluated by the Secretary for compliance with this part through such officers and employees of the Department and such experts or consultants engaged for this purpose as he determines to be appropriate. This evaluation may take into account, among other pertinent factors, the apparent risks to the subjects, the adequacy of protection against these risks, the potential benefits of the activity to the subjects and to others, and the importance of the knowledge to be gained.

(b) Disposition. On the basis of his evaluation of an application or proposal pursuant to paragraph (a) of this section and subject to such approval or recommendation by or consultation with appropriate councils, committees, or other bodies as may be required by law, the Secretary shall (1) approve, (2) defer for further evaluation, or (3) disapprove support of the proposed activity in whole or in part. With respect to any approved grant or contract, the Secretary may impose conditions, including restrictions on the use of certain procedures, or certain subject groups, or requiring use of specified safeguards or informed consent procedures when in his judgment such conditions are necessary for the protection of human subjects.

§46.416 Cooperative Activities.

Cooperative activities are those which involve institutions in addition to the grantee or prime contractor (such as a contractor under a grantee or a subcontractor under a prime contractor). If, in such instances, the grantee or prime contractor obtains access to all or some of the subjects involved through one or more cooperating institutions, the basic DHEW policy applies and the grantee or prime contractor remains responsible for safeguarding the rights and welfare of the subjects.

(a) *Institution with approved general assurance.* Initial and continuing review by the institution may be carried out by one or a combination of procedures:

(1) Cooperating institution with approved general assurance. When the cooperating institution has on file with DHEW an approved general assurance, the grantee or contractor may, in addition to its own review, request the cooperating institution to conduct an independent review and to report its recommendations on those aspects of the activity that concern individuals for whom the cooperating institution has responsibility under its own assurance to the grantee's or contractor's Institutional Review Board. The grantee or contractor may, at its discretion, concur with or further restrict the recommendations of the cooperating institution. It is the responsibility of the grantee or contractor to maintain communication with the Boards of the cooperating institution. However, the cooperating institution shall promptly notify the grantee or contracting institution whenever the cooperating institution finds the conduct of the project or activity within its purview unsatisfactory.

(2) Cooperating institution with no approved general assurance. When the cooperating institution does not have an approved general assurance on file with DHEW, the DHEW may require the submission of a general or special assurance which, if approved, will permit the grantee or contractor to follow the procedure outlined in the preceding subparagraph.

(3) Interinstitutional joint review. The grantee or contracting institution

may wish to develop an agreement with cooperating institutions to provide for an Institutional Review Board with representatives from cooperating institutions. Representatives of cooperating institutions may be appointed as ad hoc members of the grantee or contracting institution's existing Institutional Review Board or, if cooperation is on a frequent or continuing basis as between a medical school and a group of affiliated hospitals, appointments for extended periods may be made. All such cooperative arrangements must be approved by DHEW as part of a general assurance, or as an amendment to a general assurance.

(b) *Institutions with special assurances.* While responsibility for initial and continuing review necessarily lies with the grantee or contracting institution, DHEW may also require approved assurances from those cooperating institutions having immediate responsibility for subjects.

If the cooperating institution has on file with DHEW an approved general assurance, the grantee or contractor shall request the cooperating institution to conduct its own independent review of those aspects of the project or activity which will involve human subjects for which it has responsibility. Such a request shall be in writing and should provide for direct notification of the grantee's or contractor's Institutional Review Board in the event that the cooperating institution's Board finds the conduct of the activity to be unsatisfactory. If the cooperating institution does not have an approved general assurance on file with DHEW, it must submit to DHEW a general or special assurance which is determined by DHEW to comply with the provisions of this part.

§46.117 Investigational New Drug 30-Day Delay Requirement.

Where an institution is required to prepare or to submit a certification under §§46.11, 46.12, 46.13, or §46.14 and the application or proposal involves an investigational new drug within the meaning of The Food, Drug, and Cosmetic Act, the drug shall be identified in the certification together with a statement that the 30-day delay required by 21 CFR 312.1(a)(2) has elapsed and the Food and Drug Administration has not, prior to expiration of such 30-day interval, requested that the sponsor continue to withhold or to restrict use of the drug in human subjects; or that the Food and Drug Administration has waived the 30-day delay requirement: *Provided, however,* That in those cases in which the 30-day delay interval has neither expired nor been waived, a statement shall be forwarded to DHEW upon such expiration or upon receipt of a waiver. No certification shall be considered acceptable until such statement has been received.

§46.118—Institution's Executive Responsibility.

Specific executive functions to be conducted by the institution include policy development and promulgation and continuing indoctrination of personnel. Appropriate administrative assistance and support shall be provided for the Board's functions. Implementation of the Board's recommendations through appropriate administrative action and followup is a condition of DHEW approval of an assurance. Board approvals, favorable actions, and recommendations are subject to review and to disapproval or further restriction by the institution officials. Board disapprovals, restrictions, or conditions cannot be rescinded or removed except by action of a Board described in the assurance approved by DHEW.

§46.119 Institution's Records; Confidentiality.

(a) Copies of all documents presented or required for initial and continuing review by the Institutional Review Board, such as Board minutes, records of subject's consent, transmittals on actions, instructions, and conditions resulting from Board deliberations addressed to the activity director, are to be retained by the institution, subject to the terms and conditions of grant and contract awards.

(b) Except as otherwise provided by law information in the records or possession of an institution acquired in connection with an activity covered by this part, which information refers to or can be identified with a particular subject, may not be disclosed except:

(1) With the consent of the subject or his legally authorized representative; or

(2) As may be necessary for the Secretary to carry out his responsibilities under this part.

§46.120 Reports.

Each institution with an approved assurance shall provide the Secretary with such reports and other information as the Secretary may from time to time prescribe.

§46.121 Early Termination of Awards; Evaluation of Subsequent Applications and Proposals.

(a) If, in the judgment of the Secretary an institution has failed materially to comply with the terms of this policy with respect to a particular DHEW grant or contract, he may require that said grant or contract be terminated or suspended in the manner prescribed in applicable grant or procurement regulations.

(b) In evaluating applications or proposals for support of activities covered by this part, the Secretary may take into account, in addition to all other eligibility requirements and program criteria, such factors as: (1) Whether the applicant or offeror has been subject to a termination or suspension under paragraph (a) of this section. (2) whether the applicant or offeror or the person who would direct the scientific and technical aspects of an activity has in the judgment of the Secretary failed materially to discharge his, her, or its responsibility for the protection of the rights and welfare of subjects in his, her, or its care (whether or not DHEW funds were involved), and (3) whether, where past deficiencies have existed in discharging such responsibility, adequate steps have in the judgment of the Secretary been taken to eliminate these deficiencies.

§46.122 Conditions.

The Secretary may with respect to any grant or contract or any class of grants or contracts impose additional conditions prior to or at the time of any award when in his judgment such conditions are necessary for the protection of human subjects.

SUBPART B—ADDITIONAL PROTECTIONS PERTAINING TO RESEARCH, DEVELOPMENT, AND RELATED ACTIVITIES INVOLVING FETUSES, PREGNANT WOMEN, AND HUMAN IN VITRO FERTILIZATION

Source: 40 FR 33528, Aug. 8, 1975, unless otherwise noted.

§46.201 Applicability.

(a) The regulations in this subpart are applicable to all Department of Health, Education, and Welfare grants and contracts supporting research, development, and related activities involving: (1) The fetus, (2) pregnant women, and (3) human *in vitro* fertilization.

(b) Nothing in this subpart shall be construed as indicating that compliance with the procedures set forth herein will in any way render inapplicable pertinent State or local laws bearing upon activities covered by this subpart.

(c) The requirements of this subpart are in addition to those imposed under the other subparts of this part.

§46.202 Purpose.

It is the purpose of this subpart to provide additional safeguards in reviewing activities to which this subpart is applicable to assure that they conform to appropriate ethical standards and relate to important societal needs.

§46.203 Definitions.

As used in this subpart:

(a) "Secretary" means the Secretary of Health, Education, and Welfare and any other officer or employee of the Department of Health, Education, and Welfare to whom authority has been delegated.

(b) "Pregnancy" encompasses the period of time from confirmation of implantation until expulsion or extraction of the fetus.

(c) "Fetus" means the product of conception from the time of implantation until a determination is made, following expulsion or extraction of the fetus, that it is viable.

(d) "Viable" as it pertains to the fetus means being able, after either spontaneous or induced delivery, to survive (given the benefit of available medical therapy) to the point of independently maintaining heart beat and respiration. The Secretary may from time to time, taking into account medical advances, publish in the Federal Register guidelines to assist in determining whether a fetus is viable for purposes of this subpart. If a fetus is viable after delivery, it is a premature infant.

(e) "Nonviable fetus" means a fetus *ex utero* which, although living, is not viable.

(f) "Dead fetus" means a fetus *ex utero* which exhibits neither heartbeat, spontaneous respiratory activity, spontaneous movement of voluntary muscles nor pulsation of the umbilical cord (if still attached).

(g) "*In vitro* fertilization" means any fertilization of human ova which occurs outside the body of a female, either through admixture of donor human sperm and ova or by any other means.

§46.204 **Ethical Advisory Boards.**

(a) Two Ethical Advisory Boards shall be established by the Secretary. Members of these Boards shall be so selected that the Boards will be competent to deal with medical, legal, social, ethical, and related issues and may include, for example, research scientists, physicians, psychologists, sociologists, educators, lawyers, and ethicists, as well as representatives of the general public. No board member may be a regular, full-time employee of the Federal Government.

(b) One Board shall be advisory to the Public Health Service and its components. One Board shall be advisory to all other agencies and components within the Department of Health, Education, and Welfare.

(c) At the request of the Secretary, the appropriate Ethical Advisory Board shall render advice consistent with the policies and requirements of this Part as to ethical issues, involving activities covered by this subpart, raised by individual applications or proposals. In addition, upon request by the Secretary, the appropriate Board shall render advice as to classes of applications or proposals and general policies, guidelines, and procedures.

(d) A Board may establish, with the approval of the Secretary, classes of applications or proposals which: (1) Must be submitted to the Board, or (2) need not be submitted to the Board. Where the Board so establishes a class of applications or proposals which must be submitted, no application or proposal within the class may be funded by the Department or any component thereof until the application or proposal has been reviewed by the Board and the Board has rendered advice as to its acceptability from an ethical standpoint.

(e) No application or proposal involving human *in vitro* fertilization may be funded by the Department or any component thereof until the application or proposal has been reviewed by the Ethical Advisory Board and the Board has rendered advice as to its acceptability from an ethical standpoint.

§46.205 **Additional Duties of the Institutional Review Boards in Connection with Activities Involving Fetuses, Pregnant Women, or Human in Vitro Fertilization.**

(a) In addition to the responsibilities prescribed for Institutional Review Boards under Subpart A of this part, the applicant's or offeror's Board shall, with respect to activities covered by this subpart, carry out the following additional duties:

(1) Determine that all aspects of the activity meet the requirements of this subpart;

(2) Determine that adequate consideration has been given to the manner in which potential subjects will be selected, and adequate provision has been made by the applicant or offeror for monitoring the actual informed consent process (e.g., through such mechanisms, when appropriate, as participation by the Institutional Review Board or subject advocates in: (i) Overseeing the actual process by which individual consents required by this subpart are secured either by approving induction of each individual into the activity or verifying, perhaps through sampling, that approved procedures for induction of individuals into the activity are being followed, and (ii) monitoring the progress of the activity and intervening as necessary through such steps as visits to the activity site and continuing evaluation to determine if any unanticipated risks have arisen);

(3) Carry out such other responsibilities as may be assigned by the Secretary.

(b) No award may be issued until the applicant or offeror has certified to the Secretary that the Institutional Review Board has made the determinations required under paragraph (a) of this section and the Secretary has approved these determinations, as provided in §46.115 of Subpart A of this part.

(c) Applicants or offerors seeking support for activities covered by this subpart must provide for the designation of an Institutional Review Board, subject to approval by the Secretary, where no such Board has been established under Subpart A of this part.

§46.206 General Limitations.

(a) No activity to which this subpart is applicable may be undertaken unless:

(1) Appropriate studies on animals and nonpregnant individuals have been completed;

(2) Except where the purpose of the activity is to meet the health needs of the particular fetus, the risk to the fetus is minimal and, in all cases, is the least possible risk for achieving the objectives of the activity;

(3) Individuals engaged in the activity will have no part in: (i) Any decisions as to the timing, method, and procedures used to terminate the pregnancy, and (ii) determining the viability of the fetus at the termination of the pregnancy; and

(4) No procedural changes which may cause greater than minimal risk to the fetus or the pregnant woman will be introduced into the procedure for terminating the pregnancy solely in the interest of the activity.

(b) No inducements, monetary or otherwise, may be offered to terminate pregnancy for purposes of the activity.

§46.207 Activities Directed Toward Pregnant Women as Subjects.

(a) No pregnant woman may be involved as a subject in an activity covered by this subpart unless: (1) The purpose of the activity is to meet the health needs of the mother and the fetus will be placed at risk only to the minimum extent necessary to meet

such needs, or (2) the risk to the fetus is minimal.

(b) An activity permitted under paragraph (a) of this section may be conducted only if the mother and father are legally competent and have given their informed consent after having been fully informed regarding possible impact on the fetus, except that the father's informed consent need not be secured if: (1) The purpose of the activity is to meet the health needs of the mother; (2) his identity or whereabouts cannot reasonably be ascertained; (3) he is not reasonably available; or (4) the pregnancy resulted from rape.

§46.208 Activities Directed Toward Fetuses in Utero as Subjects.

(a) No fetus *in utero* may be involved as a subject in any activity covered by this subpart unless: (1) The purpose of the activity is to meet the health needs of the particular fetus and the fetus will be placed at risk only to the minimum extent necessary to meet such needs, or (2) the risk to the fetus imposed by the research is minimal and the purpose of the activity is the development of important biomedical knowledge which cannot be obtained by other means.

(b) An activity permitted under paragraph (a) of this section may be conducted only if the mother and father are legally competent and have given their informed consent, except that the father's consent need not be secured if: (1) His identity or whereabouts cannot reasonably be ascertained, (2) he is not reasonably available, or (3) the pregnancy resulted from rape.

§46.209 Activities Directed Toward Fetuses Ex Utero, Including Nonviable Fetuses, as Subjects.

(a) No fetus *ex utero* may be involved as a subject in an activity covered by this subpart until it has been ascertained whether the particular fetus is viable, unless: (1) There will be no added risk to the fetus resulting from the activity, and (2) the purpose of the activity is the development of important biomedical knowledge which cannot be obtained by other means.

(b) No nonviable fetus may be involved as a subject in an activity covered by this subpart unless: (1) Vital functions of the fetus will not be artificially maintained except where the purpose of the activity is to develop new methods for enabling fetuses to survive to the point of viability, (2) experimental activities which of themselves would terminate the heartbeat or respiration of the fetus will not be employed, and (3) the purpose of the activity is the development of important biomedical knowledge which cannot be obtained by other means.

(c) In the event the fetus *ex utero* is formed to be viable, it may be included as a subject in the activity only to the extent permitted by and in accordance with the requirements of other subparts of this part.

(d) An activity permitted under paragraph (a) or (b) of this section may be conducted only if the mother and father are legally competent and have given their informed consent, except that the father's informed consent need not be secured if: (1) his identity or whereabouts cannot reasonably be ascertained, (2) he is not reasonably available, or (3) the pregnancy resulted from rape.

§46.210 Activities Involving the Dead Fetus, Fetal Material, or the Placenta.

Activities involving the dead fetus, mascerated fetal material, or cells, tissue, or organs excised from a dead fetus shall be conducted only in accordance with any applicable State or local laws regarding such activities.

§46.211 Modification or Waiver of Specific Requirements.

Upon the request of an applicant or offeror (with the approval of its Institutional Review Board), the Secretary may modify or waive specific requirements of this subpart, with the approval of the Ethical Advisory Board after such opportunity for public comment as the Ethical Advisory Board considers appropriate in the particular instance. In making such decisions, the Secretary will consider whether the risks to the subject are so outweighed by the sum of the benefit to the subject and the importance of the knowledge to be gained as to warrant such modification or waiver and that such benefits cannot be gained except through a modification or waiver. Any such modifications or waivers will be published as notices in the Federal Register.

SUBPART C—GENERAL PROVISIONS

§46.301 Activities Conducted by Department Employees.

The regulations of this part are applicable as well to all research, development, and related activities conducted by employees of the Department of Health, Education, and Welfare, except that each Principal Operating Component head may adopt such non-substantive procedural modifications as may be appropriate from an administrative standpoint. [40 FR 33530, Aug. 8, 1975]

ADDITIONAL REGULATIONS ENACTED AFTER OCTOBER 1, 1975

Title 45—Public Welfare

SUBTITLE A—DEPARTMENT OF HEALTH, EDUCATION, AND WELFARE

PART 46—PROTECTION OF HUMAN SUBJECTS

Fetuses, Pregnant Women, In Vitro Fertilization

On August 8, 1975, final regulations were published in the Federal

Register (40 FR 33526) concerning research, development, and related activities involving fetuses, pregnant women, and human *in vitro* fertilization.

Section 46.207 thereof provides in pertinent part that: "No pregnant woman may be involved as a subject in an activity covered by this subpart unless: (1) The purpose of the activity is to meet the health needs of the mother and the fetus will be placed at risk only to the minimum extent necessary to meet such needs. . . ." This is consistent with Recommendation No. 2 of the National Commission for the Protection of Human Subjects of Biomedical and Behavioral Research (40 FR 33547). Section 46.206, however, states that: "No activity to which this subpart is applicable may be undertaken unless: . . . (2) Except where the purpose of the activity is to meet the health needs of the particular fetus, the risk to the fetus is minimal. . . ." Since §46.206 sets forth general limitations applicable to the entire subpart, it unintentionally confines the scope of the aforequoted portion of §46.207 to research involving minimal risk to the fetus despite the clear aim

of §46.207 to permit research involving greater than minimal risk to the fetus where necessary to meet the health needs of the mother. The amendment set forth below is intended to correct this error.

In view of the limited purpose of the amendment, the Department finds that good cause exists for dispensing with a notice of proposed rulemaking.

Accordingly, section 46.206(a) of Subpart B of Part 46 of Title 45 is amended to read as follows:

§**46.206 General Limitations.**
(a) *****
(2) Except where the purpose of the activity is to meet the health needs of the mother or the particular fetus, the risk to the fetus is minimal and, in all cases, is the least possible risk for achieving the objectives of the activity.

Dated: October 9, 1975.

Theodore Cooper,
Assistant Secretary for Health.

Approved: October 31, 1975.

David Matthews,
Secretary.

[FR Doc. 75-29845 Filed 11-5-75; 8:45 am]

 *Appendix V*

Human Experimentation in the Armed Forces

Recent disclosures in the press that the armed forces (and the Central Intelligence Agency) has conducted clandestine experiments with LSD-25, an hallucinogenic drug, demonstrate the need for analyzing the role of the military in the area of human experimentation.[1] Some of this research was merely sponsored by the Army, while other research used military personnel as subjects of the experiments.[2] It has also been indicated that some subjects of these experiments were given hallucinogens without their knowledge.[3]

According to a statement of Charles C. Ablard, General Counsel of the Department of Army, the Army became interested in hallucinogenic agents in the early 1950s when intelligence reports showed that other governments had purchased large quantities of these drugs.[4] This, in addition to other information, presented a serious threat, according to Mr. Ablard. He said

> [I]t indicated that a major portion of our deterrent forces could be rendered helpless—and defenseless—by drugs which were odorless, colorless and tasteless. It also reflected that our most sensitive security matters could be unknowingly compromised. But perhaps of even greater significance, it indicated that an alternative to nuclear weapons might be available; a weapon which might render large forces helpless—but only temporarily) and without any permanent damage to those forces and none to their surroundings.[5]

As a result of this, the Army commenced research on hallucinogenic drugs. At least thirteen research contracts were negotiated by the Army, spanning the period between 1951–1970. The first of these contracts was received by the New York State Psychiatric Institute, which was to conduct experiments on mescaline derivative drugs. During these experiments, Harold Blauer, a patient at the Institute, was administered the experimental drug and died a short time later. There is no indication in the records that his consent was obtained prior to the administration of the drug.[6]

Between 1955 and 1967 the Army conducted numerous in-house studies of psychedelics, using military and civilian personnel as subjects. Most of the tests were conducted at the Edgewood Arsenal in Maryland, although a number of them were done at other Army installations. The purpose of the research was to determine the effect of LSD on soldiers' ability to perform various military functions. In December 1957, sixteen men, when under LSD influence, were tested while operating a radar van. During the same period, soldiers under the influence of LSD were observed assembling and disassembling their rifles, performing skin decontamination procedures, and playing vollyball. Fifty-nine men at Fort Bragg were administered LSD and then tested while they conducted a meteorological survey, ground survey, and 40 mm artillery drill.[7] Although Army records refer to the subjects of these experiments as volunteers, it is not certain how much information they received concerning the possible effects of the drug and the nature of the experiment. It is also not clear whether or not the subjects' superiors coerced them into participating in these studies.[8]

Finally, testing was done on military intelligence personnel to determine if the administration of LSD could be used as a method of obtaining information during interrogation.[9] Subjects were advised that they would undergo a series of physical and mental tests to determine how they reacted to a specific "material." They were not informed as to the exact properties of the material, its potential application to the intelligence field, or the time, method, or location of administration. Subjects were told they could terminate their participation at any time.

Thus, the Army was interested in three different aspects of LSD use. First, it was interested in discovering its general properties; second, its effect on combat personnel; and third, its effect on intelligence personnel. Due to a lack of documentation, however, it is not always clear whether informed consent was obtained from the subjects, although in a number of instances it appears certain that such consent was not obtained.

The scope of biomedical and behavioral research conducted by the armed services has extended to a variety of fields that have a potential impact on the military. Some areas of research have been more general and could have benefited civilian populations. Military researchers have investigated the use of electrical anesthesia in surgery, bone transplantation in the treatment of severe facial wounds, the development of a meningitis vaccine to protect recruit populations, and the development of new antimalarial drugs.[10] Other studies have been conducted that deal with specific military problems such as the testing of physiological techniques to improve tolerance to sustained high acceleration forces encountered in combat aircraft, and the conduction of body heat loss in cold-water diving in various protective suits.[11] Research has also been performed in an attempt to find antidote drugs to counteract chemical weapons.

The basic problem that arises in the context of experiments on military personnel is whether or not they can give informed consent. Or to put it another way, are military personnel members of a captive population? There are indications that soldiers are not entirely free to determine whether or not to obtain medical treatment. It appears that, if a person in the military service refuses to submit to a medical or surgical procedure that is necessary to enable that person to perform his military duties, he would be subject to disciplinary procedures, including trial by court martial.[12] Certainly this rule should not apply to strictly experimental procedures. However, the armed forces do not seem to be a stronghold of free will, and, indeed, the effective running of the military requires a population that is prepared to take orders in a virtually unquestioning manner. One study will illustrate why it is especially difficult to determine voluntarism in the context of military research.

This study, entitled "Biomedical Study of Military Performance at High Terrestrial Elevation."[13] was designed to analyze the performance of soldiers suddenly transported from sea level to 12–16,000 feet. An area in Colorado with an average elevation of 12–13,500 feet was selected as the site of the study. The Third Special Forces Group at Fort Bragg provided troops for the study. While they conducted maneuvers, the soldiers were observed by biomedical personnel, and the troops were required to periodically fill out questionnaires with eleven items concerning their symptoms and subjective feelings. During the five days at high altitude, twenty-two of the 122 men had to be evacuated due to illness or injury, and over half received medication from aid men. A number of men had difficulty breathing and had abnormal sensations in their limbs. There was one fatality and four injuries resulting from lightning. One soldier developed a case of hemoptysis (pulmonary hemorrhage). At sea level there were only two casualties among 125 men performing the same maneuvers.

In any event, serious and discomforting effects occurred which were quite foreseeable. There is no indication that these troops were given any information regarding the effects of this sudden exposure to high altitudes, or that they were asked if they wished to participate in this study.

The question arises as to whether the Army has any obligation to obtain informed consent from these troops prior to conducting these maneuvers. Certainly, the general practice is not to ask soldiers if they wish to go out on maneuvers. If this exercise were merely conducted as a training procedure in which there were no biomedical personnel present, and in which no data were being collected, probably no one would argue that the superior officers were obligated to obtain the consent of the troops prior to sending them out on maneuvers.

Many studies have been conducted in an attempt to reduce the incidence of certain diseases that seem to abound on military bases. In one study *every* recruit who arrived at Keesler Air Force Base was given a single dose of either an experimental vaccine or a placebo.[14] Apparently none of the 13,892 recruits were given the choice of participating or not participating in this study.

A similar study was conducted on Marine recruits who were given live type-four adenovirus vaccine.[15] If the vaccine appeared to be effective in the prevention of certain diseases that often reached epidemic proportions in training camps, it is not clear that the recruits could have refused to take it.[16]

The problem of disregard for the rights of subjects in experimentation conducted by or for the military does not seem to result from the lack of guidelines, but from lack of respect for these guidelines. Even the Surgeon General of the Army has stated:

[T]here is evidence that sound ethical principles directed in past and present DOD [Department of Defense] regulations appear not always to have been followed, particularly in the 1950's. Where this has been true, I believe that the problem has not been lack of guidelines but lack of compliance with them.[17]

The Secretary of Defense first promulgated guidelines concerning the use of human volunteers in experimental research in 1953.[18] As they were classified Top Secret, the extent of their circulation would have been somewhat limited. These guidelines were specifically adopted to protect subjects of research in the fields of atomic, biological and/or chemical warfare. Although not specifically mentioned, the guidelines adopted the language of the Nuremberg Code, requiring voluntary informed consent, limiting the use of human subjects to those cases in which there are no other methods available to conduct the study, limiting the degree of risk that is permissible, and permitting the subject to withdraw at any time.

Since 1953 the Army,[19] Air Force[20] and Navy[21] have all adopted regulations concerning the protection of human subjects. For the most part they adopt the Department of Health, Education and Welfare standards for the protection of human subjects.[22] The Army and Navy regulations adopt the D.H.E.W. definitions of risk, set forth the detailed requirements for obtaining informed consent, require prior review of all experimental protocols, and state other D.H.E.W. safeguards. The Army appears to exempt the following from its regulations:

> a. Research and non-research programs, tasks, and tests which may involve inherent occupational hazards to health or exposure of personnel to potentially hazardous situations encountered as part of training or other normal duties, *e.g.*, flight training, jump training, markmanship training, ranger training, fire drills, gas drills and handling of explosives.
>
> b. That portion of human factors research which involves normal training or other military duties as part of an experiment, wherein disclosure of experimental conditions to participating personnel would reveal the artificial nature of such conditions and defeat the purpose of the investigation.[23]

Thus, the high terrestrial elevation study discussed earlier might be exempt from these regulations as that experiment might only subject the soldiers to risks inherent as part of training.

The Army regulations are quite detailed in regard to the protection of special subjects. Children may not be used as research subjects unless the child's parent or guardian gives "effective third party consent," and the purpose of the research is concerned with the diagnosis, treatment, prevention or etiology of conditions not found in adults, or involves a condition from which the child is presently suffering, provided that he will receive a direct benefit and there has been adequate prior testing, or the information cannot be obtained from any other class. The child must be consulted, and if capable of understanding what it is he is to be subjected to, may refuse to participate.[24] There are similar guidelines for the use of prisoners[25] and the institutionalized mentally infirm[26] as human subjects. Prisoners of war may never be used as research subjects.[27]

Although the military has adopted detailed regulations regarding human experimentation, it is not clear how much concern actually exists for the protection of human subjects. Many subtle pressures can be brought to bear on military personnel and an important part of military training is to teach individuals to take orders and to satisfy the wishes of superiors. The literature in this entire field is very limited and conclusions are impossible to draw due to this lack of information.

One additional problem in this area is that military personnel can not sue either the United States or the Army physicians for injuries that might be caused by that physician.[28] There is a fear that suits against superior officers could lead to a breakdown in discipline. A serviceman cannot sue a military physician for malpractice even after he has been discharged from the service.[29] Thus, any self-restraint that a physician might adopt due to the fear of being sued as a result of his actions is absent in the military setting.

From this brief discussion of military research few conclusions can be drawn. Although the armed forces have adopted regulations pertaining to the protection of human subjects, past experience demonstrates that such regulations are not always complied with. It is also not clear when military personnel can be ordered to encounter hazardous conditions, and when they must consent to encountering such conditions. Finally, the fear of suit by an injured subject will not act to restrain military researchers, since such suits cannot be brought by injured military personnel.

Due to a lack of information in this area, it is incumbent that further research be done to determine what sort of research has been and will be conducted, and to determine the rights of subjects who are members of the armed forces.

REFERENCES

1. Ashley, The Other Side of LSD, New York Times Magazine, Oct. 19, 1975, p. 40; New York Times, August 19, 1975, p. 37.

2. New York Times, July 23, 1975, p. 17; Boston Globe, July 17, 1975, p. 1.

3. Boston Globe, *id.*

4. Statement before the Subcommittee on Administrative Practices and Procedure of the Senate Judiciary Committee and the Subcommittee on Health of the Senate Labor and Public Welfare Committee, September 10, 1975, p. 3.

5. *Id.* at 4.

6. *Id.* at 7.

7. *Id.* at 12.

8. *Id.* at 12–13.

9. *Id.* at 13.

10. Statement by Lieutenant General Richard B. Taylor, M.D., the Surgeon General, Department of the Army, before the Subcommittee on Administrative

Practice and Procedure of the Senate Judiciary Committee and the Subcommittee of Health of the Senate Labor and Public Welfare Committee, Sept. 10, 1975, pp. 5-7.

11. *Id.* at 7.

12. Johnson, Civil Rights of Military Personnel Regarding Medical Care and Experimental Procedures, 117 Science 212, 213 (Feb. 27, 1953); Levin, Some Legal Aspects of Military Preventive Medicine, 129 Mil. Med. 439 (1964).

13. Dusek and Hansen, Biomedical Study of Military Performance at High Terrestrial Elevation, 134 Mil. Med. 1497 (1969).

14. Mogabgab, Protective Efficacy of Killed Mycoplasma Pneumoniae Vaccine Measured in Large-Scale Studies in a Military Population, 108 Am. Rev. of Resp. Dis. 899 (1973).

15. Gutekumst, White, Edmondson and Chanock, Immunization with Live Type 4 Adenovirus: Determination of Infectious Virus Dose and Protective Effect of Enteric Infection, 86 Am. J. of Epid. 341 (1967).

16. Levin, *supra* note 12.

17. *Supra* note 10 at 9.

18. Memorandum for the Secretary of the Army, Secretary of the Navy, Secretary of the Air Force from the Secretary of Defense, (Feb. 26, 1953), Appendix I to Statement of the Surgeon General of the Army, *supra* note 10.

19. United States Army Medical Research and Development Command Regulation, 70-25 (Oct. 8, 1975).

20. Naval Medical Research and Development Command Notice 3900 (Nov. 3, 1975).

21. Air Force Regulation 169-8 (Aug. 19, 1974).

22. 39 Fed. Reg. 18913 (May 30, 1974).

23. Army Regulation No. 70-25 (3.a) (July 1974).

24. *Supra* note 19 at 1-10-1.

25. *Id.* at 1-10-2.

26. *Id.* at 1-10-3.

27. *Id.* at 1-5-2 (1).

28. Feres v. U.S., 340 U.S. 135 (1950); Bailey v. Van Buskirk, 345 F.2d 298 (9 Cir. 1965).

29. Kennedy v. Maginnis, 393 F. Supp. 310 (D. Mass. 1975).

❋ *Appendix VI*

H.E.W. Draft Working Document on Experimentation with Children

APPENDIX VI

38 Fed. Reg. 31746 (Nov. 16, 1973)

SUBPART B—ADDITIONAL PROTECTIONS FOR CHILDREN INVOLVED AS SUBJECT IN DHEW ACTIVITIES

Section 46.21 *Applicability*. (a) The regulations in this subpart are applicable to all Department of Health, Education and Welfare research, development, or demonstration activities in which children may be at risk.

(b) The requirements of this subpart are in addition to those imposed under subpart A of this part.

Section 46.22 *Purpose*. It is the purpose of this subpart to provide additional safeguards in reviewing activities to which this subpart is applicable inasmuch as the potential subjects in activities conducted thereunder might be unable fully to comprehend the risks which might be involved and are legally incapable of consenting to their participation in such activities.

Section 46.23 *Need for legally effective consent*. Nothing in this subpart shall be construed as indicating that compliance with the procedures set forth herein will necessarily result in a legally effective consent under applicable State or local law to a subject's participation in any activity; nor in particular does it obviate the need for court approval of such participation where court approval is required under applicable State or local law in order to obtain a legally effective consent.

Section 46.24 *Definitions*. As used in this subpart:

(a) "DHEW activity" means:

(1) The conduct or support (through grants, contracts, or other awards) of biomedical or behavioral research involving human subjects; or

(2) Research, development, or demonstration activities regulated by any DHEW agency.

(b) "Subject at risk" means any individual who might be exposed to the possibility of harm—physical, psychological, sociological, or other—as a consequence of participation as a subject in any DHEW activity which goes beyond the application of those established and accepted methods necessary to meet his needs.

(c) "Child" means an individual who has not attained the legal age of consent to participate in research as

313

determined under the applicable law of the jurisdiction in which such research is to be conducted.

(d) "DHEW" means the Department of Health, Education, and Welfare.

Section 46.25 *Agency Ethical Review Board; composition; duties.* (a) The head of each agency shall establish an Ethical Review Board, hereinafter referred to as the "Board," to review proposals for research, development, and demonstration activities to which this subpart is applicable, as well as to advise him or her on matters of policy concerning protection of human subjects. The Board shall be composed of research scientists (biomedical, behavioral, and/or social), physicians, lawyers, clergy, ethicists, and representatives of the public. It shall consist of 15 members appointed by the agency head from outside the Federal Government. No more than one-third of the members may be individuals engaged in research, development, or demonstration activities involving human subjects.

(b) It shall be the function of the Board to review each proposed activity to which this subpart applies, and advise the agency concerning the acceptability of such activities from the standpoint of societal need and ethical considerations, taking into account the assessment of the appropriate Primary Review Committees as to: (1) The potential benefit of the proposed activity, (2) scientific merit and experimental design, (3) whether the proposed activity entails risk of significant harm to the subject, (4) the sufficiency of animal and adult human studies demonstrating safety and clear potential benefit of the proposed procedures and providing sufficient information on which to base an assessment of the risks, and (5) whether the information to be gained may be obtained from further animal and adult human studies.

(c) The Board shall review the procedures proposed by the applicant to be followed by the Protection Committee, provided for in §46.26 of this subpart, in carrying out its functions as set forth in §46.26. In addition, the Board may recommend additional functions to be performed by the Protection Committee in connection with any particular activity.

(d) In decisions regarding activities covered by this subpart, the agency shall take into account the recommendations of the Board.

Section 46.26 *Protection Committees; composition; duties.* (a) No activity covered by this subpart will be approved unless it provides for the establishments by the applicant of a Protection Committee, composed of at least five members so selected that the Committee will be competent to deal with the medical, legal, social and ethical issues involved in the activity. None of the members shall have any association with the proposed activity, and at least one-half shall have no association with any organization or individual conducting or supporting the activity. No more than one-third of the members shall be individuals engaged in research, development, or demonstration activities involving human subjects. The composition of the Protection Committee shall be subject to DHEW approval.

(b) The duties of the Protection Committee, proposed by the applicant, and reviewed by the agency including the Ethical Review Board shall be to oversee: (1) The selection of subjects who may be included in the activity; (2) the monitoring of the subject's continued willingness to participate in the activity; (3) the design of procedures to permit intervention on behalf of one or more of the subjects if conditions warrant; (4) the evaluation of the reasonableness of the parents' consent and (where applicable) the subject's consent; and (5) the procedures for advising the subject and/or the parents concerning the subject's continued participation in the activity. Each subject and his or her parent or guardian will be informed of the name of a member of the Protection Committee who will be available for consultation concerning the activity.

(c) The Protection Committee shall establish rules of procedure for conducting its activities, which must be reviewed by DHEW, and shall conduct its activities at convened meetings, minutes of which shall be prepared and retained.

Section 46.27 *Certain children excluded from participation in DHEW activities.* A child may not be included as a subject in DHEW activities to which this subpart is applicable if:

(a) The child has no known living parent who is available and capable of participating in the consent process: *Provided,* That this exclusion shall be inapplicable if the child is seriously ill, and the proposed research is designed to substantially alleviate his condition; or

(b) The child has only one known living parent who is available and capable of participating in the consent process, or only one such parent, and that parent has not given consent to the child's participation in the activity; or

(c) Both the child's parents are available and capable of participating in the consent process, but both have not given such consent;

(d) The child is involuntarily confined in an institutional setting pursuant to a court order, whether or not the parents and child have consented to the child's participation in the activity; or

(e) The child has not given consent to his or her participation in the research: *Provided,* That this exclusion shall be inapplicable if the child is 6 years of age or less or if explicitly waived by the DHEW; or

(f) The Protection Committee established under §46.26 of this subpart has not reviewed and approved the child's participation in the activity.

Section 46.23 *Activities to be performed outside the United States.* In addition to satisfying all other applicable requirements in this subpart, an activity to which this subpart is applicable, which is to be conducted outside the United States, must include written documentation satisfactory to DHEW that the proposed activity is acceptable under the legal, social, and ethical standards of the locale in which it is to be performed.

H.E.W. Proposed Rules on Experimentation with Prisoners

APPENDIX VII
39 Fed. Reg. 30654–55 (Aug. 23, 1974)

SUBPART D—ADDITIONAL PROTECTIONS PERTAINING TO ACTIVITIES INVOLVING PRISONERS AS SUBJECTS

§46.401 Applicability.
(a) The regulations in this subpart are applicable to all Department of Health, Education, and Welfare grants and contracts supporting research, development, and related activities involving prisoners as subjects.

(b) The requirements of this subpart are in addition to those imposed under the other subparts of this part.

§46.402 Purpose.
It is the purpose of this subpart to provide additional safeguards for the protection of prisoners involved in activities to which this subpart is applicable, inasmuch as, because of their incarceration, they may be under constraints which could affect their ability to make a truly voluntary—and uncoerced decision whether or not to participate in such activities.

§46.403 Definitions.
As used in this subpart:

(a) "Secretary" means the Secretary of Health, Education, and Welfare or any other officer or employee of the Department of Health, Education, and Welfare to whom authority has been delegated.

(b) "Prisoner" means any individual involuntarily confined in a penal institution. The term is intended to encompass individuals sentenced to such an institution under a criminal or civil statute and also individuals detained in other facilities by virtue of statutes or committment procedures which provide alternatives to criminal prosecution or incarceration in a penal institution.

§46.404 Additional Duties of the Organizational Review Committee Where Prisoners are Involved.
(a) In addition to the responsibilities prescribed for such committees under Subpart A of this part, the applicant's or offeror's organizational review committee shall, with respect to activities covered by this subpart,

317

carry out the following additional duties:

(1) Determine that there will be no undue inducements to participation by prisoners as subjects in the activity, taking into account such factors as whether the earnings, living conditions, medical care, quality of food, and amenities offered to participants in the activity would be better than those generally available to the prisoners;

(2) Determine that (i) all aspects of the activity would be appropriate for performance on nonprisoners, or (ii) the activity involves negligible risk to the subjects and is for the purpose of studying the effects of incarceration on such subjects;

(3) Determine that the application or proposal contains adequate procedures for selection of subjects, securing consents, monitoring continued subject participation, and assuring withdrawal without prejudice, in accordance with §46.405 of this subpart;

(4) Determine that rates of remuneration are consistent with the anticipated duration of the activity, but not in excess of that paid for other employment generally available to inmates of the facility in question, and that withdrawal from the project for medical reasons will not result in loss of anticipated remuneration; and

(5) Carry out such other responsibilities as may be assigned by the Secretary.

(b) Applicants or offerors seeking support for activities covered by this subpart must provide for the designation of an organizational review committee, subject to approval by the Secretary, where no such committee has been established under Subpart A of this part.

(c) No award may be issued until the applicant or offeror has certified to the Secretary that the organizational review committee has made the determinations required under paragraph (a) of this section.

§46.405 Establishment of a Consent Committee.

(a) Except as provided in paragraph (c) of this section, no activity covered by this subpart may be supported unless the applicant or offeror has provided an assurance acceptable to the Secretary that it will establish a consent committee (as provided for in the application or offer and approved by the organizational review committee and the Secretary) for each such activity, to oversee the actual process by which individual subjects are selected and their consents secured, to monitor the progress of the activity (including visits to the activity site on a regular basis) and the continued willingness of the subjects to participate, to intervene on behalf of one or more subjects if conditions warrant, and to carry out such other duties as the Secretary may prescribe. The duties of the consent committee may include:

(1) Participation in the actual process by which individual subjects are selected and their consents secured to assure that all elements of a legally effective informed consent, as outlined in section 46.3 of this part, are satisfied. Depending on what may be prescribed in the application or offer approved by the Secretary, this might require approval by the committee of each individual's participation as a subject in the activity or it might simply call for verification (e.g., through sampling) that procedures prescribed in the approved application or offer are being followed.

(2) Monitoring the progress of the activity and the continued willingness of subjects to participate. Depending on what may be prescribed in the application or offer approved by the Secretary, this might include: visits to the activity site, identification of one or more committee members who would be available for consultation with subjects at the subjects' request, continuing evaluation to determine if

any unanticipated risks have arisen and that any such risks are communicated to the subjects, periodic contact with the subjects to ascertain whether they remain willing to continue in the study, providing for the withdrawal of any subjects who wish to do so, and authority to terminate participation of one or more subjects with or without their consent where conditions warrant.

(b) The size and composition of the consent committee must be approved by the Secretary, taking into account such factors as: (1) the scope and nature of the activity; (2) the particular subject groups involved; (3) whether the membership has been so selected as to be competent to deal with the medical, legal, social, and ethical issues involved in the activity; (4) whether the committee includes a prisoner or a representative of an organization having as a primary concern protection of prisoners' interests; (5) whether the committee includes sufficient members who are unaffiliated with the applicant or offeror apart from membership on the committee; and (6) whether the committee includes sufficient members who are not engaged in research, development, or related activities involving human subjects. The committee shall establish rules of procedure for carrying out its functions and shall conduct its business at convened meetings, with one of its members designated as chairperson.

(c) Where a particular activity involves negligible risk to the subjects, an applicant or offeror may request the Secretary to modify or waive the requirement in paragraph (a) of this section. If the Secretary finds that the risk is indeed negligible and other adequate controls are provided, he may grant the request in whole or in part.

§46.406 Special Restrictions.

Persons detained in a correctional facility pending arraignment, trial, or sentencing or in a hospital facility for prearraignment, pre-trail, or pre-sentence diagnostic observation are excluded from participation in activities covered by this subpart, unless (a) the organizational review committee finds that the particular activity involves only negligible risk to the subjects and (b) the activity is therapeutic in intent or relates to the nature of their confinement.

§46.407 Activities to be Performed Outside the United States.

Activities to which this subpart is applicable, to be conducted outside the United States, are subject to the requirements of this subpart, except that the consent procedures specified herein may be modified if it is shown to the satisfaction of the Secretary that such procedures, as modified, are acceptable under the laws and regulations of the country in which the activities are to be performed and that they comply with the requirements of Subpart A of this part.

Note: The recommendations of The National Commission for the Protection of Human Subjects of Biomedical and Behavioral Research on prison research can be found at 42 Fed. Reg. 3076 (Jan. 14, 1977).

H.E.W. Proposed Rules on Experimentation with the Institutionalized Mentally Disabled

APPENDIX VIII

39 Fed. Reg. 30655-56 (Aug. 23, 1974)

SUBPART E—ADDITIONAL PROTEC-
TIONS PERTAINING TO ACTIVITIES
INVOLVING THE INSTITUTIONALIZED
MENTALLY DISABLED AS SUBJECTS

§46.501 Applicability.

(a) The regulations in this subpart are applicable to all Department of Health, Education, and Welfare grants and contracts supporting research, development, and related activities involving the institutionalized mentally disabled as subjects.

(b) Nothing in this subpart shall be construed as indicating that compliance with the procedures set forth herein will necessarily result in a legally effective consent under applicable State or local law to a subject's participation in such an activity; nor in particular does it obviate the need for court approval of such participation where court approval is required under applicable State or local law in order to obtain a legally effective consent.

(c) The requirements of this subpart are in addition to those imposed under the other subparts of this part.

§46.502 Purpose.

It is the purpose of this subpart to provide additional safeguards for the protection of the institutionalized mentally disabled involved in activities to which this subpart is applicable, inasmuch as: (a) they are confined in an institutional setting where their freedom and rights are potentially subject to limitation; (b) they may be unable to comprehend sufficient information to give an informed consent, as that term is defined in §46.103; and (c) they may be legally incompetent to consent to their participation in such activities.

§46.503 Definitions.

As used in this subpart:

(a) "Secretary" means the Secretary of Health, Education, and Welfare or any other officer or employee of the Department of Health, Education, and Welfare to whom authority has been delegated.

(b) "Mentally disabled" includes those institutionalized individuals who are mentally ill, mentally retarded, emotionally disturbed, or senile, regardless of their legal status or basis of institutionalization.

(c) "Institutionalized" means confined, whether by voluntary admission or involuntary commitment, in a residential institution for the care or treatment of the mentally disabled.

(d) "Institutionalized mentally disabled individuals" includes but it not limited to patients in public or private mental hospitals, psychiatric patients in general hospitals, inpatients of community mental health centers, and mentally disabled individuals who reside in half-way houses or nursing homes.

§46.504 Activities Involving the Institutionalized Mentally Disabled.

Institutionalized mentally disabled individuals may not be included in an activity covered by this subpart unless;

(a) The proposed activity is realted to the etiology, pathogenesis, prevention, diagnosis, or treatment of mental disability or the management, training, or rehabilitation of the mentally disabled and seeks information which cannot be obtained from subjects who are not institutionalized mentally disabled;

(b) The individual's legally effective informed consent to participation in the activity or, where the individual is legally incompetent, the informed consent of a representative with legal authority so to consent on behalf of the individual has been obtained; and

(c) The individual's assent to such participation has also been secured, when in the judgment of the consent committee he or she has sufficient mental capacity to understand what is proposed and to express an opinion as to his or her participation.

§46.505 Additional Duties of the Organizational Review Committee Where the Institutionalized Mentally Disabled are Involved.

(a) In addition to the responsibilities prescribed for such committees under Subpart A of this part, the applicant's or offeror's organizational review committee shall, with respect to activities covered by this subpart, carry out the following additional duties:

(1) Determine that all aspects of the activity meet the requirements of §46.50(a) of this subpart;

(2) Determine that there will be no undue inducements to participation by individuals as subjects in the activity, taking into account such factors as whether the earnings, living conditions, medical care, quality of food, and amenities offered to participants in the activity would be better than those generally available to the mentally disabled at the institutions;

(3) Determine that the application or proposal contains adequate procedures for selection of subjects, securing consents, protecting confidentiality, and monitoring continued subject participation, in accordance with §46.506 of this subpart; and

(4) Carry out such other responsibilities as may be assigned by the Secretary.

(b) Applicants or offerors seeking support for activities covered by this subpart must provide for the designation of an organizational review committee, subject to approval by the Secretary, where no such committee has been established under Subpart A of this part.

(c) No award may be issued until the applicant or offeror has certified to the Secretary that the organizational review committee has made the determinations required under paragraph (a) of this section.

§46.506 Establishment of a Consent Committee.

(a) Except as provided in paragraph (c) of this section, no activity covered by this subpart may be supported unless the applicant or offeror has provided a separate assurance acceptable to the Secretary that it will establish a consent committee (as provided for in the application or offer and approved by the organizational review committee and the secretary) for each such activity, to oversee the actual process by which individual subjects are selected and consents required by this subpart are secured, to monitor the progress of the activity (including visits to the activity site on a regular basis) and the continued willingness of the subjects to participate, to intervene on behalf of one or more subjects if conditions warrant, and to carry out such other duties as the Secretary may prescribe. The duties of the consent committee may include:

(1) Participation in the actual process by which individual subjects are selected and their consents secured to assure that all elements of a legally effective informed consent, as outlined in §46.3, are satisfied. Depending on what may be prescribed in the application or offer approved by the Secretary, this might require approval by the committee of each individual's participation as a subject in the activity or it might simply call for verification (e.g., through sampling) that procedures prescribed in the approved application or offer are being followed.

(2) Monitoring the progress of the activity and the continued willingness of subjects to participate. Depending on what may be prescribed in the application or offer approved by the Secretary, this might include: visits to the activity site, identification of one or more committee members who would be available for consultation with subjects at the subjects' request, continuing evaluation to determine if any unanticipated risks have arisen and that any such risks are communicated to the subjects, periodic contact with the subjects to ascertain whether they remain willing to continue in the study, providing for the withdrawal of any subjects who wish to do so, and authority to terminate participation of one or more subjects with or without

their consent where conditions warrant.

(b) The size and composition of the consent committee must be approved by the Secretary, taking into account such factors as: (1) the scope and nature of the activity; (2) the particular subject groups involved; (3) whether the membership has been so selected as to be competent to deal with the medical, legal, social, and ethical issues involved in the activity; (4) whether the committee includes sufficient members who are unaffiliated with the applicant or offeror apart from membership on the committee; and (5) whether the committee includes sufficient members who are not engaged in research, development, or related activities involving human subjects. The committee shall establish rules of procedure for carrying out its functions and shall conduct its business at convened meetings, with one of its members designated as chairperson.

(c) Where a particular activity involves negligible risk to the subjects, an applicant or offeror may request the Secretary to modify or waive the requirement in paragraph (a) of this section. If the Secretary finds that the risk is indeed negligible and other adequate controls are provided, he may grant the request in whole or in part.

§46.507 Activities to be Performed Outside the United States.

Activities to which this subpart is applicable, to be conducted outside the United States, are subject to the requirements of this subpart, except that the consent procedures specified herein may be modified if it is shown to the satisfaction of the Secretary that such procedures, as modified, are acceptable under the laws and regulations of the country in which the activities are to be performed and that they comply with the requirements of Subpart A of this part.

Index

Abandonment, 10
Abelard, Charles C., 305
Abortion, see Procedures: Abortion
Aden v. Younger, 165, 167, 226
Advocate, Patients Rights
   see also Third Party
      22, 38, 241, 261
Aetna Insurance Company v. University of Washington, 269
Aiken v. Clary, 164
Air Force, see Research: In Armed
   Forces
Allen, David. 232
American Board of Surgery, 218
American Heart Association, see
   Medical Organizations: American
see also Licensing Boards
American Medical Association, see
   Medical Organizations: American Medical Association
Anderson, In Re, 159
Andy, Orlando, 223
Anesthesia
   see also Operations
   Use and Administration of, 12, 19,
      40, 71, 72, 78
Anonymous v. State. 167
Aplastic Anemia, see Diseases:
   Aplastic Anemia
see also Transplants: Tissue and
   Organ
Arlington Hospital and School, 142
Armed Forces
   Research In, see Research: In Armed
      Forces

Army, department of, 130
Arnold, et al, 107
Artificial Heart, see Implants and
   Artificial Devices
Assault and Battery, 21, 27-29, 30,
      44, 51-52, 54, 68, 71, 77, 78,
      119, 160, 219
Asthma, see Diseases: Asthma,
   Respiratory
see also Diseases: Respiratory
Atomic Energy Commission
   see also Price Anderson Act, 47, 274
Atomic Reactor Safety Study, see
   Atomic Energy Commission
Autonomy, see Self Determination
   see also Privacy
Aversive Conditioning Program, see
   Behavior Modification
Ayd, Frank, 107
Ayers v. Ciccone, 120

Baldor v. Rogers, 10
Ballantine, Thomas, 223
Barnard, Christiaan, 16
Battery, see Assault and Battery
Beecher, Henry, 37, 78, 222, 236
Behavior Modification
   see also Psychosurgery, Prisoners:
      Motives for Joining Research
      Groups
   116, 117, 119-128
   Use in Mentally Infirm, see also
      Institutionalized Persons, 159,
      169
Behavioral Research, see Research

Belger v. Arnot, 160
Biomedical Study of Military Per-
    formance at High Terrestrial
    Elevation
  see also Research: In Armed Forces
  307
Bishop v. Shurly, 71
Blackstone's Commentaries, 66
Blauer, Harold, 306
Blood, drawing of
  see also Procedures, Treatments
  30, 32, 78, 92, 129, 182, 196
Blood Gasses, see Blood, drawing of
Blood Transfusions
  see also Blood, drawing of
  69, 145
Bok, Sissela, 198, 199, 206
Bonner v. Moran, 1, 77, 78, 86, 93
Brady v. United States, 118, 119
Breach of duty, See Duty, dereliction
    of
  see also Doctor Patient Relationship
Breggin, Peter, 219
British Medical Research Council, 79,
  95
Brown, Bertram, 218
Brown, Gerald, 228
Brown, James S., 143
Buck, Carrie, see *Buck v. Bell*
Buck v. Bell, 175–77
Buttonow, In Re, 162

California Medical Facility at Vaca-
    ville
  see also *Mackey v. Procunier*
  122
Cancer, see Diseases: Cancer
Capron, Alexander, 33, 36, 78
Caro Residential Center for Mentally
    Retarded, 148
Causation
  see also Negligence, Malpractice
  30, 31
Central Intelligence Agency, see
    Research: In Armed Forces
Centrello v. Basky, 74
Chemotherapy, see Research: Drug
    Use In
Children, see Minors
Cingulotomy, see Psychosurgery
Clark, In Re, 69, 91
Clonce v. Richardson, 124, 125, 127
Coercion
  see also Doctor Patient Relationship,
    Duress, Fiduciary Relationship,
    Prisoners: Motives for Joining

Research Groups, Undue Influ-
    ence
  110, 113–117, 133, 150, 154
Compensation for Harm, see Damages
  see also Indemnification
Competence, see Institutionalized
    Persons, Forms, Risks, Minros
Confidentiality
  see also Privacy
  227
Consent Review Committee, see
    Institutional Review Board
Constraint, unlawful, see Duress
Cook v. Oregon, 178
Cooley, Denton, 11–14, 16
Cornford, F.M., 75
Covert Sensitization, see Behavior
    Modification
Criminal Actions
  see also Assault and Battery, Mal-
    practice, Negligence
  28
Curran, William, 78, 95

Damages, 9, 19, 28, 44, 54, 68, 70,
  71, 77, 92, 227, 257–274, 310
  Psychological, 32, 45, 49, 54
Davis, Jefferson, 15
Decision Making, see Risks
  see also Doctor Patient Relationship
De minimis non curat lex, 50
Department of Defense, see Research:
    In Armed Forces
Depo-Provera, see Research: Drug Use
    in
Diagnosis, mistakes in
  see also Psychosurgery
  230, 231
Diagnostic Testing, 4, 5
Dietrich v. Northampton Hostpital,
  200
Dimethlsulfoxide
  see also Research: Drug Use in
  109
Disclosure
  see also Risks: Comprehension of
  29, 34, 44, 219
Diseases
  Aplastic Anemia, 85
  Asthma, 92
  Cancer, experiments on, 20
  Cholera, experiments on, 113, 115
  Dysentery, experiments on, 113
  Gastro Intestinal, experiments on,
    63
  Glomerular Nephritis, 81

Hepatitis, experiments on, 179, 180
Influenza, experiments on, 113
Malaria, experiments on, 104-109, 113, 115, 116, 307
Meningitis, experiments on, 140, 307
Pellagra, experiments on, 116
Polio, experiments on, 45
  vaccine for, 93
Respiratory, 92, 115
Rocky Mountain Spotted Fever, 113
Shighella, 113
Typhoid, experiments on, 113
Von Recklinghausen's, experiments on, 69
Yellow Fever, experiments on, 259
District of Columbia Training School, experiments in, 140
Doctor Patient Relationship, 17, 19, 20, 27-29, 35, 42, 47, 53, 119, 152, 153, 155, 257, 272
Downs Syndrome, 180
Drugs
  see also Research: Drug Use in
  Test requirements of, 64
  Use in children, 63, 64
Duty
  see also Doctor Patient Relationship, Fiduciary Relationship
  Assignment of, 4, 5, 9, 54
  Definition of, 29
  Dereliction of, 9
Duress
  see also Coercion, Prisoners: Motives for Joining Research Groups, Undue Influence
  110, 111, 114, 115, 117

Edgewood Arsenal in Maryland, experiments in, 306
Electro Convulsive Therapy, see Electro Shock Treatments
Electro Shock Treatment
  see also Behavior Modification, Psychosurgery
  122, 129, 160, 163-65, 167-170, 227-230
Emancipated Minor, see Minor: Emancipated
Emergency
  see also Standard Medical Practice
  31, 70, 77, 164
Epilepsy
  Temporal lobe, 232
Ethical Review Board, see Institutional Review Board

Ethical Guidelines on Consent
  see also Doctor Patient Relationship, Institutional Review Board, Risks: Disclosure of
  49, 50, 66, 79, 105, 195

Faradic Aversive Conditioning, see Behavior Modification
Farber v. Olkon, 167
Farinelli case, see *Nathan v. Farinelli*
Federal Employees Compensation Act, 262
Federal Laws and Regulations Concerning Consent
  see also Research: Federal Guidelines on
  8, 14, 42-44, 49, 88
Fiduciary Relationship
  see also Doctor Patient Relationship, Minors
  30, 33, 54, 112, 117, 127, 133-140, 152-153, 155, 172-173
Fletcher, Joseph, 198, 200
Folsom State Prison of California
  see also *Mackey v. Procunier*, 122
Food and Drug Administration
  see also Research: Drug Use in
  222
Food Drug and Cosmetic Act, 63
Fort Bragg, see Research: In Armed Forces
Fox v. Piercey, 111
Frazier v. Levi, 172
Freedom, see Self Determination
Freeman, Walter
  see also Psychosurgery
  216, 217-218
Freund, Paul, 36, 63, 75, 87, 107
Fraud
  see also Coercion, Forms, Fraud: Use of, Malpractice, Risks: Nondisclosure of
  38, 42
Forms
  Blanket Consent, 12, 14, 18, 175
  Coercion with signing, 18, 20, 148
  Comprehension of, 42, 44
  Fraudulent use of, 38, 39
  In experimentation, 38, 134, 141-143
  Reliability of, 42, 43, 54

Gallegos v. Colorado, 74
Goffman, Erving, 147
Goldberger, 116
Green Committee, see Green, Dwight

Green, Dwight, 116
Graft Versus Host Disease, see Transplants: Tissue and Organ
Gray, Bradford, 38, 44
Guardians, see Minors: Guardians for

Halushka v. University of Saskatchewan, 18, 33
Hand, Learned, 220, 221
Hardy, James D., 16
Harkin, Dwight, 15
Hart v. Brown, 82
Haynes v. Harris, 119, 120
Health Education and Welfare
  see also Federal Laws Concerning Consent
  14, 130, 131, 133, 234, 309
  Organizational Review Committee of, 131, 242
Health Policy Program of the University of California
  (San Francisco) School of Medicine, 116
Helsinki, Declaration of, 8, 76, 156
Hepatitis, see Diseases: Hepatitis
  see also Willowbrook State School
Haley v. Ohio, 74
Horacek v. Exon, 145
Howard, Clara, see *Bonner v. Moran*
Howard v. Fulton-Dekalb Hospital Authority, 174
Hyman v. Jewish Chronic Disease Hospital, see Jewish Chronic Disease Hospital: Experiments in

Immunization, see Procedures: Immunization and Vaccination
Implants and Artificial Devices
  see also Transplants
  Tissue and Organ, 37
  Artificial Heart, 12-16, 22
  Kidney transplants, 46
  Left Ventricular Assist Device (L.V.A.D.), 16, 17
In Re, see case name
Incompetent Persons, see Minors
  see also Institutionalized Persons
Indemnification
  see also Damages
  258-274
Infectious Disease Area, of Maryland House of Corrections, 113, 114
Ingelfinger, Franz
  see also New England Journal of Medicine
  243

Injury, see Damages
Institutional Review Board, 43, 95, 208, 224, 232, 240-243
Institutionalized Persons
  see also Prisoners, Minors
  47, 81, 84-86, 90, 96, 105, 139-183
  Motives for Research on, 140, 182, 222
  Competence of, 154, 166, 173
  Rights of, 146, 150, 163, 170, 172, 177, 178, 183, 207, 244, 273
    Involuntarily Committed, 151, 155, 160, 161-162, 167, 225-226
Insurance
  see also Malpractice
  28, 38, 51
International Law
  see also Nuremberg Code, Helsinki; Declaration of
  8, 130
Interrogation of Prisoners, see *Miranda v. Arizona*
Investigational New Drug Application (IND), see Research: Drug Use in
Involuntary Commitment, see Institutionalized Persons: Involuntary Commitment of
Iowa State Medical Facility, 122, 123, 163
Irwin v. Arrendale, 121
Ivy, Andrew, 104-106

Jewish Chronic Disease Hospital
  Experiments in, 19-21, 33
Jobes v. Michigan Department of Mental Health, 181
Jonas, Hans, 35

Kaimowitz v. Department of Mental Health, 126, 127, 148-150, 163, 221, 224, 226, 227-229, 239, 242
Karp, Haskel, 11-16
Katz, Jay, 19, 33, 36
Keesler Air Force Base
  Experiments in, 308
Keeton-O'Connell Plan, 263
Kefauver-Harris Amendments, see Food, Drug and Cosmetic Act
Kennedy Hearings on Human Experimentation
  see also Brown, James S.
  143, 259
Kidney Transplants, see Transplants: Tissue and Organ

Knecht v. Gillman, 122, 123, 125, 134, 163
Koch, Richard, 180

LSD, see Research: Drug Use in
Lacey v. Laird, 71
Lafayette Clinic (Michigan), 149
  Experiments in, 224
Lasagna, Louis, 258
Law Enforcement Assistance Admin-
  istration, 239
Lawler, Richard, 15
Left Ventricular Assist Device
  (L.V.A.D.), see Implants and
  Artificial Devices
Legal Incapacity, see Minors
Licensing Boards
  see also Medical Organizations
  5, 20
Life Threatening Situation, see
  Emergency
Liotto, Domingo, 11, 12
Lobotomy, see Psychosurgery

Mackey v. Procunier, 122, 125, 128, 134, 163
Mahoney, Maurice, 196, 197
Maiming, see Risks: Unacceptable
Maine Medical Center v. Houle, 69
Malaria, see Diseases: Malaria
Malpractice, 9, 14, 22, 29, 38, 217, 218, 220, 260-261, 271, 310
Maryland House of Corrections
  see also Infectious Disease Area:
  Experiments in
  113, 115
Massachusetts Department of Mental
  Health Task Force (on Psycho-
  surgery), 223
Massachusetts General Hospital, 223
Massachusetts Institute of Technology, 236
Massachusetts Medical Society, 231
Mature Minor, see Minors: Emanci-
  pated
Mayhem
  see also Risks: Unacceptable,
  Psychosurgery
  224
McAuliffe v. Carlson, 145
Meachum v. Fano, 125
Mechanic, David, 49, 50
Medical Center for Federal Prisoners
  see also *Clonce v. Richardson*
  124
Medical Committee on Human Rights, 225

Medical Malpractice Insurance
  see also Malpractice
  264, 265
Medical Organizations
  see also Licensing boards, American
    Hospital Association
  Committee on Ethics, 16
  American Medical Association
    ethical guidelines of, 9, 156
    endorsements of, 10
Medical Terminology
  abuse of, 13, 14
  use of, 13
Meningitis, see Diseases: Meningitis
Mental Patients, see Institutionalized
  Persons
Mentally Handicapped, see Institu-
  tionalized Persons
Mentally Ill Persons
  see also Institutionalized Persons
  168
Merriman, J.E., 18, 19
Michigan Department of Mental Health
  see also *Jobes v. Michigan Depart-
    ment of Mental Health*
  224-225
Milieu Therapy, see Behavior Modifi-
  cation
Military Law
  see also Nuremberg Code, Research:
    In Armed Forces
  7, 8
Military Personnel, see Research: In
  Armed Forces
Minors
  As Donors, 9, 268
  Emancipated, 70, 73, 75, 77
  Federal Regulations Concerning,
    95, 96, 309
  Financial Responsibility for, 71
  Guardians for, 8, 9, 90, 91, 94, 96
    limitations of, 68, 70, 94, 156
  Guidelines for, 64-67, 72, 92, 94-
    95, 103, 147, 153, 182, 219,
    229, 244
  State laws concerning
    see also State Laws Concerning
      Consent
    74, 79, 95, 96, 207
Miranda v. Arizona, 34, 117, 118
Mirsky, Allan F., 235, 237, 238
Mitchell v. Robinson, 164
Mitford, Jessica, 116
Money
  As Motive for Joining Research, see
    Prisoner: Motives for Joining
    Research

Moniz, Egas
  see also Psychosurgery
  216
Moore, In Re, 176
Moore, Joseph Lee, see *Moore, In Re*
Multiple Target Procedure
  see also Psychosurgery
  227
Mutilation, see Risks: Unacceptable
  see also Psychosurgery

National Commission for the Protec-
    tion of Human Subjects of
    Biomedical and Behavioral
    Research
  see also Research: Federal Guidelines
    on
  195, 208, 210-211, 240-242
National Heart and Lung Institute
  Guidelines for testing devices, 14
National Institute of Mental Health,
  218
National Institutes of Health, 218,
  223, 259-260
National Research Act of 1974
  see also National Commission for
    the Protection of Human Sub-
    jects of Biomedical and Be-
    havioral Research
  215
Nathan v. Farinelli, 87-88, 90, 268
Navy, see Research: In Armed Forces
Negligence, 5, 9, 27-29, 54, 92, 217,
  219, 220, 257, 262, 264, 270
Neilson v. Board of Regents, 92
New England Journal of Medicine, 231
*New York Health and Hospitals
    v. Stein,* 164
*New York State Association for Re-
    tarded Children v. Carey*
  see also Willowbrook State School
  181
New York State Psychiatric Agency,
  306
No-Fault Liability
  see also Insurance
  262-274
Nuclear Energy, see Atomic Energy
    Commission
  see also Price Anderson Act
Nugent, Arthur
  see also California Medical Facility
    at Vacaville
  122
Nuremberg Code, 1, 2, 6-7, 18, 21,
  22, 44, 76-79, 104, 139, 150,
  156, 225, 257, 308

Nuremberg Trials
  see also Nuremberg Code
  78

Operations
  see also Procedures, Standard Medi-
    cal Practice, Treatments
  Artificial heart, 13
  Plastic surgery, 71
  Psychosurgery, see Psychosurgery
  Tables of, 46
  Tonsilectomy/Adenoidectomy, 68
Organ Donation, see Treatments
  see also Implants and Artificial De-
    vices
Organizational Review Committee of
    Health Education and Welfare,
    see Health Education and Wel-
    fare: Organizational Review
    Committee of
Orzack, Maressa, 235
Oserezki, N.I., 216-217

Pain
  Intractable, see also Psychosurgery
  232, 235
Pain and Suffering, see Damages
*Palm Springs General Hospital v.
    Martinez,* 144
Parens Patriae, doctrine of, 154, 160,
  161, 168, 174, 178
Parents, see Minors: Consent for
Passivity, see Psychosurgery
Patient Doctor Relationship, see
    Doctor Patient Relationship
Patients Rights Advocate, see Advo-
    cate Patients Rights
Pedophiles, experiments on, 116, 117
Peek v. Ciccone, 119
Peel, John, 210
Peel Report, see Peel, John
Peer Review, see Institutional Review
    Board
Perinatal Research, see Research:
    Perinatal
Pescinski, In Re, 84, 89
Pharmaceutical Manufacturers Associ-
    ation, 114
*Planned Parenthood of Central
    Missouri v. Danforth,* 72
Plymouth, see *Taunton v. Plymouth*
  see also Minors
Polio, see Diseases: Polio
*Porter v. Toledo Terminal Railway
    Company,* 74
Positive Reinforcement, see Behavior
    Modification

Prenatal Research, see Research:
     Fetal
Price Anderson Act
  see also Atomic Energy Commission
  47, 266–268, 270, 273, 274
Price v. Sheppard, 167, 169
Primitive Laws Concerning Consent,
     64–67, 75
Prisoners
  see also Institutionalized Persons
  Forcible Administration of Medica-
     tion to , 119, 120
  Motives for Joining Research
     Groups, 107, 108, 110–113,
     115, 118, 119, 128, 132–134
  Research on, 20, 103–134, 171,
     242, 244
  Waiver of Rights of
     see also Waiver of Rights
     117, 118, 130
Prisoners of War
  see also Nuremberg Code, Helsinki;
     Declaration of
Privacy
  see also Confidentiality, Doctor
     Patient Relationship, Fiduciary
     Relationship
  35, 166, 202, 227, 231, 233, 240,
     266
Procedures
  see also Operations, Standard
     Medical Practice, Treatments
  Abortion, 66, 72, 73, 195, 197–206,
     208
  Immunization and Vaccination, 45,
     260
  New and Experimental, 2–4, 19, 20
  Nontherapeutic, see also Research:
     Therapeutic and Nontherapeutic
     79, 179, 200, 276
  Sterilization, see Sterilization
  Therapeutic, 79, 179
  Vasectomy, see also Sterilization
     71
Proxy
  see also Institutionalized Persons,
     Minors
  63–99, 147, 153, 165, 167, 170,
     172, 182, 204, 240, 309
Providence Hospital, 149
Psychedelic Drugs, see Research:
     Drug Use in
Psychological Damages, see Damages
Psychosurgery, 17, 67, 126, 127, 148–
     151, 160, 163, 165–167, 170,
     215–244
  Effects and Risks of, 216–219

Federal Laws Concerning, 215, 228,
     233
State Laws Concerning, 226, 228,
     233, 242
Use in Aggression, 225
Public Health Service, see Research:
     Federal Guidelines On
Punitive Damages, see Damages

Quackery
  see also Malpractice, Standard
     Medical Practice
  9, 10, 17, 31
Quinlan, Karen A. (In the Matter of),
     69, 90, 91

Ramsey v. Ciccone, 120
Ramsey, Paul, 198
Rappaport v. Stott, 85
Reasonable Disclosure, see Disclosure
Recklessness, see Risks: Unacceptable
Reed, Walter, 259
Reemtsma, Keith, 15
Relf v. Mathews, 158
Relf v. Weinberger, 158
Report of the Secretary's Commission
     on Medical Malpractice
  see also Malpractice
  261
Research
  see also Risks
  Animal Studies in, 14, 16, 106, 141,
     208
  Drug Use in, 126, 140, 144, 148,
     156, 160, 161, 163, 197, 231,
     260, 305, 306, 308
  Federal Guidelines on
     see also National Commission for
     the Protection of Human Sub-
     jects of Biomedical and Behav-
     ioral Research
     see also National Research Act of
     1974
     14, 131, 208, 210, 211, 244, 261,
     270, 309
  Fetal, 195–211
     guidelines for, 198–201, 204, 207
     perinatal, 195–211
  Fraud in, 5, 306
  In Armed Forces, 305–310
  Nontherapeutic, 94, 180, 205, 207,
     209, 272, 274
  Preparation for, 36, 37, 208, 209,
     243
  Racism in, 15, 259–261
  "Reasonable Theory" in, 3

Requirements in, 37, 63, 131, 155,
227
State laws Concerning, see also State
laws Concerning Consent
128, 130, 146, 177 206
Therapeutic, 94, 205, 206, 271, 275
Research Review Committees, see
Institutional Review Boards
Retarded Person
see also Minors, Institutionalized
Persons
77, 83, 147
Review Committees
see also Institutional Review Board
228, 229
Richardson, In Re, 83, 90, 173
Richardson, Mary, 15
Rights, Waiver of, see Prisoners:
Waiver of Rights of
Risks
see also Procedures, Standard
Medical Practice, Treatments:
Alternatives to
11, 16–19, 34, 35, 47, 54, 103,
108, 182
Acceptable, 50, 67, 90, 115
Assumption of, 19–21, 30, 73–75,
82, 90, 92, 95, 108, 149, 153,
164, 165, 169, 199, 204, 206,
219, 224, 225, 232, 233, 241,
257, 258, 273, 306
Comprehension of, 19, 20, 30, 38,
42, 44, 68, 70, 73–75, 81, 82,
90, 92, 95, 149–153, 162, 164,
165, 169, 199, 224, 225, 232,
238, 241, 257, 262, 273, 306
Disclosure of, 32, 37, 39, 42, 45,
46 (table), 48, 49
Involuntary, 47
Qualification of, 40, 45, 95
Unacceptable, 50–52, 90, 104, 115
Roe v. Wade, 72, 121, 195, 201–204,
206
Routine Procedures
see also Standard Medical Practice
20
Rush, Boyd, 15

Saikewicz, Joseph, 156, 157
St. Luke's Episcopal Hospital of
Houston, Texas, 12, 13
Sallmaier, In Re, 178
Sampson, In Re, 69
*Schloendorff v. Society of N.Y.
Hospitals,* 28, 33, 121
Seiferth, In Re, 69
Self Autonomy, see Self Determina-
tion

Self Determination
see also Doctor Patient Relation-
ship, Fiduciary Relationship,
Risks: Assumption of
28–30, 33–35, 39, 41, 53, 54, 88,
104, 119, 153
Self Scrutiny, see Research: Prepara-
tion for
Shock Therapy, see Electro Shock
Treatments
Side Effects, see Untoward Events
see also Risks
Simmons, Henry, 259, 260
Skinner v. Oklahoma, 177
Smith v. Baker, 120
Smith, Louis, see *Kaimowitz v. De-
partment of Mental Health*
Southam, Chester, 20
Special Populations, see Institution-
alized Persons, Minors, Prisoners
Special Treatment and Rehabilitation
Training (S.T.A.R.T.), see
Clonce v. Richardson
Standard Medical Practice
see also Procedures
9, 25, 45, 241
Deviations from, 2–5, 19, 28, 31, 32,
38, 40, 169, 216, 217, 223, 241,
272
State Board of Social Protection (of
Oregon), see *Cook v. Oregon*
State Laws Concerning Consent, 2–5,
38, 53, 80, 83, 89, 92
State v. Bass, 220
Sterilization
see also Operations, Procedures,
Treatments
46, 139, 158, 172, 173, 175–179
Stetler, Joseph C., 114
Strong, R.P. Colonel, 106
Strunk v. Strunk, 81, 83, 86, 88, 90,
174
"Subject at Risk"
see also Risks, Doctor Patient Re-
lationship
49
Substituted Judgment, Doctrine of,
81, 91
Surgery, see Operations
Swine Flu Vaccine, see Procedures:
Immunization and Vaccination

Taunton v. Plymouth, 70
Terminally Ill Patients, 11, 14–16, 69,
157, 198
Termination of Pregnancy, see Pro-
cedures: Abortion
Testing, see Diagnostic Testing

Teuber, Hans-Lukas, 236, 237, 238
The T.J. Hooper, 220, 221
Therapeutic Privilege
  see also Doctor Patient Relationship,
    Risks, Forms
  22, 29, 30, 32, 44, 54
Third Party
  see also Advocate: Patients Rights,
    Minors: Consent for
  22, 241, 243, 309
Tissue Transplants, see Transplants:
    Tissue and Organ
Token Economy Programs, see
    Behavior Modification
Torts
  see also Negligence, Malpractice
  28, 68, 265
Transplants
  see also Implants and Artificial
    Devices
  Tissue and Organ, 9, 46, 72, 80,
    81–86, 90, 91, 93, 95, 173, 175,
    219, 222, 268, 269
Treatments
  see also Diseases, Operations, Pro-
    cedures, Standard Medical Prac-
    tice
  Alternatives to, 11, 28, 29, 34, 40,
    43, 129, 182
    233, 273
  Choice of, 4, 44
  Nontherapeutic, see also Research:
    Nontherapeutic
    13
  Novel and Unorthodox, 11, 182,
    272
  Quality of, 4
  Refusal of, see also Self Determina-
    tion
    30, 32, 165, 259
  Termination of, 69, 90
  Therapeutic, see also Research:
    Therapeutic
    13
Tucker, Ruth, 15
Tuskegee Study
  see also Research: Racism In
  259–261

Undue Influence
  see also Coercion, Duress
  110, 112, 114–117, 133
Uniform Anatomical Gift Act, see
    Transplants: Tissue and Organ
United States Medical Center for
    Federal Prisoners

  see also *Peck v. Ciccone*
  121
University of Mississippi Medical
    Center
  Human Investigational Committee
    of, 223, 224
Untoward Events
  see also Risks
  43, 108
Urban Information Interpreters, 116

Vacaville, see California Medical Cen-
    ter Facility at Vacaville
Vaccination, see Procedures: Immuni-
    zation and Vaccination
Valenstein, Elliot, 234–236
Vasectomy, see Procedures: Vasec-
    tomy
  see also Sterilization
Vecchione v. Wohlgemuth, 145
Venipuncture, see Blood; Drawing of
Verdicts, see Damages
Volenti non fit injuria, 51, 73
Voluntary Commitment, see Institu-
    tionalized Persons
Voluntariness, see Prisoners, Institu-
    tionalized Persons
Von Rechlinghausen's Disease, see
    Diseases

Wantonness, see Risks: Unacceptable
Washkansky, Louis, 16
Watts, James
  see also Psychosurgery
  216–218
Whitbread, Ex parte, 88
Whitree v. State, 161
Willowbrook State School, 179–183
Wilson v. Lebman, 164
Workers Compensation, 262, 265,
    266, 269, 270
Winters v. Miller, 160
Wolff v. McDonnell, 123, 124
World Federation of Mental Health,
    216
Wright, Millard
  see also Psychosurgery
  216
Wyant, G.M., 18, 19
Wyatt v. Aderholt, 158
Wyatt v. Stickney, 169–172, 181, 229

Yellow Fever, see Diseases: Yellow
    Fever
Yetter, In Re, 145
Younts v. St. Francis Hospital, 72

About the Authors

George J. Annas has been Director of Boston University's Center for Law and Health Sciences for the past four years. During that time the Center has earned a national reputation in the fields of patient rights, health regulation and health law education. He holds degrees in economics, law, and public health from Harvard University. He is Assistant Professor at Boston University School of Medicine and Vice-Chairman of the Massachusetts Board of Registration and Discipline in Medicine, and has previously written books on *The Rights of Hospital Patients* (1975) and *Genetics and the Law* (1976). With his co-authors on this volume, Professor Annas is currently working on a book on *The Rights of Doctors, Nurses, and Allied Health Professionals.*

Leonard H. Glantz is currently a Staff Attorney at the Center for Law and Health Sciences, Boston University School of Law, and an assistant professor in the Department of Socio-Medical Sciences, Boston University School of Medicine. He has served on two Institutional Review Boards, and has taught graduate level interdisciplinary courses on the regulation of human experimentation. In addition to his work in this area, Mr. Glantz has published many articles on a variety of medicolegal issues, most recently concentrating in the area of health planning and regulation. He holds degrees in psychology and law from Boston University.

Barbara F. Katz is currently an instructor at Boston University School of Law. She received a B.A. in English and a J.D. from

Boston University, where, until recently, she was a staff attorney at the Center for Law and Health Sciences. She has also taught courses in law and medicine at Boston University's School of Medicine and Metropolitan College, and at Harvard University's Radcliffe Institute, as well as published numerous articles in the field.